Lafayette Ltd

Essays in Czech History

by

R. R. BETTS

UNIVERSITY OF LONDON
THE ATHLONE PRESS
1969

Published by
THE ATHLONE PRESS
UNIVERSITY OF LONDON
at 2 Gower Street London WC1
Distributed by Tiptree Book Services Ltd
Tiptree, Essex

Australia and New Zealand
Melbourne University Press

Canada
Oxford University Press
Toronto

U.S.A.
Oxford University Press Inc
New York

485 11095 4

Printed in Great Britain by
ROBERT CUNNINGHAM AND SONS LTD
LONGBANK WORKS
ALVA

EDITORIAL PREFACE

The fates conspired to deny to the world of scholarship any book from the pen of the late Professor R. R. Betts. The manuscript which he had prepared for a monograph on Jan Hus and the Czech reform movement was destroyed with the accompanying notes and papers in an air raid during the Second World War and for various reasons could not be reconstructed later. After the war he apparently had in mind a book on the social and economic history of the Czech lands in the Middle Ages and a short history of Bohemia. But teaching and administrative duties, the preparation of articles and other short studies, and growing ill-health prevented him from settling down to produce them, and at the time of his death in May 1961 neither had been written. Even his collaboration with Professor Denys Hay on *Europe in the Fourteenth and Fifteenth Centuries* in the Longmans 'History of Europe' series was suddenly halted early in a sabbatical summer term taken to give him more time to write; and when he died he had finished only two chapters, one of which was still in draft and had to be revised and recast.

The present volume brings together his major historical essays now scattered among a number of scholarly journals and *Festschriften*. We have omitted several of minor importance or of mainly topical interest, his contributions to the *New Cambridge Modern History* which are easily accessible, and his many book reviews, obituaries, encyclopaedia articles, and occasional pieces. For all their seeming diversity in title and approach, the essays included really treat the same subject and are linked together through Jan Hus on whom Professor Betts focussed his scholarly concern during the whole of his life. Their chief themes are Hus's beloved university founded only a few decades before his birth; the vital intellectual currents in European thought which stirred and propelled the ideas of Hus and his predecessors (among whom Betts took particular interest in the rather neglected figure of Matěj of Janov); Hus's leading associates in the work of reform; and the social and economic structure of Hussite Bohemia seen against a European background. Even the essay on Masaryk is relevant in this connexion. For was he not the most eloquent exponent of the Hussite idea in recent times?

As each of the essays reprinted here was written to stand on its own, there is naturally some overlapping of content when they are brought together in book form. This is inevitable, and we have not set ourselves to remove it. We have corrected a few minor factual errors and printing mistakes and have made the footnote references conform to a pattern appropriate to a book. Naturally we have altered no statement of opinion even when we thought it likely that the author himself might have favoured revision. Wherever we have inserted anything in the text or the footnotes we have indicated it by the use of square brackets. We have substituted an English translation for Latin passages in the original text and have transferred the Latin to the footnotes. We have also added a selected list of works on late mediaeval Czech history cited in the text.

We wish to express our warm thanks to Professor G. R. Potter for writing an introduction to this volume. He is an old friend of Professor Betts and a fellow worker in the field of late mediaeval history. We are also grateful to the Board of the Athlone Press for undertaking its publication; to the officers of the Athlone Press for advising on the preparation of the manuscript; to Mr D. Chrkaste of the British Museum for compiling the index; and to Dr P. Skwarczyński of the School of Slavonic and East European Studies of the University of London, Dr A. N. E. D. Schofield of the British Museum, and Professor N. Zacour of the University of Toronto for helping with various points of detail.

G. H. Bolsover
Peter Brock
Otakar Odložilík

September, 1968

ACKNOWLEDGEMENTS

For permission to reprint the essays included in this volume grateful acknowledgements are made to the Royal Historical Society; to the Editors of the following journals: *History* (London), the *Slavonic and East European Review*, the *University of Birmingham Historical Journal*, and *Universitas Carolina, Historica* (Prague); and to Messrs Frederick Muller Ltd and the Oxford University Press. Full particulars of the original place and date of publication are given in the bibliography of Professor Betts's published writings on pages 307-9 below.

The Editors of *Past and Present* to whom acknowledgement is also made wish the following note to be published in connexion with the essay on 'Social and Constitutional Development in Bohemia in the Hussite Period':

CONTENTS

Reginald Robert Betts: A Memoir

By G. R. POTTER

REGINALD ROBERT BETTS was born in the ancient city of Norwich, Norfolk, England, the son of Robert F. and Gertrude Betts, on 30 October 1903. The family had long connexions with both the city and the county; his father was a schoolmaster who, by hard private study, had obtained teaching qualifications and a university degree, much more of a rarity in those days than it has since become. Later he entered educational administration and was for a short time Director of Education for the city.

It was a deeply religious and strongly nonconformist—Liberal home background: his father had suffered some persecution because of a refusal to pay rates to support Church of England schools of whose tenets he disapproved, and he became a well-known figure in nonconformist circles. 'Reggie' went to the nearest elementary school, the excellent George White School, whence, with Mousehold Heath just behind him, redolent of memories of Robert Ket, the sixteenth-century rebel, and George Borrow, the writer, he could look down on the ancient castle, cathedral, Guildhall and many-towered flint churches of his city. It all helped to implant a love and understanding of the Middle Ages into a sensitive and alert boy. There were family memories of the past as well—his grandfather would tell him of the Crimean War or of the magnificent Victorian funeral of Bishop Stanley in 1849.

From the George White School Reginald won a coveted entrance scholarship to the Norwich School, an ancient foundation of King Edward VI, which counted Archbishop Parker, Edward Coke, Lord Nelson and Rajah Brooke of Sarawak among its earlier pupils, and where the boys assembled for prayer every day in a former fifteenth-century chantry chapel in the shadow of the great Norman cathedral.

Rejecting the hopes of his father and his headmaster, the Reverend W. F. Brown, that he would interest himself in mathematics or science, he showed instead an inclination to Latin and Greek, then already on the decline in a school which lost its best masters in rapid succession for service in the First World War. There was, however, one genius among his teachers, W. J. Blake (father of Mr Robert Blake, Student of Christ Church, Oxford, whose lives of Bonar Law and of Disraeli have received wide approval). The elder Blake had the ability to bring out the best in his pupils, and his teaching of history made the school a nursery of university scholars and historians. Betts secured many prizes and was a popular figure, in spite of the fact that he played no games. In early youth he was the victim of rheumatic fever which left his heart permanently weak and sometimes meant long periods in bed. He was a good speaker, and his thin delicate features caused him more than once to be cast for feminine parts in the annual school Shakespeare play.

In 1922 he secured an Entrance Scholarship to New College, Oxford, and was diverted to *Literae Humaniores*, 'Greats', in which he obtained a second class in 1925 and then in 1926, in one year instead of the normal two, first class honours in the final Honours School of History. His special subject was the Reign of Richard II, which led him to look carefully into the relations between England and Bohemia during that reign which had, up to then, been somewhat superficially studied from the West. Dr E. F. Jacob, also a New College man, suggested to him that he should learn Czech, of which he obtained an easy and complete mastery, and he turned his thoughts to ecclesiastical history. Like his father, he was now a Methodist lay preacher, a teetotaller and a non-smoker. He was, however, attracted to Marxist teaching, became persuaded that religion was the opium of the people, ceased to attend church and, a little ostentatiously, became a moderate beer-drinker and cigarette-smoker.

Disappointed in an attempt to obtain a Fellowship at All Souls, he taught history for a short time at Winchester College, so natural for a New College Scholar, and did some tutorial work in Oxford. In 1929 he became for two years an Assistant Lecturer at Liverpool and colleague of another fourteenth-century scholar, Miss May McKisack, and in 1931 he succeeded the writer of this memoir as head of the Department of Medieval History at the Queen's University of Belfast.

There he worked quietly at the career of Jan Hus and reached the conclusions which he summarised for scholars in his paper 'English and Czech influences on the Hussite Movement', published in 1939 in the *Transactions* of the Royal Historical Society, of which he was a Fellow. Happily married to one he had known from schooldays, with two children, he moved in 1934 to the Chair of History at University College, Southampton and to a physical and intellectual climate which suited him better than the dour Protestantism of Ulster. He was invited to undertake, and took immense pains over, a course of extramural lectures for adult (Workers' Educational Association) students in Southampton on British religious movements in the nineteenth century. With working-class movements he was always in sympathy, and conditions in Southampton, which suffered much from the unemployment of the thirties, hardened his own now advanced political thinking. He had a heavy load of university teaching and administration, and at the same time he continued his Czech studies with characteristic enthusiasm.

The war of 1939-45 brought him many duties. The overseas radio service of the B.B.C. was greatly expanded and, at the suggestion of his friend R. W. Seton-Watson, he was made Assistant Editor, then Editor, of the Czechoslovak service and finally editor to the European Service, spending much time travelling between Southampton and his headquarters at Bush House, London. His own anonymous broadcasts to the Czech people were very effective. He had completed his study of Jan Hus and his predecessors (particularly Matěj of Janov) when all his papers and books were destroyed by enemy action, and he was never able to re-write it, or to produce the short *History of Bohemia* of which it was a central theme.

In the dark days of 1944 the University of Birmingham appointed him Professor of History in succession to Sir Keith Hancock, and, amid many difficulties and some ill health, he threw himself with zest and enthusiasm into making the Birmingham School of History one of the best in the country. He secured the creation of an additional Professorship and helped to inaugurate the *University of Birmingham Historical Journal*, to the first number of which he contributed an article on Jerome of Prague. It fitted in well with his special subject lectures on the conciliar movement and also with his growing interest in mediaeval political theory.

After only two years at Birmingham, however, he was offered the Masaryk Chair at the School of Slavonic and East European Studies in the University of London, which he accepted, partly because it promised the opportunity of frequent visits to Prague which he had come to know and esteem like his native Norwich. This hope was not entirely fulfilled when political events interfered to make travel to Eastern Europe more difficult and, although he appeared to have mastered much of his early physical weakness, he always had to proceed with care.

He was, however, now doing the work that he most wanted to do and at the same time he was in touch with every important Czech visitor to London and with the heterogeneous groups of students who came to see him at the Senate House at all stages of academic and intellectual development. Many of them were older men and women in dealing with whom he found his continued interest in adult education of increasing value.

He was now at the centre of affairs: he had less general teaching to do, and much less examining (of which he had done a good deal for the Oxford and Cambridge Schools Examination Board in the past), but committee work multiplied. The School of Slavonic and East European Studies grew steadily in numbers and resources: its history department prospered under his firm and persuasive leadership. He pressed the School's claims wherever good will and assistance might be forthcoming, and he watched with eager anxiety the coming and consequences of the Communist revolution in what had once been the Kingdom of Bohemia. Every newspaper, periodical and pamphlet that came into the School's library, which he helped so much to expand, was read and absorbed.

All the time he was writing and steadily widening his intellectual horizon. One original authority after another was perused, annotated and assessed. He could write fine nervous English prose, incisive and to the point; the niceties of historical scholarship were always there without any parade of excessive learning; his footnotes were intentionally reduced to a minimum. The editors of the *New Cambridge Modern History* were well aware that they must turn to him for the sections dealing with Hungary, Bohemia and Poland, particularly in their complicated constitutional aspects, and his contributions were not the least original in their volumes. He did not live to revise the proofs of the narrative of the Habsburg Lands in the later seventeenth century but it indicated how wide and deep his knowledge had become.

Although in interests he remained a mediaevalist to the end, he was an active supporter of the Royal Institute of International Affairs with whose aims and purposes he was very much in sympathy. He liked meeting people and he had a gift for exposition both verbally and in writing. Among many pieces of writing easily overlooked are the articles which he contributed to the new edition of *Chambers's Encyclopaedia*, especially that on 'History', which is a splendid exposition of a general theme. Politics concerned him a great deal. As a student, Aristotle had meant more to him than to most men (which is partly why he understood the University of Prague so well); at Birmingham his lectures on political theory were long remembered, and from the liberalism of his early days he moved far to the left. In some measure, perhaps, this enabled him to assess with sympathy and understanding what was happening in the regions of the former Habsburg dominions. This he showed in the volume, *Central and South East Europe 1945-48*, which the Royal Institute of International Affairs produced under his editorship.

Above all, it is as an exponent of the history of Bohemia in the Middle Ages that he has a permanent place among those who have made enduring contributions to the history of Europe. English readers, at any rate, understand the Hussite movement the better as the result of his researches and thought, much of which is presented in this volume.

ABBREVIATIONS

Č Č M	*Časopis českého musea* (Prague)
Čs Č H	*Československý časopis historický* (Prague)
Erben	K. J. Erben (ed.), *M. Jana Husa sebrané spisy české*
Hardt	H. von der Hardt (ed.), *Magnum oecumenicum Constanciense concilium*
Historia et monumenta	J. Hus, *Historia et monumenta Joannis Hus atque Hieronymi Pragensis*
Höfler	C. Höfler (ed.), *Geschichtschreiber der hussitischen Bewegung*
Klicman	L. Klicman (ed.), *Processus judiciarius contra Jeronimum de Praga habitus Viennae a 1410-12*
Palacký, *Documenta*	F. Palacký (ed.), *Documenta Mag. Joannis Hus*
Regulae	Matěj of Janov, *Regulae veteris et novi testamenti*
Sedlák	J. Sedlák, *Studie a texty k náboženským dějinám českým*

I

The University of Prague: 1348

IT WOULD BE a grave dereliction of academic piety were any journal of Slavonic studies to ignore the sixth centenary of the foundation of the university of Prague; for the journal of the London School of Slavonic and East European studies to do so would be ingratitude for the many material and spiritual benefits which it owes to the people, the presidents and the scholars of Czechoslovakia.[1] These few pages are an expression of our admiration and gratitude to the university of Prague for six hundred years of work and achievement, by an attempt to assess in general terms the part played by the university in the history of European education, particularly during the critical years of social and cultural transformation which coincided with the first two centuries of the life of the university.

When in 1346 Charles of Luxemburg usurped the imperial throne of Lewis the Bavarian and succeeded his father, John, on the throne of Bohemia, there were already many universities in Europe; for two hundred years there had been *studia generalia* in Salerno, Bologna and Paris where the higher study of medicine, law and philosophy had respectively flourished. In a society which was becoming rapidly more wealthy and whose needs were becoming daily more complicated, the need and the opportunity for a higher education was such that in the thirteenth century the schools of Paris and Bologna were swelled to bursting point. The careers in state and church open to the trained lawyer, doctor or clerk were so many and so profitable that the qualifications which a university could give were eagerly sought after by rich and poor. To the rich, a degree was a profitable investment for a son or a younger brother, or for a

[1] [This study was originally published in 1948 in the *Slavonic and East European Review*.]

canon or prebendary who was ambitious for prelatical honours and emoluments or high office in the court of king or prince; to the poor man of ability and industry the university offered, often at little cost, the high road which led by the *licencia ubique docendi*, through papal provision or aristocratic patronage, to benefices and offices of all sorts. But not only did the universities provide the means for satisfying the ambitious, they also, in the words of Charles's foundation charter, 'set out a table of welcome for those who incessantly hunger after the fruits of learning'. The appetite for knowledge grows with feeding; late mediaeval Europe could afford to feed that appetite, and the universities were an efficient instrument for its satisfaction. It is therefore not surprising that the universities which grew up spontaneously, those of Salerno, Bologna, Reggio in Italy, Paris and Montpellier in France, Oxford in England and Valladolid in Spain, should soon have become so full of aspirants for learning and degrees that they spilled over into neighbouring towns; there were secessions which led to the establishment of new *studia* at Vicenza, Arezzo, Padua, all early thirteenth-century children of Bologna; Padua in its turn became the parent of the university of Vercelli. A similar secession from Paris produced a new university at Angers, and Cambridge was the child of Oxford dissensions. In the course of the thirteenth century the fame and prosperity of those cities wherein universities had spontaneously generated or whither they had been transplanted aroused the envy of the other cities who began to petition prince or pope for the grant of a charter, for it was coming to be assumed that the granting of the licence to teach everywhere was a privilege that could not be adopted by every self-constituted group of teachers and students. The jealousy of established *studia generalia* allied itself with the growing pretensions of pope and ruler to limit and control the development of the new vested interest in learning and education. Nevertheless the hundred and thirty years which separated Innocent III from Charles IV saw a great increase in the number of chartered universities: the rich cities of Italy secured papal foundation for the universities of Piacenza, Rome, Perugia, Treviso and Pisa; the rulers of Castile and Aragon thought no papal assent necessary to them and founded universities by royal charter at Palencia,

Salamanca, Seville and Lerida; the university of Portugal, so long unsettled between Lisbon and Coimbra, was founded in 1290 by the joint action of King Diniz and Pope Nicholas IV. In France, too, it was co-operation between municipality and pope which led to the proliferation of universities: Toulouse, Avignon, Cahors and Grenoble had all received papal charters before Charles IV became emperor.

There were two other universities in existence besides those already mentioned when Charles IV succeeded: one the peripatetic university of the Roman Curia, and the other the university of Naples, the only university founded by an emperor. It had been chartered by Frederick II in 1224 during and as part of his struggle with the Papacy. No succeeding emperor, whether Hohenstaufen, Plantagenet, Castilian, Habsburg, Naussauer, Luxemburger or Wittelsbach, had founded a university.[2] Not that there was ever any doubt of his ability to do so; as king of Bohemia and *a fortiori* as emperor he had as much right to charter a university as any king of Castile or Aragon. It is true that the Avignonese popes would have resisted any attempt of Charles's predecessor Lewis of Bavaria to charter a university, not because Lewis was emperor but just because John XXII denied Lewis's claim to the imperial dignity. But before Charles not even the emperors who had been most friendly to the popes, such as Rudolf I, had sought his help in the establishment of a *studium generale*.

Therefore it remained the fact that of the thirty universities which existed in Europe in 1346, thirteen were in Italy, six in France, six in the Iberian peninsula, two in England, and one moved about with the papal court; only the not very distinguished universities of Avignon and Grenoble were in territory that, except for Italy, could in any sense be called imperial. Germany, Switzerland, the Low Countries, Poland, Bohemia, Hungary, Scandinavia, the Balkans and Russia had not a university among them.[3]

It is possible to explain this extraordinarily lop-sided develop-

[2] The anti-emperor Frederick of Austria had granted a charter to Treviso in 1318, but it is doubtful if the university of Treviso survived the year of its foundation.

[3] The university of Constantinople hardly attained and certainly did not survive the Latin conquest of the thirteenth century.

ment of the universities of Europe in part by saying that higher education is an expensive social luxury which cannot exist without economic prosperity and the leisure which prosperity can provide. In that sense it was natural that the universities should appear in the towns of Lombardy and Emilia, in Languedoc and in the burgeoning communes of the Loire and the Seine. But this is not the whole solution of the problem. Palencia, Coimbra and Lerida had universities, and yet they were not noticeably wealthy as compared with Ghent or Cologne or Florence which had none. Economic considerations are not enough to explain why great universities should have established themselves in the bleak backwaters of Cambridge or even in the remote country town of Oxford while Nürnberg and Hamburg, Breslau and Venice, Prague, Cracow and Buda remained in unchartered darkness.

Undoubtedly political factors must also be taken into account. In war the arts are dumb, and though it would be grossly inaccurate to describe thirteenth-century Italy as peaceful, yet it is true that western Europe had long been free from foreign invasion, while the Mongol invasion and devastation of Russia, Poland, Silesia and Hungary had left state and society in eastern Europe in ruins in which no learned corporation could hope to thrive. Germany, though she had been free of all external danger since the middle of the tenth century, had been subject to the destruction, expense and insecurity of civil war ever since the premature death of Henry VI in 1197. During the devastating conflicts of Welf and Staufen, of Wettins, Ascanians and Wittelsbachs, of Babenbergers, Luxemburgers and Habsburgs there was little opportunity for universities to take root and grow, though one would have thought that conditions there were no more unfavourable than in the Italy of Frederick II and Charles of Anjou. Also, it must be remembered, though there were no universities in Germany before the reign of Charles IV, there was nevertheless a great deal of learning there: Cologne, where Thomas Aquinas studied and where Albertus Magnus and Duns Scotus taught, was a focus of philosophy and theology equal to Paris and Oxford long before it received its university charter in 1388. No university of Europe in the first half of the fourteenth century could show a trio of scholars who could challenge the brilliance of Marsiglio of Padua, Jean of Jandun and William of Occam at the court of Lewis of Bavaria.

It seems to me therefore that neither social nor economic considerations, nor both together, completely explain why the development of universities was so long confined to countries west of the Rhine and south of the Alps. The Rhineland, Swabia and Bohemia were as prosperous as France and England, more prosperous than Spain; Bohemia, apart from the heavy but transient calamity of 1278, had known internal and external security and growing prosperity since 1197; Germany was not more troubled by war than Italy. Therefore, as it seems to me, the lateness of university development in the lands between the Rhine and the Oder is due in large measure to historical accidents: to the fluctuating struggle for supremacy between Welf and Staufen between 1197 and 1214; to the long absences of Frederick II and his hostility to urban privilege; to the nonage of Conrad IV and Conradin; to the absenteeism of Richard of Cornwall and Alfonso of Castile; to the rapidity with which the imperial office passed from Habsburg to Nassau and back, from Luxemburg to Bavaria, all within less than half a century; and finally to the accident of the great quarrel between Lewis IV and the papacy, for no German community would be likely to seek a university charter from the French pope in Avignon, nor from the German sovereign who was for so much of his reign excommunicate.

There was indeed one country in central Europe where a university might have been expected to develop before the fourteenth century, namely, the kingdom of Bohemia, which had been immune from Mongol invasion,[4] and which had been preserved by the strong hand of the last four Přemyslid rulers from the barbarisation of civil conflict. Indeed King Václav II had about 1294 proposed the establishment of a *studium generale* in Prague, but the Bohemian nobles, to whom a university meant Roman law and the doctrine of royal supremacy, opposed the project 'lest they should perchance lose the fruits which they

[4] Part of the Mongol host it is true marched through Moravia on its way from Silesia to Hungary, but its transit was complete within a fortnight, and anyhow, it did not touch Bohemia.

had been hitherto accustomed to gather by their unwarranted innovations'.[5] Despite such jealous feudal opposition it seems probable that a royal university foundation would have appeared at Prague decades before 1348 had it not been for the murder of Václav III in 1306 and the long period of dynastic strife between Habsburg, Carinthian and Luxemburg claimants to the throne and of its occupation for thirty-six years by the absentee and unclerkly John of Luxemburg.

The accession of Charles IV made the creation of a central European university inevitable; he had for a dozen years been regent of Bohemia and had already come to realise that the position and condition of Bohemia would provide the only sound basis for his imperial plans. Prague must be the metropolis of the empire, and the metropolis must have a *studium generale* to provide for the spiritual and administrative needs of the Christian empire. There was indeed no obstacle to the establishment of the university of Prague. Charles had been the pupil of Pope Clement VI and was his friend and ally. Charles was a man of culture and learning and had first-hand experience of the university of Paris: he and his kingdom were rich and could well afford the endowment of chairs and colleges.

Everything went smoothly with his project: on 26 January 1347, the pope granted a bull in which, at the request of Charles, king of the Romans, he agreed 'that it would be advantageous to his hereditary kingdom of Bohemia and to the other neighbouring regions and lands, where there was no *studium generale*, to have one, and that the metropolitan city of Prague, situated in the middle and in the healthiest part of the kingdom, visited by people from divers lands, and abounding in food and the other necessaries of life, was most suited for such a *studium generale* since there had long been a *studium particulare* there'.[6] On 7 April 1348, Charles IV in Prague issued the Golden Bull of Foundation as king of the Romans and king of Bohemia, and on 14 January 1349, at Eisenach confirmed all the privileges of the university by his imperial authority.

[5] Such was the opinion of the monastic writer of the Zbraslav chronicle.

[6] This bull of Clement's and the two foundation bulls of Charles are now most conveniently to be found in V. Chaloupecký, *The Caroline University of Prague*.

In these two bulls Charles made it clear that it was primarily Bohemia and only secondarily the empire whose welfare he wished to promote, 'for more particularly our heartfelt love of our hereditary kingdom of Bohemia impels us to exalt it more generously by especial titles of privilege, for it is as a green garden to our eyes and the personal delight of our majesty'. The king was anxious that 'the faithful subjects of our realm who hunger unceasingly for the fruits of knowledge should not be forced to beg of others, but should find a table prepared for them in their own country. They should not have to satisfy their desires by begging in foreign lands, but should deem it glorious to invite foreigners to come to participate in the sweetness of such a grateful savour.'

Here we have expressed the dual function which Charles wanted his new foundation to perform: to provide a centre for the education of his Bohemian people, and to attract thereto men of distinction from the rest of the empire, and even the rest of Christendom.

Indeed it was the historical function of the university of Prague first to plant there the fruit of the academic achievement of France and Italy, and then to scatter the seeds of the tree of knowledge throughout Germany, Austria, Poland and Hungary.

The very constitution of the university illustrated the richness and diversity of its inheritance. Charles endowed it with 'all the privileges, immunities and liberties which the doctors and scholars as well of Paris as of Bologna by royal authority are wont to use and enjoy'. The details of the constitution he wisely left undefined, and it was the wisdom of the first chancellor, Archbishop Arnošt of Pardubice, which first gave form and order to the new *studium* in his statutes of 1360. At first the *studium* was a university of both masters and scholars, seeking to combine the aristocratic character of Paris with the democratic character of Bologna. But experience showed that it was impossible for teachers and taught to share control; by a curious compromise in 1372 the *studium* split into two universities, one, that of the lawyers which contrived to model itself on the student university of the Bologna law school, the other the university of the three faculties of arts, theology and medicine which steadily became more like the university of Paris, excluding all the students from all but formal participation in its government, and which came more and more under the sole control of the council of masters elected by masters. But it was not only constitutions that Prague took from the older universities. Though there were some Czechs, who, having been educated in Paris or in Italy, were from the beginning capable of lecturing in Prague, it was necessary for Charles to write to the general chapters of the monastic orders to invite them to send teachers to Prague. Master Stephen, who was the first to lecture in canon law in the university, and Master Walter, who was among the first in arts and medicine, were both graduates of Bologna. Though among the names of the first lecturers known to us there are none obviously French, yet the host of erudite Germans who at first flooded all four faculties had most of them been educated at Paris, where they and such Czechs as Vojtěch Raňkův, Matěj of Janov and Jan of Jenštejn, had all been members of the English nation.

It was not only Paris and Bologna that Charles brought to central Europe; less directly and less immediately the university of Oxford played its part in moulding education at Prague and among the children of Prague. The prescribed text-books in arts included the *Poetria Nova* of Gottfried Anglicus, the *Tractatus de sphaere* of John of Halifax (Johannes de Sacrobosco), the *Computus cyrometricalis*, probably by the same author, and the *Perspectiva communis* of the Englishman Johannes Pisanus. More than that the German doctors who came from Paris to Prague were to a man disciples of the British nominalistic school of Occam and Duns, just as a generation later their Czech successors in the university were influenced by Wyclif's philosophical writings to champion the neo-Augustinian realism of Oxford; indeed, after 1409, through the influence of Hus and Jerome [Jeroným] Prague threw off the tutelage of Paris and became more Oxonian than Oxford itself.

One thing which made the rôle of Prague very important was the fact that from its foundation it contained all four faculties; the majority of its predecessors in Italy and France particularly had been predominantly law schools, some of which had never developed studies in the free arts beyond the grammar school stage, and most of which had never had a faculty of theology at all, for the popes long sought to maintain the theological monopoly of Paris. But Prague came fully fledged to life; it was intended to stand beside Paris as a centre of theological study and beside Oxford as a centre of philosophy and mathematics; as for the faculty of medicine, of which we hear very little before the sixteenth century, it was probably no better or worse than medical faculties anywhere else at the time.

But the greatness of Prague lies not so much in what it received as in what it gave. The seedling planted in the broad virgin field of central Europe speedily propagated itself as soon as it became mature. Charles himself was not anxious for rivals to Prague to be planted in Germany, and indeed sought to prevent the establishment of the university of Vienna, and did prevent its having a faculty of theology; the three other universities which Charles founded or refounded by imperial charter were far away from Prague at Siena, Pavia and Orange. Indeed, apart from Vienna, no university was established in the Germanic part of the empire while Charles lived. But the ineffectiveness of his successor, Václav, permitted ambitious princes to seek the renown and profit of establishing universities in their states, and, in that time of papal schism, there was always one pope willing to purchase the prince's support by granting the bull of foundation. This proliferation of universities in the German lands was made possible by the difficulties of the German masters at Paris, who, since the outbreak of the schism, found it profitless to apply to the Avignon pope whom Paris recognised for benefices in Germany where he had no control. Albert of Helmstedt went from the Sorbonne to be the first rector of the university of Vienna in 1365; the great nominalist philosopher Marsilius of Inghen went from Paris to become rector of the new university of Heidelberg in 1384. But Prague also made a most important contribution to the beginning of the higher education of Germany. The learned, prolific and famous Heinrich Totting of Oyta came in 1366 from Erfurt to lecture in the faculty of theology at Prague; from 1377 to 1382 he was teaching in Paris; he returned to Prague and after three years went in 1385 to the university of Vienna where he spent the last fourteen years of his life. Totting's compatriot and contemporary, Konrad von Soltau, came to Prague as a student about 1365, and stayed to become rector in 1384; in 1387 he went to assist in the establishment of the new university of Heidelberg. To the same university went a great Prague theologian and reformer of the next generation, the Silesian Nicholas Magni of Jauer, who spent twenty-five years of his life in the university of Prague and thirty years (1402-1432) in that of Heidelberg. Perhaps the most eminent of the German scholars of Prague, was the probable author of the notable *Speculum aureum de titulis beneficiorum*, Albrecht Engelschalk of Strübing. He matriculated at Prague about 1370, graduated bachelor and master in both arts and theology, was a fellow of the Charles college, twice dean of arts and once rector; he too, sometime after 1402, left for the university of Vienna. The extent to which Vienna was populated from Prague is revealed by the number of witnesses described as 'formerly student of Prague, now student of the university of Vienna' who gave evidence when Jerome of Prague was tried for heresy in that city in 1410.

There is one other university, not in the empire, which owes much to Prague in its early years—the university of Cracow, first founded by Kazimierz III of Poland in 1364, and then after a period of trouble and obscurity, refounded by Władisław Jagiełło and Queen Jadwiga in 1397. Hitherto many subjects of the Polish monarchs had gone to study at Prague, where, together with the Silesians, they constituted the Polish 'nation'. Some of them came home to assist in the establishment of Cracow. Jan Isner, after twenty years in Prague, became *scholasticus* in Poznań and in 1401 transferred to Cracow, to which he bequeathed his valuable library, in which were the works of Aquinas, Duns Scotus, Holkot, Totting and Matthias of Cracow; there, in the same year, the Silesian Matthew of Liegnitz, after nearly thirty years in Prague, joined him. Even more eminent was the renowned Matthias of Cracow himself; he had gone to Prague about 1360, pursued the long *cursus* there until in 1381 he became professor of theology. In 1391 he went home to Cracow, and three years later went on to become a professor in Heidelberg; the eminence of the service to church reform which he performed by his *De squaloribus curiae romanae* was such that not even his sycophancy to the pope when at the end of his life he became bishop of Worms could undo it.

I know no direct evidence that Prague scholars assisted in the foundation of the other universities which were chartered in the fourteenth century in central Europe—Erfurt (1379), Pécs (1367), Cologne (1388) and Buda (1389); but I have little doubt that a collation of promotion lists would show that scholars from Prague played their part here too. But the largest and most immediately successful contribution of Prague to German education was involuntarily made, the result of hostility rather than solicitude. Gradually the number and influence of the Czech masters at Prague had been increasing, and they gained a preponderance of numbers when the foundation of the German universities both made it unnecessary for Germans to go to Prague, and attracted Germans from Prague. But still the three preponderantly Germanic nations at Prague, the Bavarian, Saxon and 'Polish' could and did outvote the Czech nation. At length in 1409 the national desire of the Czechs to be masters in their own university, the increasingly bitter quarrel between the reformist, Wiclifite Czech realists and their conservative German nominalist opponents, and the anger of King Václav at the refusal of the German masters to support him in his plans to heal the schism, led to the publication of the royal decree of Kutná Hora, which gave three votes to the Czechs and one to the Germans. Such a position of inferiority the Germans refused to tolerate, and about a thousand of them, masters and students, shook the dust of the heretical Slav city from off their feet, of whom over forty masters and four hundred students and bachelors accepted the invitation of the two margraves of Meissen to found a university at Leipzig; the rest went perhaps to Heidelberg, Cologne or Vienna.

The departure of the Germans transformed the character of the university of Prague as thoroughly as the expulsion of the Germans after 1945 has transformed the Czechoslovak republic. It put an end to the ecumenical character of the university, which henceforth played a great part in the history of the Czech nation, but did so in opposition to the rest of Europe. The Hussite schism crippled the university constitutionally and narrowed its interests for long to theological and ecclesiastical polemics. After a halcyon period in the sixteenth century Habsburg imperialism and Jesuit counter-reformation stifled and distorted the university; Maria Theresa and Joseph II completed its denationalisation. Not until 1882 did the Charles university again take its proper place in the academic world. In its restored vigour it once more begat and nurtured a promising family: the Comenius university of Bratislava, the Masaryk university of Brno and the Palacký university of Olomouc. As it enters, not with the happiest auguries, on its seventh century of life, we who also boast ourselves the heirs of Masaryk can but say amen to the benediction which President Beneš pronounced in the university on 7 April this year [1948]; it was to prove his last visit to Prague, and his words were his *Nunc Dimittis*. This is what he said:

Three years after the most terrible war in human history, the peace that we yearn for with all our hearts does not exist between the nations. If this natural human yearning, along with the desire for freedom of belief, science, thought, and vocation, is to be fulfilled, it is imperative to cultivate and to attain a universal freedom of the spirit—the essential condition of all genuine spiritual life. This freedom, which is founded on man's respect of man and on common tolerance, and which has always had its home in our university, will, God willing, lead the Charles University once more, and all of us with it, to a truly prosperous and happy future.

II

The University of Prague: The First Sixty Years[1]

LIKE so much else of the creative work of Charles IV, the university of Prague was affected by his ambiguous position as both king of Bohemia and Holy Roman emperor. He thought good to publish the Golden Bull of Foundation not only on 7 April 1348 in Prague as king of Bohemia, but also on 14 January 1349 in Eisenach as king of the Romans and emperor elect. Thus from the start the university had a dual

[1] BIBLIOGRAPHICAL NOTE. The basis for the study of the early history of the university of Prague is still *Monumenta historiae universitatis Carolo-Ferdinandeae pragensis*, edited by A. Dittrich, A. Spirk *et al.*, 3 vols (Prague, 1830-48), and *Děje university pražské*, by W. W. Tomek (Prague, 1849), published in celebration of the fifth centenary of the university. To Tomek's pioneer work this article is inevitably greatly indebted. A select list of other publications valuable for the study of the history of the university between 1348 and 1409 is given below:

W. Erman and E. Horn, *Bibliographie der deutschen Universitäten*, 3 vols. (Leipzig, 1904).

F. C. Dahlmann and G. Waitz, *Quellenkunde der deutschen Geschichte*, 9th ed. (Leipzig, 1931), pp. 206-17.

H. Rashdall, *The Universities of Europe in the Middle Ages*, new edition, 3 vols. (Oxford, 1936), ii, pp. 211-30.

F. Paulsen, 'Die Gründung der deutschen Universitäten im Mittelalter', *Historische Zeitschrift*, xlv (1881).

Statuta universitatis pragensis (Feiertag, 1796).

V. J. Nováček, 'Prameny zakládací listiny university pražské', *ČČM* (1890), pp. 226-38.

Monumenta vaticana res gestas bohemicas illustrantia, ed. L. Klicman, i, 405 (letter of Clement VI, 26 Jan. 1347).

Sammlung ungedruckter Nachrichten, ed. J. W. Hoffmann, ii, 222.

Archivum coronae regni Bohemiae, ed. V. Hrubý, ii, no. 62 (The Golden Bull of Foundation).

O. Placht, *Zakládací listina university Karlovy v Praze* (Prague, 1931).

A. Blaschka, 'Das Prager Universitätsprivileg Karls IV', *Jahrbuch des Vereines für Geschichte der Deutschen in Böhmen*, iii (1932).

[Footnote continued on next page]

function: it was to serve as a *studium generale* for the 'faithful inhabitants of this Bohemian kingdom, that they may not have to go to distant parts of the world to beg from others the desire of their hearts', but at the same time Charles hopes that 'others, strangers, might be invited to participate in its delights'. It was ever Charles's policy to give substance to his imperial position by developing the resources of his Bohemian patrimony, and therefore the university of Prague was designed to serve primarily Bohemia and incidentally the empire. It is clear from the

[Footnote continued]

G. E. Guhrauer, 'Die Anfänge der Prager Universität', *Deutsche Vierteljahrsschrift*, iii (1848).

K. Spiegel, 'The Origin of the University of Prague', *Catholic Historical Review*, ix (1929).

F. Doelle, 'Ein Fragment der verlorengegangenen Prager Universitätsmatrikel aus dem 14. Jahrhundert', in *Miscellanea Francesco Ehrle* (Rome, 1924), iii.

W. W. Tomek, 'O počtu studentů v učení pražském ve 14 století', *ČČM* (1846).

B. Varsík, 'Slováci na pražskej universite do konca stredoveku', *Sborník filosofické fakulty university Komenského*, iv (Bratislava, 1926), p. 38.

K. Domin, V. Vojtíšek, and J. Hutter, *Karolinum-statek národní* (Prague, 1934).

A. Bachmann, 'Der älteste Streit zwischen Deutschen und Tschechen an der Prager Universität', in *Historische Vierteljahrsschrift*, vii (Leipzig, 1904).

V. Novotný, *Náboženské hnutí české ve 14. a 15. stol.* (pp. 96-125 deal with the German and Polish masters at Prague.)

E. Stein, 'Mistr Jindřich z Bitterfelda', *Český časopis historický*, xxxix (1933), pp. 36-56, 259-96, 473-504. (The same author also has an article on the philosophical disputes in the university in *ČČH* (1947), which was not available in this country when this article was written.)

F. Ryšánek, 'Husovy rektoráty universitní', *Listy filologické* (1930).

O. Odložilík, *Štěpán z Kolína* (Prague, 1924).

C. Höfler, *M. Johannes Hus und der Abzug der deutschen Professoren und Studenten aus Prag, 1409* (Prague, 1864).

F. Matthaesius, 'Der Ausgang der deutschen Studenten aus Prag', *Mitteilungen des Vereines für Geschichte der Deutschen in Böhmen*, liii (1915).

F. M. Bartoš, 'V předvečer kutnohorského dekretu', *ČČM*, cii (1929).

Incidental light is thrown on the early history of the university by Novotný and Kybal's *M. Jan Hus*, Klicman's *Processus iudiciarius contra Jeronimum de Praga*, and the article on Jerome of Prague later in the present volume.

[In 1948, on the occasion of the six hundredth anniversary of the university's foundation, three studies on its history were published in Prague in English. V. Chaloupecký, *The Caroline University of Prague: Its Foundation, Character and Development in the Fourteenth Century*; O. Odložilík, *The Caroline University 1348-1948*; V. Vojtíšek and D. Líbal, *The Carolinum, Pride of the Caroline University*. See also F. Kop, *Založení university Karlovy v Praze* (Prague, 2nd ed., 1948). For recent works on the university, see the bibliography in F. Kavka, *Stručné dějiny university Karlovy* (Prague, 1964). Mention should be made, however, of F. Seibt, 'Johannes Hus und der Abzug der deutschen Studenten aus Prag 1409', *Archiv für Kulturgeschichte*, xxxix (1957), pp. 63-80.]

bull of foundation that Charles did not think of the university as a specifically Czech institution; Prague in particular and the lands of the Bohemian crown (which included Silesia and Lusatia) were so impregnated with Germanity that Charles's views and plans were inevitably not racial but national.

This dual function of the university as being both a national and an imperial institution affected the whole of its development and character down to the departure of the Germans in 1409.

As Tomek realised when he wrote his history of the university a hundred years ago, it could not have been purely Czech, even had that been Charles's desire. There was not a sufficient supply of boys of Czech birth and speech equipped with a sufficient knowledge of Latin and numerous enough to fill it; neither from the nature of the case were there enough educated Czechs to staff it. We know the names of only a few of those who lectured in the university during its first twenty years, but, among them, of the earliest professors of theology the Augustinian friar Nicholas and the Franciscan Albert seem to have been Germans, as do also Dytherus de Wydera, Hermann of Winterswyk, Heinrich of Stade, Rutger of Lippe, Hermann of Ravensburg, Gerard of Osnabrück, and Konrad von Soltau among the first lecturers in the faculty of arts. Nevertheless, such native scholars as there were seem to have been employed from the first. It is probable that Stephen the archbishop's chancellor, who is the first known professor of canon law in the university, Balthasar and Walter, the first professors of medicine, as well as Fridman of Žitov, Jenko of Prague, Nicholas of Moravia, John of Drštka, and Lewis of Prague, all of whom were lecturing in the faculty of arts before 1372, were all Bohemians or Moravians; whether they were Czechs is a different matter. The first Bohemian whose name appears in the admittedly incomplete list of rectors is Fridman of Žitov in 1376; the first indubitably Bohemian rector of the law school is Henry of Štvolenka in 1378; and though the second name in the list of deans of the faculty of arts is again that of Fridman, yet, as Tomek points out, of the thirty-five deans of arts from 1368 to 1384 only five were members of the *nacio bohemica*, but which of them were Czechs and which of them were Bohemian Germans it is impossible to determine. Of the twelve rectors of the law school between 1372 and 1378 two only were of the Bohemian 'nation', and one of them, Nicholas Greunher, was a member of one of the richest German merchant families of Prague.

In this connexion it is interesting that even after the foundation of the university many Czech students continued to seek their education elsewhere than in Prague. Vojtěch Rankův (Adalbertus Ranconis), who later became eminent as *scholasticus* of the Prague cathedral chapter, was educated at Paris and perhaps also at Oxford; Archbishop Jan of Jenštejn and Matěj of Janov were also distinguished members of the university of Paris, and none of the three was ever, as far as we know, a student or teacher at Prague, though Jenštejn was *ex officio* as archbishop chancellor of the university. Of the two other Czech leaders of the Bohemian reform movement in its first period Jan Milíč was apparently never a member of any university, and Tomáš of Štítný, even if he was a student of Prague, never graduated.

The difficulty of adequately staffing the new university, whether from native or foreign resources, probably accounts for much of its obscurity during the first twenty years after 1348, as well as for the paucity of the sources for that period of its history. It seems that Charles deliberately refrained from a detailed prescription of the constitution of the university, except to indicate that in the main it should follow the example of Paris, and that the teachers and students should have 'all the rights and liberties of the universities of Paris and Bologna'. That ambiguous provision and the probability that from the first the archbishop of Prague was the chancellor of the university, and that its chief officer was an elected rector, is all that we know of the original constitution of the university. For the rest the founder was apparently content to let time and experience and the wisdom and discretion of Archbishop Arnošt of Pardubice develop the constitution as seemed good and convenient. It was not even laid down by Charles whether the university should basically conform to the Parisian or the Bolognese model, that is, whether it should be a corporation of masters on the French and English pattern, or a corporation of students electing their own rector and employing their teachers, of the type which prevailed in Italy and Scotland. While Paris was a *universitas magistrorum* and Bologna a *universitas scholarium*, Prague was a *universitas magistrorum et studentium*. This meant that sovereign authority in the university rested, in theory at least, in the *generalis congregacio* of all members of the university, such congregations being at first summoned whenever there was need; later they were held twice a year, on 8 September and 12 March. Technically, only congregation could alter or add to the statutes of the university. But it was inconsistent both with the aristocratic temper of the later fourteenth century and with the efficiency of university business that so large and democratic a body should maintain its effective sovereignty. Gradually control passed into the hands of the council, composed at first of eight persons elected by the four 'nations', and later of all the doctors and masters. It is characteristic of the constitutional temper of the age that the original function of the council of eight, limited to the promulgation of *conclusa*, had by 1391 become by custom the right to legislate decisively by the process of submitting the *conclusa* of the council for acceptance by the congregation as *statuta*. By the end of the century the aristocratic transformation was complete: the university had become a corporation of masters, and the function of the congregation was merely the passive one of listening to the moral exhortations of the rector and of being informed what dues and fines had to be paid.

But while in this respect the university of Prague came to conform to the Parisian model, in another the Bolognese example prevailed. The preponderant interest in the study of civil law at Bologna since the twelfth century had led in that university to the establishment of an independent law school. This example inspired the jurists at Prague from the first to assert peculiar claims, and the earliest statutes provided that if the rector was an artist the vice-rector should be a jurist. It seems too that the jurists regarded with alarm the growing authority of the masters at the expense of the students. The increasing tension came to a head in 1372 in a quarrel between the faculty of law and the artists and theologians of Charles College about the possession of some house property in Prague. The rector decided in favour of the jurists, but the college appealed successfully to the chancellor. The consequent dissatisfaction of the jurists led to a schism, for the jurists seceded from the university and set themselves up as a separate single-faculty university, whose rector was the dean of the faculty of law. The life of this law university, which apparently continued as a separate institution until 1419,[2] was a peculiar one. It was predominantly a school of canon law, for the study of civil law never attracted many students in Bohemia, where Roman law was not current. Also the law university, like its Bolognese prototype, maintained its democratic character in the sense that it was always a corporation of students, and that its rector was usually a student or a bachelor. Of its thirty-seven rectors only two are definitely known to have been masters of arts, only three bachelors of canon law, and one is recorded as having had both degrees. But while the law university was democratic in the academic sense, it was singularly aristocratic in the social origins of its rectors, amongst whom there were a dozen scions of the noble houses of Germany, Bohemia, Silesia, and Poland, and even more canons, provosts, and deans from all over central Europe. In the former group occur the names of Jan, count of Pernštejn; John, count of Hohenlohe and canon of Babenberg; Medek of Schellenberg; Smylo of Wyczów; and Jaroslav of Pořešín; among the prelatical rectors of the law university were Nicholas of Kossczol, canon of Breslau; Charles Haguini, archdeacon of Upsala; Peter Capler, provost of St Cross at Breslau; John de Burn, provost of St Stephen's at Bamberg and canon of Bamberg, Herstfeld, and Speyer; Stephen of Manicz, canon of Olomouc and Brno; Mroczko, canon of Płock; Nicholas Greunher (six times rector between 1381 and 1404), first *scholasticus* and then dean of the Vyšehrad; John Pauli, archdeacon of Lund and canon of Roskilde; and half a dozen more.

The organisation of the main university followed more or less the pattern already existing at Paris and Oxford. The archbishop of Prague was *ex officio* chancellor. Arnošt of Pardubice, the first chancellor, had much to do with the shaping of the infant university and with the framing of its first statutes. His

[2] The list of its rectors as given in the *Monumenta universitatis pragensis*, ii, I, ends with the year 1419.

successors confined themselves to ceremonial functions, to hearing appeals from the rectorial court, and to the nomination of the vice-chancellor. The vice-chancellor was usually drawn from the archbishop's clerical entourage and his chief function was the appointment of examiners on the nomination of the faculties.

The chief executive, judicial, and financial officer was the rector. At first the rector was elected annually, but before 1384 the office had become half-yearly. The rector was chosen by that system of elaborate indirect election which the universities had learnt from the Italian communes. Each 'nation' elected one person, and those four elected seven others from the whole university indifferently, and those seven then chose five others who actually elected the rector, either unanimously or by a majority. They might choose any member of the university, in theory, even a student, as long as he was of legitimate birth, a *clericus*, unmarried, not a regular, and of honest report. The rector exercised full jurisdiction over all members of the university in the court which he normally held every Tuesday and Thursday. He had to publish statutes and take oaths of obedience. For his maintenance he received a third of all payments for letters given under the seal of the university and a third of matriculation fees. He was assisted by two collectors, an elected vice-rector, and the university council, the body which before the end of the century had come to be composed of all the regent masters and to be the effective governing body of the university, always excepting the law university.

After the schism of 1372 the main university consisted of three faculties only: the free arts, medicine, and theology. The organisation of the faculties developed slowly: the first dean of arts appears only in 1367, and we have no certain information about deans in the faculties of medicine and theology before 1392. It seems that the organisation of the faculties was first prescribed in the statutes of Archbishop Arnošt of 1360, but we can only deduce what those statutes contained from the revision made by the faculty of arts in 1390 and from subsequent *novellae*. The regent masters in the faculty of arts elected a dean every six months, at first by an open vote, later by secret ballot (*scrutinium*), and finally by an electoral committee (*compromis-*

sum). The dean was assisted in the administration of the finances of the faculty by elected collectors and assessors, and in the licensing of extraordinary lecturers by *dispensatores*. Supreme authority in the faculty lay with the whole body of masters of arts, but gradually all effective control came into the hands of the actual teachers, the *magistri regentes in actu* who composed the faculty council and dealt with faculty business in their regular Saturday meetings. In the absence of direct information we must assume that the faculties of medicine and theology developed a similar organisation to that of the faculty of arts.

The *cursus* of the student in arts in Prague was that normal in the Parisian type of university: matriculation, two years of study, presentation to the faculty, the first examination, and admission to the degree of bachelor. Until 1377 candidates were placed in order of merit, but thereafter this custom was dropped because richer candidates had been bribing the beadle to put them at the top of the list. The new bachelors, unless they were very poor, had to pay a *bursa* of 20 groats to the faculty for a certificate of graduation. If the bachelor wanted to continue his studies, he had yet to be presented for 'promotion', which took place on the next following Ember day, when the candidate was presented by his master to the faculty. There he had to make oral reply to a *sophisma* which was propounded to him; thereupon followed the posing of the *questio*, to which he replied with his *determinacio*, the successful accomplishment of which completed the elaborate process. After an interval of not less than two years more the bachelor who had performed all the necessary exercises might present himself for examination for the master's degree. If he satisfied the examiners, they presented him to the chancellor for the *licencia docendi*, which cost him 38 groats. The licence did not of itself make the recipient a master of the faculty; for that the further processes of graduation, promotion, and inception were necessary. Some licentiates never graduated, probably because they could not afford the fees. Masters of other universities might be admitted *ad eundem gradum* if they took the necessary oaths and made the prescribed payments. Jerome of Prague, for example, after he had graduated as a bachelor at Prague, was given leave of absence to continue his studies abroad. He went to England and some time later graduated as a master in Paris, proceeded to the same degree at Heidelberg and Cologne, and when he returned to Prague was admitted there as a master without further examination. Only after the completion of his course in arts could the master proceed to read theology and pursue the long road of *cursor* and *baccalaureus formatus* to the mastership or (if he was a teaching master) to the professorship in theology.

Before his death Charles IV endowed the university with the beginnings of a collegiate system. In 1366 he founded the Charles College or Carolinum for twelve masters of arts, two of whom had also to be graduates in theology and the rest students of that subject. The college was first established in the house of Lazar the Jew in the Old Town, and was richly endowed by the king. In 1386 the college was removed to the more commodious premises of John Rotlev's house near St Havel's Church in the very centre of the city, where what is left of it still remains. Rotlev, who was master of the mint, had built his house at great cost: it had 141 windows, and was built round two courts. Not only did the fellows live there, but it provided every facility for holding all the functions of the faculties of arts and theology and there were rooms set apart for the meetings of the congregation and council of the university, as well as the *stuba facultatis artium* and the *stuba Saxonum*. In the Great Hall, the *nobile collegii, quod theologicis deputatum est actibus, palatium*, were held promotions and disputations.

In 1366 King Charles also converted the collegiate chapel of All Saints on the Hrad into a college of the university by ordaining that as the existing canons died off they should be replaced one by one by the senior fellow of the Carolinum. In this way All Saints became eventually a college of professors of theology. Charles provided them with a common lodging by the gift of a house near St Nicholas's Church in the Old Town.

The collegiate system was further extended by the conversion of certain monastic houses into communities of regulars teaching and studying in the university. The Dominican school of St Clement's (which was to become the Jesuit Clementinum in the sixteenth century) was incorporated in the university in 1383; from the earliest days there were professors resident in the Franciscan school at St James's; and when Milíč's foundation, the hospice for repentant harlots called 'Jerusalem', was handed over to the Cistercians in 1374, they made it a college of the university for members of their order.

Charles IV's son and successor, Václav IV, was also a munificent patron of the university. In 1380 he founded the College of King Wenceslas. Like the Carolinum it seems to have been exclusively for artists and theologians, who had living-quarters and lecture-rooms there. At the Wenceslas College lived and studied some of those who were to become protagonists of the Bohemian reform movement, as we know from a note in the tractate against the four articles of Prague written by John-Jerome: 'Therefore we, the young Bohemian students of Prague—Jan Hus and Jerome [of Prague] along with Jakoubek [of Stříbro] and Marek [of Hradec] and others—dwelt in the College of King Wenceslaus.'[3]

The other faculties also had their colleges: the jurists were given in 1373 a house in the Old Town which Charles bought from his chamberlain, Pešlín; in 1383 new law schools were built in its courtyard and close by a *commune auditorium universitatis iuristarum.* It was probably Charles, too, who established the medical school in what is now Kaprá Street in the Old Town.

These colleges were primarily for teachers of the university. Undergraduates seem to have lived in private houses. We do not know much about their way of life, though occasionally the sources give us a glimpse of it, such as is provided by the evidence which the eighteen-year-old Kaspar Weinstein gave at the trial of Jerome at Vienna in 1410. When he was asked what he knew of the alleged excommunication of Jerome at Prague in the previous year, Weinstein replied

> that he had heard from students and townsmen that Jerome, Hus, Páleč and their companions had been excommunicated. Asked who those students and laymen were, he said that he could not remember, but that he heard about it in the Old Town of Prague in the house of a furrier with whom he was lodging [*cum quo steterit in expensis pro tunc*]. When he was asked how he had heard of the excommunication, he said: 'I had just returned from the disputation when my landlord said to me: "Why have the judges and sheriffs [*scabini*]

[3] [Translated from the Latin by Peter Brock.]

paid a visit to your schools today? Have you heard any news?" I replied that I knew nothing, and they said: "We have heard that Páleč, Jan of Ješenice, Marek, and in particular Jerome and Hus and others have been excommunicated, because they have been saying that the Bread is not the Body of Christ, and that there is a universal ass." '

Though most of the students seem to have lived in inns and private lodgings, some lived in endowed hostels, like the *domus pauperum studentium* by St Valentine's Church in the Old Town.

From its foundation until the end of the fourteenth century the leading men in the university were foreigners. It was the German, Silesian, and Polish masters and professors who were most distinguished as scholars and teachers. Some of them wrote much; a few of them wrote with vigour and eloquence; but none made a really important contribution to theology, philosophy, or science. Prague before 1400 followed Paris in that it looked at the Church and society with the sceptical eye of the fashionable nominalist. The Prague teachers were as ready as any in Europe to take up the cudgels against superstition and ignorance; many of them shared in the contemporary revival of interest in the person and passion of Christ; some were critical of the laxity of the morals of the regulars, the prelates, and the laity; a few were advocates of frequent communion of the laity. Some of the Prague masters achieved a European reputation, not as scholars of the order of Duns Scotus, Ockham, Bradwardine, Wyclif, or Gerson, but as valuable expositors or commentators. The most eminent of this not very distinguished school of the Prague nominalists were Heinrich Totting of Oyta (he was a German from Oldenburg); Konrad von Soltau, probably a Hanoverian; Jan Isner, a Pole; Nicholas Magni of Jauer, a Silesian; the Dominican Heinrich of Bitterfeld; and Albert Engelschalk of Strübing, a member of the Bavarian 'nation'. Such men did valuable work in expounding the newly rediscovered scientific and political works of Aristotle and his successors. For example, Heinrich Totting wrote *Questiones phisicorum Aristotelis*; Konrad von Soltau wrote *Dicta super Porphirium* and *Commentum super predicamenta Aristotelis*. The [Silesian] German professor Matthias of Liegnitz wrote *Questiones super libros ethicorum Aristotelis*; Engelschalk wrote *Disputata phisicorum Aristotelis*. This same group of teachers also poured out a mass of commentaries on the gospels, the Song of Songs, the psalter, and the epistles, and all of them produced with varying degrees of unoriginality their statutory commentaries on the four books of the *Sentences* of Peter Lombard. Konrad von Soltau's *Exposicio* of the *Sentences* achieved a reputation outside Prague. Their most important contribution to the questions that then most agitated men's minds were Heinrich Totting's *De Contractibus*, *Dicta et responsa cuidam religioso*, and *Questio an concepcio beatae Mariae debeat celebrari*; Konrad von Soltau's *Utrum mater domini, beata virgo, fuerit in peccato originali concepta*; Nicholas Magni's tractates on the passion of Christ and monastic vows. Heinrich of Bitterfeld, perhaps the ablest of the whole group, wrote *De contemplacione*, *Exposicio cantici canticorum mystica*, *De confessionibus et proprio sacerdote*, *Magisterium Christi in septem artibus liberalibus*, and *De crebra communione vel quod licite possit cottidie communicari laycus devotus*. The two books produced by Prague scholars which produced the greatest stir and which are of the greatest interest to the historian are the *Speculum aureum de titulis beneficiorum*, the work of either Engelschalk or Matthias of Cracow, and Matthias of Cracow's undisputed and radical *De squaloribus curiae romanae*, neither of which was published until its author had left Prague for some years.

These two works were not produced until after the turn of the century, and their character indicated a definite shift of interest and achievement from purely philosophical and theological to moral and ecclesiastical questions. This transition in the university of Prague is accompanied by, and is in part due to, the decline of German preponderance in the university and to the steady advance in numbers and prestige of the new generation of Czechs who had reached magisterial status. Since the foundation of the first German and Polish universities (Cracow in 1364, Vienna in 1365, Erfurt in 1379, Heidelberg in 1386 and Cologne in 1388) the number of students at Prague had diminished; also many of the foreign masters of Prague went to assist in the establishment of the new universities in their native lands. Correspondingly the number of Czech students and masters increased both relatively and absolutely.

An important step was that the Czechs in 1384, after exacerbated litigation, secured eleven out of the twelve fellowships in the Carolinum. Another factor in the decline of the Germans at Prague, particularly of the west Germans of the 'Bavarian nation', was the election in 1400 of Ruprecht, elector palatine, as rival king of the Romans to Václav, an event which caused most Germans to cease to look on Prague as the capital of the empire, the 'metropolis of the world', as Matěj of Janov had called it. Nevertheless, even as late as the period 1390 to 1408 the *nacio bohemica* was still only one-fifth part of the university.

Yet comparatively few as they were, the Czech masters were already beginning to make a name for themselves, and, with the support of the king, the queen, the archbishop, and the citizens, to exercise an ever-growing influence. The first Czech to occupy a leading position in the university was Stanislav of Znojmo. He was a lecturer in the arts faculty in 1391, dean in 1395, and provost of the Carolinum in 1400. What makes him particularly important is that in his commentary on the *Sentences* of Lombard he took his stand on the basis of Wyclifite realism, and thus inaugurated that philosophical schism which thenceforward set the Czech realists in opposition to the German nominalists. From 1490 onwards Czech names begin to appear more often in the lists of university dignitaries: Jan Eliáš was rector in 1393, Jan of Moravia in 1394, Štěpán Páleč in 1400, Jan Hus in 1402; Přibislav of Jesenice was dean of arts in 1391, Štěpán of Kolín in 1493, Stanislav in 1395, Ondřej of Český Brod in 1396, Daniel of Prague in 1398, Páleč in 1399, Hus in 1401, Křišt'an of Prachatice in 1403, and Řehoř of Prague in 1405. The Czechs now began to feel that they were entitled to a greater part in the councils of the university than was allowed to them by the constitution, which gave but one vote to the Bohemian 'nation' against the three enjoyed by the Bavarian, Saxon, and Polish nations. The growing feeling of national injustice was expressed eloquently by Jerome of Prague during his trial at Constance in 1416. When he was charged with having broken his oath to preserve the constitution of the university he said:

I am condemned by none but my fellow Bohemians, the German Bohemians; the reason for their hatred is this: the Czechs are descended from the Greeks, and as there was hatred between the Greeks and the Teutons, so it continued until the kingdom came into the hands of the Emperor Charles IV. This same Charles, being king of Bohemia, saw that it was a rich country, not lacking in food, gold or silver, but only in educated men, and that his subjects had to go outside the realm to acquire learning, to Paris and other places to get the degree of master or doctor. Therefore the Lord Charles, wishing to endow the kingdom of Bohemia and the city of Prague, founded and built a university there. In that university many Germans secured prebends and fellowships, so that the Czechs had nothing. And when a Czech had graduated in arts, if he had no other means of livelihood, he had to go to the towns and villages and earn his living by teaching in some private school. The Germans were in complete control of the university of Prague and of all its benefices; they held the seal of the foundation and all the insignia. Also they had three votes in the university, namely the Bavarian and the Saxon and more than half the Polish vote, for the Silesians, who were reckoned among the Polish nation, were all Germans, so that the true Poles were only a minority therein. Whatever the Germans wanted in the university was as good as done. The [Czech] Bohemians could do nothing.[4]

Czech national feelings were exacerbated by the conflict between Ruprecht and Václav and by Benedict IX's withdrawal of recognition of Václav's position as emperor elect in 1403. The divergence between Czechs and Germans in the university became a gulf during the disputes which accompanied the condemnation of the forty-five Wyclifite articles in 1403. In 1408 the German masters determined to assert their authority by charging Matěj of Knín with Wyclifite heresy; the Czechs took up the challenge by securing the election of Knín to perform the honourable function of *Quodlibetarius* for the ensuing year.

The crisis came in 1409. King Václav was committed to supporting France in a policy of neutrality between the rival popes Gregory XII and Benedict XIII until the projected council of Pisa should have made a decision. It was the realisation that the German masters would not support him in that policy of neutrality, not the arguments of Jerome and Hus, that convinced Václav that an international university could

[4] Hardt, iv, 757-8.

not be relied on to support a national policy. On 18 January Václav published the Decree of Kutná Hora:

Although every man is bound to love his fellow man, yet that love must be founded on settled affection. Wherefore it is not right to give a stranger precedence over a compatriot, for true love begins with oneself . . . Since, then, reliable information has reached the king that the German nation, which has no right of citizenship in the Bohemian kingdom, has in all the business of the university arrogated to itself the use of three votes, while the Bohemian nation, the true inheritor of this land, has and uses only one; and whereas the king considers it wrong and most unfitting that foreigners and strangers should enjoy in abundance the favours that belong to the natives of the country, who feel themselves oppressed by so hurtful a deprivation, he commands the rector and the university that hereafter the Bohemian nation, in all the councils, courts, examinations, elections and all other activities and proceedings of the university, shall . . . enjoy the right to three votes, and in virtue of this privilege shall preserve that right for ever in peace and without hindrance.

For a few months the German masters resisted. The rector and the dean, Henning Baltenhagen and Albert Warrentrappe, both Germans, refused to surrender their offices at the normal term. The king decided to act drastically. He sent his minister, the Lord Mikuláš of Lobkovic, and the consuls of Prague to the Carolinum; the rector and dean were compelled to give up their seals, and the royal command was read out that the king had appointed master Zdeněk of Labouně, his secretary, as rector, and master Simon of Tišnov as dean of the faculty of arts.

Thus by royal act the imperial university of Charles was nationalised. The German masters departed, bitter and resentful against all Czechs and Wyclifites, to Leipzig and Erfurt. Henceforward the university of Prague served, not the needs of the Holy Roman empire, but of the Czech nation. It became the instrument of schism and the leader of the nation in its fight against the anathemas of the church and the crusading hosts of Sigismund.

The departure of the Germans from the university was not the end of the achievement of Charles's foundation. In other European universities their nationalisation in the fifteenth and sixteenth centuries was much more damaging than that of Prague, which avoided the narrowness that characterised Paris during and after the reign of Louis XI, and the subservience of Tudor Oxford and Cambridge. It is true that after 1409 the function of Prague was less ecumenical, but the task that it was called upon to fulfil while the nation was fighting for its national and ecclesiastical independence was such that it called for the best efforts of the council and members of the university.

Between 1409 and 1415 the philosophical and religious disputes were continued with increasing acrimony, but the partisans of both sides were now Czechs. Hus was elected rector for the second time in October 1409 and was henceforth the acknowledged leader of the realists and reformers; behind him stood a group of zealous *Wiclifistae*, the radical and statesmanlike Jakoubek of Stříbro, the judicious Marek of Hradec, the ardent and eloquent Jerome of Prague. The party of opposition, drawn from the better-endowed Prague clergy, secular and regular, reinforced later by some of Hus's former friends who were frightened into reaction by the dangers into which their own former radicalism had taken them, rallied to Archbishop Zbyněk. The conflict raged round the questions of universals, the validity of the sacraments of unworthy priests, and the remanence of the material bread after the consecration of the Host. The archbishop solemnly burnt all the writings of Wyclif he could collect; the reformers in the university replied by a series of tractates defending each of Wyclif's philosophical treatises. They played a leading part in the fight against the indulgence granted to assist John XXIII in his war with Ladislas of Naples.

In this atmosphere of excited theological and ecclesiastical controversy there developed within the university the men who were to lead the nation during the years from 1419 to 1452, when there was no king in Prague and when the university virtually governed the country through its control of the Utraquist consistory. In Jakoubek of Stříbro, Jan of Příbram, and above all in Jan Rokycana the legacy of Charles justified itself: sound learning and godly conversation in the university endowed the Czech nation with men who guided and governed it in its most difficult and glorious age.

III

The Great Debate about Universals in the Universities of the Fourteenth Century

When the official of the bishop of Passau was examining Jerome of Prague in 1410 on a charge of heresy, one of the witnesses, a former student of Prague, summed up the whole issue in the words: 'We heard him say in a sermon that there is a universal ass.' University students have a genius for reducing the complex arguments and guarded conclusions of their teachers to such simple terms, and Kaspar Weinstein, not then eighteen years of age, was not the first to crystallise the learning and argumentation of a century into a line in a student's notebook. For this question of universals is the form which the fundamental and still unresolved riddle of all philosophy took in the period when the university of Prague was growing to maturity.

If Jerome of Prague, in agreement with Hus and Stanislav of Znojmo, with Wyclif and Anselm, with Augustine and Plato, was right in his thesis that there is a universal ass, if there is a quality of asininity by virtue of participation in which every individual ass is an ass, there follows a whole theory of being, of reality, a whole metaphysic and epistemology totally different from that which must ensue if one assumes with the opponents of Jerome that there exist only individual asses, and that asininity and all other universal terms are merely words, descriptive conveniences that correspond to nothing that is real. On the other hand if, as Wyclif and his fellow neo-Augustinians, English and Czech, maintained, universals are real, and not merely concepts or intellectual artifacts, if universals have a real existence independently and prior to the individual manifestation of them, then reality is a timeless and changeless universe of realities imperceptible by the senses, not susceptible to mensuration or to human manipulation and experiment; only universals such as humanity, justice, goodness, eternity, infinity, corporeality, substance, sweetness, whiteness, softness are real; the only individual real is God; on the other hand, individuals such as Socrates, just actions, and good men or deeds, this moment and this place, or the white, sweet, soft bread that is consecrated in the host, are merely temporary and transient manifestations of the supersensual reals. Real bread is the substance of every piece of bread, that essence which is imperceptible to the senses, without which that which looks, feels, tastes, or smells like bread is not bread at all. A perceptible individual is composed of a substance, and those accidents whose fortuitous and temporary coherence in it make it perceptible. But the grouping of accidents does not make a thing what it is, and therefore the registration of perceptible accidents (the work of the scientist) can afford no certain knowledge of the thing in itself, which can only be known by an act of non-sensual and non-rational comprehension. A thing may look, feel, taste, and smell like bread, but its substance may be really the body of Christ. A man may be to all outward appearance a pope, bishop, priest, or king, but may be really Antichrist or a tyrant. From this it follows that accidents are not themselves perceptible (for they are mere qualities) unless they cohere in a substance, for individuation only comes by the inherence of accidents in substance. This conclusion led to one of the fundamental problems which perplexed and obscured fourteenth-century philosophical thought, that of annihilation. Orthodox eucharistic theory required that the act of consecration of the Host should annihilate the substance of the bread, and replace it, without effect on its accidents, with the substance of the body, without the appearance of the accidents of the body. It was when realist philosophers reached this stage in their argument that they divided: only the more radical and fearless of them either at Oxford or Prague were willing to follow Wyclif to the heretical and subversive conclusions that were bound to follow on the denial of every possibility of annihilation.

Like the realists, the nominalists of the fourteenth century were started on their course by Duns Scotus's trenchant and penetrating statement of the dilemmas of knowledge, individualism, and determination. By insisting that God is pure will Duns Scotus had appeared to make a distinction between the knowledge and actions of man which are inspired by the inscrutable will of God and those human opinions and actions which result from the restricted activity of man's reason. The successors of Duns at Paris, notably William of Occam, Marsilius of Inghen, Buridan, and John Maulfeld (whom Jerome of Prague at Heidelberg said were *non dialecticos, sed diabolicos hereticos*) went on to argue that there are two ways of cognition: inspiration or revelation, and ratiocination on the basis of sense-perception. Thence it was not far to talk of two sorts of truth; truths of faith and truths of reason, and even to the position that a thing might be true in faith and false in reason or vice versa. The Occamists who pursued this line of thought were easily led to concentrate their attention on the perceptible and the rational, wherein human thought could play a conscious and active part, ceasing to follow Aquinas in his attempt to rationalise the revealed mysteries of the faith.

It is this concentration of attention on the perceptible world which is the characteristic of the neo-nominalism of the fourteenth century, and what most sharply distinguishes it in practice from realism. The nominalists were content to leave the mysteries and problems of theology unresolved. They would not follow Bradwardine into making up their minds on the subject of predestination and free will; the functions of grace and faith in the salvation of the individual they left for Luther, Calvin, and the Tridentine fathers to pronounce upon; they refused to follow Wyclif in seeking a logically consistent explanation of the mystery of transubstantiation. Such things were for the Paris doctors above and beyond reason, which, they believed, could only profitably attend to those things known through the senses.[1] This does not mean that the nominalists were all cold, intellectual rationalists. Indeed, the very fact

[1] In part, this refusal to attempt to rationalise the whole of the faith was the Franciscan reaction to the Dominican thesis, expounded by Aquinas, that even the profoundest revealed mysteries were not illogical or insusceptible of rational explanation.

that they assigned so large a part of the universe to the supra-rational led some of them to seek knowledge thereof by contemplation and mystical exercise. This explains how Gerson could be at once the most eminent nominalist and the most eminent mystic of the early fifteenth century. But for the most part the nominalists were concerned with things as they appear. It is the externals of the church and of religion which absorb their attention: rites, ceremonies, vestments, the words of the sacraments, and the propriety of the externals of the sacramental acts. They are interested in the canon law, the jurisdiction of the church, and its disciplinary and financial machinery. All these things are rationally knowable and therefore susceptible of amendment. Hence the nominalists are ardent reformers; it is Gerson and d'Ailly who believe in the general council as an instrument for the reform of the church in its head and members. The nominalistic habit of mind also led the university teachers of the fourteenth century to judge men and institutions by what they appeared to be, and not to seek to make windows into men's souls. To them what a man is can only be judged by what he does or says; how but by his works shall a man know that he or his neighbour is saved? To the German masters at Prague Wyclif's thesis that dominion is founded on grace, was in the first place nonsense, because prelates and magistrates obviously, and even rightly, exercised dominion irrespective of their state of grace; in the second place it was an anarchical doctrine, for as God alone knows whether any man is predestined to salvation or foreknown to damnation, to deny efficacy to the sacraments of an unworthy priest or to the judgements of a graceless magistrate is to leave every man uncertain whether he has been effectively baptised, confirmed, married, communicated, absolved, ordained, or anointed; unless it is accepted that a man is given authority by observable symbols and ceremonies, any man will be able to refuse to accept the orders of the magistrate or the verdict of the courts. In practice, if only God knows whether a man in fact has ecclesiastical or political authority, the individual will set himself up as a judge of his superiors. The nominalists realised to the full that the sovereignty of the individual means anarchy. For whereas Hus might have been right in his condemnation of John XXIII (had not the council itself charged him with murder, adultery, simony, corruption, and heresy?), what is to be said when Milíč identifies so estimable a person as Charles IV with Antichrist, and Matěj of Janov extends that designation to the whole body of prelates and regulars?

It is easy to understand how it was that the realists begat the heretical reformers of both Bohemia and Germany, and that the nominalists were the fathers of Constance who believed that it was possible at one and the same time to reform the church and to burn Hus and Jerome. The realist faith in the reality of universals and human knowledge as a participation in universal reality implied a faith in the rationality of the whole universe; therefore any effective reformation could not be concerned with externals only, but must concern itself with what underlies phenomena. Inevitably Matěj of Janov's criticisms of the behaviour of churchmen, his condemnation of the abuse of images and pictures, of clerical avarice, and of the abuses of prelatical and papal power led Hus to adopt the thesis of Wyclif's *De ecclesia* and *De potestate papae*, that the very basis of a church founded on the donation of Constantine and the assumptions of the canon law was unsound. The logic which drove the realists into heresy and schism can be illustrated by a passage from Matěj's *Regulae veteris et novi testamenti* (lib. iii, tract. 5, dist. 8, cap. 1) compared with what Hus wrote. Matěj, in a chapter headed 'How fearful are the limbs of Antichrist', wrote about prelatical tyranny thus:

The locusts' teeth (Apoc. ix, 3) are the hard precepts of governors to them that are under them, which may truly be called heavy burdens bound on men's shoulders. For by these commandments of man multiplied without number and beyond what their subjects can bear, these proud and cruel tyrants work oppression, demand full performance, and thus they appear as lions, and not worthy of love like a gentle lamb. Therefore their precepts and instructions have been not undeservedly likened to a circus of raging lions which rend and devour rather than to sheep that chew the cud, for, in the fashion of proud women they are puffed up against their subjects and they lord it over the clergy, not making themselves ensamples to the flock, as Christ did, who said: 'Learn ye of me, for I am meek and lowly of heart'; nor are they humble in proportion to their greatness, but rather the more ardent and bold after the manner of the kings of the Gentiles who lord it over those whom they rule. Therefore 'Round about his teeth is terror', and they say not: 'I beseech you in the mercy of God, dear brother', or: 'I ask you, brethren', but their word is: 'Strictly commanding you, we demand', or: 'We excommunicate you now and hereafter', and: 'Whosoever does not do this and not otherwise, let him know that he shall incur the wrath of almighty God and His saints, that is, anathema', and other like things. Whereby they go against the teaching of wisdom, like lions in the house, turning out their servants.

Lo how these same men, multiplying their innovations, decreeing and affirming their precepts, as if they were a circle of sharp teeth, have confirmed these things under penalty of mortal sin, have published them to the people and openly imposed them on men's consciences, making more discussion and examination of them than of the commandments of God.

For today they are more concerned if a priest chance to omit prime before the celebration of the mass, or if he say mass not according to the order and custom they have laid down, than if the priest is a liar, a drunkard, avaricious or anything of that sort. They make more conscience of it if in the mass the priest says a versicle or response or alleluia otherwise than the rubric enjoins, than if he is a frequenter of taverns, or uses those lips which ought to 'keep knowledge' for hours or days at a time in speaking vanities or the works of man. And so it is of many other things, whose number is without end.[2]

Despite all the radicalism of his criticism Matěj remained a moralist; he was always ready to profess his obedience to the teaching of holy church, and to recant at the behest of his superiors any error they detected in his writings. But during the twenty years after he wrote these words in 1389 the Bohemian realists had discovered that the corruption of morals was but a particular manifestation of what they regarded as an error in first principles, the error that saw supreme authority in the church as it then was, and not in its head. The following well-known passage written by Hus in 1412 well illustrates the nature and result of this development in revolutionary realist thinking:

[2] This passage is characteristic of Matěj. He makes his point by a syntactically complicated cento of Biblical phrases: in this case from the Apocalypse, Matthew, Jeremiah, Job, I Peter, Luke, Ecclesiasticus, and Malachi.

Lo, I rely on this most holy and fruitful example of the Redeemer and, from the heavy oppression, wrongful sentence, and pretended excommunication of the pontiffs, scribes, pharisees and judges sitting in Moses' seat I appeal to God, committing my cause to Him. I follow in the footsteps of my Saviour Jesus Christ as did the great and holy patriarch of Constantinople, John Chrysostom, from the crafty Council of bishops and clerics; as Andrew, blessed in hope, bishop of Prague and Robert of Lincoln, when they were harmfully oppressed, humbly and healthfully appealed from the Pope to the supreme and most just Judge, who is never moved by fear, nor turned aside by love, nor seduced by gifts, nor deceived by false witnesses.

I hope therefore that all the faithful of Christ, and especially the princes, barons, knights, vassals and other inhabitants of the kingdom of Bohemia will understand and sympathise with me in this pretended excommunication which I suffer mainly through the instigation of my rival and adversary Michael de Causis, formerly incumbent of the church of St Adalbert in the New Town of Prague; an excommunication which was given and fulminated by Peter of S. Angelo, cardinal deacon of the Roman Church, as the judge deputed by the Roman pontiff John XXIII, who for two years refused to give audience to my advocates and proctors, which should not be denied even to Jew, pagan or heretic; nor was he willing to accept any reasonable excuse that I did not appear in person, nor to accept in his fatherly kindness the evidence of the university of the Studium of Prague, even with the seal and attestation of notaries public called in evidence . . .

I, Jan Hus of Husinec, master of arts, bachelor formatus of sacred theology of the university of Prague, priest and preacher appointed to the Chapel called Bethlehem, make hereby my appeal to the Lord Jesus Christ, the most just judge who knows, protects and judges, makes plain and unfailingly rewards the just cause of every man.[3]

The nominalists were not constrained to make any such fatal advance from moral criticism to ecclesiastical revolution. Matthias of Cracow could damn the 'squalor of the court of Rome' with an eloquence of detail no less thorough than that of Wyclif and much more scurrilous than that of Hus. But Matthias of Cracow was in the nominalist tradition: his judgements were based on what he knew by the evidence of his

[3] 'Appellatio M. Joannis Hus a sententiis pontificis Romani ad Jesum Christum supremum judicem', in Palacký, *Documenta*, p. 464.

senses; he had learned from the Scotists and Occamists to leave the truths of faith unquestioned; to him reason was no weapon to use against revelation. Therefore while Hus went to Constance and the stake, Matthias of Cracow went to his fat bishopric at Worms, where he could attack as heretics those whom he had once joined in the clamorous chorus of moral indignation.

It was this willingness of the nominalists to be content with the observation and criticism of externals and appearances which made the effort to reform the church which they sponsored abortive. The culmination of the reformist activities of the nominalists was the council of Constance. There they made formal attack on the obvious abuses of ecclesiastical practice; pluralities, absenteeism, papal reservations of absolution, annates, the *communia servicia* and *servicia minuta*, papal collations and expectative graces, the appellate jurisdiction of the *curia*, the papal chancery and penitentiary, simony, dispensations, papal provisions, indulgences, and papal tenths. This is the list of things to be reformed by the future pope prescribed by the council in its fortieth general session on 30 October 1417, before the election of Martin V. It was a comprehensive programme and one which Wyclif and Hus would have applauded. For months the reform commission of the council laboured to elaborate it, but the poverty of their achievement is well known. It was the *curia* and the system which triumphed, and Gerson and d'Ailly feebly acquiesced in a small list of reform decrees which merely invited the pope to be sparing in his use of exemptions and incorporations. The accumulation of benefices was piously forbidden; the pope renounced his claim to the first-fruits of vacant benefices; simony was condemned once more in general terms; dispensations for the enjoyment of ecclesiastical revenues without ordination or consecration were annulled; papal tenths were only to be levied in cases of special necessity and that with the consent of the bishop of the province: finally the pope was asked to enjoin greater regularity in the dress and conduct of clerics (Decrees of the forty-third general session of Constance, 21 March 1418).

It is true that there were political and personal reasons for the failure of the council to achieve its purpose of reforming the church in its head and members. Nevertheless, no small part of this failure must be ascribed to the philosophical position of the nominalists; their refusal to examine first principles and their scepticism about general notions made them unwilling to look for the root causes of which these ecclesiastical abuses were the consequences. It was just because Wyclif and Hus and Jerome had stripped away the *adinvenciones hominum* and revealed the corruption of motive and character behind them. The fatal error of the council was to think that they could both reform the church and extirpate Wyclifism.

Gerson and d'Ailly were fully alive to the fact that their quarrel with Hus and Jerome was fundamentally a philosophical one; their theological and ecclesiastical ends were the necessary consequences of their faith in *realia ante rem.* At the very beginning of the first examination of Jerome, Gerson said: 'Jerome, when you were at Paris, you thought that in your eloquence you were an angel from heaven, and you troubled the whole university, positing many erroneous conclusions and corollaries in the schools, especially in the matter of universals and ideas and many other scandalous things.' Similarly Pierre d'Ailly got to the root of the matter when he said to Hus during his examination on 7 June 1415: 'We cannot judge in accordance with your conscience, but only in accordance with what has been proved and deduced against you and what you have confessed.'

Nevertheless, while it seems probable that reformation was impossible on the principles of the nominalists, their achievement in the fourteenth century was not entirely barren. It has been the fashion ever since the time of Francis Bacon to look on Duns Scotus as the father of all empty sophisms and the most uncreative of dialecticians; until recently Buridan has been known only as the ingenious propounder of logical puzzles. But the more recent researches of such men as Gilson, Landry, Longpré, C. R. S. Harris, Noel Valois, Hochstetter, and Pierre Duhem have demonstrated that the work of Duns and Occam was the beginning of the scientific revolution of the sixteenth and seventeenth centuries. The development of western Europe in the fourteenth century was already causing men, increasingly interested as they were in the visible external world, to ask questions about space, time, and matter and their measurement which could not be answered on the basis of *a priori* Aristotelian science. The needs of the clockmaker and smith, of the bridgebuilder and shipwright, of the assayer and miner, the navigator and surveyor, found no satisfaction in the works of Augustine or Anselm or even Aquinas. It was not problems of cognition but of mensuration, not metaphysics but physics, not the eternal but the apparent, which were interesting to the citizens of fourteenth-century Florence, Paris, Prague, and London. This change in the centre of interest from man's soul to his body, from ideas to things, hastened the nominalistic revolt from Anselm's idealism and Aquinas's Aristotelianism. The transference of interest from the eternal to the transient was reflected in the nominalists' interest in individuals rather than species and genera, and led to their characteristic doctrine that *generalia* are only names given by men for the sake of convenience to observed similarities in individuals. They denied that 'whiteness' had any existence apart from and independent of white things, and therefore they denied the realist thesis of *universalia ante rem*.

It was the Franciscans at Oxford who led the movement away from the rationalist idealism of Aquinas in the direction of rationalist scepticism and empiricism. The development of mathematical studies at Oxford and the experimental work of Roger Bacon paved the way. The first and decisive step was taken by another Oxford Franciscan, Duns Scotus; his faith in the absolute will of a super-rational God led him to regard only the sensible world as susceptible of rational exposition and comprehension; but in dealing with the sensible world he put aside all the assumptions of Platonic and Aristotelian deductive logic, and insisted that only that which is syllogistically demonstrable has validity. It was Duns, too, who was the protagonist of the doctrine of the freedom of the human will; in this, too, the nominalists of the fourteenth century followed him, while the realist line of succession through Bradwardine, fitzRalph, and Wyclif was led by its insistence on the eternal to the opposite doctrine of predestination.[4] It was Duns Scotus who took

[4] Belief in predestination occupied a large place in the charges made against Wyclif, Hus, and Jerome at Constance, and against Jerome at Vienna. The

the new philosophy to Paris and Cologne, where he taught from 1304 to 1308.

Duns was not a nominalist in the formal sense of the word, but it was easy for his disciples to develop his metaphysics in a nominalist sense. It was a Dominican, Durand of Saint-Pourçain, and a Franciscan, Pierre Auriol, who first restated the thesis that *generalia* have no existence apart from mind and that knowledge cannot go beyond the individual and the classification of facts. But it was an Englishman, William of Occam, who made neo-nominalism comprehensible and popular by the consistency and radicalism of his exposition. At Oxford and Paris and in Germany Occam had expounded his fundamental scepticism, metaphysical and ethical. To him the sole legitimate function of science was the description of individuals; ideals and universals were but mental acts of abstraction and imagination; the faith cannot be rationalised, it must be accepted by a pure act of faith.

On the ground which Occam had cleared of all assumption and hypothesis, his disciples began to build a new structure. At Oxford Adam Woodham and Robert Holkot pursued the mystical tendencies implicit in nominalism; at Prague the German, Silesian, and Polish masters expounded the logical side of the doctrine and interested themselves in the phenomena of contemporary religious life and practice; but at Paris Occamism bore fruit in the exploration of scientific method and physical problems. There Nicholas d'Autrecourt flatly denied the existence of *substantia*, and explored the possibilities of atomism and the nature of causation. Jean Buridan not only drew the conclusion from Duns's ethics that morality is purely relative, but went on from Occam's criticism of Aristotelian physics to explore the nature of motion, mass, and density, and the acceleration due to gravity: he poured scorn on Aquinas's system of *intelligenciae motrices*, and argued that the whole universe is governed by a uniform system of mechanical law. Albert of Helmstedt, called 'the Saxon', applied the same method of sceptical empiricism to physiography, and came to make the important distinction between the geometrical centre

charges take the form of accusations that the accused had said *Deus debet diabolo obedire*, or *Omnia de necessitate eveniunt*.

of an object and its centre of gravity. Nicholas d'Oresme in his *De celo et mundo* went even farther on the road that led to Copernicus, Galileo, and Newton: he saw that mass is the determining factor in any astronomical system, and therefore went on to argue that a body of such relatively small mass as the earth cannot be the centre of the solar system; he also adumbrated the method of analytical geometry.

Speculations of this kind were not confined to Paris. Buridan probably was one of the founders of the university of Vienna; Albert the Saxon was the first rector of that university, and was bishop of Halberstadt from 1366 to 1370. Marsilius of Inghem went from Paris in 1384 to be rector of the university of Heidelberg, where he remained till his death in 1396. To what extent the masters of Prague were aware of, or participators in, these modern physical and mathematical studies we shall not know until more of their writings have been published. What evidence we have seems to indicate that Prague lagged behind Paris, and that Heinrich Totting and Matthias of Cracow and even Bitterfeld were more interested in the moral side of nominalism than in its physical speculations. In any case, the more eminent of the German masters left Prague before the end of the century to assist Buridan, Albert, and Marsilius in the founding of the new German universities, and the rest of them departed in 1409, leaving Prague in the hands of the Czechs, among whom the realist party soon and permanently prevailed. As realism had been extinguished in Oxford with the suppression of Wyclifism, Prague was left alone to develop the implications of Wyclif's philosophical doctrines; therefore it was that only in Prague is the connexion between the realism of the fourteenth century and the Reformation of the sixteenth century unbroken.

Nominalism continued to dominate the other universities of Christendom in the fifteenth century; but the great promise of the Parisian physicists was not immediately fulfilled, partly because of the cramping effect of the policy of narrow nationalism in the universities which was universal in the fifteenth century, and partly because the Occamists became increasingly fascinated by the syllogistic problems of their verbal logic; the statement and solution of *dilemmata* and the discussion of fallacies more and more monopolised their attention; alchemical studies obtruded on physical speculation and astronomy was obscured by astrology. Nevertheless, the critical examination of Aristotelian science and the attempt to construct a cosmogony on the basis of observed facts were not entirely swamped: the nominalists had cleared much of the ground and asked many of the questions which were to make the task of the scholars of the sixteenth century possible.

Thus it was that the debate about the universal ass in the fourteenth century started two trains of thought which were to lead one to the Reformation and the other to the Renascence.

IV

The Influence of Realist Philosophy on Jan Hus and His Predecessors in Bohemia[1]

REALIST philosophy is not merely a phenomenon of the Middle Ages. It survived both the materialism and the humanism of the Renascence to burgeon again in the philosophy of the Cambridge Platonists and the Jesuits of the seventeenth century and in that of the Pietists and the school of Berkeley in the eighteenth. Mediaeval realism lived again in the Romantics, Chateaubriand, Coleridge and Newman, in the Hegelian idealists and in the Neo-Platonists of our own day. The lineage of realism also extends far into the past: begotten by Socrates and brought into the world by Plato, consecrated by the apostle Paul and Saint Augustine, mediaeval realism was formulated by two abbots of Bec and archbishops of Canterbury, Lanfranc and Anselm, and defended against an ever more menacing verbal rationalism by Saint Bernard and Saint Bonaventura, to be inherited by the mystics of the late Middle Ages.

But this thread of realist thought which links the Socratics to the idealists of today was very nearly severed in the fourteenth century. It was the abhorred shears of the nominalists which threatened it, and nominalism was the more dangerous because it was the product of the forces of an age which was dominated by the merchants, the humanists, the cynics and the materialists. The nominalists had no use for the ideas, the generalisations and abstractions, the essences, substances and universals of the

1 [The first paragraph, which summarises the main points of mediaeval 'realism', and several subsequent paragraphs, have been omitted. The Latin citations preceding notes 8, 11-14, 21, 25-7, 29, have been translated by Peter Brock.]

realists. They regarded them as nothing but a breath of air, a *flatus vocis*, a mere convenience of discourse, without reality or actuality. To the nominalist the only real was the sensible individual; he believed that human reason could occupy itself only with that which could be immediately apprehended by the eyes, the hands, the nose, the ears and the palate. It was a philosophy which was content to put the mysteries of religion on one side as being beyond the competence of reason, to accept them without question on the authority of the church alone, concerning itself for the rest solely with the sensible world. Such an approach explains why the nominalist philosophers of the fourteenth century so often ignored questions of high theology and devoted themselves to the exploration of observable phenomena. As the century progressed the nominalists interested themselves more and more with the problems of physics and physiography, and so closely were the problems they discussed related to the needs of an age of expanding bourgeois commerce that there was a great danger that the idealist philosophy of realism might succumb, suffocated in so earthy and material an atmosphere. This danger was the greater because the university of Paris had itself been seduced by nominalist philosophy; and the university of Paris in the fourteenth century was the acknowledged sovereign and arbitrator of the learned world of western Christendom. The choicest spirits of western and central Europe came to Paris to study and to teach, from Germany, Bohemia and Scandinavia, where there were, before 1348, no universities at all, from England and Scotland where there were a few universities, and even from Italy, where there were many.

The mendicant schoolmen of Oxford had blazed the trail which led from Aquinas's rationalist idealism, by way of the mathematical and experimental studies of Roger Bacon, towards scepticism and rationalist empiricism. The seeds of formal nominalism had been sown by an Oxford Franciscan, Duns Scotus, whose exaltation of God's absolute will above human reason had led him to believe that only the sensible world is capable of being rationally explained and of being comprehended by the human intellect. It was Duns Scotus, too, who brought this philosophy to Paris.

Nor was it only the French who became the apostles of the new scientific materialism. As long as there was no university east of the Rhine the Germans came by preference to Paris for their education in philosophy and theology, and when, towards the end of the century, universities had been founded in Germany, these Germans took back with them the nominalism they had learned at Paris to the newly established chairs at Heidelberg, Cologne, Erfurt and Vienna. One such was Albert of Helmstedt, called 'the Saxon', who had learnt at Paris to apply empirical methods to physiography and to distinguish between the geometrical centre of a thing and its centre of gravity. This same Albert became the first rector of the university of Vienna, of which university Buridan was probably one of the founders. Another German, a doctor of Paris, Marsilius of Inghem, himself one of the most eminent nominalists, left Paris in 1384 to become rector of the university of Heidelberg where he taught until his death fourteen years later.

The university of Prague was also born of and nourished in Parisian nominalism. Its founder, the Emperor Charles IV, was devoted to Paris and had attended lectures by its doctors, and from the foundation of the university of Prague in 1348 he had modelled it on the universities of Paris and Bologna. Since there was not at first a sufficient number of educated Czechs to fill the chairs of the new-born university, Charles IV and the first chancellor of the university, Archbishop Arnošt of Pardubice, had to invite foreigners, mostly Germans, to Prague, and some of these German professors who came to Prague had been educated at Paris. The German masters dominated the university until the end of the century. Of the four 'nations' which composed the university of Prague, two were those of the Saxons and Bavarians; the third, that of the Poles, was full of Silesian Germans. What is more, after 1378, when the university of Paris recognised the Avignonese pope, Clement VII, some of the German masters at Paris, being unwilling to remain under the jurisdiction of a pope whom they believed to be schismatic, departed for Prague. It was in this way that the young university of Prague came to be subject to nominalist philosophy during the first fifty years of its existence. Its most eminent teachers were German nominalists.[2] How far these nominalist masters in the university of Prague were influenced by the mathematical and physical savants of Paris we shall not know as long as their works lie unedited in the Prague libraries. What evidence we have seems to indicate that Prague lagged far behind Paris, and that Totting and Matthias of Cracow and even the most eminent of this group, Bitterfeld, were much more concerned with moral questions than with the physical speculations of the nominalists.

From all that we know of fourteenth-century philosophy it seems to be clear that in 1390, when the young Jan Hus matriculated in the university of Prague, almost the whole learned world was in the full flood of nominalism; it had triumphed in France, Germany and Bohemia. It looked as if idealist philosophy might disappear for ever in the darkening atmosphere which signalised the end of mediaeval spirituality and the advent of the materialism of the modern world.

But providentially as it might well seem, there remained one island of refuge for the realists from the rising tide of nominalism and by a second miracle, when that island was itself inundated by the flood, the ideas and the faith which had found asylum there escaped destruction by emigration to the other end of Europe where they could flourish lustily to defend themselves against all attacks. The first of these refuges of realism was England, the second Bohemia.

English realism was descended from that same Duns Scotus who had, somewhat unwittingly, begotten nominalism. Of the two elements in his philosophy, human reason and the will of God, the Paris masters had concerned themselves with the one, the Oxford masters, especially the seculars, with the other. It is not easy to see why the university of Oxford did not follow its sister of Paris along the road towards nominalism. Perhaps it was that the preponderance of secular masters at Oxford over the friars gave less opportunity to the Franciscan champions of nominalism and assisted the survival of the rival school of thought. It must be remembered too that Oxford long opposed the rationalism of Aquinas. But whatever the reason, English

[2] For a brief account of the work of the German masters in the university of Prague see Novotný, *Náboženské hnutí české ve 14. a 15. stol.*, pp. 96-105.

philosophy never quite forgot the idealist tradition of Anselm. The line of mystics was continued into the fourteenth century with Holkot and Hales; the controversy waged by Richard fitzRalph, chancellor of the university of Oxford and archbishop of Armagh, with the mendicants engendered in England a hostility to both the ideas and the activities of the Franciscans.[3] What is still more important, as the fourteenth century progressed the English theologians interested themselves more and more in the problem of free will and predestination. fitzRalph placed in the forefront of his theology the omniscience and the prescience of God, whereby every human creature is predestined from the beginning of time to choose either his own salvation or his own damnation. His contemporary, Bradwardine, the archbishop of Canterbury who died of the black death in the first year of his primacy, pushed the doctrine of predestination to the extremes of Calvinistic rigour; to him predestinating grace was all in all; faith and works had no place in his system of salvation. In all this the renewed study of St Augustine had a great influence. It is difficult to exaggerate the importance of this neo-Augustinianism in England at this time, and it was not only the Augustinian doctrine of predestination which attracted the English secular theologians. The whole body of St Augustine's Platonic philosophy, his idealism, his insistence on the super-temporal, the super-sensual and the ideal, penetrated the whole spirit of the Oxford realists. The uncompromising doctrine of predestination was to become the shibboleth whereby the nominalist fathers of the council of Constance recognised and condemned their realist opponents, and insistence on it or indifference to it became the criterion of distinction between the two rival schools.

Now predestination is not a fact which is capable of scientific demonstration, for the evidence of the senses will not reveal whether any individual man has been predestined to salvation or foreknown to damnation: that depends on the inscrutable will of God. A man is able to judge of the faith and the works of his neighbour, but not of his state of grace. But for fitzRalph

[3] For the place of fitzRalph in the development of Anglo-Bohemian thought see 'Richard fitzRalph, Archbishop of Armagh, and the Doctrine of Dominion' later in this volume.

and Bradwardine, and for their disciple, Wyclif, grace and the unchangeable will of God were the very essence of the relation of a man to God. It was indeed Wyclif who elaborated these ideas into the system which may be described as neo-realism. In his earliest philosophical writings, the *De ideis* and the *Summa de ente*,[4] he expounded formally his whole system of realist metaphysics, the doctrine of *universalia ante rem*, of the reality of unindividuated substance, and of the transience of the individual and of accidents. Later in his life his belief in the indestructibility of *substancia* led him to adopt the formally heretical thesis of the remanence of the substance of the bread and wine in the host after its consecration.

For a score of years Oxford philosophy was dominated by Wyclif's realism, and its position was only challenged when Wyclif incurred the suspicion of eucharistic heresy.[5] The opportunity he thereby afforded was eagerly seized on by his enemies, particularly by the friars, whom he so ferociously assailed. His realist opinions, both dogmatic and ecclesiastical, were condemned at Canterbury and Oxford, and the university was purged of his disciples. After his death in 1384 the Lollards were in part exterminated by systematic persecution and for the rest reduced to dumb obscurity. In the early fifteenth century debased nominalism ruled at Oxford with the same soul-destroying tyranny as at Paris.

But the idealism which had been as much the glory of ancient Greece as it was of the high Middle Ages was not destined to

[4] Tractates 1 and 2 of Wyclif's 'Summa de ente' have been edited by S. H. Thomson, *Summa de ente; libri primi tractatus primus et secundus* (Oxford, 1930), and tractates 3 and 4 of the first book of the 'Summa' by M. H. Dziewicki, *De ente* (London, 1909), pp. 1-48. The remaining three tractates of the first book and the whole of the second book, containing the crucial 'De universalibus' and 'De ideis' still await publication.

[5] Dr Workman would date the beginning of Wyclif's eucharistic aberration to 1379 (H. B. Workman, *John Wyclif* (Oxford, 1926), ii, 408-9) largely on the evidence of the following passage from Sermon LXIII: 'Certum quidem est quod nedum christianismus sed quodcunque regnum eius vel notanda communitas in duo dividitur, quarum prima pars quam quidam vocant Urbanitas vere concedit quod panis sacramentalis sit vere et realiter corpus Christi, alia autem pars infidelis que est longe potencior sive plurior quam quidam vocant Robertinos asserit infideliter quod hoc sacramentum non potest esse panis nec corpus Christi sed unum accidens quod ignorant' (Wyclif, *Sermones*, iv, ed. J. Loserth (London, 1890), p. 499). Dr Workman thinks that such a passage could only have been written soon after the outbreak of the Great Schism in 1378.

disappear from the face of the earth. Hardly had the torch been extinguished at Oxford than it was rekindled at Prague amidst the shadows of the oppressive nominalism which reigned there. It may be asked, why precisely at Prague, and why just at that critical moment? The explanation is not to be sought merely in the importation of Wyclif's writings into Bohemia. While Wyclif was still young and hardly known outside the schools of Oxford voices were already to be heard in Prague speaking the language of St Paul, of Augustine and Guillaume de Saint-Amour. They were the voices, not of the German doctors of the university, but of Czechs. Was this a spontaneous and parthenogenetic rebirth of realism on the very edge of Catholic Europe? In part perhaps it was. But also there was a fertilisation from the west which anticipated that which Wyclif provided. Ever since the accession of the first Luxemburg to the Bohemian throne in 1310 in the person of King John, the contacts between Bohemia and France had been close, and as long as there was no *studium generale* east of the Rhine and north of the Alps, young Czechs questing for knowledge and office had been accustomed to go to Paris to seek degrees in arts or theology. Even after the foundation of the university of Prague in 1348 this stream of young Czech scholars continued to flow to Paris and did not dry up until the outbreak of the great schism.[6] It might well be asked how it was that the Czech scholars could have acquired a bias towards realism at Paris in view of the dominance of nominalism there. The explanation of this paradox is afforded us by some invaluable indications in the lists of promotions contained in the archives of the university of Paris. It is well known that all those who came to matriculate at Paris from central, northern and eastern Europe were registered as members of the English 'nation', in which were to be found, beside the English with their known realist predilections, also the Scots and the Irish, whose place of origin was even more

[6] All the evidence seems to indicate that the university of Prague remained embryonic and not very attractive at least until its chancellor, Archbishop Arnošt of Pardubice, gave it a body of statutes in 1360. The effect of the schism for the German and Czech students at Paris, which adhered to the Avignonese pope, was to drive them to seek graduation in one of the new universities in Bohemia, Germany, Austria or Poland; otherwise they could not hope for preferment in those countries, which remained in the obedience of Urban and his successors.

remote from the centre of nominalist infection. It was in close community with this realist minority from the British Isles that the Czechs dwelt and studied. The Czech scholar Vojtěch Raňkův (Adalbertus de Ericinio), who became a regent master and later rector of Paris, had a Scotsman as his promotor in arts, and during the whole twenty years that he remained at Paris he was in close contact with his British colleagues. Jan of Jenštejn tells us that Vojtěch was also at one time professor at Oxford, which is quite possibly true, for not only did Vojtěch bequeath his property to provide an endowment to send young Czech scholars to study in Paris and Oxford, but also he was given by his contemporaries the nickname of 'Armachanus'; this is a clear indication that he was notorious at Paris as a disciple of the Oxford realist, Richard fitzRalph, archbishop of Armagh. After Vojtěch had returned to Prague and become a canon and *scholasticus* of the cathedral church of St Vitus he became the patron and friend of a group of reformers whose inspiration was Jan Milíč and of which Matěj of Janov and Tomáš of Štítný were the members most indebted to the hospitality of Vojtěch.

This same Jan of Jenštejn who tells us of Vojtěch's professorship in Oxford became while still a young man archbishop of Prague, and after a gilded and libertine youth suddenly plunged into all the rigours of an idealistic and ascetic mysticism. He too had been a member of the English nation at Paris and it is probable that the seeds which later flowered into this practical idealism were sown during his association with this coterie of British realists at Paris.

Even more important in the story of the coming of realism to Prague is Matěj of Janov. He was the first who gave to the Czech reformers a written body of teaching, a copious treasury of texts and arguments on which they could draw for their ammunition in the war which they waged against the corruption of the church of their day. The bulk of Matěj's work is contained in the five large books of the *Regulae veteris et novi testamenti*[7] which he had completed before his death in 1394.

[7] The first four books have been published as *Matthiae de Janov dicti magister Parisiensis Regulae veteris et novi testamenti* under the editorship of V. Kybal and Odložilík. The fifth book of the *Regulae* has not yet been published but I have

It was in Paris that Matěj also had gained the learning embodied in these volumes and the ideas which inspire them. He spent there ten years as student, master and rector, and such was the reputation he won that in the history of mediaeval philosophy he earned the proud title of *Magister Parisiensis*. But what is most significant for the purpose of this present study is that he returned to Prague not as a disciple of the Paris nominalists, but as an idealist, mystic and eschatologist; his inspiration at Paris had not been the physicists and physiologists of the school of Nicholas d'Oresme, but the French mystics and idealists of the thirteenth century such as Guillaume de Saint-Amour, Hugues de Saint-Victor and the author of the *Pericula novissimorum temporum*.

The following characteristic passage from the *Regulae* well illustrates the temper of Matěj's philosophy. He is speaking of the unity of the Church and says:

For there is in the church of Jesus Christ a second mode of union, that is, of adhesion or dependency of one on another, since the whole church adheres to Christ Jesus as the members to the head, as the accident to its subject, as the adjacent to its substance . . . Hence, to be sure, there can be discerned a close similitude of the union of the church or any faithful soul with Christ Jesus. For, as the whole being [*esse*] of the accident depends on the essence of the subject, so, as the Philosopher says: 'The being of the accident is the existence in the subject.' So indeed the whole being of grace and the blessedness of the Christian soul or the whole church stems from the being of Christ, from adhesion to Jesus Christ through faith, hope and charity. And, just as the more strongly the accident inheres and the deeper it is rooted in its subject, the more it communicates the being of the subject and is removed from non-being, so the church and any rational soul, the more strongly it adheres to the incarnate Word and the more profoundly it is rooted in faith, hope and charity, so much the more it abounds in the being of grace and of its own proper good . . . And again, as it is in its subject that the accident is generated and corrupted, is augmented and diminished, the subject remaining motionless, so any spirit remains permanently in a state of grace.[8]

been privileged to consult the transcript of the Olomouc MS made by Odložilík. The classical study of Matěj is V. Kybal, *M. Matěj z Janova*.

[8] *Regulae*, ii, 150-1: 'Est eciam in ecclesia Jhesu Christi secundus modus unionis, scilicet adhesionis vel dependencie unius ad alterum, quoniam tota ecclesia adheret Christo Jhesu quasi membra suo capiti, quasi accidens suo subiecto, quasi adiacens

This is obviously not the language of a nominalist of the school of Occam or Buridan, but of a realist, a realist perhaps more Aristotelian than Platonic, but one who is much nearer to St Augustine or Wyclif than to Gerson or Pierre d'Ailly. It is the same with the whole body of Matěj's writings.[9] It is true that he is not much concerned with questions of pure metaphysics and logic, but nevertheless all his mysticism and apocalypticism, all his moral and reforming zeal, all his exalted faith in the virtues of the eucharist are impregnated with a philosophy which refuses to be limited by what is sensible and which sees everything *sub specie eternitatis*. Nothing reveals better Matěj's realism and his affinities in this respect with both Wyclif and Hus than his doctrine of the church. He talks of it as a 'beloved city, the bride of the lamb, the betrothed of the crucified Jesus, the one dove, the unique and beautiful beloved one of the son of God', and his realist philosophy forbids him to recognise the church in any one of the three *ecclesiae particulares* which competed for the allegiance of Christendom in his day. Like Wyclif and Hus, Matěj also refused to accept the denotation of the church as a totality made up of the rival popes, officious cardinals, proud and ambitious bishops, selfish and

sue substancie . . . Hinc quippe potest magna similitudo elici unionis ecclesie vel cuiuslibet anime fidelis cum Christo Jhesu. Nam sicut totum esse accidentis dependet ab essencia subiecti, ita ut dicit Philosophus: "Accidentis esse est in subiecto esse," ita eciam totum esse gracie et beatificum anime christiani vel tocius ecclesie dependet ab esse Christi, ab inhesione Jhesu Christo per fidem, spem et caritatem. Et quemadmodum accidens, quanto forcius inheret et profundius radicatur in suo subiecto, tanto magis communicat esse subiecti et remotum est a non esse, sic ecclesia et quelibet anima racionalis, quanto forcius adheret verbo incarnato et intimius radicatur fide, spe et caritate, tanto magis habundat esse gracie et sui boni proprii . . . Et iterum, sicut accidens in subiecto suo generatur et corrumpitur, augetur et diminuitur, subiecto manente immobili, ita anima quelibet in esse gracie permanente.'

[9] Matěj's formal realism may be illustrated by a quotation like the following: 'Philosophi posuerunt duo principia omnium intrinseca, scilicet actum, et illud est forma, quam ego voco hic regulam et materiam precise suscipientem illum actum intrinsece, quod placet michi hic nominare corpus rectum. Unde Aristoteles primo de anima: "Anima est actus primus corporis organici phisici, potencia vitam habentis." Est igitur regula illa, secundum quam res unaquaque regitur, forma intrinseca rei, non tamen illa, que est hic assumpta ad inquirendum, quoniam ista non est aliud ab ipsa re, quoniam est intrinseca et que dat esse rei secundum philosophum et format ipsam rem ad numerum, pondus et mensuram, et quia illa varia est in rebus et multiplex secundum diversitatem specierum' (*Regulae*, ii, 6).

lazy monks, worldly and avaricious friars, ignorant and carnal priests, who in his opinion made up the visible church in his day.[10] As a good realist he thinks of the church as a real idea, unlimited in space or time, always the same in its essence however its accidents may change. Such a conception of the church prompted his constant appeal to the example of the primitive apostolic church, and it also inspired his conception of Antichrist as an idea or a malefic spirit rather than as a living individual as Milíč did when he pointed to the Emperor Charles IV as Antichrist.

Near the beginning of his great treatise Matěj of Janov propounded a fundamentally realist principle as the basis of his whole enquiry. He states it in these words:

And even if relative knowledge is transmuted in the same spirit or in different spirits, universal and abstract knowledge, remaining one, is not changed. And although sense experience and the cognition of individual things is changeable, yet knowledge of universal, necessary propositions remains ever the same. We come to knowledge of these universal propositions through the working of the reason and gathering of many individual facts into one spiritual one. Again, these universal propositions are thus indeed firmly brought together through the working of the judgment of reason, into certain propositions more general in their knowledge of truth, and fewer in number. And they are again reduced to still fewer and more general, until one comes to the first principle of any science, the unique and

[10] Compare with Wyclif's and Hus's idealist conception of the Church the following passages from Matěj's *Regulae*: 'Civitas illa magna orbis christianorum in tres partes de facto est conscissa, scilicet Romanorum ad meridiem, Grecorum ad orientem, Francigenarum ad occidentem. Quorum Romani dicunt: "Hic est ecclesia et hic est Christus." Franciqene dicunt: "Non ita est, sed nos sumus ecclesia, et hic est Christus." Et Greci erecti pertinaciter inquiunt: "Mentimini vos et vos, sed nos sumus ecclesia, et hic est Christus." . . . Ecce obscuritas solis et lune, ut eciam civitas posita supra montem abscondatur et sit obnubilata, quod videri non potest, in tantum, ut ex infinita multitudine christianorum non facile non posset inveniri, quod sit ita certus, ubi est unica vera dei ecclesia' (*Regulae*, i, 294-5). 'Sancti et electi, qui faciunt unitatem in Christo Jhesu et unam ecclesiam, sunt divisi vel facti diversi adinvicem et adversi . . . Sed scisma factum est in ecclesia malignancium vel inter christianos et primum sacerdotes et clericos amatores huius mundi, qui utique spiritum Jhesu crucifixi neque ipsius amorem dignum et verum habentes, suam propriam gloriam et admiracionem in hominibus posuerunt, estimantes questum esse pietatem, quibus aliquid simile contigit, veluti illis, qui dicebant: "Ego sum Cephe, ego vero Pauli, ego autem Apollo" ' (*Regulae*, ii, 157).

general, that, according to the investigators of such things, is called the subject of attribution in knowledge or the most general type. And they have subtly represented it as something that ought to be simple.[11]

This is clearly a statement of a principle of scientific method very different from that of the nominalists, who concerned themselves merely with perceptible individuals, and who saw nothing in the individual except a complex of accidents.

While it is true that Matěj of Janov is at one with nominalists such as Matthias of Cracow, the author of the *De squaloribus curiae romanae*, in denouncing the superstition, venality, and immorality of the clergy, these moral strictures of the nominalists were the products of their arid legalism and scientific scepticism, while the moral ardour of Matěj and his disciples was inspired by devotion to the ideal and by high-minded wrath against every infraction of universal and eternal order.

Matěj's realism appears most clearly in his fervid sacramentalism, in that mystical and passionate devotion to the eucharist which impelled him to see in the frequent communion of the laity that famous 'thirteenth rule' *pro discrecione spirituum*, and the most effective instrument for restoring to the church its lost unity and purity and for bringing back every sinful soul to Christ the crucified. (These are all typical Matthian phrases.) To illustrate the metaphysical realism of Matěj's eucharistic teaching it will suffice to quote the following extract from the second *tractatus* of the first book of the *Regulae*.

And how wonderful is this sacrament, how good and beautiful, which is always without change or diminution, and all may plenti-

[11] *Regulae*, ii, 17: 'Et licet sciencia relativa transmutetur in eadem anima vel in diversis animabus, sciencia tamen universalis et abstracta, manens una, non mutatur. Et quamvis experiencia sensitiva et congnicio rerum singularium varietur, sciencia tamen proposicionum universalium necessariarum perpetue non mutatur. Ad quarum proposicionum universalium scienciam pervenimus per discursum racionis et multorum singularium in unum spirituale conleccionem. Que iterum proposiciones universales sic stabiliter vere ad quasdam proposiciones magis communes in sua sciencia et veritate et pauciores per operacionem iudicii racionis colligguntur, et ille iterum ad pauciora et magis communia rediguntur, donec veniatur ad primum principium cuilibet sciencie unicum et commune, quod secundum perscrutarores talium subjectum attribucionis in sciencia vel genus generalissimum vocatur, et illud esse debere aliquod inconplexum subtiliter descripserunt.'

fully partake of it. It is always whole. And while it is always being created, it always remains completely and perfectly generated. And remaining the same as always and unchanged, it becomes according to its own mode the continually renewed sacred bread, which gives life to this world and to him who walks in the way of God. Thus in everything is this awe-inspiring sacrament wonderful, good and most lovely.[12]

It was not only those Czechs who studied at Paris who thought and wrote in this way. Matěj's own beloved master, the first of the Czech reformers, the saintly and mystical Jan Milíč of Kroměříž uses the same sort of words and ideas. Since he had never been to any university Milíč never learned to clothe his realism in the logical formulae of the schools, but it is none the less evident for that. The two great volumes of his sermons (still awaiting publication), entitled *Abortivus* and *Gratiae dei*, with all the long citations of the bible and the fathers with which they are filled, are replete with that idealism which Augustine and St Paul alike inherited from Plato. Milíč had the utmost contempt for the new science of the nominalists, as can be seen from the following passage from the *Gratiae dei*:

Then, when Christ did this with his disciples, the Jews spoke against him, saying: 'What in the world is this new doctrine!' And indeed it is still new. For the masters and the monks and the philosophers and the logicians contemplate great things while trading in, and fishing for, fat prebends and prelacies, and creating—every year almost—a new logic and then destroying it, [and speaking] ancient lies in ancient tongues . . . And some believe in fate and in predestination denying free will, and still others say that the world has existed since eternity or that the first matter was co-eternal with the very beginning of things. And meanwhile the unlettered rise up speaking in new tongues and reach heaven, while they with their doctrines sink down into hell with their author. As Augustine says On Psalm

[12] Ibid., i, 127: 'Et quemadmodum hoc sacramentum est mirabile, bonum et pulchrum, quod sine sui mutacione et minucione semper at ab omnibus in copia manducatum, semper est integrum; et cum semper generetur, semper persistit summe et perfecte generatum; et semper manens idem et antiquum, fit modo sibi proprio continue nowus panis celestis, qui dat vitam huic mundo et digne deo ambulanti: ita per omnia est mirabile, bonum et pulcherrimum hoc terrificum sacramentum.'

CXLI: 'Who is Aristotle? He trembles in the inferior regions.'[13]

Milíč also expresses the same contempt for the science of the schools in the volume of sermons which he modestly entitled *Abortivus*:

For [Augustine] knew that the intellect gets nothing from its own exercise unless it is given from above by God. Thus when the blessed Ambrose at the outset of [Augustine's] conversion had given to him the prophet Isaiah to read, he threw it aside, because he could not understand its beginning. Where then are those who say: 'No one can perfectly understand theology, unless through Physics and Logic [i.e. of Aristotle]. Behold Augustine, who without contrivance comprehended the liberal arts, being a philosopher could not understand the beginning of one prophet, whom however fishermen and other simple men understood completely. Therefore, theology can be understood by the humble, the theology that at one time could not be understood by the proud philosopher Augustine; but later, through the humble Augustine, understanding was granted from the dew of the divine benediction.'[14]

Milíč's moral zeal, his exalted asceticism, the apocalyptic fervour which inspires his *Libellus de Antichristo*, all reflect a habit of mind which is ever occupied with that which is eternal

[13] Jan Milíč, 'Gracie dei', pars hiemalis. Codex universitatis Pragensis, D.20, f. 84b-85a. Quoted in Kybal, *M. Jan Hus*, ii, 1, 121. 'Quod cum Christus cum discipulis faciebat, dicebant Iudei contra eum: "Quenam doctrina hec nova." Certe et nunc nova est, quia magistris et religiosis et philosophis et loycis [logicis] magna contemplantibus et magnas prebendas et prelaturas venantibus et piscantibus, et omni anno fere novam loycam facientibus et iterum destruentibus et antiquis linguis antiqua mendacia [loquentibus] . . . , aliis fato credentibus, aliis predestinacioni et libero arbitrio detrahentibus, aliis mundum ab eterno fuisse vel materiam primam primo principio coeternam fuisse dicentibus, surgunt interim indocti et linguis locuntur novis et rapiunt celum, et illi cum doctrinis suis demerguntur in infernum cum suo auctore, sicut Augustinus dicit Super Psalmo CXLI: "Quis est Aristoteles? Aput inferos contremiscit." '

[14] Jan Milíč, 'Abortivus', MS Codex universitatis Pragensis, D.37, f. 199a: 'Sciebat enim [Augustinus] quod nichil ex industria intellectus haberet nisi desuper datum a deo. Unde cum beatus Ambrosius sibi in principio sue conversionis Ysayam prophetam ad legendum dedisset, abiecit eum, quia principium eius intellegere non potuit. Ubi sunt qui dicunt: "Nemo potest perfecte intellegere theologiam nisi per physicam et loycam." Ecce Augustinus, qui sine ingenio intellexit artes liberales principium unius prophete intelligere non potuit existens philosophus quem tamen prophetam piscatores et alii simplices totum intellexerunt. Potest ergo ab humilibus theologia intelligi que per superbum philosophum Augustinum aliquando intelligi non valebat, sed postea per humilem Augustinum fuit ex rore benedictionis divine optime intelligencia.'

and universal. He stands with St Bridget of Sweden and St Catherine of Siena, as far removed as possible from the French and German nominalists. It must be admitted that this realism of Milíč owes nothing to the inspiration of the English realists either at Oxford or Paris; its roots go much deeper, beyond Occam, Aquinas and Abelard, to Augustine, Ambrose and Chrysostom, to the idealism of the gospels and the Hebrew prophets. It seems probable that Milíč's biblical realism had more influence on Matěj of Janov and others who recognised in Milíč their inspirer and their master than any of the English before Wyclif.

Milíč's sermons and Matěj's writings together provided a body of teaching and an armoury of arguments which moulded the thought and directed the actions of a whole generation of reformers who followed them in the last years of the fourteenth century. By that time native Czechs had grown up to take their rightful place as leading teachers in the university of Prague. Two Czech masters, Stanislav of Znojmo and Štěpán Páleč, forged realist philosophy into a weapon with which to combat the supremacy of the German and Silesian nominalists in the university.[15] It was the easier for them to do so because a rich storehouse of realist philosophy had just arrived in Prague in the shape of the metaphysical and logical works of John Wyclif. Hus has recorded that he first became acquainted with them in 1398, and that he himself copied the *De materia et forma*, the *De ideis* and the *De universalibus* at that time.[16] Wyclif's

[15] Compare a remark of Páleč: 'As in a man guilt and holiness come not from the body, but from the soul, so also in the mystical body of the Church guilt and holiness come not from any material parts but from the forms. The Church Militant is and is called holy since its form remains always holy and unalloyed.' Štěpán Páleč, 'Contra Johannis Husi tractatum de Ecclesia', in Sedlák, ii, 203-4. Páleč's desertion of the Wyclifite camp laid him open to charges of nominalistic verbalism; see Hus on Páleč's later scriptural literalism: 'What is the purpose of all this quacking, my good story-teller, if the words and vowels or written letters which you call Holy Scripture, are only dead things? Again, leaving things, you turn to meanings and tropes and then you sidle off like a crab.' ('K čemu ta kachna, dobrý fiktore, jestliže slova a samohlásky nebo psané literky čili písmenka, jež zoveš Písmem sv., jsou věcí neživou? Již, zanechávaje věcí, obracíš se k znamením a výrazům, zpět ustupeju jako rak.') Hus, 'Contra Páleč', quoted by Kybal, *M. Jan Hus*, ii, 1, 45. To Hus the Bible is *res animata*, 'the book of life which judges itself', Kybal, ibid.

[16] All three of these tractates of Wyclif are unfortunately among those parts of the 'Summa de ente' which still await publication.

realism was so categorical and uncompromising and it accorded so well with the native predilections of the Czech masters that it was inevitable that they should have found it much to their taste. Immediately the implicit realism of Milíč, Matěj and Štítný became explicit, equipped with all the mechanism of a system of formal logic. It did not therefore lose its earlier ethical and mystical character. The Czechs used the dialectic they learned from Wyclif to sharpen their weapons for the fight against clerical abuses and the materialism of their German rivals at the university.

Wyclifite realism profoundly influenced all the protagonists of the early Hussite movement: Stanislav and Páleč, Jan of Jesenice, Jakoubek of Střibro and Marek of Hradec, as well as Jerome of Prague who, like Hus, was burned at Constance for his realist heresies. There is no room in this article to deal with them all, and it must suffice to refer to the solemn annual university debates called *quodlibetae*,[17] and to say something to illustrate the realism of Jan Hus and Jerome of Prague.

It is not surprising that Hus did not entirely escape the nominalism which dominated the university of Prague when he began his studies in the faculty of arts. For example, before he came under the influence of Wyclif Hus was willing, like Occam and the other nominalists, to acknowledge that the teaching of the church had a dogmatic authority beside that of the bible. 'I venerate', he wrote, 'all the general and particular councils, the decreta and decretals, the canons and constitutions as far as they are explicitly and implicitly consonant with the law of God.'[18] He was also prepared to give great weight to both *veritas a sensu cognita* and *veritas elaborata ab infallibili racione*,[19] and he was unwilling to follow Plato so far as to limit the source of all true knowledge to divine inspiration alone. Hus's realism always remained more moderate than

[17] See particularly *Magistri Johannis Hus Quodlibet*; disputationis de quolibet Pragae in facultate artium mense Ianuario anni 1411 habitae Enchiridion, edidit Bohumil Ryba. This *Quodlibet* indirectly owes much to another book by an Englishman, Walter Burley's 'De vita et moribus philosophorum'.

[18] Hus, 'Elucidatio fidei', in *Historia et monumenta* (1558), i, 48b (60a/b).

[19] 'Omnis veritas in religione Christi sequenda et solum ipsa vel est veritas a sensu corporeo cognita, vel ab intelligencia infallibili inventa, vel per revelacionem cognita, vel in divina posita scriptura.' Hus, 'De ecclesia', ibid., i, 220b.

that of Wyclif or even Stanislav of Znojmo. Stanislav, up to the time of his recantation, was so zealous a devotee of Wyclif, even of his errors and heresies, that he was willing to follow him to the pinnacle of the realist edifice, the doctrine of the remanence of the substance of the bread and wine in the consecrated host. Such extremes were too much for Hus. The fathers of Constance agreed that in the matter of eucharistic heresy he had never erred.

Nevertheless Hus was a realist even though he never pushed realism to its extremes. His judges at Constance had no doubt about this, and they put his metaphysical errors at the head of the articles of condemnation. The fathers knew that anyone who taught that the universal church is the totality of the predestined was highly dangerous to the actual church.[20] For if all the predestinate and only the predestinate are members of the church, then God alone knows who are members of the church, and it is impossible to conduct the day-to-day administration of a society when it is impossible to ascertain who are its members. The realism which Hus taught would have dissolved the visible church into a number of individuals, and the church has always most feared and most severely punished those heresies which might lead to schism. The council was justified in seeing in Hus a realist very dangerous to the church such as it was in the later Middle Ages. Now faith in the priority of the ideal to the material, faith in the universality and permanence of truth inspired everything Hus did and said. In his *De corpore Christi* he wrote: 'Real faith, by which the faithful adheres firmly to Catholic virtue, is concerned not with visible things but with invisible.'[21] In his *Exposition of the Faith*, written in Czech, he says: 'The first Czech who explained the Greek word ἐκκλήσια understood it wrongly, for he stupidly translated it by the word "kostel" or "cierkev", which would mean that the bride of the lord Jesus Christ is a stone church

[20] 'Unitas autem ecclesie catholice consistit in unitate predestinacionis cum singula eius membra sunt unum predestinacione et in unitate beatudinis, cum singuli eius filii sunt in beatitudine finaliter uniti. In presenti eciam eius unitas consistit in unitate fidei et virtutum et in unitate charitatis.' 'De ecclesia', cap. 2, in *Historia et monumenta* (1558), i, 198b (246a).

[21] Hus, *Opera omnia*, i, 18: 'Fides proprie, qua fidelis adheret firmiter virtuti katholice, est de non apparentibus et de invisibilibus.'

or a building made of wood. But if he had explained that this word ἐκκλήσια means an assembly (*sbor*) they would not have made this mistake.'[22]

Hus's realism culminates in his conception of the church, and it is just therein that its importance for the future development of Hussitism lies. Hus had always been opposed to the nominalist doctrine of the church as expounded by such as Pierre d'Ailly.[23] Among the articles of accusation charged against Hus at Constance, the first charged him with having said: 'There is only one holy universal Church, which is the totality of the predestined', and the third: 'The foreknown [i.e. to damnation] are not part of the church, for no part finally falls away from it, since the predestinating love which binds them does not fail.' Article 5 ascribes to Hus the opinion:

The foreknown, although sometimes in grace according to present righteousness, nevertheless is never part of the holy church, and the predestinate [i.e. to salvation] always remains a member of the church, even though he sometimes falls away from the prevenient grace, but not from the grace of predestination.[24]

Michal of Německý Brod, the most inveterate of Hus's accusers at Constance, charged him with having maintained a realist view of the church in these words:

Thirdly, he errs concerning the church, and above all, in that he does not concede that the church signifies the pope, cardinals, archbishops, bishops, and clergy subject to them, and that he says

[22] Hus, 'Výklad víry', in Erben, i, 24.

[23] Compare d'Ailly's statement: 'Tanta est ecclesie catholice auctoritas, quod omnis illa et sola Scriptura firmiter est credenda de necessitate salutis, quam ipsa [*sc.* Ecclesia] recipit, approbat et tradit tamquam catholicam et divinam' (quoted by L. Salembier, *Petrus de Alliaco* (Lille, 1886), p. 308) with Hus: Jiní pak bludie, rkúc, že papež jest cierkev svatá, a jiní, že kardinálové s papežem, a jiní, že všichni kněžie spolkem, a jiní, že všchni křesťané.' (Some err, saying that the pope is Holy Church, others saying that it is the cardinals with the pope, others that it is all the priests together, others that it is all christians.) Hus, 'Výklad víry', Erben, i, 25.

[24] Quoted in Kybal, *M. Jan Hus*, ii, 1, 283. [Translations are taken from *John Hus at the Council of Constance*, ed. M. Spinka (New York and London, 1965), pp. 260, 261.] 'Presciti non sunt partes ecclesie, cum nulla pars eius finaliter excidit ab ea, eo quod predestinacionis caritas, que ipsam ligat, non excidet.' 'Prescitus, etsi aliquando est in gracia secundum presentem iusticiam, tamen nunquam est pars sancte ecclesie, et predestinatus semper manet membrum ecclesie, licet aliquando excidat a gracia adventicia, sed non a gracia predestinacionis.'

that this meaning is extorted by scholars and is by no means tenable. This error comes out clearly in his treatise on the church.[25]

For Hus, such a definition of the church by denotation of the individuals who compose the ecclesiastical hierarchy was quite inadequate. It was the connotation of things he always sought and he wished to know what the church was in its essence without restriction of space or time. In the course of one of the sermons which he preached in the Bethlehem Chapel in Prague he defined the church in these terms:

But as to what this church may be, it is often said that it is the aggregation of all the holy elect, those living on this earth and those sleeping and triumphant. And that other [church] is divided into separate parts consisting of those gathered according to kingdoms, but none of them is the church universal.[26]

One important result of this conception of the church was that Hus did not feel bound to identify the church with one of the three rival churches of that time of schism. If for him the church was a 'congregation of certain men in the charity of God'[27] it was also true that

the universal Church of Christ's believers militant here on earth is spread throughout the world wherever there are believers in Christ, whether in Spain under Benedict, or in Apulia and the Rhineland under Gregory, or in Bohemia under John XXIII, in accordance with the words of Matthew, xviii, 20: 'Where two or three are gathered together in my name, I am in the midst of them.' Whether the papacy consists of three or four popes the Church is still one in Christ, one in faith, hope and love.[28]

[25] Palacký, *Documenta*, pp. 195, 289 and 226: 'Tertio errat circa ecclesiam, et primo, quod non admittit quod ecclesia significet papam, cardinales, archiepiscopos, episcopos et clerum eis subditum, et dicit illam significacionem extortam a scholaribus et nullatenus esse tenendam. Patet iste error manifeste ex tractatu suo de ecclesia.'

[26] Hus, 'Betlemská kázání', Codex universitatis Pragensis, III, B.20, quoted in Kybal, *M. Jan Hus*, ii, 1, 251-2: 'Quid autem sit ista ecclesia dictum est sepe, quia est aggregacio omnium sanctorum electorum, hic viancium et dormiencium et triumphancium. Et illa dividitur in parciales aggreganciones secundum regna, sed nulla illarum est ecclesia universalis.'

[27] Hus, 'Expositio prime epistule ad Corinthos', in *Historia et monumenta* (1558), ii, 83a (131a).

[28] Hus, 'Contra Páleč', ibid., 260b-261a (325b-326a), quoted by Kybal, *M. Jan Hus*, ii, 1, 249-50.

This conception of a 'mystical universal body of churchmen, which is truly made up of Christ and the company of the predestined' was the faith with which Hus inspired his disciples and his legacy to his followers. But Hus was not the only author of this faith. Earlier than he Tomáš of Štítný had expounded similar realist ideas not only in the Czech language, but also in simple and striking terms which even unlearned laymen could understand. Of equal importance was Jerome of Prague. In his *Recommendacio artium liberalium* pronounced at the famous 'Quodlibet' of 1409,[29] in his disputation with master Vlk (Lupus) in the same year,[30] before his judges at Vienna in the year 1410,[31] and above all during his examination by Pierre d'Ailly and Jean Gerson on the eve of his condemnation to the stake, Jerome showed himself a realist of the school of Wyclif, at the same time more systematic and more eloquent than Hus himself. His scholastic eminence is evidenced by the fact that the council insisted, even more than it had done in the case of Hus, on the metaphysical errors and heresies of which, according to his accusers, Hus was guilty. At the very beginning of the examination of Jerome, Gerson, chancellor of the university of Paris and doyen of the nominalists, said to him: 'Jerome, when you were at Paris, you thought in your eloquence you were an angel from heaven, and you troubled the whole university by posing many conclusions and corollaries in the schools, especially in the matter of universals and of many other scandalous things.'[32]

But even more neatly than the reverend chancellor, a simple student of Prague, Kaspar Weinstein, had five years earlier at Jerome's trial in Vienna expressed the heinous crime of Jerome and all the realists in these words: 'We heard him say in a sermon that there is a universal ass.'[33] Anyone who believes that there is a universal ass must also believe that there is a universal church and a universal truth. That is the faith for which Hus and Jerome suffered at the stake; that is the faith they bequeathed to their compatriots Jakoubek of Stříbro, Rokycana,

[29] Text in Höfler, ii, 112-28 (where it is ascribed to Hus).
[30] Text in Sedlák, ii, 229-58.
[31] Klicman, *Processus judiciarius contra Jeronimum de Praga.*
[32] Hardt, iv, 217-18.
[33] Klicman, p. 29.

Mikuláš of Příbram and to Peter 'Engliš', to Žižka and Prokop the Bald, and to all the 'warriors of God' who fought and died in this faith under the banner of the chalice. Their faith in the reality of the ideal has never failed among the Czechs; it was the inspiration of Petr Chelčický and of the whole community of the Unity of Bohemian Brethren down to the days of Comenius, who in the long years of his exile spread it throughout the world.

V

Some Political Ideas of the Early Czech Reformers[1]

THE religious reformers who lived and worked in Bohemia during the half century before the death of Hus in 1415 were none of them political thinkers of the first order. Political thought was not a field in which they were ambitious or, indeed, very much interested. For Jan Hus and his predecessors the fundamental problem of their day was essentially a moral one, and they saw its solution above all in a change of heart, not in a political revolution or *coup d'état*. That is why none of them wrote a formal treatise on political science. They merely touch on political questions incidentally. Even if every mention they make of politics were collected and analysed, it would still not amount to any new or profound system or to any revolution in political thought. It is nevertheless perhaps worth while to attempt a short study of the political thinking of the earlier Czech reformers, not so much for what it was in itself, but because it afforded the foundations on which, after Hus's death, the edifices of the Hussite state and church were erected. On the political philosophy of the early Czech reformers, occasional and unsystematic as it was, was built the first nation in western Europe to proclaim and practise the doctrine of the supremacy of the state in all things, spiritual as well as temporal, or, perhaps one should say, the doctrine of the identity of the nation state and the national church.

The clues to the political thought of the founders of Hussitism are scattered through such works as the sermons of Jan Milíč,[2]

[1] [The Latin citations preceding notes 6, 8, 9, 15-19, 25-29, 31, 32, 34, 35, 38, 39, 41, have been translated by Peter Brock.]

[2] The two sets of Milíč's 'Postillae', or sermons for Sundays and Saints' Days throughout the year exist in the still unpublished manuscripts of his 'Abortivus' and 'Gracie dei'.

the *Regulae veteris et novi testamenti* of Matěj of Janov,[3] the books of Christian instruction which Tomáš of Štítný wrote for his motherless children and his layman's *postilla* in the vernacular, entitled 'Sermons for Sundays and Saints' Days',[4] and in almost all the innumerable tractates and sermons of Hus, as well as in his more systematic works such as his commentary on the *Sentences* of Peter Lombard and his *De ecclesia*.[5] The writings of some of Hus's contemporaries such as the two renegade Wyclifites Stanislav of Znojmo and Štěpán Páleč, of Hus's first spiritual successor Jakoubek of Stříbro, and above all the little that has survived of the orations and disputations of Jerome of Prague (Jeronym Pražský) provide some indication of the sum of political ideas which were bequeathed to the militant generation of the Hussites.

A philosophical system is usually the product of three factors: the heritage of the past, the particular genius of the individual philosopher, and the material, moral and political circumstances in which he wrote.

In what they took from the past the Czech reformers appear to have shown a truly catholic receptivity. They reproduce the political ideas of the fathers of the church and of the schoolmen of every complexion and sect, whether they be Caesarian or papalists, Thomists or Scotists. The influence of the ideas of Marsiglio of Padua and William of Occam appears side by side with that of Innocent III and Agostino Trionfo. But from this gallimaufry of references and quotations, often very difficult to reconcile, there emerge certain predilections and tendencies. In the first place the Czech reformers show a preference for the political authority of the bible, especially as it is expressed in the gospels and in the epistles of Paul and Peter. In this regard it is not without importance that both apostles insisted on the doctrine that the powers that be are ordained of God, that political authority is of divine origin, and that therefore civil obedience is a Christian duty. Hus and his friends ever insisted that the evangelical admonition to render unto Caesar the

[3] See Ch. IV, note 7 above.

[4] Tomáš of Štítný, *Spisy*, číslo 2: *Řeči nedělní a sváteční* (Prague, 1929); *Knížky šestery o obecných věcech křesťanských* (Prague, 1852); *Besední řeči* (Prague, 1897).

[5] Hus, *Exposicio quattuor librorum sentenciarum Petri Lombardi*, ed. V. Flajšhans (Prague, 1903-4) and 'De ecclesia' in *Historia et monumenta* (1715), i, 243-318.

things that are Caesar's was still valid in the fifteenth century, and that the readiness of the Son of God to submit to the civil authority of Pontius Pilate was a standing rebuke to the proud refusal of the prelates and priests of their day to be submissive to the authority of emperors and kings.

Hus most clearly stated the scriptural basis of his political theory that the state has power to rule and discipline the clergy in the reply he wrote to an anonymous champion of clerical immunities in 1411:

Kings and temporal lords ought to begin by punishing an injury to God by the clergy, because the latter gone astray infects the rest of the Christian body like a root, according to Augustine and Bede, or like a stomach, according to Chrysostom.

This duty, too, is made clear from the law that we should love God by punishing injuries to him. To this end indeed, according to the apostle, Romans 13, the power has been given them [i.e. kings and temporal lords], as otherwise by consent they might sin treasonably . . . Since, therefore, kings and secular lords, according to the apostle as above, are ministers of God, serving him in this matter, to this end they bear the sword, and receive tribute, that they may punish those who do evil. And they are sent for this purpose in order to punish, according to the witness of Peter the apostle, I Peter ii. And priests ought, for the sake of God, to be subject to every human creature, whether to the king as ruler or to his governors, as much as they are sent by him, because such is the will of God.[6]

Next to the authority of the bible the Hussites put that of Augustine, in politics as in everything else. From him they learned to see in the state, in the institution of private property, and in the subjection of man to man, instruments decreed by the divine will for the punishment and reform of man in his

[6] 'Replica M. Johannis Hus contra occultum adversarium' (*Historia et monumenta*, 1715, i, 169): 'Reges et domini temporales debent vindicando dei injuriam a clero incipere, quia ipse perversus ut radix, secundum Augustinum et Bedam, vel ut stomachus, secundum Chrysostomum, inficit residuum corporis christiani.

Patet autem hoc debitum ex lege dilectionis dei, vindicando ejus injurias. Ad hoc enim secundum apostolum ad Romanos 13 data est eis potestas, cum aliter peccarent proditorie ex consensu . . . Cum igitur reges et seculares domini juxta apostolum ubi supra, ministri dei sunt, in hoc ipsum servientes, et ad hoc gladium portant et tributa accipiunt, ut vindictam faciant in eis qui malum agunt et ad hoc missi sunt, ut vindicent, teste Petro apostolo I Petri 2. Et sacerdotes debent subjecti esse omni humanae creaturae propter deum, sive regi tanquam praecellenti, sive ducibus, tanquam ab eo missis, quia sic est voluntas dei.'

fallen state. The Augustinian political creed of the Czech reformers was clearly and fully expounded by one of the earliest of them, Matěj of Janov, in the third book of his *Regulae*.[7] While to Matěj the state is the 'Beast' of the Apocalypse, he yet believes with Augustine that it is part of the divine plan and exercises its fearful authority with God's approval:

And it is granted to it, to the aforesaid beast, which has two horns like a ram's, that 'he had power to give life unto the image of the beast', that is, that it should have the power and authority of spirituals, 'that the image of the beast should speak' [Rev. xiii, 15], that is, that it may establish constitutions and the doctrines and laws of men for the purpose of acquiring riches and glory and may promulgate them throughout the length and breadth of the church.[8]

It is pure Augustinian political theory when Matěj says:

And so it stems from God's ordinance that the hard-hearted and worldly populace should be punished harshly and that it should groan in subjection to the iron yoke of tyrants, since God allows a hypocrite to rule on account of the people's transgressions and, according to the apostle, all power is from the lord God.[9]

But all this is the commonplaces of mediaeval political theory, a store of ideas shared by the whole of Christendom. Nevertheless on this common basis each Christian country had built up its own domestic traditional pattern of thought. In Bohemia this tradition was at the same time both Erastian and sacerdotal. In the thirteenth century the state had waged war against the

[7] e.g. 'Docendus est populus christianus, quod primum et ante omnia Christo Jhesu sit subditus et illum et maxime portet et glorificet in corpore suo, sibi ex animo obediat et eius preceptis, dehinc omnibus suis superioribus obediat propter Christum Jhesum in illis, que promovent ad Christum vel que non contradicunt virtutibus et sapiencie Christi Jhesu, quoniam in veritate ad hoc solum sunt positi reges et principes christiani, ut promoveant in populo christiano Christi sanguine redempto non se ipsos, sed amorem et timorem Jhesu Christi.' *Regulae*, iv, 207.

[8] *Regulae*, iv, 123: 'Et datum est illi, prefate bestie, que habet duo cornua similia agni, "ut daret spiritum imagini bestie", id est ut haberet potestatem spiritualium at auctoritatem, "ut loquatur ymago bestie", id est ut condat constituciones, doctrinas hominum et leges super et pro acquirendis diviciis et gloria et ea late longeque per ecclesiam divulgaret.'

[9] Ibid., ii, 229-30: 'Ex dei itaque ordinacione venit, quod crudelis et mundialis populus puniatur dure et gemat subditus iugo ferreo tyrannorum, quoniam propter peccata populi deus permittit regnare yppocritam, et secundum apostolum omnis potestas a domino deo est.'

immunities and pretensions of the church as fiercely, and as unsuccessfully, in Bohemia as in twelfth-century England. But it seems that in the days of Hus the Czechs remembered less the pertinacious struggle of Bishop Ondřej of Prague against Přemysl Otakar I than they did the Slavonic rite that the popes had withdrawn from them, the national struggle against German invaders and intruders, and the contribution which had been made by such lay princes as St Václav, St Ludmilla and the good King Charles of Luxemburg in the edification of the Czech nation and church. It must also be remembered that in the course of the fourteenth century preachers and reformers in Bohemia, such as the anonymous author of the *Malogranatum*, Konrad Waldhauser, Vojtěch Raňkův, Engelschalk, Matthias of Cracow, and above all Jan Milíč, had built up a tradition of moral zeal and ethical criticism which became and remained the characteristic and strength of Hussitism. It is just because the early Bohemian reformers were so passionately concerned about the moral and religious crisis of their day that unlike Wyclif or the French conciliarists they never systematised a Czech political philosophy which they could bequeath to the Hussite state and church.

Far more important was the influence of the foreign body of political ideas which profoundly affected the Czech reformers of the early fifteenth century, above all that of John Wyclif and of the Irishman, Richard fitzRalph, archbishop of Armagh, who had been the first to elaborate the principles on which Wyclif had constructed the system which he expounded in his treatises on divine and civil dominion and on the office of the king.[10] These writings of the radical English theologian attracted the interest of the Czechs in the first place because the cornerstone of fitzRalph's and Wyclif's system was the principle that moral rectitude is a condition of civil and ecclesiastical author-

[10] For consideration of the nature and extent of the influence of Wyclif and fitzRalph, see M. Spinka, *John Hus and the Czech Reform*; also 'English and Czech Influences on the Hussite Movement' and 'Richard fitzRalph, Archbishop of Armagh, and the Doctrine of Dominion' in the present volume.

The relevant texts by John Wyclif are: *Tractatus de dominio divino* (in which is printed the first half, i.e. books i-iv, of fitzRalph's 'De pauperie Salvatoris'), ed. R. L. Poole (London, 1890); *Tractatus de civili dominio*, ed. R. L. Poole, 4 vols. (London, 1885-1904), vol. i; *Tractatus de officio regis*, ed. A. W. Pollard and Charles Sayle (London, 1887).

ity. This principle of dominion founded on grace, with its corollary that no priest or magistrate has either the power or the right to exercise the functions of his office if he is in a state of mortal sin, was eagerly accepted by the Czech reformers because it provided a theoretical rationalisation of their crusade against the immorality of office holders in church and state.[11] The second political principle of Wyclif's which attracted the Czechs was that it was both the right and the duty of the state to reform the church, by force if need be, and even by the confiscation of the property of the church.[12]

It has to be remembered that these Wyclifite doctrines were not known in Bohemia before the first decade of the fifteenth century, when Jerome of Prague, Mikuláš Faulfiš and Jiří of Kněhnice brought back the copies of Wyclif's polemical writings which they had made during their visits to England. But even before Jerome's return to Prague in 1402 there already existed in Bohemia a corpus of political ideas which the Czechs had themselves developed. It was the impact of the precise, systematic and radical political ideas of Wyclif on the still imprecise, cautious and vaguely formulated political ideas of the Czech reformers which produced the political system of Jan Hus and his fellows.

The very fact that Konrad Waldhauser, the pioneer of the reform movement in Prague, had been invited by King Charles to transfer his revivalist activities from Vienna to

[11] fitzRalph stated the principle in these words: 'Racionaliter potes inferre quod caritas sive gracia primo homini in origine sua sibi collata fuit previa causa dominii et causa cuiusque actus huius dominii . . . unde nullus de stirpe ipsius primi parentis seminalis filius, donec a peccato mundetur et graciam gratificantem receperit, istud dominium potest recipere seu habere.' 'De pauperie Salvatoris', in Wyclif, *De dominio divino*, p. 348.

'Dominus rerum non est aliquis nisi gracia iustificante sit iustus', ibid., p. 441.

Wyclif applies the principle to the civil magistrate in the words: 'nullum civile dominium est iustum simpliciter, nisi in naturali dominio sit fundatum; sed nemo habet naturale dominium pro tempore quo peccat mortaliter.' Wyclif, *De civili dominio*, i, 37.

[12] 'Bona materialia . . . sunt valde extranea et accidentalia ecclesie, ut stater pisci, et fluxibilia sicut aqua; sunt necessaria tegumenta et alimenta, et sic foret ad perfeccionem ecclesie si preter media usui cleri forent ad usus alios resecata. Et hec sentencia movit me ad dicendum quod domini temporales possunt aufferre bona temporalia ab ecclesia delinquente, contra quod instant quidam scolastice et alii pueriliter quando deficiunt argumenta.' Wyclif, *De officio regis*, pp. 185-6; cf. pp. 154-5 and 210-11.

Prague had created from the start a presumption in favour of the right and the duty of the civil power to concern itself with the morals of its subjects. But Waldhauser's disciple and successor, the former notary of the royal chancery who was transformed by his fervent exhortations into the zealous evangelist, the ascetic, mystic, zealous saint of the Czech reform movement, Jan Milíč, never saw either in the king or in the secular arm, which he had renounced, a possible instrument of reformation. On the contrary, Milíč on one occasion denounced Charles IV as Antichrist in person.[13] Milíč saw no remedy for the evils which he believed to presage the imminent end of the present dispensation except in repentance, the exercise of virtue and the frequent participation by the laity in the communion of the Eucharist. In as far as he had any hope at all that the cataclysm might be prevented, it was not in the secular arm, but in a general council of the church, whereto Milíč exhorted Pope Urban V from his prison in Rome.[14] One who believed as ardently as did Milíč that the end of the world was at hand had no need of a political philosophy.

It was much the same with the last of the eminent reformers before Hus, Tomáš of Štítný, country gentleman and lay preacher. He too was primarily a moralist and a mystic and saw no need to formulate the problems of sovereignty or the relations of church and state. The fact that Štítný had a long-standing grudge against King Václav IV for having robbed him of part of his estates prejudiced him against civil supremacy.

It was Matěj of Janov who was the first of the Czechs to bring some precision into the political thinking of the reformers. So much oppressed was he by the sense of the evils and sins which were corrupting the whole body of Christians that he was driven to explore the possibility of means of reformation, and he could not avoid the question whether it would not be

[13] Matěj of Janov, 'Narracio de Milicio' in *Regulae*, iii, 361: 'Hic indutus zelo quasi toraci, imperatorem predictum aggressus, digito indicavit et dixit sibi coram omnibus, quod ille sit magnus Antychristus. Propter quod carceres et vincula diutive est perpessus.'

[14] 'Suade igitur summo pontifici, ut faciat consilium generale in Roma, in quo omnes episcopi accipiant modum corrigendi suos et suorum defectus, et certas personas dent religiosas et seculares, mittendas ad predicandum . . .' Milíč, 'Libellus de Antichristo' in Matěj of Janov, *Regulae*, iii, 380.

after all necessary to appeal to the secular power if the church were to prove to be unwilling to reform itself. As has been said above, as far as formal political science is concerned in respect of the origin, nature, parts and end of the state, Matěj was completely orthodox and never went outside what had been taught by the apostles and St Augustine. But there was one aspect of political science on which Matěj had formed strong opinions, which were not without influence on his successors. Matěj, who was writing the *Regulae* between 1384 and 1394, was living in a society much troubled by lack of order, in a world where princes and lords played the tyrant over lesser folk. The proud and ambitious magnates of Bohemia respected neither the king nor the law; Hungary was for twenty years the victim of a civil war waged between the Luxemburg and Angevin factions, neither of which knew the meaning of mercy; Italy was at the mercy of *condottieri* who had become princes, and France was in the hands of the malign uncles of a mad king. It is therefore not surprising that Matěj had little respect for the civil power and little hope in it for the reformation of society and the church. In his exposition of the 'Beast' of the Apocalypse with its ten horns and seven heads Matěj well expresses his sense of the political crisis of his day:

For truly there are in Christendom many kingdoms, principalities and duchies without mutual respect, harmony or unity, in this age in regard to which that vision of the Beast is fitting. Indeed they are more divided from each other on account of their disregard fo government and their disobedience and dissension. Nay, they are divided and turned against each other to such a degree that they destroy one another in deadly and implacable fashion, up till now, with such cruelty and carnage that greater are not seen from the beginning of the world nor ever will be seen hereafter, that is in a people of one religion and one God and lord Jesus Christ. In this way they show themselves worse than all the kingdoms and peoples of the heathen that have preceded them since the creation of the world and have existed in various kingdoms, as, for instance, under the rule of the Chaldeans, and the Persians, of Syria and of the Romans, where the like things are never seen or heard of: namely, that the people who worship one and the same God and are moved and governed by one law, one faith, one priesthood have carried out on one another so many massacres, so many schisms and dissensions as in these times indeed is generally seen and done . . .

For although every kingdom and people of the present age are replete with almost every crime, nevertheless in wonderful fashion indeed one may see every kingdom labouring more in one deadly sin, as the French in pride, the Flemings and Rhinelanders in luxury, the Germans or Teutons in avarice, the Bohemians and Poles in gluttony, and similarly in regard to the rest, if they are each in turn scrutinised.[15]

Matěj is driven to the unhappy conclusion that the secular arm is either too much corrupted by tyranny or too much weakened by dissension to be an instrument either for the defence or the reformation of the church:

And through this an extraordinary and most monstrous thing comes to pass: the left hand in the same body taking precedence over the right hand as a support, when, as in all things, it ought to assist the chief hand in the body and help and comfort it. And behold this same other hand is made an obstacle to, and oppressor of, its liberty, destroying it along with its jurisdiction, glory and honour.[16]

From all this it is abundantly clear that Matěj had no wish to exalt the state at the expense of the church; to him the state is

[15] *Regulae*, iv, 208-9: 'Multa etenim sunt in Christianitate regna, multi principatus et ducatus, nullum habencia respectum adinvicem, nullam concordiam, nullam connexionem in tempore hoc, cui ista visio bestie est coaptata, sed magis scissa ab invicem propter negligenciam inperii et inobedienciam ac discessionem, ymmo sunt contra alterutrum divisa et adversa in tantum, ita ut mutuo se exicialiter et inplacabiliter destruant usque modo tanta crudelitate et tanta strage, ut non sint vise maiores ab inicio mundi, nec unquam post sint future, videlicet in populo unius religionis et unius dei et domini Jhesu Christi, per hoc deteriores se esse exhibentes omnibus regnis et populis gencium precedentibus ab origine mundi, que sub variis regnis prefuerunt, utpote sub regno Caldeorum, Persarum, Syrie, Romanorum, in quibus nunquam visum vel auditum est simile, quod puta populus unius et eiusdem dei emulator, una lege, una fide, uno sacerdocio actus et gubernatus, tantas strages, tanta scismata et sediciones contra alterutrum exercuerit, sicut temporibus istis est totum visum et inpletum . . .

Licet enim quodlibet regnum et populus moderni seculi fere omnibus criminibus est repletus, nichilominus tamen est videre miro modo quodlibet regnum magis in uno vicio mortali laborare, ut Francigene in superbia, Flandri et Renus in luxuria, Almani vel Teutonici in avaricia, Bohemi et Poloni in gula, et ita de aliis, si bene singula contemplentur.'

[16] Ibid., ii, 232: 'Et per hoc mirabilis res et nimium monstruosa evenit, ut manus sinistra in eodem corpore in aminiculum manui dextre prestita, et que perinde in omnibus manui principali in corpore assistere adiuvareque ipsam debuerat et confortare, et ecce, ipsa eadem altera manus facta est manui principali ad inpedimentum et aggravamen sue libertatis, eandem depredans sua iurisdiccione, gloria et honore.'

always the 'Beast': 'Indeed that woman, that is, the multitude of hypocrites, is seen seated upon the Beast. This Beast signifies the secular, that is, the imperial and military power with all the kingdoms of Christians who are in the flesh.'[17] Matěj never questioned the supremacy of the *sacerdotium*: in the second book of the *Regulae* he says:

The right hand, that is, the priesthood, possesses the whole Christian populace, enfolds, protects and governs—and should govern—them in the first place, and in superior fashion to the left hand, that is, the royal hand or the secular arm. And always and everywhere throughout the church the first honour, and greater and speedier obedience, ought to be commanded from the common people and from the crowd by the priests rather than by the secular magistrates and princes.[18]

This superiority, says Matěj, arises from the fact that kings and princes receive their hallowing, anointment and authority to rule at the hand of the priest . . . 'And to this witness the old histories of the holy emperors and kings, as for instance Theodosius and others.'[19]

In addition to the influence exercised by the traditional corpus of political science and by moderns such as Wyclif and Matěj of Janov, the political philosophy of the Hussites was moulded by the economic, social and political circumstances in the midst of which it developed. In as far as the situation of Bohemia at the end of the fourteenth century was similar to that in England, the Hussites were content to travel along the same road as Wyclif. But in so far as there were differences between the two countries the two philosophies diverged. Bohemia indeed had much in common with England: the negligence and ignorance, the venality and immorality of priests and

[17] Ibid., iv, 198: 'Visa est autem ista mulier, id est multitudo yppocritarum, sedere super bestiam. Que bestia significat potestatem secularem scilicet imperatoriam et militariam cum universis regnis christianorum carnalium.'

[18] Ibid., ii, 227: 'Manus dextra, id est sacerdocium, primum et principalius possidet populum totum christianum, ambit, munit et gubernat et debet gubernare, quam manus sinistra, id est manus regia vel brachium seculare. Et primus honor et maior prompciorque obediencia a plebibus et a vulgo debet inpendi sacerdotibus quam iudicibus et principibus secularibus semper et ubique per ecclesiam.'

[19] Ibid., ii, 229: 'Et ad hoc faciunt hystorie veteres sanctorum imperatorum atque regum, utpote Theodosii et aliorum.'

prelates, monks and friars, as described by Chaucer and Langland, were much like the moral disorders that are revealed by the synodal decrees of the archbishops of Prague and the denunciations of Janov and Štítný. That is largely why Hus, Stanislav of Znojmo, Jakoubek of Stříbro and Jerome of Prague welcomed the writings of Wyclif with such enthusiasm. They saw in him a brother in arms in a common war. But since the almost contemporary deaths of Charles IV and Edward III the courses of the two countries had begun to diverge. Under these two mighty monarchs both countries had been among the most powerful and wealthy in Europe. But while England continued to grow richer, Bohemia, dependent for its wealth almost solely on its native stores of silver in a world where bullion was steadily depreciating, had started on the cruel road of impoverishment. In the England of Richard II the peasants were ridding themselves for ever of the yoke of serfdom; in the Bohemia of Václav IV they were well on the road which led to the complete predial subjection of the peasants a hundred years later. There were also moral differences as Matěj had realised.[20] Not only did he think that the Czechs exceeded all other nations except the Poles in gluttony but also that they were unique in the pride and cruelty of their lords and knights who, for the sake of honour and glory:

Wound each other mortally, fight duels, and that with edged weapons, and often naked or half naked, quite deliberately when there was plenty of time for taking counsel, knowing full well that one or the other of them must be killed and go to hell. Sometimes they fight each other for glory, sometimes for the love of their mistresses.[21]

The peculiar ecclesiastical position of the Bohemian church also contributed to the idiosyncrasies of Czech political philosophy. In Bohemia many of the higher clergy—the canons, archdeacons, abbots and priors—were by origin and speech Germans, and

[20] See page 71 above.

[21] *Regulae*, iv, 222-3: 'Exicialiter se trucidantes, duella subeuntes, cum hastis acutis, et nudi, vel fere nudi, sese invadentes; et hoc deliberate magno tempore previo pro consiliis habendis, ubi scitum est de necessitate unum eorum interire et descendere ad infernum; qui quandoque hoc faciunt pro sua gloria, quandoque pro amore suarum amasiarum.'

it was the same at the Charles University, where two of the four 'nations' of which it was composed were German, and a third, nominally Polish, was filled with Silesians.[22] This phenomenon was largely the reason why the political thought of the Hussites was embittered by a nationalism which was at the same time both more ardent and more impotent than that of the English. There are also grounds for suspecting that the spiritual temper of the Czechs was fundamentally different from that of Wyclif and the Lollards, for the Czechs seemed more ready to surrender themselves to mysticism and to sentimental and sacramental consolations than Englishmen like Wyclif, for whom the cold rationalism of remorseless logic sufficed.

But it was above all political differences between the two nations which induced in Hus a reluctance to follow Wyclif to the end of his political programme. Wyclif had been able to formulate his political theory under the aegis of a long-established monarchy which was well accustomed to treating the church and the papacy with firmness. The kings of England were already armed with two powerful weapons with which to combat the jurisdictional and administrative pretensions of the curia, the statutes of premunire and provisors. In England there was a parliament in which the burgesses played a powerful part, a parliament which had heard with acclamation Wyclif proposing to secularise the goods of the church to alleviate the burden of taxation on the knights and citizens. What is more, England had in Richard II a king who had formed trenchant ideas on the subject of the absolute sovereignty of kings, and who said: 'The laws are in my own mouth, nay, even in my own heart.' No wonder that Wyclif in his *De officio regis* was willing to exalt the state at the expense of the church and to place his hopes for the accomplishment of reform in the king.

[22] Jerome of Prague described the situation thus: 'Et Teutonici gubernabant studium Pragense totaliter, et omnia beneficia, et tenebant sigillum fundacionis studii, et omnia clenodia dicti studii Pragensis. Et habebant in dicto studio iii voces, videlicet Bavaricam, Saxonicam, et plusquam medietatem Polonorum, cum, dixit, Slesite, qui sunt de nacione Polonica, essent omnes Teutonici: ita quod veri Poloni minorem partem habebant. Et quicquid Teutonici facerent et fecissent, in ipso studio, habebatur pro facto. Bohemi vero nihil potuerunt facere.' Hardt, iv, 758.

But Hus knew that he must not put his trust in princes. In the end it was his confidence in the safe conduct given to him by the Emperor Sigismund which was to cost him his life. It is true of course that King Václav IV and even more Queen Zofie were on the whole well disposed to Hus and reform. But Hus never forgot that on one occasion when he and Jerome proposed to Václav, who unfortunately at that moment was angling for the support of the Germans, that he should do justice to the Czechs in the matter of the university vote, Václav had called them troublers of the realm and had threatened to burn them both.[23] Besides, what hope could the reformers place in a king who had twice been made prisoner by his rebel lords and who proved incapable of preserving his imperial crown from the usurpation of Ruprecht in 1400 and of Jobst in 1410? As for the diet of the Bohemian estates, it was something very different from the English parliament. As far as I know neither Matěj of Janov nor Hus ever so much as referred to it. All in all, the mechanism of the executive instruments of the Czech state was still far too inadequate and ineffective to be the instrument for the reformation and government of the church before the revolution of 1419.

What has just been said may help to explain why Hus was less Erastian than Wyclif. It is significant that when his writings were condemned by the chancellor of the university of Oxford, Wyclif appealed to King Richard; when Zbyněk, archbishop of Prague, condemned the same writings, Hus and his friends appealed to the pope.[24] This is not to say that Hus never recognised the supremacy of the state. There were times when it looked as if the king might be both willing and able to punish the misconduct of the church. For example, on the occasion of

[23] Palacký, *Documenta*, p. 282.

[24] 25 June 1410: 'A quibus quidem mandatis, sententia et processibus prefati domini Sbynconis archiepiscopi, sicut prefertur, frivolis et nullis, imo expresse errorem in se continentibus . . . ad sanctam sedem apostolicam tunc provocavimus et appellavimus.' 'Tenor appellationis', in *Historia et monumenta* (1715), i, 113.

For Wyclif's appeal to Richard II, see *Fasciculi Zizaniorum*, ed. W. W. Shirley (Rolls Series) (London, 1858), p. 114: 'Sed post, ad suae haeresis majorem manifestationem, et suae pertinaciae ostensionem, alias publice a condemnatione cancellarii et judicio praedicto appelavit, non ad papam, vel ad episcopum, vel ordinarium ecclesiasticum, sed haereticus adhaerens seculari potestati in defensionem sui erroris et haeresis, appellavit ad regem Ricardum volens per hoc se protegere regali potestate, quod non puniretur vel emendaretur ecclesiastica potestate.'

the great quarrel about the papal indulgence of 1412, Hus published a defence of the sixteenth of the condemned articles of Wyclif: 'Whether temporal lords can by their own judgment take away temporal goods from habitually delinquent clergy.' So greatly enraged was Hus by the indulgence, the purpose of which was to provide Pope John XXIII with funds to prosecute his territorial struggle with the Christian King Ladislas of Naples, that he was moved to write as follows:

A secular lord has the power at will to take away the lands of the church, and in consequence secular lords have the power by their own judgment to take away temporal goods from habitually delinquent clergy.[25]

Since on account of their possessions the clergy are subject to emperor or king, it follows that these possessions can lawfully be taken from the habitually delinquent by such an emperor or king.[26]

'If any would not work, neither should he eat' [II Thessalonians iii, 10]. Thus the law of nature permits those having the governance of kingdoms to amend abuses growing out of temporal possessions which especially destroy their kingdoms, whether it were temporal lords or other persons who endowed the church with the temporal possessions. They may for cause take away temporal goods as a medicine, as a warning against sins—any excommunication or other ecclesiastical censures notwithstanding—since they were given only on condition, implied as it were.[27]

If, as it is thought, priests in the kingdom of Bohemia are enormous sinners, then it is the king's concern to correct these priests, since he is after God the supreme lord of the kingdom of Bohemia. But as the confiscation of their temporal goods is the mildest punishment for those who remain obdurate in evildoing, it follows that it is lawful for this king thus to take away these goods . . . and this is

[25] Hus, 'De ablatione bonorum temporalium a clericis', *Historia et monumenta* (1715), i, 148: 'Dominus secularis habet potestatem ad libitum tollere agros ecclesie, et per consequens domini seculares habent potestatem ad arbitrium suum auferre bona temporalia ab ecclesiasticis habitualiter deliquentibus.'

[26] Ibid., 148: 'Ex quo clerici ratione possessionum sunt imperatori vel regi obnoxii, sequitur quod ipsis habitualiter deliquentibus possessiones ab ipso imperatore vel rege licite possunt tolli.'

[27] Ibid., 149: ' "Si quis non vult operari, non manducet." Jus ergo naturae licentiat habentes regnorum gubernacula rectificare abusus temporalium, qui praecipue destruerent regna sua, sive domini temporales, sive quicunque alii dotaverunt ecclesiam temporalibus. Licet eis in casu auferre bona temporalia medicinaliter, ad cavenda peccata, non obstante excommunicatione vel alia censura ecclesiastica. Cum non nisi sub conditione, scilicet implicita, sunt dotati.'

equally reasonable if they conspire unlawfully to bring about the king's death or deprivation, or if they wish to betray the king to his enemies.[28]

Also, in 1411, when Zbyněk had provoked the king into taking reprisals, Hus rallied to Václav, and in a sermon on the text '*Exi in vias*' he said:

Our King Wenceslaus, in forcing the priests to preach and officiate by seizing their revenues, exercises a power given him by God . . . For if the priests followed the example of their maker, they would not complain much concerning the seizure of their revenues, not to speak of their complete confiscation, for the author of faith himself patiently underwent the impounding of his garments and did not advise drawing back from the sacrifice of his body.[29]

In another sermon, which Hus preached in the Bethlehem Chapel about the same time, he expressed himself even more explicitly about the subjection of the clergy to the state:

All men, even clerics, ought to be subject to Caesar and the princes of this world; this is evident from the words which Christ addressed to Caesar's heathen servant, Pontius Pilate: 'Thou couldest have no power against me except it were given thee from above.' Lo, power was given to princes from above, and Christ confirms their estate.[30]

In the sermon 'Exi in vias' Hus goes to the limit in the assertion of civil supremacy and quotes with approbation the words of Wyclif's *De officio regis*:

Whence the king ought by right of office to defend the law of God, by his compulsive power to subdue those in rebellion and to destroy

[28] Ibid., 150: 'Sacerdotibus in regno Bohemiae, ut supponitur, enormiter peccantibus, regis interest, cum sit post deum supremus dominus regni Bohemiae, ipsos sacerdotes corrigere. Sed cum mitissima correctio induratorum in malitia sit rerum temporalium ablatio, sequitur, quod licitum est ipsi regi ipsa temporalia sic auferre . . . et par est ratio, si in mortem regis vel in destitutionem eius illicite conspirarent, vel si regem vellent prodere inimicis.'

[29] Hus, Sermo 'Exi in vias', *Historia et monumenta* (1715), ii, 74-5: 'Rex noster Wenceslaus compellendo sacerdotes ad praedicandum et officiandum per arestationem censuum, exercet a deo sibi concessam potestatem . . . Si enim sacerdotes exemplum autoris sui respicerent, non murmurarent multum de arestatione censuum, non dico ablatione, ipse enim autor fidei patienter sustulit ablationem suarum vestium, et non praecepit cessationem ab oblacione sui corporis.

[30] Quoted by Kybal, *M. Jan Hus*, ii, 361-2.

the adversaries of the law of God throughout his kingdom. And any who resist kings in this respect resist the will of God, according to the apostle, Romans xiii. And he who does this is a king wise like Solomon in the Old Testament, who deposed the high priest, as is shown in I Kings ii concerning Abiathar, who was deposed, and Sadoch the high priest, whom the king placed in office. This indeed was more than to deprive bishops of their temporalities, and yet he did this, and on this account was Solomon a king who prospered in peace and his kingdom was ruled in the virtue of the Lord. And on account of this threefold office which the king ought to discharge to his God, God bestows on the king a threefold good, that is, worldly prosperity and worldly power, the respect of the world, even from his chief priest, and finally blessedness according to the degree with which he has faithfully served his God.[31]

But this categorical doctrine of the supremacy of the temporal power which Hus expounded during the great crisis of 1411 and 1412 did not represent either his normal or his final opinion. Usually Hus was far too much dazzled by the glory and honour of the church which Christ himself had founded and had made His elect and cherished bride, and he was usually too much filled with that fear and detestation of civil tyranny which he had learnt from Matěj of Janov to be willing to deny the supremacy of the church outright. In this regard, what he said on the subject of his excommunication in 1408 is significant:

One who disobeys pope, archbishop or other of his superiors is excommunicated, as I am now excommunicated. And since every excommunication is to be feared, even if it is unjust, as Gregory says in his homily on Easter, therefore, in order to avoid excommunica-

[31] *Historia et monumenta* (1715), ii, 74: 'Unde rex debet ex vi sui officii defendere legem dei, per potestatem coactivam compellere rebellantes, et in regno suo destruere legi dei adversantes. Et qui resistunt in isto regibus, voluntati dei resistunt, secundum apostolum, Romanorum 13. Et istud executus est rex sapiens Salamon in veteri testamento deponendo summum pontificem, ut patet 3[1] Regum 2 de Abiathar deposito, et Sadoch summo sacerdote, quem posuit loco sui. Hoc autem fuit magis quam auferre temporalia ab episcopis, quod et fecit, et propter hoc fuit Salamon rex pacificus, et regnum suum in virtute domini prosperatum. Et propter istud triplex officium quod rex debet solvere deo suo, Deus regi tribuit triplex bonum, scilicet, prosperitatem mundanam, et seculi potestatem, honorificentiam mundi, etiam a suo praecipuo sacerdote, et finaliter beatitudinem, secundum gradum, quo fideliter servivit deo suo.'

tion one should in all things obey pope, archbishop or other superior.[32]

Nevertheless, although Hus was generally ready to recognise the authority of the church, even over the laity, in matters of faith and conscience, he still found it very difficult always to submit to the actual church of his day. He could not believe that an archbishop who condemned the works of Wyclif to be burned indiscriminately, or a pope who forbade preaching in the Bethlehem Chapel, or even a general council which demanded that he should renounce heresies and errors that he had never held, was speaking with the voice of the true church.[33]

The last question of political theory which can be discussed here, and perhaps the most important of all in the history of Hussitism, is that of *dominium.* This doctrine had been enunciated by Richard fitzRalph in the middle of the fourteenth century in these terms:

Whence it appears to me that no one being in mortal sin has true lordship over other creatures according to God, but ought justly to be called a tyrant or thief or robber, although he may retain the name of king or prince or lord through possession or hereditary succession, or on account of the approbation of the people subject to him or of some other human law. But truly he does not have lordship, until he repents and the grace of penitence places him in a state acceptable to God . . . seeing that the approbation of the people alone is insufficient to make him king or prince over the people unless God approves his state.[34]

[32] Hus, 'De obediencia' in Sedlák, *M. Jan Hus,* p. 146*: 'Non obediens pape, archiepiscopo vel alteri suo preposito excommunicatur, sicut ego iam excommunicor, et cum omnis excommunicacio sit timenda, eciamsi sit iniusta, ut dicit Gregorius in omelia de octava Pasche, igitur propter excommunicacionem vitandam est omnino pape, archiepiscopo vel alteri preposito obediendum.'

[33] Early in his career Hus had said in his lectures on the canonical Epistles: 'Si quis praelatione utatur in malum, praecipiens aliquid contra legem dei vel praecipiat actus peccatorum, non actus virtutum.' *Historia et monumenta* (1715), i, 254.

[34] Richard fitzRalph: *Summa domini Armacani in quaestionibus Armenorum,* ed. J. Sudoris (Paris, 1512), lib. x, cap. 4: 'Unde mihi videtur nullus existens in peccato mortali habet aliarum creaturarum verum dominium apud deum sed tyrannus aut fur sive raptor merite est vocandus, quamvis nomen regis aut principis aut domini propter possessionem seu propter successionem hereditariam aut propter approbacionem populi sibi subiecti aut propter aliam legem humanam retineat, nec verum habet dominium donec peniteat et penitencie gracia eum in statum deo acceptum instituat . . . quoniam sola approbacio populi ut super populum rex fiat aut princeps non sufficit nisi deus approbet eius statum.'

John Wyclif developed the implications of this thesis in his treatise on Civil Lordship, where he summed it up thus:

A man being in grace, according to which he can in his own person enjoy the perpetual inheritance of a kingdom and any portion of the world, and then stooping to sin with which the usership of anything is incompatible, loses whatever before he might have had, even if by natural habit an imperfect being may hold in ambiguous fashion many possessions. And thus grace is not irrelevant to, but the very basis of, lordship. Just as natural potency and the act of procreation, aside from extreme instances, is the source of paternity, so, I say, grace is necessary to exercise, and in consequence for all, true lordship.[35]

In modern terms, this means that the exercise of office or authority and the enjoyment of property should be conditional on a subjective qualification. If this principle were accepted, nobody, be he pope, bishop, priest or friar, king, judge, landlord or merchant, has any right to exercise the functions of his office or trade in virtue of any act of consecration, election, ordination, or by right of inheritance, purchase, conquest, gift or charter. It was a doctrine to unmake popes, trample the bishops underfoot, cripple monasticism, and provoke political and social revolution. The fathers of Constance, who themselves condemned this doctrine in Hus and Jerome, used it without acknowledgment to snatch the fisherman's ring from the finger of John XXIII, to whom they denied the right to continue to be pope because he was a 'simoniac, a notorious dilapidator of the Church, and a scandal to the Church because of his notorious evil life'.[36] This same doctrine that authority is founded on grace was employed by the Czechs in 1419 to reject the claims of Sigismund to the Bohemian throne and ultimately, in 1458, to choose as their king George of Poděbrady, a mere gentleman without the faintest shadow of hereditary right. When Martin

[35] Wyclif, *Tractatus de civili dominio*, i, 24-5: '[Homo] existens in gracia, secundum quam potest in persona propria gaudere perpetuo hereditate regni et cuiuslibet partis mundi, et decidens in peccatum, cui repugnat usus cuiuslibet usibilis, perdit quodcunque quod prius habuerit; licet habicione naturali inperfecta habeat equivoce multa bona: et sic gracia non est inpertinens sed fundamentum dominii. Sicut naturalis potencia et actus procreandi preter extrema principiant paternitatem, sic, inquam, gracia requiritur ad usum, et per consequens ad omne verum dominium.'

[36] Hardt, iv, 185-6.

Luther, a century after the death of Hus, proclaimed the priesthood of every Christian man, he too was saying nothing more than that it is not rite, but faith and virtue which convey title to office.[37] The doctrine of *dominium ex gracia* is equally the basis of John Locke's theory of a terminable contract between the state and its subjects. In truth the fourteenth century elaboration of the doctrine of *dominium* was nothing but an essay in discovering a new basis for authority and property in a society which was in a condition of rapid development. In the late fourteenth century it was no longer easy to base authority solely on custom, law, investiture and prescription. New men and new classes were challenging the vested interests of the small aristocratic group which had hitherto monopolised power. The merchants, bankers, wool traders, corn factors, the Bardi, the d'Ursins, the Medici, the Philpots and de la Poles, intelligent and ambitious parvenus all of them, were looking for a new principle of right which would authorise the able and the industrious in ousting the incompetent and sterile.

Jan Hus and his collaborators knew this radical and subversive doctrine of dominion well. The question for the historian is how far they accepted it. Sometimes Hus seems prepared to go all the way with his English preceptor. In his treatise *Nullus est dominus civilis* Hus wrote:

Lordship is formally understood as the guise of rational nature, according to which those are named to be set in authority over a servant. In this manner a man is called a civil lord whether he has been set in authority over his servant rightly or wrongly. These considerations being noted we may suppose the following: No one, so long as he is in mortal sin, simply possesses jurisdiction over any gift of God . . . thus, clearly, if for any period anyone holds such jurisdiction unjustly, he for the same reason does not possess this simply and justly; . . . Mortal sin, since it corrupts nature, much more clearly corrupts its every mode or accident, so that if the life of a man is unjust, he thus lives out all things unjustly. Then every action of his is unjust since he does not act otherwise than he lives.[38]

[37] Hus anticipated Luther in one of his Bethlehem sermons: 'Everyone who, like Zacharias, enters into the temple of the Lord to place the incense, sacrificing Christ on the altar of his heart, is symbolically a priest. Of such a priest John Chrysostom says: "Every holy man is a priest, but not every priest is a holy man."' Quoted by Kybal, *M. Jan Hus*, ii, 314

[38] Hus, 'Nullus est dominus civilis', in *Historia et monumenta* (1558), i, 159-60:

> It is not possible that an unjust person have dominion over any one, unless in such manner as one unjustly has lordship, or rather tyrannises, when he unjustly occupies the property of another. Thus no one is justly a civil lord while he is in mortal sin.[39]

At other times Hus saw the dangers implicit in the doctrine of dominion. If a sinner has no power or authority there can never be any certainty that the sacraments have been effectively performed. No one can ever be certain that he has been lawfully married, that he is not a bastard, that he has been lawfully communicated or ordained or anointed. If the sacramental power of every priest is subjectively determined, where then is the church? Not in the pope, cardinals and hierarchy, because they may be all foreknown to damnation or rendered incompetent by mortal sin; not in the whole body of the baptised, because either baptiser or baptised may be outside the church for the same reason.[40] Wyclif and Hus alike knew well that if the sacraments cannot give an effective indication of the denotation of the church, the church can only be the unknown totality of the predestined:

> Thirdly, the church is the community of the predestinate . . . And

'Dominium intellectum formaliter est habitudo nature racionalis, secundum quam denominantur suo praefici servienti, quomodo dicitur homo civilis dominus, dum bene vel male praeficitur servienti. Istis notatis fit suppositio ista: Nemo ut est in peccato mortali habet justitiam simpliciter ad aliquod bonum dei . . . sic videlicet, si aliquis pro aliquo tempore injuste occupat, non habet illud simpliciter juste pro eodem; . . . mortale peccatum, cum inficit naturam, multo evidencius inficit omnem modum vel accidens ejusdem, ut si vita hominis sit injusta, ita quod injuste vivit, tunc quaelibet operacio ejus est injusta, cum non aliter operatur quam vivit.'

[39] *Historia et monumenta* (1715), i, 161: 'Non est possibile injustum alicui dominari, nisi ut sic injuste dominetur vel potius tyranniset, cum injuste occupat aliena, ergo nullus est juste dominus civilis, dum est in peccato mortali.'

[40] Hus's opponent Štěpán Páleč saw this dilemma clearly when he said in his *De ecclesia*: 'Alias si in malo prelato non esset vera potestas sed pretensa, ille error sequeretur, quod si papa vel prelatus non sequitur vitam Christi, sed est in peccato mortali et male vivens, non est papa vel prelatus. Quia cum non sit verus papa vel prelatus sed falsus, non est papa vel prelatus. Sed hoc est graviter errare, in quo errore sui [i.e. Hus's] discipuli generaliter sunt conclusi, non considerantes, quod sicut stat aliquem esse malum hominem vel christianum et cum hoc esse bonum vel verum magistrum in officio vel artificio, sic stat esse aliquem malum hominem et christianum et esse bonum vel verum papam vel prelatum. In primo est malicia vite, in secundo est bonitas vel veritas officii, que simul se compaciuntur.' Štěpán Páleč, 'De ecclesia' in Sedlák, *M. Jan Hus*, p. 254*.

thus the said church is twofold; one part is the church triumphant, which is the multitude of the predestinate reigning with the father. And it is called triumphant because it has triumphed over the vices of Satan. The second part of the holy mother church is the church militant, which is the multitude of the predestinate on their earthly pilgrimage. It is indeed called militant, because it employs the army of Jesus Christ against the flesh, the world and the devil. And the bishops are, through the holy spirit, the rulers of this church . . . And a third part of the holy mother church is the sleeping church, which is the multitude of the predestinate sleeping in purgatory. It is indeed called sleeping because there it is not active in advancing blessedness.[41]

The fathers of Constance realised that this was the fundamental ecclesiastical heresy of the Wyclifites. When the commissioners of the council enumerated the heretical and erroneous articles of Wyclif which Jerome of Prague had been propounding from one end of Europe to the other, they accused him of having said: 'If a bishop or a priest is in a state of mortal sin, he does not ordain, consecrate the elements or baptise. If the pope is foreknown of God to damnation or is a mortal sinner, he has no power over the faithful given to him by God, unless perchance it be given to him by Caesar . . . The prayers of the foreknown are without effect . . . Temporal lords can at their pleasure seize the goods of habitual delinquents.'[42]

The Emperor Sigismund also, during the examination of Hus, shrewdly observed the anarchism latent in the doctrine of *dominium*. Hus was being charged with having written in his *Replicatio contra magistrum Stephanum Palecz*: 'If a pope, bishop or prelate is in mortal sin he is at that moment neither pope,

[41] Hus, Sermo 'Diliges Dominum', *Historia et monumenta* (1715), ii, 40: 'Tertio modo Ecclesia est praedestinatorum universitas . . . sic autem dicta ecclesia bipartitur et una pars est ecclesia triumphans, quae est multitudo praedestinatorum regnantium in patria. Dicitur autem triumphans quia in viciis Sathanae triumphavit. Secunda pars sanctae matris ecclesiae est ecclesia militans, quae est multitudo praedestinatorum viancium. Dicitur autem militans, quia contra carnem, mundum et diabolum exercet militiam Jesu Christi. Et istius ecclesiae per spiritum sanctum episcopi sunt rectores . . . Tertia pars sanctae matris ecclesiae est ecclesia dormiens, quae est multitudo praedestinatorum in purgatorio dormientium. Dicitur autem dormiens quia ibi non est in actu beatitudinem promerendi.'

[42] 'Articuli Johannis Wicleff quos Hieronymus Pragensis revocavit.' Hardt, iv, 508-10.

bishop nor prelate.' Hus boldly replied to the accusation by saying: 'Truly he who is in mortal sin has in the eyes of God no just right to be a king.' The fathers, exultant that Hus had added treason to heresy, hastily summoned Sigismund from the embrasure where he was conversing with the Count Palatine and Frederick of Hohenzollern, that he might hear Hus repeat these damning words, whereupon Sigismund gave the one decisive answer to the doctrine of dominion, saying: 'Jan Hus, no man lives without sin.'[43]

As a matter of fact, Hus had not used the words with which he was taxed. What he had written was: 'A bad pope, bishop, prelate or priest is an unworthy minister of the sacraments through which God baptises, consecrates or otherwise works for the well-being of the Church',[44] which is something very different from the Wyclifite doctrine which was put into his mouth. Hus and his Bohemian friends knew well that it was impossible to put the doctrine of dominion strictly into practice, for to have done so in the condition of morals in the fifteenth century would have been to deprive the church of its pastors and the state of its rulers and servants. Hus at Constance retracted the Wyclifitism of his *De ecclesia* and expressed his final opinion that the power of a pope who does not conform himself to Christ and Peter in morals and conduct is in fact deprived of all merit and reward which he himself might have gained therefrom but does not gain, but he is not thereby deprived of his office.[45] Jerome of Prague, when he was heard by the council for the last time, took up the same position, saying: 'Even if the pope be a usurer and a fornicator, nevertheless, as a priest he does consecrate the elements, even though he himself profits not therefrom'.[46] This theory, that an evil priest operates the sacraments to the good of the recipients, but to his own damnation, is a return to the older Czech tradition which Matěj of Janov

[43] This instructive incident is recounted by Hus's friend and biographer, Petr of Mladoňovice in his 'Relatio', Palacký, *Documenta*, pp. 299-300.

[44] Ibid., p. 299: 'Malus papa, episcopus, prelatus vel sacerdos est indignus minister sacramentorum, per quem deus baptisat, consecrat vel aliter ad profectum sue ecclesie operatur.'

[45] Ibid., pp. 291-2: 'Potestas in tali papa frustratur, quantum ad meritum vel premium, quod deberet ex illa consequi et non consequitur, sed quoad officium non.'

[46] Hardt, iv, 752 (Jerome's reply to article XIX).

had preached in his *Regulae*.[47] By adopting such moderate views as to the relations of morality and authority Jan Hus bequeathed to the Hussites a dogma which at the same time embraced the critical moralism of Wyclif and avoided the anarchism implicit in the philosophy of the English heretic.

[47] 'Nichilominus tamen inter sacerdotes ad missas celebrandas non multum instatur in presenti nec multum exquiritur, quis inter presbyteros sit dignus missam celebrare, vel quis indignus, neque eciam fit ita rigida repulsio a missis celebrandis indignorum sacerdotum, neque eciam fit ita diligens inquisicio vel eleccio dignorum sacerdotum, sed dummodo sacerdos legitime ordinatus existat, qualis sit in moribus suis vel in vita, non curatur et gratum habetur, si et quando vult missam sanctam celebrare.' *Regulae*, v, 162.

VI

The Place of the Czech Reform Movement in the History of Europe

BETWEEN 1350 and 1450 there took place in Bohemia a profound and violent revolution in its moral, religious and political life. It has long been recognised, especially by the Czechoslovaks, that in the history of their own country this movement was decisive in shaping its character and destiny, and they have devoted much patient and scholarly labour to its elucidation. From the time of Palacký the orthodox school of Czech historians has seen in the Czech reform movement the flowering of that sense of morality and nationality which it regards as the essence of Czech history. Others, especially Pekař and Sedlák, while recognising its importance, have been less enthusiastic, and more ready to see the harm done by self-isolation and schism, or more inclined to regard the reform movement as an aberration.[1] Some German scholars also have studied it: Lechler with much sympathy and understanding; Höfler and Loserth with a scholarship marred by animosity against all things Slav in general and Czech in particular.[2] English historians, better acquainted with the German than with the Czech language, have until recently been too ready to accept the German assessment and therefore to think of the movement as beginning with Hus, and of Hus as but an echo of Wyclif. But hitherto Czechs and Germans alike have been mainly interested in the movement as a chapter in Czech history, as leading to

[1] The more important general treatments in Czech of the Czech reform movement are: F. Palacký, *Dějiny národu českého*; V. Novotný, *Náboženské hnutí české ve 14. a 15. stol.*; F. M. Bartoš, *Husitství a cizina*; V. Novotný and V. Kybal, *M. Jan Hus, život a učení*; J. Sedlák, *M. Jan Hus*. Cf. J. Pekař, *Smysl českých dějin*.

[2] G. V. Lechler, *Johannes Huss*; C. Höfler, *Geschichtschreiber der hussitischen Bewegung in Böhmen* (*Fontes rerum austriacarum*, Abt. i, ii, vi, vii); J. Loserth, *Huss und Wiclif* (2nd ed.). For a corrective see M. Spinka, *John Hus and the Czech Reform*.

the establishment of a national Church under a national king.

Yet the movement is clearly more than that; it is an integral part of the history of Europe. The Czech reform movement cannot be rightly appreciated unless it is looked at as a part of a social, moral and political revolution affecting the whole continent, nor can the history of Europe be rightly understood without an understanding of the particular manifestation in Bohemia of the general revolution.

We are today beginning to understand how fundamental and influential was that transference of economic and political power from the owners of land to the owners of personal property, which made the commercial revolution of the fourteenth and fifteenth centuries no less historically decisive than the industrial revolution of the nineteenth. Government was passing out of the hands of landed proprietors into those of the Bardi, Medici, Ursins, de la Poles, Philpots, and the merchants of Venice, Ghent, Cologne, Lübeck, Novgorod and Prague; the chanceries of popes, emperors and kings were becoming powerful bureaucracies of middle-class commercially minded men; the possession of goods and money was becoming more decisive than the ownership of forests and castles; ships and harbours, roads and bridges, letters of credit and bills of exchange, loans and banks and bankers, were becoming the decisive factors in the new society. It is true of course that land and the landowner were not yet completely deposed from their former hegemony, especially in Spain, Poland and Hungary, and that for centuries the majority of the people in even the most progressive states would continue to earn their livelihood from the land. But the power of capital was such that a handful of bankers and merchants could direct the destinies of whole communities. The centres of political power were now determined by considerations of communications and the siting of mineral wealth. That is why Prague in the fourteenth century became suddenly the 'imperial metropolis', as Matěj of Janov described it.[3]

What attracted Charles IV, Luxemburger and Francophile as he was, to make Bohemia the centre and mainstay of his Empire was his conscious realisation that this inheritance from

[3] *Regulae*, iii, 357.

his Czech mother alone of all his dominions could provide him with the wealth and men to make his rule effective; not to mention his unconscious appreciation of the value of the silver and gold, the salt, glass and leather of the country, of the industry and skill of its mixed, energetic and enterprising population, as well as of the central position of Prague, towards which and from which led the highways of the Elbe, the Oder and the Danube, and where the route from the Adriatic to the Baltic crossed that from the Bosphorus to the English Channel. The rapid development of the commerce and industry of Prague was both the cause and the consequence of the fact that from 1346 to 1410 here was the imperial capital, where German-speaking merchants in the Old Town were challenged and stimulated by the rapid growth of the New Town, which Charles founded and filled with artisans and craftsmen of Czech speech. And towns have ever been the forcing grounds of social progress and political revolution. Members of this new and growing class figure in almost every incident of the reform movement. It was the German burghers of Prague who so filled the Týn church to hear Konrad Waldhauser's denunciation of the greed and idleness of the monks and the worldliness and avarice of the friars that he had to preach in the great square outside; it was the Czech artisans and shopkeepers who flocked to hear Milíč preach in their own language at St Giles's in the Malá Strana, and their sons whom he instructed in Latin in the art and duties of a preacher at St Nicholas's in the Old Town. When Milíč preached that the wars and pestilences of his own day, the division of nation against nation, the avarice and self-indulgence of clergy and laity alike, were all signs that the abomination of desolation was already set in the holy place, that Antichrist was at hand, and that the year of the prophet Daniel was already come, he was merely stating in the terms of apocalyptic the historical fact that he was living in an age of revolution, and that an ecclesiastical and moral order designed for an agricultural, feudal, unnational society was breaking down in the new commercial and nationalist society in which he and his hearers were living.[4] When Tomáš of Štítný wrote

[4] See Jan Milíč of Kroměříž, 'Libellus de Antichristo', in Matěj of Janov, *Regulae*, iii, 368-81.

his books on morality and religious education in Czech rather than Latin, it was because he was unconsciously impelled to appeal to an audience of literate but unscholastic townsfolk and county gentry that was typical of the new age. As the reform movement grows and develops, more and more do we find that the middle classes play a part. For example among those who strove to preserve Milíč's refuge for repentant prostitutes, known as 'Jerusalem', for its original purpose after his death, besides the lord of Rožmberk, Matěj of Janov and various priests, we find Angelo the apothecary,[5] Machuta 'the cloth cutter', and Kříž 'the shop-keeper'.[6] The same Kříž 'kramář' was the moving force in the founding of the chapel of 'Bethlehem' in 1391 as a centre for preaching, and from its pulpit Jan Protiva, Štěpán of Kolín, and finally Hus himself were to stir the Praguers to a practical and enduring zeal for reform. In the stormy years after Archbishop Zbyněk took active steps against the 'Wyclifites' of Prague in 1408, the Praguers, supported by King Václav IV and egged on by the fiery eloquence of Jerome of Prague, broke out into a series of anticlerical riots which well illustrate the incompatibility of the vested interests of the church and the dissatisfaction of a bourgeoisie becoming conscious of its strength. This may be illustrated from Petr of Mladoňovice's account of the examination of Hus at Constance on 7 June 1415:

It was also charged against him that his scandalous and erroneous sermons caused a great sedition in the city of Prague, and by reason of the guile and guilt of Jan Hus many notable and catholic god-fearing men were forced to go and hide outside the city; there ensued slaughter, robberies, sacrilege and other horrible and execrable acts, of which Jan Hus was the cause and in which he participated. He replied that the riots were not due to him, but to the interdict imposed for two miles round Prague by Archbishop Zbyněk when the king and the university declared their neutrality [as between the rival popes Gregory XII and Benedict XIII], for

[5] This Florentine, who had settled in Prague, and who had introduced Cola de Rienzi to Charles IV there, is an interesting example of the fruitful intercourse between the great commercial centres of Europe at this time.

[6] These are the people addressed in the letter of Vojtěch Raňkův, written just before his death, asking them to resist the efforts of the Cistercians to take over 'Jerusalem'. See Novotný, *Náboženské hnutí*, pp. 140-1.

Zbyněk having despoiled the tomb of St Wenceslas fled to Roudnice, whither the prelates and clergy followed him; for they refused to obey the king and carry on divine service, but fled, and so others took over their affairs [the king confiscated their revenues], 'but', Hus said, 'not by my order or under my leadership'.

And Náz said: 'No, reverend fathers, it was not out of disobedience to the king's wishes, but because of the robberies the clergy had suffered that they asked the archbishop to impose the interdict, and that was why they were despoiled.'

And the cardinal of Cambrai [Pierre d'Ailly], commissioner and judge at this hearing, said: 'I must testify at this point. When I was riding from Rome, certain prelates from Bohemia met me, and when I asked them what the news was there, they replied: "O, most reverend father! It is bad: all the clergy have been robbed of their prebends and have been ill treated." '[7]

From the long list of charges made against Jerome of Prague in May 1416, it is possible to supplement this picture. When the papal indulgence was preached in Prague in 1412 there were organised demonstrations in the parish and monastic churches; the preachers were interrupted and the protesters made public denials of the right of the pope to use such means to raise money for his war against Ladislas of Naples. Three of the interrupters were arrested by the magistrates of the Old Town (probably German 'patricians') and, despite a deputation from the university which pleaded that they should be leniently treated, they were speedily and secretly beheaded, not in the usual places under the pillory, but clandestinely and surrounded by a strong guard—'for fear of the people', as the contemporary chronicler records. When the corpses were discovered, a huge mob of weeping and angry citizens and students escorted them to the Bethlehem chapel, where they were honoured with the rites customarily paid to martyrs.[8] The same articles charged against Jerome tell also of another organised demonstration in Prague, when a student standing in a cart and dressed like a prostitute, and with the hated bull of indulgence suspended round his neck, was escorted by a tumultuous crowd, to whom he leeringly offered his wares, all round the city to the market

[7] Petr of Mladeňovice, 'Relatio', in Palacký, *Documenta*, pp. 282-3.
[8] 'Articuli dati in causa fidei contra Hieronymum de Praga', in Hardt, iv, 676.

place of the Old Town, where the dummy bull was publicly burnt.[9] During the same year, 1412, and again in 1414, this campaign of organised demonstrations against what had come to be regarded as the worst instruments of clerical extortion and superstition was directed against crucifixes, which were plastered with human dung, and relics, which were snatched out of their coffers and trampled underfoot under the eyes of the friars who had them on show in order to attract the offerings of the devout.[10]

These scenes of protest and disorder in Prague are closely parallel to what was happening at much the same time in other centres of the adolescent bourgeoisie, to the murder of Archbishop Sudbury by Wat Tyler's mob in 1381, to the violent attack on the privileged and established order of things by the Cabochiens in Paris in the years 1411 to 1413, to the rising of the 'Ciompi' against the patrician oligarchy of Florence in 1378, or to the revolt of Ghent against the count of Flanders in 1382.

To some extent we are confirmed in the view that the Bohemian reform movement was part of the general European middle-class revolution when we examine the social provenance of the leading reformers. Jan Milíč was a Moravian who retained his provincial accent even after he had been a civil servant for four years, and the fact that between 1358 and 1362 he was successively registrator, corrector and notary in Charles IV's chancery is symptomatic of the close connexion between the new bureaucracy, the bourgeosie, and the reformers. Tomáš of Štítný and Matěj of Janov were sons of country gentlemen who came to the city; Petr Chelčický was of even humbler rural origin, and as he embodies a later stage of the reform movement, he may to some extent be held to voice the sentiments of the peasantry, which had not shared in the victory of the middle classes embodied in the Utraquist and Taborite parties. Hus was born in a village, but, coming as he did to the university of Prague while still an adolescent, he became and remained a typical Praguer. The embodiment of the bourgeois character of the reform movement is Hus's dear friend, admirer, and fellow-martyr Jerome, whose only other name was

[9] Ibid., 672. [10] Ibid., 672-4.

'de Praga', 'Pragensis'; he is 'Jeronym Pražský', almost the incarnation of the volatile, restless, zealous, reckless and inconstant city. Though he wandered, led by his *ardor discendi*, to Oxford, Paris, Heidelberg, Cologne, Jerusalem, Buda, Vienna, Cracow, Vitebsk, and Pskov, he ever returned to the country and city he loved so well. Though it is difficult to tell how true are the uncontrollable charges made against him by his accusers at Constance that he was the ringleader in all the excesses of the anti-clerical riots, the burning of the indulgence, the honouring as martyrs of the three youths who were executed, the organising of the insults to friars, crucifixes and relics, yet enough is clear from his own admissions to make it obvious that he was that sort of natural popular leader whom times of urban revolution breed, a more noble-minded Wat Tyler or Caboche, a more spiritually minded Étienne Marcel or Philip van Artevelde. He admits that he slapped the mouth of the Dominican Beneš of Innem who insulted him. (His accusers said that 'he slapped Beneš's face in the public streets in the presence of a crowd of people, and Jerome drew his knife and would have struck him therewith, and probably have killed him or mortally wounded him, had he not been prevented by master Zdislas of Zvířetice'.)[11] Another incident in Jerome's career as an agitator is instructive both as to the goings-on in Prague and the views of his accusers as to what was good evidence:

Similarly it is charged against Jerome that in the year 1412 in the month of September on St Wenceslas' day in the Carmelite monastery he did command, procure and instruct certain laymen to throw on the ground certain relics which were placed there by a friar who was begging alms for the fabric, . . . and Jerome entered the monastery violently and took prisoner the friar Nicholas who was saying that Wyclif was a heretic who had been reproved by the Church, and led him away captive with two other friars of the same monastery. These two he handed over to the magistrates of the city who put them in the prison of the New Town[12] among the thieves and robbers. But the friar Nicholas he kept in his own custody in prison for several days, and tortured him in devious ways. And not content with that, Jerome took him out in a boat on the river Vltava which

[11] Ibid, 641-2.

[12] The magistrates of Nové Město were probably Czechs, not Germans as were those of the Staré Město.

flows strong and wide near to Prague, tied him to the end of a rope and threw him overboard, saying to the said friar some such words as these: 'Now tell me, monk, was Master John Wyclif a holy and evangelical doctor or not?' wishing to force him to revoke those words he had spoken in the pulpit against Wyclif. And Jerome would certainly have drowned the friar had not help come from one of his followers and members of his household, who freed him from his great peril.

To this charge Jerome replied: 'When I entered the monastery I found the two monks quarrelling with two citizens whose servant they had imprisoned. While I was talking calmly with them, many armed men rushed on me with swords. As I had then no weapon with me I snatched a sword from a layman who was standing by and defended myself as best I could against them. Afterwards I handed over two monks to the magistrate, and one I kept for myself.'[13]

Though the Czech reform movement was fundamentally a social phenomenon, it was of course not consciously so. The realisation that the world was upside down, which manifested itself in Milíč's apocalyptic and in Matěj of Janov's plea for a return to the apostolic age, was largely subconscious. Nevertheless here and there we do observe a conscious social sense even in the early stages of the movement. Konrad Waldhauser, the Austrian preacher, whom Charles IV brought to Prague in 1363 and who was the master and inspiration of Milíč, made a bitter attack on the levying of burial dues and the traffic in the privilege of being buried in monasteries or friaries.[14] This is a part of the programme which nearly all of his successors embraced; and it neatly anticipates that attack on mortuary dues, which was the first gesture of the English Reformation parliament of 1529. The protests against the sale of indulgences, against the exploitation of popular superstition to extract money in return for the benefits conferred by relics and thaumaturgic statues and pictures, and against the charging of fees for the ministration of the sacraments, are in part a protest against the materialisation of religion and the cult of *adinvenciones hominum*, and in part the revolt of the townsmen against exploitation by a clerical caste whose functions were becoming stereotyped and

[13] I have conflated the articles of accusation in Hardt, iv, 641, with the additional articles, ibid., 666-7.

[14] Novotný, *Nabożenské hnutí*, p. 60.

of a value that was decreasingly apparent. The same can be said of the protests which we find uttered by Hus and others against the feudal legal system, which gave the lord the right to inherit the property of a tenant who died without direct heirs.[15] But it would be surprising if we could find evidence that the early reformers had a detailed social programme for the emancipation of the serf and the labourer. In the first place, serfdom did not become legally complete in central Europe before the end of the fifteenth century, and in the second the early stages of the reform movement were so predominantly urban that the social condition of the peasantry did not impinge on its conscience. Indeed except for Chelčický and the Unity of Brethren, all the Hussite parties so identified themselves with the townsmen and the gentry that they viewed the increasing subjection of the peasantry with indifference at the best. Hus's social philosophy was completely orthodox: it is the duty of the *laboriosi* to work to support the clergy and the *majorates*, and it is the duty of the clergy and lords to obey God's commandments.[16] Such is the theme of Hus's preaching in Bethlehem. Of course all the reformers wax indignant at the way God's poor are robbed by priests who curse for tithes, and who use alms originally intended for the poor to adorn their churches and themselves; but this is pure moral indignation, not due to any feeling that there ought not to be any poor.

In considering the social aspects of the reform movement we must bear in mind that the merchants and craftsmen were not the only beneficiaries of the commercial revolution. The advent of an economy of production for sale and profit also favoured the professional farmer, the man who owned freehold hereditary land, which he farmed with serf labour, and the produce of which he sold to the towns. These country gentry, the Pastons of England, the *vladyky* of Bohemia and Moravia, the *szlachta* of Poland, the innumerable 'nobles' of Hungary—were the economic counterpart of the towns: the landlords fed the towns and the towns supplied the landlords with their clothes, tools, weapons, ornaments and luxuries. These country gentry were pushing themselves into the English house of commons, the

[15] Ibid., pp. 138, 139, 255.

[16] Kybal, *M. Jan Hus*, ii, 361.

Spanish cortes, the Bohemian diet; they monopolised the government of the Hungarian counties and the Polish provincial diets, whence they were sent as delegates to the national parliaments.

As the reform movement in Bohemia develops and begins to spread outside the city and university of Prague, so do the gentry become increasingly involved in it. When Hus in 1412 went into voluntary exile from Prague in order to save it from the interdict his excommunicated presence would have incurred, he spent two years in the towns and the manor houses of the Bohemian countryside, the effect of which can be seen in the loyal support he received from the Bohemian gentry at Constance. There his comfort and safety were the constant care of Jan of Chlum, Jindřich of Lacenbok and Václav of Dubá, which was but an earnest of the letters of indignation and protest which, after Hus's death, were signed by scores of nobles and gentry of Bohemia and Moravia.[17] The measure of support which Hus had from this class was clearly expressed during the council, much to the alarm of the Emperor Sigismund, who was heir-presumptive to the kingdom of Bohemia. The political significance of the passage has long been recognised, but it is worth repeating here as evidence that the reformers had the support not so much of a nation as of a social class.

The cardinal of Cambrai said to Hus: 'Master John! when you were brought to the bishop's palace we asked you how you had come and you said you had come here freely; and that had you not wanted to come neither the king of Bohemia nor the lord king of the Romans could have compelled you to come.' And the master replied: 'Indeed I said that I came here freely, and had I not been willing to come, there are so many great lords in the kingdom of Bohemia who love me, in whose castles I might have lain hidden, that neither that king nor this could have forced me to come here.' The cardinal nodded his head and his countenance somewhat changed and he said: 'See this hardihood!' And lord Jan [of Chlum], when some of

[17] The letter of 2 Sep. 1415 (Hardt, iv, 495-7; Palacký, *Documenta*, pp. 580 ff.), was signed by 61 persons 'in pleno concilio magnatum, baronum, procerum, et nobilium regni Bohemie et marchionatus Moravie'. They pledged themselves 'legem domini nostri Jesu Christi ipsiusque devotos, humiles et constantes predicatores, usque ad effusionem sanguinis . . . defendere'. The letter of 30 Dec. 1415 was signed by 432 nobles and gentlemen.

those standing by murmured, said to them: 'He is speaking the truth; I am but a poor knight in our kingdom, and yet I would have been quite willing to entertain him for a year, let who will like it or not, so that they could not have got him. And there are many and great lords who love him, who have strong castles where they could have harboured him for as long as they liked, even against both their kings.'[18]

Sigismund was to realise the truth of Jan of Chlum's assertion when he and his Hungarian forces tried to seize Bohemia in 1420, when these 'many and strong' nobles roundly defeated him at Sudoměř and Vítkov.

It is also worthy of remark that it was not only the Czech gentry who stood by Hus at Constance. The Polish delegates also befriended him. In a letter which Hus wrote describing the first day of his trial, 5 June 1415, he said: 'Some cried out: "Let him be burned!", and especially Michael de Causis, whom I heard. I felt that I had not one friend in this whole crowd of clergy, except "Pater" and one Polish doctor, whom I knew.'[19] And earlier, on 14 May, when Petr of Mladoňovice had organised a complaint to the council about the barbarous treatment of Hus in prison, in addition to the names of the Czech signatories there are those of Zawisza Czarny of Garbów, the most famous Polish knight of that time, Janusz of Tulisków, castellan of Kalisz, and the Polish lords Boruta, Dunin, Balicki and others.[20] That Czech reformist ideas spread early to Poland is well known; and it is probable that Jerome's activities in Cracow in 1413, when he engaged in a great public disputation in the university,[21] and when he accompanied Grand Duke Witold of Lithuania on a great progress to Vitebsk, Pskov and Wilno, had much to do with winning the sympathy of the Polish gentry. Jerome may have performed much the same function in Hungary and Austria, where his activities were thus described by the official of the archbishop of Passau:

What rumour had already reported was recently plainly announced to us on behalf of the university, namely that a certain master of arts,

[18] Petr of Mladeňovice, 'Relatio', in Palacký, *Documenta*, p. 283.

[19] Palacký, *Documenta*, p. 105.

[20] Ibid., pp. 258, 556; Hardt, iv, 188.

[21] Described in a letter of Albert, bishop of Cracow, of 2 April 1413, Palacký, *Documenta*, p. 506.

called Jerome of Prague, implicated in certain Wyclifite errors con demned by the apostolic See, careless of his soul's safety, was bold to disseminate these errors in Heidelberg, in Prague and in Hungary, where he was many times ignominiously confuted by the faithful of Christ and supporters of orthodox belief. And now he has made his way to the glorious university of Vienna, our beloved mother in whom is no wrinkle of duplicity . . . in order to infect with his perverse doctrine the hearts of the weak . . . and to propagate even wider his erroneous sect.[22]

More precisely the articles charged against Jerome at Constance said:

The same Jerome in Hungary, in Buda, in the presence of the most serene prince and lord Sigismund, king of the Romans and of Hungary, in the royal chapel of the castle of Buda, in the year 1410, on the Thursday before Easter—he, being a layman, dressed in lay habit and wearing a long beard, in the presence of the lord king and of many reverend fathers, bishops and other prelates and of others of diverse estates, publicly preached many things scandalous and erroneous in the faith, and also heresies about the sacrament of the altar, and other things contrary to church order and offensive to pious ears, whence might follow sedition and popular commotions made by temporal lords against the clergy.[23]

It is interesting to speculate why the seeds thus promisingly sown in Poland and Hungary failed to take permanent root. Bishop Albert of Cracow ironically said after Jerome's departure from Poland: 'Our land seems to be too arid to receive the seed that he sows and to bear fruit, because the simple people are not able to understand his dogmas; much less can the lands of the Lithuanians and Russians do so.'[24] The bishop was right in so far as Poland was less affected by the commercial revolution than was Bohemia. When the *szlachta* later succeeded in excluding the Polish towns from foreign trade and from the diet, they so enfeebled what would have been the best forcing ground of reform that the movement, which had shown much early promise, was easily nipped in the bud by cardinal Oleśnicki, after the death of those early patrons of the reformers, Queen Jadwiga and Grand Duke Witold.

[22] Klicman, p. 37. [23] Hardt, iv, 673.
[24] Palacký, *Documenta*, p. 506.

In Hungary, though apparently Hussite ideas did for a time get some hold in the German-Slovak mining towns, they were almost obliterated when the feeble civic life of Hungary was emasculated by the triumph of the Hungarian nobility and the choking up of the Danubian trade routes by the advance of the uncommercial Turk.

The moral disease that afflicted Europe in the later Middle Ages was the inevitable concomitant of the social crisis. The moral code that had been effective for the preservation of a purely agricultural society was proving inadequate to solve the new moral problems presented by an economy of buying and selling. Gregory the Great's *Magna moralia* had nothing to say about the ethics of capital, banking, market prices, rates of interest, partnership and company promoting. The moral code which had justly condemned the money-lender in the interests of the peasant farmer was now hampering the development of commercial and industrial credit, and was therefore being evaded with the help of all sorts of sophistries and fictions. The attempt to apply the moral code of one type of society to another basically different inevitably resulted in widespread disobedience to ancient precepts. In such circumstances morality could not but become convention rather than conviction. It was an atmosphere in which precept ceased to coincide with practice even in the preceptor. Salvation from the prevalent sense of sin was sought in conformity to outworn rules, in external acts, in works rather than faith. How universal the moral disease was can be seen in nearly all contemporary writers: in Chaucer's 'Miller's Tale' and 'Clerk's Tale', in the second part of the *Roman de la Rose*, in Boccaccio's *Decameron*; how desperate was the search for a remedy appears in Langland's *Piers Plowman*, in the visions and prophecies of St Bridget of Sweden and St Catherine of Siena. The immense volume of polemical literature produced by the murder of Louis of Orleans in 1407 and the problem of the right or wrong of tyrannicide illustrates the acuteness of the moral crisis and the failure of the conscience of Christendom assembled at Constance to give any lead at all.

The Czech reform movement was an integral part of this general European phenomenon. The disease was as bad in

Bohemia as it was in Tuscany or England; the protests of Waldhauser, Milíč, Matěj of Janov and Hus were as eloquent and trenchant as those of Wyclif, fitzRalph, Petrarch or Gerson. One passage from the *Regulae veteris et novi testamenti* of Matěj of Janov must serve to illustrate the Czech share in this European concert of moral indignation.

This outward appearance and splendour of earthly things which is contrived for the pleasure of the flesh, the delights of the eye and the pride of life by Christians who are lovers of this world . . . is the figure of the Beast with horns [Revelation xvii] . . .

Look for example at those noble esquires who make their honour and their boast in their fathers after the flesh, but not at all in Christ Jesus, and who take more emulous pride in their noble birth than in the fact that they are of the generation of Jesus Christ. So hot do they get about it that they perpetrate deeds that can without qualification be described as Beastly. For the honour of their birth and breeding they wound each other mortally, fight duels, and that with edged weapons, and often naked or half naked, quite deliberately when there was plenty of time for taking counsel, knowing full well that one or the other of them must be killed and go to hell. Sometimes they fight each other for glory, sometimes for the love of their mistresses. Anyone who has his eyes open cannot help seeing that such creatures are not men, and certainly not Christians, but ferocious and irrational beasts.

As I began to say the whole outward appearance of the dress and body of such men is the exact representation of the Beast with horns . . .

Women too, by a wonderful dispensation, also strive to be horned in their outward appearance, so that they also publicly display themselves as perfect beasts; for with great art and much labour they build up their headdress into at least three sharp horns, one on their foreheads and one on either side, And then they make two other horns on their bosoms by making their breasts stick out, even if they are naturally flat-chested, by the fashion in which their gowns are cut . . . Finally these women bear two horns on their feet in the shape of the long pointed shoes they wear, as anyone can see.[25]

From that Matěj goes on to a circumstantial account of the immodesty of the contemporary dress of both men and women that can be paralleled in a hundred sermons being preached at

[25] *Regulae*, iv, 222-4.

the same period all the way from Paul's Cross to the Týn church of Prague. And so it is with the remedies that the Czech reformers have to prescribe: at the same time when Matěj was pleading in pulpit and tractate with the people of Prague for a turning from the vanity and hypocrisy of the *adinvenciones hominum* to *Jhesus crucifixus*, to the bible, and to the sacramental grace of frequent communion in the saving body of Christ, the Lollards were taking the vernacular bible and the apostolic evangel to the people of England. Not till Jerome brought Wyclif's *Dialogus* and *Trialogus* from Oxford to Prague at the turn of the century did Czech reformers realise that they were not fighting a lone battle. But the discovery that the *doctor evangelicus* had fought the same battles as those in which they were engaged made the Czech reformers welcome him, even to the extent of making his very words their own.

The remedy for moral disorder in the fourteenth and fifteenth centuries was inevitably sought in terms of religion, as an answer to the age-old question: 'How shall a man be saved?' The revolutionaries everywhere were answering: 'Not by works alone; not by absolution and penance, not by indulgences or miracle-working relics and images; not by vain repetitions and outward acts, *but* by a change of heart, penitence and not penance, by the indwelling of the Spirit.' It was this religious sentiment that underlay the whole of the great controversy of the philosophers in the schools during the fourteenth century, the battle between nominalism and realism. Led by the great Franciscan schoolmen, from Roger Bacon, through Duns Scotus, and Occam, philosophy had adjusted itself to the changing order of things, by concentrating its attention on the sensible world, dismissing ideas and abstractions as mere *flatus vocis*, setting apart the world of faith from that of reason, as something which man must accept as revelation, but beyond rationalisation. This nominalism had become the current philosophy especially at the acknowledged centre of European thought, the university of Paris, where its leading exponents at the beginning of the fifteenth century were Jean Gerson, chancellor of the university, and Pierre d'Ailly, later cardinal of Cambrai. But while this new nominalism, with its interest in the perceptible and the measurable and its adumbrations of the scientific method and spirit, was itself the response to the needs of a developing commercial society, it singularly failed to give an answer to the specifically moral and religious question of the day. It is true that the rationalism of the nominalists made them zealous enemies of superstition and exposers of thaumaturgy; but that was purely destructive work; they had little positive contribution to make to the solution of psychological or spiritual problems. Therefore, though nominalism was firmly entrenched in Paris and in the new German universities then being established at Heidelberg, Cologne, Leipzig and Vienna, it never succeeded in getting such mastery in the universities of either Oxford or Prague. In Oxford there was a rival philosophical development. It too stemmed from Duns Scotus, but followed him on that side of his teaching which had exalted will above reason, and the intense ethical interests of a series of seculars in the university of Oxford, Richard fitzRalph, Bradwardine, Holkot and Wyclif, pursued this line towards a neo-Augustinian theology and psychology, which led Bradwardine into uncompromising predestinarianism, and Wyclif very near to it. In the realm of metaphysics this alternative development became a new Realism, insistent on the reality of universals, of which Wyclif was the most able and eminent exponent in Europe.

At the same time a similar philosophical divergence was manifesting itself at Prague, where metaphysical debate was exacerbated by national animosity. Modelled as it was on the universities of Paris and Bologna, looking as it did to Paris as a place to which its own able scholars should go for further study, it was inevitable that from its foundation in 1348 the university of Prague should be inclined towards Parisian nominalism. Indeed its first two generations of eminent scholars were nominalists—Heinrich Totting, Konrad von Soltau, Johann Marienwerder, Jan Isner, Matthew of Liegnitz, Nicholas of Jauer, Heinrich of Bitterfeld, and Albert Engelschalk. They were all enemies of superstition and zealous moralists; but their writings are marked by the negative aridity of nominalism, and they were all Germans or Germanised Silesians. But towards the end of the fourteenth century we begin to see the beginnings in Prague of an Augustinian, ethical and realist reaction. What its origins were and whether it goes back beyond the arrival of Wyclif's philosophical works about 1391 are matters on which more research is necessary. What is clear is that the philosophical schism was from the beginning tied up with the opposition of the Czech 'nation' in the university to the dominant Bavarian, Saxon and Polish (Silesian) nations. The champions of Wyclif's realism—Stanislav of Znojmo, Marek of Hradec, Štěpán Páleč, Hus, and Jerome—were all Czechs. Why there should have been this parallel philosophical and national dichotomy, I cannot say; there is a temptation to ascribe it unscientifically to some inherent quality in the Slavs which found the idealism of the realists more congenial than the rationalism of the nominalists: but I am inclined to believe that the Czech scholars were ready to pick any bone with their German colleagues, and that they found in realism and Wyclif a potent force with which to attack the specific moral and political problems of their own day and their own country. How closely philosophical and national considerations were interlocked can be seen in the battle royal of the scholastic war which was fought out in the great university debate of 1409. In the presence of the ambassadors of the duke of Brabant, the consuls of the Old Town, and a vast concourse of doctors, masters and students, Matěj of Knín opened his *quodlibet* on the theme 'Whether it is necessary to posit universals apart from things if the harmony of the world is to be sensible'. Knín had but recently been charged with Wyclifite errors before archbishop Zbyněk, and such was his unpopularity with the German nominalist masters that they had to be ordered to attend by King Václav himself. The three days of debate culminated in the famous speech made by Jerome, the so-called *Recommendatio artium liberalium* which established his reputation for eloquence, though it is less a formal exposition of realism than an attack on the German masters, a defence of the orthodoxy of the Czechs, and a plea for the right of students to study Wyclif, even though some of what he wrote had been officially condemned.[26] With a charac-

[26] For an account of Knín's *Quodlibet* see Novotný, *M. Jan Hus*, i, 301-13. Jerome's speeches at the *Quodlibet* and at its continuation in his debate with Blažej Vlk a few weeks later are all that we have of Jerome's continuous composition. These speeches are published in Höfler, vol. ii, pp. 112-28 (there wrongly ascribed to Hus), and Sedlák, *Studie a texty*, ii, pp. 215-62.

teristic sense of the dramatic Jerome concluded his oration by producing and reading the notorious Oxford letter of 1406, which purported to give the official support of that university to Wyclif's orthodoxy.

Knín's *quodlibet* was the last act of the undivided university of Prague, for a fortnight later, 18 January 1409, King Václav issued the decree of Kutná Hora which transferred the majority of votes from the Germans to the Czechs, and led to the departure of the German masters to Leipzig and Erfurt. Henceforward the Czechs, and therefore Wyclifite realism, were supreme at Prague, and the philosophical controversy was not renewed until Hus and Jerome went to Constance, there to defend their views.

It is clear that to many of the fathers of the council the most serious charge against Hus and Jerome was their realism. With some justice they felt that it was the realist refusal to believe that accidents could subsist without continuity of substance which had led Wyclif into the heresy that the material bread and wine remain after the consecration of the elements in the sacrament of the altar. Though Hus had steadfastly refused to pursue his philosophical Wyclifitism to that logical conclusion, and though the sentence of condemnation on Jerome expressly admitted his eucharistic orthodoxy, nevertheless Gerson and his fellows were convinced that realism was inherently likely to lead to the heresy of remanence. This connexion between the philosophical and doctrinal aspects of the problem is well illustrated by the following passage from Mladoňovice's *Relatio* (proceedings of 7 June 1415):

Further it is alleged that Jan Hus in June 1410 and at other times in the chapel called Bethlehem and at other places in the city of Prague did preach to the people there assembled many errors and heresies both from the books of the late John Wyclif and out of his own obstinacy and guile, and that he did teach, maintain and defend them, and chiefly this, that after the consecration of the Host on the altar material bread remains. And they adduced witnesses on this point: doctors, prelates, parish priests, etc. And the master, calling God and his conscience to witness, replied that he had not said or maintained any such thing . . . Then the cardinal of Cambrai taking up a paper which he said had come into his hands late on the previous day, and holding it in his hand, asked master John whether he held that universals exist apart from things; and he replied that he did, as St Anselm and others had done. Then the cardinal argued: 'It follows then that after consecration the substance of material bread remains; for, once the consecration has been made, while the bread is changed and transubstantiated into the body of Christ, as you admit, either the general substance of material bread remains, or not. If it does, then my point is proved; if not, it follows that on the ceasing to be of the individual piece of bread, the universal also ceases to be.' Hus replied that the universal does cease to be in this individual material bread, when it is thus changed or passes into the body of Christ or is transubstantiated, but nevertheless the universal remains the subject of other individuals. Then a certain Englishman got up and tried to prove that Hus's argument proved that material bread does remain. And the master said: 'That is the sort of childish argument which boys learn in schools, and its falsity is self-evident . . .'[27]

With this may be compared the charges made against Jerome, first at the Vienna trial of 1410 and then at Constance in 1416, though in Jerome's case the argument was that his realism led to Trinitarian rather than to eucharistic heresy. For example at Vienna Johann of Vohburg gave evidence that Jerome had written: 'Universals must be predicated of the divine mind . . . quality is extrinsically present in virtue of the form of things; for every quality is determined by the substantial form which it follows, and is therefore the instrument of its action or the decoration of its subject, and so quality is essentially conserved by substantial form.' To us the chief fault of such opinions may well seem the obscure jargon in which they were expressed, but the church rightly sensed Wyclifitism and the danger of heresy and schism. Had Wyclif not been led on by his philosophy to challenge not only sacramental dogma but also the authority of the church? He had said that if the church taught a doctrine of transubstantiation which was metaphysically impossible, the church was wrong; if the church misused indulgences, excommunication, reservations, tithes and tenths, then the church must be opposed. Wyclif had asked a question which perplexed men were asking throughout

[27] Palacký, *Documenta*, pp. 266-7.

Christendom—'Where is the Church? In the greedy, corrupt, sinful, ambitious Curia of Rome or Avignon, or in the whole body of Christ's elect?' The dual and the triple schism in the west, added to the ancient eastern schism, made this question topical and urgent. Since 1409 there were three persons, each claiming to be Christ's vicar, each proclaiming the other two to be usurpers, schismatics and heretics, each maintaining a court as costly to one-third of Christendom as before 1378 the one curia had been to the whole. In England Wyclif was driven to advocate that after the death of Urban VI the English should live without a pope 'as the Greeks do'. For a generation the rulers and universities of France, Germany, Spain and Italy agitated the question of how the schism could be ended, and many were driven to accept the sovereignty of the general council as the only solution. In Bohemia Matěj of Janov was forced to exclaim:

This great city of the world of Christians is severed into three parts, that of the Romans in the south, the Greeks in the east, and the French in the west. The Romans say: 'Here is the Church and here is Christ.' The French say: 'It is not so, for we are the Church and Christ is here.' And the Greeks continually say: 'Ye lie, both of you, for we are the Church and Christ is here.' See how the Gospel is literally fulfilled which says: 'In those days they shall say to you, Lo, here is Christ, or there.' Behold how the sun and moon are darkened so that even the city that is set on a hill is hid and covered in darkness that it cannot be seen, in such a way that of the infinite multitude of Christians it would not be easy to find one who is certain where the one true Church of God is . . .

I myself believe that Christ is in the Roman obedience. But what I say I say in relation to the whole body of those who were formerly called Christians, and I speak relatively to the certainty in the primitive Church of the saints where it was well known where was the Church and where was Christ. But today there is no such certainty as to which part of Christendom Christ is in that anyone would be so bold as to be willing to die for it.[28]

It is from such a fundamental and general perplexity that Hus's doctrine of the church evolves. The fact that his *De ecclesia* follows Wyclif almost verbatim through much of its

[28] *Regulae*, i, 294-5.

course is not so much evidence of Hus's lack of originality, as Loserth would have it, as evidence that the disease from which Bohemia was suffering was general. The Hussite movement was in no sense an isolated manifestation of some idiosyncrasy of the Czech character, but the local form taken by revolt against the social, moral, philosophical, religious and ecclesiastical confusion of the general European revolution. That in Bohemia alone in the fifteenth century it resulted in a successful and enduring national schism was due in part to the advanced economic condition of the country, in part to the fact that its aspirations for religious autonomy came to be involved in the struggle against the political claims of the Emperor Sigsmund to subordinate the interests of Bohemia to the needs of his disorderly and bankrupt empire, and in part to the spiritual and military leadership of Hus and Žižka. Nevertheless even the Hussite wars and the national monarchy of George of Poděbrady are not an aberration from the highroad of historical development in Europe, as was to be seen when, a hundred years after the death of Hus, Luther, Henry VIII, Zwingli, and Calvin took half Europe along the path that the Czechs had already travelled.

VII

National and Heretical Religious Movements from the End of the Fourteenth to the Middle of the Fifteenth Century

THE heretical and schismatic movements of the period between the beginning of the western schism in 1378 and its end in 1449 can be regarded as either the culmination of the scattered, diverse and evanescent heresies of the Middle Ages, or as the first chapter in the history of the national, organised and permanent heresies of the modern age. In that they are both mediaeval and modern they form a fitting conclusion to [a] study of popular piety and heresy in the Middle Ages.[1]

In the period of the great schism and in the experiment in the conciliar government of the western church there was much potentially heretical sentiment in most of the countries of the Latin rite. The materialist speculations of the Averroists and nominalists in France, the Netherlands and the Rhineland, the continuing revolutionary eschatology of the later Joachimites, the Fraticelli and the Flagellants in central and southern Europe, the dispersed but numerous remnants of Manichaeism and Bogomilism, of Picards, Waldensians, Humiliati in Germany, Bohemia, Austria and Italy, and the near-heresy of the German mystics, of Beghards, Beguines, Brethren of the Common Life and Brethren of the Free Spirit, all provided a multitude of possible centres of crystallisation of popular heretical opinions and practices.

There was nothing new in the extent and activity of doctrinal

[1] [This essay was originally published in English, but with an Italian title: 'Correnti religiose nazionali ed ereticali dalla fine del secolo XIV alla metà del XV.']

and ecclesiastical criticism or of spiritual discontent and readiness to experiment. What was new, and what gives to popular heresy in this period its historical significance, was that for the first time there existed in western Christendom economic and political forces which could, given the right conjunction of moments, be able to crystallise heresy into permanent heretical communities, strong enough to survive the assaults of the forces of religious unity and conformity.

The two centres where this identification of nationalism and heresy manifested itself first were England and Bohemia. In England the birth of the national schismatic state proved, in the latter part of the fourteenth century, to be abortive; in Bohemia the marriage of the nation and heresy was more successful, and there in the first half of the fifteenth century was born a society which survived and which managed to preserve both its national and ecclesiastical independence of church and empire long enough to see other and more lusty national churches securely established on the principles which the Hussite state had been the first to exemplify in practice.

Bohemia indeed affords us our best and most instructive opportunity of studying the relations between popular religion and heresy at the end of the Middle Ages, for the vigour and success of Hussite heresy made it a topic of great and wide interest. Its adherents and its opponents alike described and discussed it and there is a vast contemporary literature both of apology and criticism. Because the Hussites and their enemies realised that here was something either of great promise or of great danger it is in Bohemia that we get the best view of the religious life of a whole nation, even of its peasants and urban poor, and can observe most clearly how a popular heresy could influence its faith and conduct.

The heretical movement was much more a concern of the whole nation in Bohemia than in any similar movement anywhere else before the sixteenth century, more than had been Catharism in Languedoc, more popular by far than Wyclifitism was in England. Much as Wyclifitism and Hussitism had in common they differed greatly in the extent of their domestic success. Wyclif was influential because he had powerful supporters in people like John of Gaunt and the Queen mother, but that support was never widespread nor did it survive Wyclif's later theological temerities.

The university of Oxford was never united behind Wyclif, as the university of Prague was, after the departure of the German masters in 1409, behind Hus. The lay lords who toyed with Wyclif's political and ecclesiastical ideas were never more than a small faction, and when once his theological heresies had been announced and condemned, the court, the parliament, the Lancastrian faction and the university dropped him, and though he was himself allowed to die in peaceful rustication, his Lollard followers were persecuted out of existence by the government of Henry IV, so unsure of itself that it played a leading part in securing the ultimate condemnation of Wyclif at the council of Constance in 1415.

What we know of the temper of the peasants and townsfolk who took part in the English peasants' revolt of 1381 is enough to indicate that there was ground as fertile for the flourishing of the seeds of religious discontent as there was to be in Bohemia forty years later. But the English revolt was purely social and political. The monasteries of St Albans and Bury St Edmunds were attacked as rapacious landlords and as the opponents of civic liberties, not because they were the abode of idle, ignorant and sinful monks; Sudbury, the archbishop of Canterbury, was murdered by Wat Tyler's men not because he was a bad Christian (he was indeed no worse than many and better than some) but because as lord chancellor he appeared in the eyes of the people as the embodiment and chief executive of a legal and social system which they found obstructive and tyrannous. It was not about the archbishop of Canterbury but about the archbishop of Prague that a mob sang in the streets:

Bishop Zbyněk, a b c d,
Burnt the books but could not read
What was written in them.

When Bishop Zbyněk burnt the books
And canon Zdeněk lit the pyre
He brought great shame on all the Czechs;
Woe will it be to all bad parsons.

It is well known that the one preacher who took a leading

part in the English peasants' revolt, John Ball, preached a gospel of social equality rather than of religious reformation. Social revolt and Lollardy never coincided in England, for the Lollards began their itinerant labours after the peasants' revolt had been effectively and finally quelled, and therefore Lollardy never became a mass or national movement; the English church and the English government from 1384 were allied against Lollardy so effectively that it was confined to a tiny minority of the nation and the Lollards were either forced to recant or executed, while Lollardy, if it survived at all, could but languish underground. No people or nation in the fifteenth century was more orthodox than England.

For these reasons the study of Wyclif and the Lollards cannot throw much light on the relations of heresy and popular religion. What work has recently been done on the subject either, like that of Professor Edouard Perroy,[2] merely serves to make clear that Wyclifitism was not typical of English life and thought and that its importance, at least for English history, has been exaggerated, or it is devoted to the study of Wyclif as an individual thinker, isolated in his extreme anarchism and influential only in so far as his ideas were exported to luxuriate in the much more fertile soil of Bohemia. The editorial labours, actual and promised, of Professor Harrison Thomson and Miss Beryl Smalley will make it possible to study the development of Wyclif's realistic scholasticism, but neither Professor Thomson's edition of Wyclif's *Summa de ente*, nor the editions of his *De ideis* and *De trinitate* which Professor Thomson and I are respectively preparing,[3] nor the *Commentary on the Sentences* which Miss Smalley has recently discovered are likely to do more than illuminate the philosophical basis of his theological aberrations.

For all these reasons it is to Bohemia rather than England to which we must look for light on popular religious movements of heretical character in the closing decades of the Middle Ages. The Hussite wars were fought as vigorously and as ruthlessly

[2] E. Perroy, *L'Angleterre et le grand schisme d'occident* (Paris, 1933).

[3] Wyclif, *Summa de ente; libri primi tractatus primus et secundus*, ed. S. H. Thomson (Oxford, 1930). [These promised editions of Wyclif's unpublished writings have not been completed.]

with the pen as with the sword. From 1403, when the archiepiscopal chancery of St Vitus's Cathedral in Prague first launched an organised assault on the champions of Wyclif in the Charles University there was poured out a spate of controversial pamphlets, tractates, sermons and systematic treatises from both sides. We have therefore a mass of literature, much of it arid, much of it obscure and repetitive, but nevertheless unique in its massive concentration on a small number of theological, ecclesiastical and moral themes; and concealed in this mountain of published and unpublished material there are to be discovered occasional clues to the effect of Wyclifite and Hussite heresy on popular religious belief and practice. Much of this material has long been in print: the majority of Hus's Latin writings was published by Lutheran presses at Brunswick and Nürnberg in the sixteenth century.[4] The great compilations of ecclesiastical documents of the seventeenth and eighteenth centuries gave us much more, from both sides, in the collections of Goldast,[5] Orthuinus,[6] Raynaldus,[7] Lenfant,[8] Mansi[9] and von der Hardt.[10] The revived interest of Czechs in their own history in the age of national revival gave us a second vast instalment of texts. As fast as the Protestants and Czech nationalists such as Dobner,[11] Palacký,[12] Erben,[13] Goll,[14] Novotný and Kybal[15] edited the works of Hus, of his predecessors and followers, so on the other side the Catholic and Austrian scholars such as Höfler,[16]

[4] *Historia et monumenta* (1558).

[5] M. Goldast, *Monarchia S. Romani Imperii*, 2 vols. (Hanover and Frankfurt, 1611-14).

[6] Orthuinus Gratius, *Fasciculus rerum expetendarum et fugiendarum*, ed. E. Brown, 2 vols. (London, 1690).

[7] O. Raynaldus, *C. Baronii Annales ecclesiastici continuati*, ed. J. D. Mansi and D. Georgius (Lucca, 1738-59).

[8] J. Lenfant, *Histoire du concil de Constance*, new edition, 2 vols. (Amsterdam, 1721).

[9] Mansi, *Sacrorum conciliorum nova et amplissima collectio.*

[10] Hardt, *Magnum oecumenicum Constantiense concilium.*

[11] G. Dobner, *Wenceslai Hagek a Liboczan Annales Bohemorum*, i-vi (Prague, 1761-82).

[12] F. Palacký, *Geschichte von Böhmen*, ii and iii (Prague, 1839, 1845).

[13] *M. Jana Hus sebrané spisy české*, ed. K. J. Erben.

[14] J. Goll, *Quellen und Untersuchungen zur Geschichte der Böhmischen Brüder.*

[15] V. Novotný and V. Kybal, *M. Jan Hus, jeho život a učení*; Novotný, *M. Jana Husi korespondence a dokumenty.*

[16] C. Höfler, *Geschichtschreiber der hussitischen Bewegung in Böhmen.*

Loserth,[17] Flajšhans[18] and Sedlák[19] supplemented their work, not only by their publication of writings of the opponents of the Hussites, but also by the edition of Hussite texts which the Czech patriots had either missed or ignored. This work was not only continued by the scholars of the first Czechoslovak republic, notably Bartoš,[20] Krofta,[21] Pekař,[22] Urbánek[23] and Odložilík,[24] but it is happily continuing today. It is true that the polarity of interest in the Hussite movement has changed since 1948, but fortunately for Hussite scholarship, the present day Marxist historians in Czechoslovakia and Russia profess a great interest in the movement, which they see not as a mighty moral and religious revolt but as the 'superstructure' to fundamental social and economic stress and crisis, as a significant chapter in the history of class war. While the two dominant Marxist mediaevalists in Prague, Josef Macek[25] and František Graus,[26] are rewriting the history of Hussitism in this sense a number of scholars who survived the purge of 1948 is encouraged to continue to publish texts especially in as far as they throw light on the social and economic aspects of the movement or illustrate its popular character. Fortunately for scholarship the references to social conditions in the writings of the Hussite propagandists and apologists are so occasional that it is necessary to publish the masses of purely theological and homiletic material in which they are embedded. For example, it is fashionable to regard Jan of Želiv [Jan Želivský], *ci-devant* monk and radical agitator, as the best exponent of the revolutionary and popular character of the Hussite movement in its early stages. We have therefore been given an admirably edited text of his sermons,[27] which in fact throws more light on popular homiletics than on the class

[17] J. Loserth, *Huss und Wiclif*, 2nd ed. (1925).

[18] Hus, *Opera omnia*, ed. V. Flajšhans *et al.*

[19] J. Sedlák, *M. Jan Hus.*

[20] The invaluable contributions of F. M. Bartoš to Hussite studies are too numerous to be listed here. Special reference may be made to his *Literární činnost M. J. Husi.*

[21] K. Krofta, 'Jan Hus', *Cambridge Medieval History*, viii.

[22] J. Pekař, *Žižka a jeho doba.*

[23] R. Urbánek, *České dějiny*, Part iii.

[24] O. Odložilík, see above, page 49 note 7.

[25] J. Macek, *Husitské revoluční hnutí*; *Husité na Baltu a ve Velkopolsku*; *Tábor v husitském revolučním hnutí.*

[26] F. Graus, *Chudina městská v době předhusitské*; *Český obchod se suknem ve XIV. a počátkem XV. století*; *Dějiny venkovského lidu v době předhusitské.*

[27] J. Želivský, *Dochováná kazání z roku 1419*, ed. A. Molnár.

war. Similarly there has recently been published by the evangelical theological faculty in Prague the last considerable work of Jan Hus, the sermons in the vernacular which he composed during his exile from Prague in 1413[28]; Bohumil Ryba admirably edited *Magistri Johannis Hus quodlibet*.[29] Very useful for the study of the popular aspect of Hussitism is the publication of the texts of the earliest Hussite religious verse and hymns.[30] It should also be mentioned that Ferdinand Hrejsa has been allowed to complete his vast *History of Christianity in Czechoslovakia* since the February events of 1948.[31] It is interesting that these recent contributions to Hussite historiography are predominantly the work of Protestant theologians and historians; Catholic Czechoslovak scholars are not in a position to continue their part in the work to which before the last war they made valuable contributions.

From this mass of Hussite and anti-Hussite literature which has been poured out in an almost perpetual stream ever since the invention of the printing press, what can we discover about the state of popular religion and the effect on it of heresy at the end of the Middle Ages in central Europe?

First it must be emphasised that the people of Bohemia were not irreligious or wanting in piety in the latter half of the fourteenth century. In this regard we tend to be deceived by the fact that most of the tracts written and sermons preached are of necessity critical of contemporary habits. Those who feel that all is reasonably well with the church and religion are not so eager to rush to pen and paper as are the more mordant and restless spirits who, angered by some particular or local abuse, are blind to the virtues of their society. Even Dante found it easier to describe hell than heaven, and Chaucer knew his public well enough to include only one saint amongst his Canterbury pilgrims. Robert Brinton, bishop of Rochester, whose sermons from the years 1372 to 1384 have just been published,[32] and who was an outspoken opponent of Wyclif, is

[28] Hus, *Postille, vylozenie svatých čtení nědelních*, ed. J. B. Jeschke (Prague, 1952).

[29] *Magistri Johannis Hus quodlibet*, ed. B. Ryba (Prague, 1948).

[30] J. Daňhelka (ed.), *Husitské písně* (Prague, 1948).

[31] F. Hrejsa, *Dějiny křesťanství v Československu.*

[32] *The Sermons of Robert Brinton, Bishop of Rochester (1373-89)*, ed. M. A. Devlin (London, 1954).

very critical of churchmen and the state of religion in his day. But a careful reading even of the critical literature makes it quite clear that, in Bohemia at least, there was a widespread piety among all classes of society, at the king's court, in the cathedral chapter and the university, as well as amongst the middle classes of town and country, as well as in the homes of the peasants. Jan Hus, who was of the poorest peasant stock, records how out of his dire poverty as an undergraduate in Prague he contributed to an indulgence. Matěj of Janov, the most forthright of the critics of religious life in Bohemia during the years 1370 to 1390, throws some interesting light on the upbringing of a son of a country gentleman, especially of the place occupied by the bible in his education. 'The bible', he says,

> from my youth have I greatly loved and called my very friend and bride . . . soon was my spirit fixed in lasting love of the bible. And indeed I confess that, from my youth up into old age and decline, whether on the road or at home, when busy or when idle, still this love has not left me.[33]

Matěj was in this respect, of course, one of a privileged minority for not only were the majority of his fellow countrymen illiterate, but also the text of the bible in Czech in the middle of the fourteenth century was fragmentary and copies of it were rare.

A fuller picture of a pious home, that of a country gentleman of southern Bohemia, is given us by Tomáš of Štítný. He was an educated layman who wrote in the vernacular a series of treatises on religion and conduct, primarily for the benefit of his children, household and neighbours. All that he wrote was of great importance because it spread a knowledge of the principles of the Christian faith amongst large numbers of his fellow countrymen by providing handbooks for family religion, in which were excellent translations of the Lord's prayer, the creeds, the ten commandments and of long passages of the scriptures and the fathers (he translated much of St Augustine into Czech). Incidentally he tells us something of religious life in his parents'

[33] *Regulae*, i, 12. [Translated from the Latin by Peter Brock.] 'A iuventute mea adamavi, et vocavi ipsam amicam et sponsam meam . . . mox aglutinata anima mea biblie in amore perpetuo; ubi fateor, quod a iuventute mea non recessit a me usque ad senectam et senium neque in via neque in domo, neque dum occupabar, nec cum ociabar.'

and his own household. In his treatise 'On general Christian matters',[34] he says: 'From my youth I was able to hear about Christian matters from my father and my mother, whereby I gained some knowledge of the scriptures.' A rare glimpse of a family council is afforded us by Štítný in his chapter on 'the widowed state'[35]. 'I always remember how sometimes when I thought of marrying I paid no attention to what I had heard from childhood from my grandmother, who was a very good woman of great and virtue; she used to say: "O good Lord! how is it that widows have a greater reward than married folk? How much better and more comfortable an estate we widows have than we had in marriage!" ' Addressing his motherless children Štítný says:

Never forget your mother, for she brought you up in zealous love, with greater care than many mothers show; pray diligently that God may deign to be merciful to her and give her her reward. For though by God's will she has departed this life, let not her memory and her love fade from your hearts. And as you love her so, remember that you can never fully repay your father and mother.[36]

Of the Christian housewife he says:

Every housewife should occupy herself with her hands so that the devil never finds them idle; she should do so too that she may have wherewith to give alms and may be able thereby to do God's service; but she should not give large alms without her husband's knowledge, but only so much as she knows he is willing she should give. When I say that the housewife should not be idle, I do not mean that she is to work on holy days; in pious thoughts and words, in godly instruction of her household and neighbours, therein she shall have occupation on holy days . . . And she who would be a good housewife should so conduct herself as to avoid evil words, to be in mutual love with her husband, to be a good example to her children and her neighbours.[37]

A final glimpse of this pious household is afforded us in Štítný's chapter 'Of other temptations of the devil':

God-fearing people, knowing that the devil is diligent to tempt people when they are at meat, before they sit down to table first

[34] Tomáš of Štítný, *O obecných věcech křesťanských.*
[35] Ibid., 83. [36] Ibid., 43. [37] Ibid., 106.

commend themselves to God, always asking for his help in everything. And also religious people read to each other at mealtimes, lest they engage in idle conversation, listening to what is read. So should every Christian man do when he sits at table . . . For thus they can have something useful to their salvation to talk about at meat, so that the devil cannot move them to evil speech; and thus when they take bodily nourishment they may also nourish their souls with good and profitable conversation.[38]

From many hints provided by our documents we get a similar picture of a society where religious exercise was common and piety widespread. Jan Milíč, for most of his adult life an official in the royal chancery, knew the bible almost by heart. Archbishop Zbyněk of Prague was so greatly concerned about the time and money spent on long pilgrimages that he sent a commission of enquiry to report on the validity of claims made for the holy blood at Wilsnack in Brandenburg. Among the objects most frequently pawned by unemployed labourers in Prague were crucifixes—evidence of their existence even if not of the esteem in which they were held. In the sixth and seventh decades of the fourteenth century such vast crowds flooded to hear the Austrian friar, Konrad Waldhauser, preaching in German in Prague that the Týn church was not big enough to hold them. The same was true when Jan Milíč began to preach in the vernacular. Milíč's hostel for reclaimed prostitutes had a success far greater than that which had attended the Empress Theodora's similar enterprise in Constantinople; Milíč's protégées became and remained devoted attendants at frequent communion, unlike Theodora's who were driven by boredom and frustration to throw themselves into the Bosphorus. The speed and extent of the moral reformation effected later by Hus and his friends witnesses to the existence of popular opinion and practice which was by no means unprepared or unsympathetic.

This is not to say that all was well with the spiritual health of the people. There were abuses. Many of the prelates and the religious were idle, ignorant, worldly or vicious. Much religion was superficial; many continued to seek salvation by external acts which to them had little spiritual significance. Not only the mordant Matěj of Janov, but also the humane and charit-

[38] Ibid., 201.

able Tomáš of Štítný make it clear that superstition was rife. Štítný returns again and again to the vanity and wickedness of witchcraft, spells and potions. The cult of the saints and their relics was often crude and materialistic. Štítný threatens with the pains of hell those who 'collect bones beneath the gallows or cut bits off the flesh of those who have been hanged; those who baptise frogs, mandragoras or bones, or who consecrate mistletoe'.[39] In his exposition of the decalogue he says: 'But many honour the saints only for temporal gain, in truly heathen fashion; for example, St Stephen so that they may have success with horses, or St Fortunatus and his companions so that they may become rich, or St John the Divine, whom they call Burjan, that it may not hail . . . Surely St Stephen has something better to do than to concern himself with horses! Were there no horses before St Stephen? Who looked after them then?'[40]

Such then was the milieu into which Hussitism came in the early decades of the fifteenth century. The relation between the religion of the people and the heretics was one of mutual influence. Hus, his fellow martyr Jerome of Prague, Jakoubek of Stříbro the founder of Utraquism, Nicholas (Mikuláš) of Pelhřím the popularly elected 'bishop' of the Taborites, the military leaders Jan Žižka and Prokop the Bald, the architects of the Hussite church and state Jan Rokycana and George of Poděbrady, even Petr Chelčický and the other begetters of the Unitas Fratrum, were all creatures of the social and spiritual environment of the society in which they grew up. The essential features of Hussite heresy: its essentially moral character, its biblicism, its passionate interest in the eucharist, its eschatological and chiliastic elements, even its Erastian tendencies, were all determined by the condition and temper of the country in which they worked. What is of interest here is the way in which the ideas as formulated by the Hussite writers and preachers interacted with the religious temper of the people and in which popular religion developed from the interplay of idea and practice.

The supreme historical interest of Hussite heresy is that it was the first body of heretical thought to become identified with a

[39] Ibid., 8. [40] Ibid., 109.

successful experiment in national independence. From the very first it was associated with opposition to German dominance in the Bohemian church and the university of Prague, as Jerome of Prague made clear in his defence before the council of Constance in May 1416. It may be argued that it was largely because the German masters who dominated the Charles University up to 1409 were disciples of Parisian nominalism that the Czech masters unanimously embraced the opposing realism of Wyclif, the idealistic element in which was in any case congenial to the unscientific temper of people to whom the sophistication of Ockham could mean little. The political character of the religious movement was emphasised by the course of events. The letter of protest against the condemnation and burning of Hus issued by an assembly of all the important officers of state and the assembled nobility in the autumn of 1415 is chiefly remarkable for its insistence that the council of Constance by its deeds had insulted the kingdom of Bohemia and margravate of Moravia. What the Czech magnates were protesting against was the supra-national authority claimed by the council much more than its claim to a theological supremacy. An accident made the identification of heresy and the claim to political independence real and enduring.

In 1419 King Václav IV of Bohemia died without a direct heir to his territories of Bohemia, Moravia, Silesia and Lusatia. His next of kin was his brother Sigismund, king of Hungary and king of the Romans: in the former capacity he was suspect to the Czechs as one who might exploit the wealth of Bohemia to serve the interests of Hungary; as king of the Romans and emperor elect, he was the patron of the council, which the Czechs regarded as the murderer of their best-beloved son and the slanderer of their nation, and also the embodiment of the principle of the supranational authority of the empire. When therefore in 1420 Sigismund came to Prague with a largely Magyar army determined to seize the lands of the crown of St Wenceslas by force and hereditary right, the Czech people opposed and expelled him. The Hussite wars which thus began were an inextricable confusion of religious and nationalist elements; German patricians were expelled from Prague; German and Czech miners mutually massacred each other in the silver mines; the doctrine of elective monarchy became indissolubly connected with the claim to religious independence; during the periods of kinglessness, from 1419 to 1436 and from 1439 to 1453, the country was in fact jointly ruled by estates of lords and burgesses and the consistory of Hussite clergy and university masters. In such circumstances it is not surprising that Hussitism became in practice Erastian: the estates elected Rokycana and two other priests to the episcopal office, and many believed that they should ordain and confirm without waiting for consecration and confirmation, which church and pope consistently denied them. The estates, predominantly lay as they were, became the ultimate authority which gave legislative force to the theological decisions of ecclesiastical assemblies, which were deemed to be valid for Catholic as well as for Utraquist Czechs. Among the more radical Hussites the laicisation of the church and the doctrine of the priesthood of every Christian man proceeded to extreme lengths: in the chiliastic assemblies of 1419 and 1420 the yeomen and peasants of south-western Bohemia and the Adamites of the south established religious democratic republics which anticipated those of the Anabaptists a century later. In the radical communities of Tábor, Žatec, 'Horeb' and Slaný the laity exercised an almost presbyterian authority; the Taborite bishop, Mikuláš of Pelhřimov (the 'Biskupec' of the Council of Basel) and the Taborite clergy were popularly elected with little regard to the sacrament of orders; Žižka, the layman, exercised a spiritual authority as great as the military authority of Prokop, the priest. The Erastian character of Hussitism was enshrined in that one of the four articles of Prague which demanded the punishment of public sin; henceforward sin was regarded as crime, without distinction.

Closely associated with this was the Hussite attitude to ecclesiastical property and the religious houses. The ground had already been prepared by the infiltration and the fermentation of sentiments hostile to the material wealth of the church. Joachimite vaticinations, the arguments of spiritual Franciscans and Fraticelli, Waldensian and Picard refugees had all been at work for a century; the vague sentiment had been made concrete by Matěj of Janov in his trenchant and popular

Regulae veteris et novi testamenti; Czech scholars had made contact in Paris, perhaps even in Oxford, with 'Armachanus', Richard fitzRalph, archbishop of Armagh, and author of the famous *De pauperie Salvatoris*[41]; in about 1403 Wyclif's *Dialogus* and *Trialogus*[42] were brought to Prague and afforded to eager Czechs a powerful armoury for their war against the wealthy prelates and the religious orders. It is therefore not surprising that when the dam burst in 1419 the first manifestation of popular religious excitement was the assault on the monasteries, nunneries and friaries of Prague and its environs. The religious were expelled or murdered, the treasuries of their houses were seized and most of the buildings destroyed by fire. In the first destructive assault monasticism in nearly all Bohemia and much of Moravia was wiped out. The landed property of the orders was seized, some of it by neighbouring landlords, Catholic and Hussite alike, or by the towns, some of it even by Sigismund. It is interesting to find the king of the Romans giving monastic property to George of Poděbrady, the future Hussite successor to the Bohemian crown. The estates of the secular clergy in part suffered the same fate. Among the reasons why no archbishop of Prague was consecrated between 1431 and 1561 was that there were no archiepiscopal or capitular estates left to provide him with an income suitable to his status. The puritanical, iconoclastic, xenophobic temper which produced the catastrophic assault on the monasteries in the earliest years of Hussitism did not result from any hostility to the ascetic and contemplative life as such. During the subsequent years of Hussite history there were indications of a revival of the regular life. When Sigismund was at length restored to the Bohemian throne in 1436 the first sign of the revival of Catholicism was that some of the monks began to return to their ruined houses, especially to those on the estates of Catholic lords like Oldřich of Rožmberk, even though their estates were not restored to them. There was a Hussite monasticism too: a regular community was established in the monastery 'na Slovanech' of St Em-

[41] Richard fitzRalph, 'De pauperie Salvatoris', books i-iv, in Wycliff, *Tractatus de dominio divino*, ed. R. L. Poole (London, 1890).

[42] Wyclif, *Dialogus sive speculum ecclesiae militantis*, ed. A. W. Pollard (London, 1886); *Trialogus*, ed. G. V. Lechler (Oxford, 1869).

maus in Prague; communities of religious women, like those associated with the Hussite chapel of 'Bethlehem' in Prague, appeared as a natural expression of a popular piety that was often deepest felt by women; the groups of 'hearers' who gathered round religious leaders like Rokycana or Petr Chelčický had something of a regular character which they bequeathed to the earliest communities of the Unity of Brethren.

One of the more interesting aspects of the impact of Hussite heretical theory on the popular religious movement is that of the concept of the church in theory and in practice. The most serious of the charges which had led to the condemnation of Hus was that he had maintained and propagated the condemned Wyclifite heresy that the church is the totality of the predestined, a doctrine which followed logically on fitzRalph's and Wyclif's doctrine of dominion founded on grace, but one which was so anarchical in its implications that neither pope nor council could ever tolerate it. When the Czechs refused to accept the authority of the church, especially in the essential matter of communion in both kinds for the laity, they were driven in practice to seek a new definition of authority and the church, and it was naturally the doctrine which Hus had taken from Wyclif which appealed to them. Hussites who lived for a generation in a state of common and continuous excommunication comforted themselves with the belief that as long as they were in a state of grace no decree of council or pope could deprive them of membership of the church, to which they were elect by the eternal decree of the divine will. They never regarded themselves as heretics or schismatics, whether they were of the conservative party of Jan of Příbram who sought comprehension within the Roman church on the basis of toleration of their peculiar practice of Utraquism, or whether like the Taborites they continued to believe that by force of prayer and military might the rest of the church could be brought to accept the truth as it had been revealed to the warriors of God.

Every religious movement which rejects the authority of the church in any point is compelled, in practice at least, to decide what is for it the authority which it is prepared to obey even against the church. The Hussites had no doubts about what that authority should be—*verbum dei*: the word in the sense of the incarnate Son of God to whom Hus appealed in 1412 from his excommunication by pope and archbishop, and the word of God in the sense of the scriptures. As Matěj of Janov had written when the church was already divided and its authority ambiguous, the ultimate appeal must be not to the

> wisdom of this world or of the princes of this world, which perishes, but [to] the wisdom, which is from God, and the divinely inspired scripture, which is serviceable for teaching, for expounding, for reproving and for instructing in justice, so that the perfected man of God may be made ready for every good work.[43]

When the Hussites came into actual conflict with the authority of the church embodied in the fathers of the council of Basel they were driven to define this authority more precisely. The definition was made in the famous 'Judex Egrae', the formulation agreed on at Cheb (Eger) between the Hussite leaders and the representatives of the council, which was to be the criterion to decide the lawfulness of the claims made in the four articles of Prague: 'The praxis of Christ and his apostles, and of the Fathers who were in accord with that praxis'. The 'Cheb judge' remained the ultimate authority to which the Hussites appealed as long as Hussitism lasted. By implication it denied the continuing authority of the church; only the fathers who could be shown to have supported the Hussite conception of the apostolic church were in practice regarded as having been in accord with the *praxis Christi*. In other words, as with all Protestant heresy, the ultimate court of appeal was the conscience of the individual Christian who believed himself to know the truth. Herein lies the root cause of the fundamental and continuing disagreements of the Hussites amongst themselves.

But this attitude towards the problem of authority in faith and morals inevitably led to a cult of the scriptures which became one of the more outstanding characteristics of the religion of the people. Though there was no single translation of the bible from the Hebrew and Greek as a whole in Czech until

[43] *Regulae*, ii, 49. [Translated from the Latin by Peter Brock.] 'Sapienciam huius mundi vel principum huius mundi, que destruuntur, sed sapienciam, que ex deo est, et scripturam divinitus inspiratam, que est utilis ad docendum, ad arguendum, ad corripiendum, ad erudiendum in iusticia, ut perfectus homo dei ad omne opus bonum instructus.'

towards the end of the sixteenth century, many portions of it were current in the vernacular before 1450. But it was not that the masses read the bible; illiteracy was still general. But they heard the word quoted and expounded in innumerable sermons preached not only in pulpits, but in field, market place and camp, and above all in the homes of the gentry and master craftsmen, many of whom followed the example of Štítný and constituted themselves a lay pastorate constantly fostering by family prayer and exhortation the spiritual life of their children, neighbours, apprentices and servants. A glance at the sermons of one of the more popular preachers like Jan of Želiv will reveal that his homilies were little more than catenae of quotations from the bible, rarely interspersed by a sentence from Augustine or Gregory or a comment of his own. It can then be said that three of the most remarkable characteristics of popular Hussitism were the cult of the bible, the popularity of the pulpit and the practice of family worship—the last encouraged because of the difficulties in securing the education and ordination of Hussite clergy. There was no chancellor of the Charles University after the death of Archbishop Konrád in 1431 and, probably for that reason, no examinations in the faculty of arts until after the middle of the century; even the one surviving Czech bishop, the bishop of Olomouc, refused to ordain Hussites, who in their desperation went to Italy or even Constantinople to seek a sacrament which few of them were bold enough to consider unnecessary.

The cult of the bible and the pulpit would not by itself distinguish the popular Hussite movement from other Protestant sects or even from the Roman church. What gave it its special character and even its name was the peculiarity of its cult of the sacrament of the altar. An especial devotion to the eucharist had distinguished the Bohemian reform movement from the start. Jan Milíč had been an advocate of frequent communion of the laity, and had introduced it in his hospital of 'Jerusalem'. Matěj of Janov had made the frequent and corporal communion of the laity the thirteenth and last of his 'rules' for the revival of true religion, and the five large tomes of his *Regulae* are mainly concerned with arguing the case for frequent communion and with the exaltation of the eucharist as the best and most effective element in popular religion. Though Hus himself seems not to have placed the same emphasis on the eucharist as his predecessors or successors, he did during his last days give his blessing to the practice of giving the chalice to the laity which Jakoubek of Stříbro had already introduced in Prague. From that time Utraquistic theory and practice rapidly developed until it became the most characteristic and general feature of the Hussite movement. The demand for the chalice for the laity was the first of the four articles of Prague formulated in 1420, and when finally the council of Basel and Sigismund entered into the Compactata in 1436, the other three articles, demanding the freedom of preaching, the punishment of public sins and the restoration of the church to apostolic poverty were defined so as to be meaningless; the one concession made by the council to the Hussites was the right of those who had enjoyed the chalice to continue to do so. It was this practice alone which united the many sects into which Hussitism came to be divided, and communion in both kinds for the laity was Hussitism's most obvious and concrete bequest to later Protestantism.

Hussite theologians and the people alike tended to take the principle and practice of communion *sub utraque specie* for the laity to its logical extreme. Rokycana, as protagonist of the chalice at Basel, developed the argument from the *praxis Christi* that the cup was not only of inestimable spiritual benefit to the faithful Christian, not only his right in virtue of the words *sumite omnes ex hoc*, but also was *de precepto* and therefore not only profitable, but also necessary, for salvation. From this it followed that it should not only be given to those who desired it, but to all; that it should not only be administered by Hussite clergy, but by every priest; that it should be administered not only to adults after confirmation but also to infants immediately after baptism. It was this practice of administering the communion to children which became not only the most cherished of Hussite rites, but the subject of particular objurgation by their opponents. Celebrations of the eucharist, not only in churches, but in open places, in fields and camps of the Hussite field armies, where eager crowds of men, women and children flocked to drink of the cup and to hear its saving virtues expounded, were the life and soul of the popular religion of the Hussites. In their own tongue they sang:

> Thou gavest us His body to eat,
> His holy blood to drink.
> What more could He have done for us?
>
> . . .
>
> Let us not deny it to little children
> Nor forbid them
> When they eat Jesus' body.
>
> Of such is the kingdom of heaven
> As Christ himself told us,
> And holy David says also:
>
> 'From the mouths of small children
> And of all innocent babes
> Has come forth God's praise
> That the Adversary may be cast down.'
>
> . . .
>
> Praise God, ye children,
> Ye tiny babes,
> For He will not drive you away,
> But feed you on His holy body.[44]

While all the Hussite leaders, from conservatives like Jan of Příbram and Prokop of Plzeň to the most radical like Mikuláš of Pelhřimov and Klecanda were united by their Utraquism there was the greatest diversity amongst them both in eucharistic theory and practice. Like Hus himself the more conservative never wavered in their faithfulness to the Catholic doctrine of transubstantiation, earnestly rejecting Wyclif's heresy of the remanence of the substance of the bread and wine in the consecrated elements. But among the central mass of the Hussites, of whom Žižka, Prokop the Bald, Rokycana, Peter Payne (Petr Engliš) and Oldřich of Znojmo were typical, there developed a certain carelessness as to the metaphysics of transubstantiation, though they all insisted on a 'real' or 'sacramental' presence of Christ in the elements. In the early years

[44] Daňhelka, *Husitské písně*, pp. 108-9.

the Taborites burnt at the stake certain 'Picards' who denied all such miraculous and sacrificial qualities in the Eucharist, though later amongst the radicals there was an increasing approximation to the concept of a mere memorial celebration; to a minority the eucharist became the 'Lord's Supper', though their devotion to it was none the less for that. A similar diversity appeared in practice. The Taborite party early rejected all that they regarded as *adinventiones hominum* in all religious services: the wearing of vestments at the mass, kneeling before the host, candles, holy water, consecrated oil, the chrism of baptism, the kiss of peace. They simplified the mass to the utmost limits; their celebrations often took place in fields or unconsecrated buildings, and there was probably truth in the accusations of their enemies that the celebrants were sometimes laymen or even women. In the innumerable conferences in which the diverse sects of the Hussites strove to achieve uniformity nothing was discussed at greater length or with more acrimony than the nature of the real presence in the eucharist and the rites and vestments with which it should be celebrated. The political and military defeat of the Taborites by the conservative 'Praguers' in 1434 ensured the triumph of the ritualistic and 'Catholic' wing of the Hussites, though something of Taborite practice and theology was kept alive in the Church of the Unity of Brethren.

None of the other sacraments occupied the same place in the Hussite reform movement as did the eucharist. The sacraments of baptism and extreme unction were the subject of dispute between the two wings of the movement, but here the disagreement turned largely on ritual matters. Here too the conservative party triumphed and the use of the chrism and the sign of the cross and of god-parents in baptism were ultimately accepted. The serious difficulty in securing the ordination of Hussites to the diaconate and priesthood led some to speculate about apostolic succession and the necessity for episcopal ordination. The same difficulty led to the sending of a Hussite mission to Constantinople to explore the possibility of some kind of union between the two utraquist communions, Czech and Greek. The leader of the mission was a man whose name appears in the sources as 'Constantinus Angelicus'. It is believed by Professors Bartoš and Paulová[45] that he was in fact Peter 'Anglicus', the refugee Oxford scholar who took the name 'Constantine' after his reception into the Greek church. However that may be, the anxiety of the Emperor Constantine not to compromise the union of Florence still further by countenancing Czech heretics and the capture of Constantinople by the Turks during the process of the negotiations rendered them abortive. None but the Taborites cut the Gordian knot by resorting to ordination by the laying on of unconsecrated hands; the majority of the Hussites continued to seek the ordination of their clergy where they could, though they refused to accept the solution of their problem by acknowledging a canonically consecrated nominee of the church; they remained faithful to their choice, Rokycana, affirming that if the church would not confirm him they would have no other.

From what has been said it is clear that the formal heresies of the Hussites were not numerous. The Taborite minority indeed erred gravely in the matter of the sacrament of the altar, the apostolic succession of the priesthood, the existence of purgatory and sacerdotal privilege. But the main body of the Hussite church remained faithful to Catholic doctrine in all these things and in much besides. It is interesting to notice how many Hussite hymns were written in honour of the Virgin; Hussite iconoclasm seems not to have diminished the honour in which she was held. But the one heresy (for as such it had been condemned by the council in 1415 and as such the popes continued long to regard it), of which they were guilty, was fundamental, for their adherence to Utraquism was the denial of the sovereignty of the church to determine practice, even if the practice prescribed by the church were not that of the apostolic church and were a recent innovation. The other matters in which the Hussites differed from the church: their emphasis on election and predestination, their insistence on the right and duty of all priests and deacons to preach, their doubts about the lawfulness of ecclesiastical property, their willingness to allow the civil power much ecclesiastical and moral authority, none of these things did the Hussites ever erect into a dogma. As their agreement to the emasculation of all the articles of Prague

[45] M. Paulová, 'Styky českých husitů s cařihradskou církví', *ČČM* (1918-19).

except that on Utraquism in the Compactata of 1436 showed, they were unwilling to make any of their beliefs and practices except Utraquism a *casus schismatis*.

The abiding interest of Hussitism in the history of popular religion lies not so much in the formal heresies of the Hussites as in the experiments in popular piety to which those heresies opened the way. The lively expectation of the second advent which impelled thousands of farmers and peasants to sell all they had and to gather together in the 'cities of refuge' in south-western Bohemia, the primitive communism of those who flocked into the armed camp on the hill they called Tábor and of the Adamites whose moral and social experiment was so speedily and bloodily destroyed by Žižka's soldiers, the Cromwellian order Žižka established in his standing army, and the Calvinistic regime of moral enforcement established in Prague during the short period of Jan of Želiv's domination there, are all of great interest to students of the relationship between religion and society. Indeed the present official school of history in Czechoslovakia sees in these experiments the prime interest of what they call the 'revolutionary Hussite movement' which they regard as being fundamentally due to the 'crisis of feudalism'.[46] It is of course true that the enthusiastic peasants of the chiliastic period of the movement anticipated that the imminent reign of Christ on earth would bring amongst its benefits the abolition of rents and services and of those manorial obligations which were just beginning to become a serious burden on the peasants of central and eastern Europe. It is true too, as Dr Graus has shown,[47] that there was a growing class of ill-paid and often unemployed poor urban labourers, especially in Prague, who refused to distinguish their own and Christ's enemies during the period of popular revolt. They killed and expelled not only monks but also German-speaking patricians like those whom they defenestrated from the town hall of the New Town of Prague in 1419.

But the phase of the 'revolution of the poor' was but short-lived. A bourgeois counter-revolution in Prague deposed and beheaded Jan of Želiv; the 'old Town' of the merchants and

[46] See the writings of Macek and Graus referred to in notes 25 and 26, above.
[47] See Graus, *Chudina městská v době předhusitské*.

patricians triumphed over the Czech proletariat of the 'New Town'. From 1422 the city and university of Prague were identified with the more conservative wing of Hussitism. Even the fortified camp of the saints on Tábor rapidly became a town of craftsmen and traders, all its earlier communistic ideas and practices forgotten. The victory of the Praguers over the Taborites at the battle of Lipany in 1434 virtually put an end to the social and revolutionary phase of Hussitism. Indeed the Marxist historians regard 1434 as the end of the 'revolutionary Hussite movement'.[48] But such narrowing down of the movement to a mere twenty years is only possible to those who regard it as essentially a social and nationalist phenomenon. If it is regarded as fundamentally a religious and moral revolution, then it must be seen as enduring as long as the Hussite church retained its independence, that is until 1620, or even as a movement that still survives if, as can reasonably be done, the assumption is made that the Unity of Brethren, which has outlived persecution, proscription and exile, is an integral part of Hussitism.

The religious characteristics of Hussitism survived Lipany. Popular piety, as modified by the impact of Wyclifite and Hussite heresy, maintained the beliefs and practices which were developed during the first phase. Perhaps most important in the history of popular piety was the increasing and fruitful use of the vernacular as the instrument and vehicle of popular religion. Jan Milíč, in the earliest years of the Bohemian reform movement, had preached in Czech, and soon after his death a group of Prague citizens had founded the chapel of 'Bethlehem' for the express purpose of providing regular preaching in the vernacular. Hus, as one of the appointed Bethlehem preachers, had learnt to express himself most eloquently in his own language: it was in Bethlehem that he and Jerome of Prague introduced the notorious 'new hymns' and versifications of parts of the liturgy in Czech. Towards the end of his life, especially after he had been driven from Prague into the countryside, Hus wrote and preached more and more in the language of the simple people. Tomáš of Štítný had provided in his translations and original works a corpus of excellent

[48] See Macek, *Husitské revoluční hnutí.*

religious and moral literature, and at the same time had devised and developed the vocabulary for the discussion of theology and philosophy; in his hands Czech prose first became mature. Hus (if it was in fact he) made a most valuable technical contribution by providing a simplified and uniform spelling of the Czech language in his *Orthographia Bohemica*.[49] The younger generation of Hussite scholars and preachers increasingly used the vernacular for all communications except those addressed to other scholars or to alien bodies such as the council of Basel.

It was only on this basis of the ready use of the vernacular that Hussitism could become and remain popular. That it did so is proved by the abundance of hymns and religious verse which was produced and which was the most lively element in both public and private worship. Many of these religious poems are controversial or even satirical; many of them are versifications of biblical passages or of the liturgy; but most of them are purely pietistic, even 'salvationist' in tone. There are hymns to the Virgin cheek by jowl with those in honour of 'holy Master Jerome' and of 'Mistr Jan Hus':

> Thou, beloved Hus,
> whom Czechs must have in love,
> since they know not where else to find
> so virtuous a preacher.

But above all the Czechs honoured in song *Jhesus crucifixus* and his saving love on Calvary and in the sacrament of the altar. This outburst of religious verse was accompanied by a corresponding development of music, the history of which was written a generation ago by the man who is today [1955] communist minister of education in the Czechoslovak people's republic, Zdeněk Nejedlý.[50] It has been convincingly argued that not the least of the legacies bequeathed by Hussitism to German Protestantism was the *Choral*, the supreme achievement of the blending of religious verse and folk music.

[49] Hus (?), *Orthographia Bohemica* (A. V. Šembera, *M. Jana Husi Ortografie česká*). The problem of its authorship is discussed by J. Zubatý in *Naše Řeč*, iii, 99.

[50] Z. Nejedlý, *Počátky husitského zpěvu*; *Dějiny husitského zpěvu za válek husitských*. Cf. Macek, 'Zdeněk Nejedlý a husitství', *ČsČH*, I, i (1953).

Finally it should be remarked that the moral element which had characterised the reform movement in Bohemia from the first maintained its force, despite recourse to the murder of monks, cruel punishment of foreign and domestic prisoners of war, and the looting of the property of monasteries and chapters at home and that of helpless Germans and Hungarians who were the victims of the great Hussite raids. Even during the worst of these excesses the war on prostitution, drunkenness, gambling, magic, immodest dress and profanity was maintained by the Hussite leaders and congregations. These puritanical attitudes were taken over and further developed by the Unity of Brethren in a way that anticipated the pacifist and quietist views and practices of the Quakers. The violence and the ruthlessness of the Hussites during the early years of civil and foreign war may be explained, though not excused, by the very strength of their conviction that the Czechs were the nation elected by God to purge Christendom of His enemies. It was in that faith that they sang their most famous song:

> Ye who are warriors of God,
> and of His law,
> pray God for help
> and put your hope in Him
> that in the end ye shall for ever triumph with Him.

VIII

English and Czech Influences on the Hussite Movement

THIS paper[1] is a preliminary study of the relative indebtedness of the Hussite movement in Bohemia to the English reformers of the latter half of the fourteenth century on the one hand, and the native Czech predecessors of Hus on the other; but it will also raise questions of historical method and of the influence of nationalism on modern historiography.

I do not pretend that it is the result of the investigation of any large mass of unpublished material, but I would excuse my temerity in flouting that most sacred article of modern historical faith that only in the holy rite of reading manuscripts which no one has ever bothered to look at for four hundred years, lies the scholar's salvation, by this plea: the revival of Czech nationalism in the past hundred years, based as it was by Palacký on the study of the history of the Czech people and given an immense impetus by the emancipation of the Czechs in 1918, has resulted in the editing of an ever-increasing volume of texts and a welling flood of monographs, biographies, and full-grown histories, which most English historians have had little time to digest. It is therefore in a humble attempt to interpret a small fraction of this output, that fraction which perhaps most nearly touches our own history, that I have written this paper, and I do so with a hearty readiness to acknowledge my constant indebtedness to such patient, scholarly, and able editors and authors as Palacký himself, Emler, Tomek, Flajšhans, Sedlák, Klicman, J. B. Novák and Kamil Krofta, Vlastimil Kybal, Václav Novotný, Otakar Odložilík, F. M. Bartoš, and many others, whose devoted labours have

[1] [Originally read before the Royal Historical Society (London) in March 1938. Four lines relating to this occasion have been omitted in the first paragraph.]

made a study of the reform movement in Bohemia possible.

In the enquiry which I propose to institute are involved questions of fundamental importance to an estimate of that movement. There is the question of the extent of the original contribution which Hus made to that movement: the question whether Hus was a theologian of genius, a philosopher of originality, a reformer of insight and imagination, the original of a movement which was to establish the first national Protestant church in Europe, the father of the Reformation and regenerator of his country, or whether he was merely the pale reflector of the bright light of the morning star of the Reformation, a slavish uncomprehending copyist and pirate, a mere receptacle and vehicle, a mere lifeless duct, devoid of originality and genius, undiscriminating, uncreative, a ventriloquist's doll, reproducing and distorting the utterances of his foreign master. And as a corollary to this question is involved that of the origin of the Hussite movement as a whole, the question whether it is to be regarded as the direct issue of a movement which had long been gestating in the fecund womb of Bohemia, begotten of native genius, guarded by its princes, nursed by its scholars and saints, or whether it is merely the monstrous offspring of alien intercourse, an unwished-for misconception of an unnatural union between Wyclifite heresy and Bohemian anti-Germanism, born only to torment Holy Mother church and Holy Roman empire. The dispute goes even further than this, for in the hands of historians whose national prejudices are stronger than their respect for the truth the question of the originality or indebtedness of Hus has been made a cardinal point on which turns the whole conflict between Slav and Teuton, the one party seeing in Hus one of the most illustrious exemplars of the fecundity, genius, and virtue of the Slav race, the other seeing in his servile dependence on Wyclif (a good enough Teuton, *faute de mieux*), but another example of the essentially imitative, uncreative, ineffective race of Slavs.

When what is a purely historical problem has been made the crux of such mighty issues, it is both inviting and bold for a compatriot of Wyclif to enter the lists. But I hope the sequel will prove that I do so not with any national bias, but merely to attempt to find an historian's answer to an historical question.

The usual opinions of Englishmen about central Europe in general, Bohemia in particular, and Hus most particularly, are largely derived from the work of German scholars. Indeed the sources for a study of this subject have been so little accessible until recently, and the language of the Czechs is regarded as being so laughably and insanely foreign, that it is inevitable that it should have been so. It follows from this that we have tended to adopt the view that Hus and Hussitism were almost entirely the products of the introduction of Wyclifite opinions and manuscripts into Bohemia during the thirty years which separate the death of Wyclif from the death of Hus. And, indeed, whatever the motives and deficiencies of the German students of Wyclif and Hus, it must be admitted that such men as Höfler, Buddensieg, Böhringer, Helfert, and above all Johann Loserth, have done a valuable service in demonstrating the undeniably close interdependence of the English and Czech reform movements, a connexion which Czech and Russian scholars are ever ready to admit. Indeed the internationalism that survived into the fourteenth century made such a connexion inevitable.

Let us first endeavour to estimate as concisely and precisely as possible the extent of this connexion and of Wyclif's influence on Hus.

Before that nationalisation of the universities which was one of the greatest disasters of the general nationalist tendencies of the fifteenth and sixteenth centuries, there was considerable and very fruitful intercourse between the few European universities which then existed. The extent to which students from all over Europe went to study at Paris is well known; many of the most eminent English scholars worked in French or Italian schools. And thus it was natural that the university which Charles IV founded at Prague in 1348 should draw many of its teachers from abroad, should constitute itself into 'nations', and send many of its alumni for long periods to foreign schools of learning. Such eminent Prague doctors as Heinrich Totting of Oyta, Nicholas Magni of Jauer, Heinrich of Bitterfeld, and Albert Engelschalk, were Germans; Matthias of Cracow, the distinguished author of the *De squaloribus curiae romanae*, was a Pole, as also was Jan Isner; Konrad Waldhauser himself was an Austrian. And it was to be expected that scholars of Prague should go abroad to continue their studies: Konrad von Soltau went from Prague to Heidelberg and later to Cracow; Engelschalk spent some time at Vienna; Matthias at Cracow and Heidelberg. But most important are the prolonged visits of Czech scholars to Paris. Jan of Jenštejn, archbishop of Prague, studied for many years at Paris, and his friend and client Matěj of Janov, the author of the *Regulae veteris et novi testamenti*, the monumental textbook of the Czech reform movement, spent five years at the university of Paris and earned the distinguished title of *Magister Parisiensis*.

Until the incidence of Wyclifite opinions on the university of Paris has been more closely examined than appears to have been done at present, it is difficult to say how much Wyclifite influence may have come to Prague through Paris. What, however, is more directly to the point is to discover which Czech scholars went to Oxford, and as far as I know there are only two of whom we have any evidence that they were there before the death of Wyclif; but one of these two is most important for our problem, for he was Master Vojtěch Raňkův of Ježov (M. Adalbertus Ranconis de Ericinio).[2]

Vojtěch took his master's degree in Paris in 1349, and became rector of that university in 1355, and it is probable that he also studied in Oxford.[3] However that may be, when he came to Prague he brought with him fitzRalph's *Defensorium curatorum adversus fratres mendicantes*.[4] We have further evidence of the connexion between fitzRalph and Vojtěch in two facts: in the copy of fitzRalph's *De paupertate Salvatoris seu de mendicitate fratrum*, now in Vienna, there is an inscription saying that the book belonged to Vojtěch Raňkův[5]; also it is said that Vojtěch's opponents at Paris had attacked him as being 'Armachanus',

[2] The other of the two, Johannes Moravetz, the Dominican who read for his master's degree in Oxford some time before 1348, later became papal penitentiary in Bohemia. (*Monumenta vaticana res gestas bohemicas illustrantia* (Prague, 1903 ff.), i, no. 1014; also ibid., nos. 813, 1015, 1016, 1315.)

[3] See J. Loserth in *Archiv für Österreichische Geschichte*, lvii, 11, 71, and his *Huss und Wiclif* (1925 ed.), p. 62.

[4] C. Höfler, *Anna von Luxemburg* (*Denkschriften der kaiserlichen Akademie der Wissenschaften, Philosoph.-hist. Klasse XX*) (Vienna, 1871), p. 112.

[5] Vienna, Bibliotheca Palatina, Codex 1430. See Loserth, *Huss und Wiclif* (1925), p. 45, n. 1.

that is, a disciple of fitzRalph, bishop of Armagh.[6] But what makes him even more important as a link between England and Bohemia is the well-known provision in his will, made in 1388, whereby he bequeathed scholarships 'for those wishing to study at Paris or Oxford in England either in theology or arts, but not in medicine or any other faculty'.[7] The importance of Vojtěch in the history of the Czech reform movement makes these connexions between him and fitzRalph and Oxford a most important link in the argument. This conceited and intolerant controversialist, who refused to wear the tonsure or say his hours, who never took priest's orders, was the first Bohemian polymath. He was an early nationalist, who helped Tomáš of Štítný to compile his Czech dictionary, and protected tenant farmers in their rights. He was the friend of the early reformers Waldhauser, Milíč and Matěj of Janov, and he was the protector of Milíč's house of refuge for fallen women, characteristically called by the biblical name of 'Jerusalem'. He was a great preacher, to whom was entrusted the honour of pronouncing the funeral oration over Charles IV in 1378. He attacked simony and clerics who affected lay dress. But that he was no mere slavish echo of French and English reformers is shown by a letter he wrote to Martin of Nova advocating frequent communion of the laity.

It is possible that this early interest of the Bohemians in Oxford and England may have been in some measure due to the considerably increased part that England played in European politics in the reign of Edward III, who was in frequent diplomatic relations with imperial and German princes. Similarly it was natural that English interest in Bohemia should be aroused when the Bohemian kings, already dukes of Luxemburg, became Holy Roman emperors. At first the Luxemburgers had been the allies of France and the enemies of England, but with the rapid recovery of France under Charles V the necessity of restoring the balance of power drove England to seek the alliance of the greatest of German princes. The

[6] V. Novotný, *Náboženské hnutí české ve 14. a 15. stol.*, 142.

[7] See Loserth in *Mittheilungen des Vereines für Geschichte der Deutschen in Böhmen*, xvii, 210, for the text of the will. See also R. F. Young, 'Bohemian Scholars and Students at the English Universities from 1347 to 1750', *EHR*, xxxviii (1923), 72.

common hostility of England and the Luxemburg emperor to France was increased when the outbreak of the great schism in 1378 threatened to add ecclesiastical hegemony to the already excessive power of France by the establishment of the papacy permanently at Avignon. Thus political and ecclesiastical considerations drove England and the emperor to make common cause, and resulted in a series of diplomatic exchanges which culminated in the marriage of Richard II to Anne of Bohemia, daughter of Charles IV, and sister of Hus's sovereign and protector, Václav (Wenzel), emperor and king of Bohemia.

This connexion between the two countries is made much of by German historians, who see in it another channel by which Wyclifite opinions could influence Bohemia. As early as 1871 Constantin Höfler, in a lengthy article on Anne of Bohemia, sought with great learning and some success to demonstrate the importance of these negotiations in the religious development of Bohemia, and thereby to counter Palacký's exaltation of Hus as a national hero.[8] The evidence Höfler adduced has recently been supplemented by the documents published by Professor Perroy, so that it is now more or less possible to form some estimate of the probability of an exchange of theological opinions due to this alliance.[9]

As Höfler and those who follow him have laid such considerable emphasis on the importance of these negotiations for the spread of Wyclifite ideas in Bohemia, it is perhaps as well to see what the evidence amounts to. The initiative seems to have been taken in 1379 by Urban VI, who was anxious to unite the emperor and the king of England in opposition to Clement VII. Urban used as his negotiator the notorious Cardinal Pileus de Prata.[10] A correspondence between Václav and Richard was begun in the same year whereby Václav sought to establish a union of Urbanist states against the followers of Clement.[11]

[8] Höfler, *Anna von Luxemburg*, pp. 89-240.

[9] E. Perroy, *L'Angleterre et le grand schisme d'occident* (Paris, 1933); *Diplomatic Correspondence of Richard II*, ed. E. Perroy, Camden Society, Third Series, no. 48 (London, 1933).

[10] See K. Guggenberger, *Die Legation des Kardinals Pileus in Deutschland, 1378-1382* (Munich, 1907). Cf. T. Rymer, *Foedera*, vii, 256-7, 292a, 293b, and T. Walsingham, *Historia Anglicana* (Rolls Series), ed. H. T. Riley, 2 vols. (London, 1862-4), i, 452.

[11] O. Raynaldus, *C. Baronii Annales ecclesiastici continuati*, ed. J. D. Mansi and D. Georgius (Lucca, 1738-59), vii, s.a. 1379, no. xl and xli, pp. 390-2.

Before the end of the year Michael de la Pole and Simon Burley, who had gone to Italy to arrange the marriage of Richard to Catherine Visconti, were deflected from their course, probably at the instigation of Pileus, and visited Germany[12]; there it seems they were met by William Sturry who had been sent from England with new instructions.[13] On their way back from Germany de la Pole and Burley were captured by brigands and the herald Richard Hereford had to be sent to negotiate their release.[14] It may well be that the outcome of their adventurous journey can be seen in the breaking off of the peace negotiations with Charles V in May 1380,[15] and of the marriage negotiations between Anne of Bohemia and the dauphin. In June the interchange of ambassadors between England and Bohemia began. Simon Burley, Robert Braybrooke (the future bishop of London and enemy of the Lollards), and Bernard van Zetles,[16] went to visit Václav and were absent for six months.[17] At the same time 'Borzireoge de Siryne', a Bohemian knight, came to England and was given presents by the king, and received at the Savoy by John of Gaunt.[18] At the end of the year 1380 Burley, Braybrooke, and Bernard were sent again on a more solemn embassy to make a formal proposal for Anne's hand, and this time they were accompanied by John Gilbert, bishop of Hereford, Thomas Holland, earl of Kent, Hugh Segrave, seneschal of the household, Richard Abberbury, knight of the chamber, and Master Walter Skirlaw.[19] It is worth noting that Skirlaw had been educated at University College, Oxford, and was later to be bishop successively of Coventry, Bath, and Durham.

Anne accepted Richard's offer in January 1381, and she and her mother the Empress-Dowager Elizabeth appointed three

[12] Perroy, *L'Angleterre et le grand schisme*, p. 141.

[13] Ibid., p. 141.

[14] For Hereford's mission and his companions see Public Record Office (London), French Rolls, 20 Jan. 1380 (Richard II, membrane 15).

[15] Perroy, pp. 141-3.

[16] Or 'Sedlec'; he is described in Rymer, vii, 257, as 'Miles curiae nostrae'; there is probably no connexion between this mysterious Bernard and the abbey of Sedlec in Bohemia. Cf. French Rolls, year 3, Ric. II, m. 2.

[17] *Dipl. Corr. Richard II*, no. 18. Cf. Rymer, vii, 304-5.

[18] Perroy, p. 145.

[19] Ibid., p. 147. Cf. Rymer, iv, 104-5.

Bohemian nobles, Přemysl, duke of Teschen [Těšín], Conrad Kreyger, seneschal of the household to Václav, and Petr of Vartenberk his chamberlain, as proctors to go to the king of England to make final arrangements for the marriage.[20] Václav appointed the same three nobles as his commissioners for the concluding of the alliance with England for the termination of the schism.[21] In March the English ambassadors brought the three imperial proctors to England, and Cardinal Pileus came with them with legatine powers.[22] The treaty was signed at Westminster on 2 May 1381. It cost Richard £3,000 down in the shape of the first instalment of a subsidy to Václav. Two months after their arrival the Bohemians departed, accompanied by Burley, Braybrooke, Zetles, Dagworth, Skirlaw, and three members of Richard's household, John Reynald, William Hert, and Giles de la Chambre, who were commissioned to secure Václav's ratification of the treaty.[23] After Václav had ratified it Sir John Cheyne and Lancaster Herald were sent to his court to escort Anne to England.[24] She arrived in December 1381, and was married to Richard and crowned in January 1382.

In all these comings and goings there seems but little chance that 'Borzireoge' or the three noble proctors of the emperor could have absorbed much in the shape of Wyclifite errors, unless it were through the tainted channel of John of Gaunt, who, however, seems to have been chiefly employed in ministering to their creature comforts. Nor does it seem that the duke of Teschen and his fellows would have been much interested in the niceties of Wyclif's neorealism or predestinarianism, for from what we know of them they appear to have been all essentially diplomats and courtiers, and I have not been able to find that they were in any way associated with religious movements in Bohemia. It is perhaps slightly more possible that the dozen English commissioners who visited Václav may have sown the seeds of heresy there (though in some cases it is doubtful whether

[20] Letters of procuration in the Public Record Office, E.30, 292 and 293. Cf. Rymer, iv, 105-6.

[21] P.R.O., Dipl. Docs., E. 294. Cf. Rymer, iv, 106.

[22] Perroy, p. 149. For Pileus' unpopular conduct in England, cf. *Chronicon Adae de Usk, 1377-1421*, ed. E. M. Thompson (London, 1904), pp. 2, 3; Walsingham, i, 452; Rymer, iv, 109; *Calendar of Patent Rolls*, i, 615.

[23] Perroy, p. 153. Rymer, iv, 117-21.

[24] Perroy, p. 154.

they had actually to go to Prague to find him—he did occasionally visit his German dominions). But it seems little probable that courtiers and civil servants such as Burley, de la Pole, Thomas Holland, Segrave, Abberbury, Dagworth, Reynald, Hert and their fellows had much interest in theological propaganda. It might seem more likely that the ecclesiastics Skirlaw and Braybrooke would have done so, but the responsibility for inspiring the Bohemians to religious revolt of a man like Braybrooke cannot have been very great, for he himself was an arch-enemy of Wyclif. He gave much offence to the Londoners in 1382 by refusing to annul the statute against preachers of heresy; he it was who secured the co-operation of the king against the Lollards who nailed their pamphlets on the door of Saint Paul's; it was he too who secured the recantation of Thomas Latimer and Richard Story.[25] As for Skirlaw, he was a typical civil servant, a chancery clerk and keeper of the privy seal, whose numerous preferments seem to have been the reward, not of theological, but of bureaucratic abilities.

The political connexion between England and Bohemia did not end with the marriage of Richard and Anne, but appears to have continued spasmodically until Anne's death in 1394. There was a further exchange of diplomats between 1382 and 1384 to secure the renewal of the treaty. More important for the question we are examining is the retinue which Anne brought with her, chiefly chaplains and ladies. But we know little except their names: Henry of Reybutz, priest and 'commensalis' of the queen; one 'Jacobus', her confessor; Johannes Lantgraf and Henricus Potus, knights, and that elusive Agnes whom Robert de Vere married.[26] That they were interested in Wyclif and Lollardy is never suggested by our documents. Complaints against their rapacity were made in parliament, and many of them were sent home in 1382.[27] Indeed their chief function seems to have been that of horse dealers to Richard, who sent certain of them, Rockaus, Walter and John Swartes, and Sithellius back to Bohemia to replenish his stables.[28]

[25] J. H. Round on Braybrooke in the *Dictionary of National Biography*, ii, 1151 ff.

[26] *Dipl. Corr. Richard II*, nos. 34, 57. P.R.O., Issue Roll 490, m. 14.

[27] *Rotuli parliamentorum* (6 vols.), iii, 248. Rymer, iv, 139.

[28] *Dipl. Corr. Richard II*, no. 37. P.R.O., Treasury rolls, 72, m. 21. For the un-

It has been necessary to say so much about so little because Höfler's study on 'Anna of Luxemburg' became the basis of the German and English approach to the subject of the relations between Wyclif and Husitism. But an examination of the material seems to indicate that the coincidence of these political negotiations has been made the ground for an exaggeration of their importance for the religious developments in Bohemia.

Höfler was an Austrian, and was perhaps thereby to some extent prejudiced against the Bohemians and inclined to ask, 'Can any good thing come out of Nazareth?' And that has been the more or less unconscious attitude of those German historians who followed him, and most notably of Johann Loserth.

Loserth is universally recognised as one of the most learned students of the Wyclifite movement, and he brought to the study of the relations of Hus and Wyclif a knowledge of Wyclif's theological writings almost unequalled, and his contribution to the study of the problem is the more important because it is based on so much incontrovertible fact. It has been his task to illustrate the coming of Wyclif's writings to Bohemia and the frequency of Hus's quotations from those works.

It is clear that certain of Wyclif's philosophical works reached Bohemia in the last decade of the fourteenth century, for Hus himself copied and glossed the *De materia et forma*, the *De ideis*, and the *De universalibus* in 1398.[29] But it was not until the turn of the century that Wyclif's theological writings began to filter through to Bohemia, and even then it was some years before they were known there in detail or completeness. It seems that Jerome of Prague, who spent two years in Oxford (probably the years 1399 to 1401) brought back with him to Prague the *Trialogus*, the *De eucharistia*, the *Dialogus* and the *De simonia*.[30] Certainly Tomáš of Štítný knew something about Wyclif's eucharistic views very early in the century.[31] But the main material for the study of Wyclif in Bohemia did not arrive until after the visit of Mikuláš Faulfiš and Jiří of Kněhnice to

popularity of Anne's retinue, see Walsingham, ii, p. 46; *Eulogium historiarum*, ed. F. S. Haydon, Rolls Series, 3 vols. (London, 1858-63), iii, p. 355; *Chronicon Henrici Knighton*, ed. J. R. Lumby, 2 vols. (London, 1889-95), ii, 150-1; *Mon. Westm.*, 12.

[29] Novotný, *M. Jan Hus*, ii, 59 ff.; F. M. Bartoš, *Husitství a cizina*, p. 29.

[30] Novotný, ii, 104 ff. Bartoš, op. cit., p. 32.

[31] Loserth, *Huss und Wiclif* (1925), p. 64.

England in the years 1406 and 1407.[32] They evidently not only visited Oxford and conversed with some of Wyclif's followers there, but also it seems possible that they visited Oldcastle; the copy of the *De dominio divino* they made has a note: 'Braybrug psano', and Braybrook was the manor of the Lollard Thomas Latimer and its incumbent the Lollard Robert Hoke.[33] Faulfiš and Jiří of Kněhnice not only brought back a fragment of Wyclif's tomb, but also copies they had made of the *De veritate sacre scripture*, *De dominio divino* and, most important of all, the *De ecclesia*. Either at the same time or within a few years copies of the other books of the *Summa Theologica*: the *De civili dominio*, *De officio regis*, *De potestate pape*, *De apostasia*, *De blasphemia*, *De mandatis divinis*, and the *De statu innocentie*, were also available to Hus and his fellows.[34]

From this time until the disappearance of open Lollardy in England relations between the two movements continued spasmodically. In 1410 Richard Wyche, a pupil of Wyclif who was later burnt at the stake, wrote to Hus a letter of sympathy and encouragement to the Bohemian reformers, to which Hus replied.[35] In the same year Oldcastle wrote in a similar vein to Vok of Valdštejn and Zdislav of Zvířetice.[36] Some three years later Oldcastle wrote to King Václav himself, commending to him the cause of the reformation in general and Hus in particular.[37] Of course, the Lollard who had the greatest influence in Bohemia next to Wyclif himself was Peter Payne, but as his activities in building up the Taborite party fall after the death of Hus, they lie outside the scope of this paper.

From all this it is quite clear that at least after 1407 there was abundant manuscript material in Prague for the influence of Wyclif to have its full force. No one would deny the cogency of this part of Loserth's argument; nor is it possible to controvert the next point which he makes, namely, that Hus used the writings of Wyclif extensively, quoting from them sometimes

[32] Bartoš, op. cit., pp. 40-1, 47n., 62, 110. Loserth, op. cit., pp. 65, 194-203.

[33] Loserth, op. cit., pp. 196-9. Cf. Wyclif, *Tractatus de dominio divino*, ed. R. L. Poole (London, 1890), p. 249.

[34] Loserth, op. cit., pp. 200-1.

[35] Text in Novotný, *M. Jana Husi korespondence a dokumenty*, no. 22, pp. 75-9.

[36] Text in Loserth, op. cit., pp. 210-12.

[37] Ibid., pp. 212-13.

whole paragraphs word for word, frequently introducing sentences, phrases and locutions that undoubtedly come from Wyclif, usually without acknowledgment. Indeed it would be strange if he had not done so. It must be remembered that the church in England and the church in Bohemia were parts of the same ecumenical institution, which was undergoing the same modifications and pursuing the same policy by the same means in all parts of Roman Christendom. It therefore follows that there were the same causes and symptoms of corruption and secularisation in the two countries. Thus Wyclif's spirited and cogent criticisms of the pride and ambitions of the papacy, of the officiousness and rapacity of the curia, of the worldliness and carelessness of the bishops, the devotion of the secular clergy to worldly things, their sloth, ignorance and intemperance, were eagerly read by Hus and his companions, and freely used by them in their writings. Wyclif's attack on the inordinate preoccupations of the regulars, the idleness, luxury and spiritual pride of the monks, the ambitious and greedy business of the friars, his animadversions against the abuse of relics, images, indulgences, papal reservations, ecclesiastical tenths and jubilees, were as easily applicable to the Bohemian as to the English church, and were therefore freely and gladly used by the Bohemian reformers. The great schism was as baneful in its consequences and as distressing in the doubts and misgivings it inspired to Bohemia as to England.

But there are also peculiar reasons why the subjects of Václav should have found in the works of English reformers much that was apt to their own state. The Roman church had never sat easily in either country, each of which was on the periphery of the Roman obedience, neither of which had ever been Romanised as had been Gaul, Italy, Spain and parts of Germany; to both of them the Latin of the liturgy was completely alien in a sense which was not true of the Romance-speaking countries. The underlying longing for their forbidden Slavonic liturgy on the part of the Czechs corresponded to the traditional anti-papalism which in England dated at least from the first half of the thirteenth century. Both countries had achieved a position of national unity and self-consciousness at a time when France, Germany, Italy and Spain were still at best loose federations of feudatories, and both resented therefore with the full force of adolescent national feeling their ecclesiastical, judicial and financial dependence on an alien and often hostile papacy. As Englishmen resented the supranational control expressed in the papal claims to feudal supremacy and the Johannine tribute, in papal reservations and provisions and the burdensome and galling exercise of appellate jurisdiction by the curia, so too were the Bohemians exasperated by the deposition of Václav by Boniface IX in 1403, and the refusal of Alexander V to raise the ban in 1409, and to them too the whole issue of national independence was brought home by the onerous demands expressed in papal tenths, jubilees and indulgences. The pride and pockets of Englishmen were affected by the frequent collation of absentee foreigners to benefices; in Bohemia many of the highest and wealthiest incumbencies were occupied by Germans.

While these considerations made a sympathy between Czech and English reformers natural, there were others which more particularly attracted Hus to Wyclif. Hus's first acquaintance with Wyclif was through his philosophical works, and the majesty, completeness and uncompromising courage of Wyclif's philosophical system profoundly influenced a mind already well disposed to accept its main tenets and applaud its methods. The neo-realism of Wyclif, his unhesitating and devastating attack on the 'epigonic nominalism'[38] of Ockham, Scotus and d'Ailly, his stout refusal to believe that faith and reason were irreconcilable, his original and effective use of the historical method to show the novelty and frailty of many of the claims of the contemporary church, found in the mind of Hus, already disposed towards such ways of thought by his environment and reading, an approving response. Hus, who as preacher at 'Bethlehem' had come to value highly the place of the pulpit in the Christian ministry, applauded the founder of the poor preachers of England; Wyclif's attack on the wealth of the church found amongst the disciples of Milíč a ready echo; finally Wyclif's remedy for all the ills of the church, a return to the primitive simplicity of organisation and doctrine of the apostolic church, found an eager response in Hus, the heir of

[38] I owe the phrase and much besides to Bartoš, *Husitství a cizina*, p. 27.

Milíč and Matěj of Janov who had been expounding the efficacy of the same panacea for thirty years.

Thus, when Loserth sets out parallel passages from the writings of Hus and Wyclif side by side and demonstrates thereby the frequency with which they correspond, not only in ideas but in their actual wording, it should be no cause for surprise to realise how much Hus owed to Wyclif. We must remember, too, what Bartoš has pointed out,[39] that there is nothing unusual in the way Hus quotes Wyclif at such length and without acknowledgment. Every mediaeval work of scholarship uses its authorities in just the same way. An author was not respected for his originality, but for his knowledge of the dicta of those who had treated the same subject before him, and the bulk of the theological writings of the late Middle Ages consists largely in the collection and rearrangement of lengthy extracts from the writings of others. It must be remembered too that these authorities were so universally known that the necessity of referring continually to one's sources by name was never realised; certainly Hus never dreamed that he would be deceiving his readers into thinking that what he pirated from Wyclif was his own. Nowadays we read so much and so fast and books are so numerous that we do not remember one hundredth part of what we read, and when we quote we do so deliberately and consciously, giving references because we know that the odds are that the reader will not have read the book from which we quote, or that if he has he will not recognise the passage. But before the invention of the printing press the scope and manner of men's reading were different. There were fewer books to be read, and there was time to get to know those one did read thoroughly. As often as not reading meant learning by heart. It seems to me apparent that many of the Wyclifite passages in Hus's writings are to be explained not as copying from a treatise of Wyclif but as the more or less conscious reproduction of passages which have been memorised. The fact that Hus more often gets near to Wyclif's words than quotes him verbatim,[40]

[39] Bartoš, op. cit., pp. 20-3.

[40] Cf. J. Wyclif, *Tractatus de mandatis divinis*, ed J. Loserth and F. D. Matthew (London, 1922), p. 153, with Hus, 'Expositio Decalogi', *Opera omnia*, ed. V. Flajšhans, i, 7; Wyclif, op. cit., p. 159, with Hus, op. cit., i, 7, Wyclif, *Tractatus de civili dominio*, 4 vols. (London, 1885-1904), i, 368, with Hus, 'De ecclesia',

and that he sometimes corrects Wyclif's own misquotations seems to bear this out.[41]

Hus omits whole paragraphs in the midst of passages he is quoting from Wyclif, adds remarks of his own, rearranges the material, sometimes gives references for the passages he is quoting which Wyclif himself omitted to give; sometimes he gives a sense to the quotations which was not in the original. If we can believe that Hus knew a great part of Wyclif's works by heart and quoted them from memory we can explain simply a crux which Loserth has to deal with by a very doubtful assumption. When Hus was in prison in Constance awaiting his trial he is said to have composed there his *De sufficientia legis Christi*. Loserth says that this work is so full of Wyclifite views and teaching, contains so many themes from Wyclif's tractates which correspond so literally with Wyclif's own words, that the *De sufficientia* could not have been composed by Hus in his prison at Constance, where he had no books available, but must have been written much earlier, probably before he left Bohemia.[42] Is it necessary thus to fly in the face of the evidence? We know that when Milíč was imprisoned in the Ara Coeli in Rome in 1367 he compiled there his *Sermon on the Last Day*, a work composed entirely without the help of books, which is a network of quotations from the Bible and the Fathers.[43] There is every reason to believe that Hus's acquaintance with Wyclif was sufficient for him to be capable of a similar feat of memory.

Loserth then has apparently misunderstood the whole method of mediaeval scholarship and misinterpreted the nature of the dependence of Hus on Wyclif. He flatly denies any originality in Hus, and ascribes the whole Hussite movement to Wyclif's inspiration. Invaluable as is Loserth's contribution to our knowledge of the relations of the two men, there are, however, several considerations which force us to doubt the conclusions he has drawn from the verbal comparison of their works.

Historia et monumenta (1558), i, CCI; Wyclif, *Tractatus de simonia*, ed. H. Frankel and M. H. Dziewicki (London, 1898), p. 2, with Hus, *Historia et monumenta* (1558), i, CXCIIII.

[41] Cf. Wyclif, *Polemical Works*, ed. R. Buddensieg, 2 vols. (London, 1883), ii, 666, with Hus, *Historia et monumenta* (1558), i, 175b.

[42] Loserth, *Huss und Wiclif* (1925), p. 124.

[43] Novotný, *Náboženské hnutí české ve 14. a 15. stol.*, p. 71.

In the first place Loserth was a German inhabitant of Bohemia, and that fact has determined his whole approach to the question. A member of a national minority which before 1918 dominated the Czech majority and since that year was subject to it, it was perhaps inevitable that he should have adopted the attitude which is the psychological consequence of such a relationship. The martyred Hus is the national hero of the Czech people; the champion of national liberties who expelled the Germans from the university of Prague in 1409; the man who defied Sigismund and whose spirit inspired Žižka and Prokop to lead the people to repel the attacks of the German crusaders in the Hussite wars. Philosopher, theologian, saint, patriot and martyr, his name and work were flaunted throughout Czechoslovakia as the victor in the battle of Czech against German. If then it could be shown that as philosopher and theologian and nationalist he is but the pale reflection of an Englishman, without scholarship, art, or ideas of his own, if it could be shown that the man who was burnt at Constance was but Wyclif in effigy, the idol of the triumphant and exulting Slavs would be overthrown, and the Teutonic thesis that all that there has been of greatness in Bohemia is an importation from a Teutonic source would have been vindicated. I believe that Loserth has been subconsciously perverted by considerations such as these, and that here lies the root of the inadequacy and partiality of his treatment of the problem.

The first specific charge to be made against Loserth is that he confined his collation of the works of Wyclif and Hus entirely to Hus's Latin works, and never once cites examples of Hus's indebtedness from his works in the vernacular. Indeed Loserth gives but little indication that he was acquainted with Hus's Czech writings at all. Now this is very important, because Hus had begun to preach and write in Czech[44] before the manuscripts brought back by Faulfiš and Jiří of Kněhnice had made him conversant with the main body of Wyclif's theological works, and because it was natural that in his Latin writings, where his approach is more erudite and therefore more academic, his debt to the English schoolman should be greater than in his vernacular works, where the treatment is more popular.

[44] See Novotný, *M. Jan Hus*, i, 182 ff.

Thus it is not surprising that the evidence of Wyclif's influence is much less marked in his Czech works, because he is here dealing with matters that have a more particular reference to his own country and people, and his method is not so much that of the schoolman as that of the teacher and publicist. It is interesting to observe that Loserth, while quoting certain parallelisms with Wyclif's *De simonia* to be found in such Latin works of Hus as the *De sex erroribus*[45] makes no attempt to collate the *De simonia* with Hus's treatment of the same subject in Czech, the *O svatokupectví*. This work, it is generally agreed, is amongst the best that Hus ever did. It is true that here too we find reminiscences of the *De simonia* of Wyclif, but as Novotný says, some seven-eighths of the work is original. Much of it is topical, having reference to the triple schism and to the domestic circumstances of his day.[46] Loserth's ignoring of the vernacular writings of Hus is as dangerous to a just estimate of his work as would be an account of Wyclif which ignored his English works. Not only were the Czech works of Hus profoundly influential in shaping the course of the popular movement which appeared after his death, but it is natural that they should express ideas which he had absorbed in his native air and inherited from his native predecessors.

The strong anti-Czech prejudices of Loserth are also to be seen in his arbitrary treatment of the views expressed on Hus's work by modern historians of Slavonic birth. We must realise that the German campaign to belittle Hus has its counterpart in a rival campaign waged by the foes of Germanism to emphasise his greatness. It was unfortunate that the first edition of Loserth's *Huss und Wiclif* was published in 1884, just at the time panslavism was rising to its height and Katkov was initiating his great campaign in the Moscow press against Bismarck and Austria and all things German. The Russian Slavophils were eager to seize on any example of Slavonic achievement, and Hus therefore became an object of admiration and self-congratulation throughout the Slavonic world. Russian scholars saw in Hussitism something unique, which could have only

[45] Loserth, *Huss und Wiclif* (1925), p. 182.

[46] See Novotný, *M. Jan Hus*, ii, 238-42. The text of the 'O svatokupectví' is in Erben, i, 474 ff.

flourished on Slavonic soil. The exaltation of Hus by Palacký as a Czech national hero was taken up by such Russian scholars as Yelagin, Novikov, Hilferding, Lamansky and Palmov. Loserth's attempt therefore to belittle Hus's achievements aroused an outcry in Russia, and in the Kiev *Universitetskaya Izvestiya* of May 1884 there appeared an article by Florinsky, which ably pointed out some of the weaknesses of Loserth's thesis. He pointed out that Loserth had totally ignored the religious opposition in fourteenth-century Bohemia to the Latinism of the Roman church, expressed in a movement to re-establish the use of Slavonic ritual, corporal communion of the laity, and the establishment of a Slavonic monastery by Charles IV as early as 1347. Florinsky also drew attention to Loserth's failure to deal adequately with the position of Hus in relation to frequent communion of the laity and communion in both kinds by laymen. Since the denial of the chalice to the laity in 1350 there had been a growing demand in Bohemia for its restoration. Loserth ignored the fact that Matěj of Janov had made this the basis of his teaching, and that Hus had identified himself with this purely native movement, not only, as Loserth implies, in his last tractate written in prison at Constance, but also in his *De corpore Christi* (1401) and in the *De sanguine Christi sub specie vini a laicis sumendo*.[47] Finally, Florinsky notices that the greater part of the evidence of Hus's Wyclifitism Loserth takes from the opponents of the Hussites; and that he does not take into account the sermons, instructions and letters of Hus written in Czech, which were both popular and influential; and that he ignores the great and important differences between the teaching of Hus and that of Wyclif.

Thus was the stage for this international conflict between Slav and German set, and the reputation of Hus was the trophy which was to be torn down or defended at all costs. Until German historians of Bohemia can bring themselves to read texts and monographs written in Czech and Russian they must remain at a disadvantage in the controversy; the whole

[47] Florinsky refers to works by I. S. Palmov on the question of the chalice in the Hussite movement (Petersburg, 1881) and by V. I. Lamansky on important participants in Western Slavonic education in the fifteenth, sixteenth and seventeenth centuries (*Slavyanski Sbornik* (St Petersburg), i, 1875, pp. 546 ff.).

subsequent history of this problem consists in the elaboration of the points Florinsky made; the second edition of Loserth's *Huss und Wiclif*, in 1925, made no serious attempt to meet these criticisms and has merely served to delay the proper understanding of the facts in Germany and England, where his authority is still decisive.

Let us examine Loserth's thesis in the light of the researches of recent Czech scholars.

First, attention must be drawn to the doubtful validity and the limitations of Loserth's method of the collation of texts in parallel columns. Such textual comparisons are valid only as long as they are used to demonstrate a textual dependence; all they can be made to prove is that sometimes Hus quoted Wyclif with a greater or less degree of accuracy. But to attempt to demonstrate thereby, as Loserth does, a complete dependence of ideas is to make an assumption which the evidence by no means warrants. It is one of the vices of a certain type of modern historical scholarship to become so much engrossed with the mechanical process of the detection of detailed verbal similarities as to neglect the duty of endeavouring to estimate the achievement of a man or a movement as a whole. Loserth's method also well illustrates another vice of modern historiography, namely the readiness to be tempted to ascribe to interconnexions and direct influence movements in different countries which were the independent product of similar conditions and developments. The truth appears to be that the reform movement in Bohemia had already developed very considerably before a single one of Wyclif's manuscripts was known there and that those common features of the religious life of Christendom which we have already noticed had produced a reaction and a demand for reform in Bohemia similar in many respects to what was happening in contemporary England and quite independent of it. Thus when Wyclif's works were introduced into Bohemia the ground was already well prepared, men's minds had been educated by a distinguished line of autochthonous reformers to greet Wyclif, not so much as a leader and master, but rather as a fellow-worker in a neighbouring vineyard, overgrown with much the same weeds as those with which the Bohemians were only too well acquainted.

Of course the similarity between conditions in Bohemia and those in England was not complete. There were differences in national temperament, in the political and social background, in the mental inheritance and environment of the two nations, which established important differences between the ideals and methods of the two reform movements. A brief examination of this native background and an enumeration of the vital differences between the beliefs and methods of the Hussite movement and English Wyclifitism must therefore be undertaken.

The rapid publication of the writings of the pre-Hussite Bohemian reformers is daily making clearer how much Hus and Hussitism owed to Bohemians who worked and wrote and died years before a single manuscript of Wyclif reached Bohemia. The task of verbally collating the voluminous works of Hus with the even more voluminous works of his native predecessors has hardly yet begun, but even so a reading of such works as have become available makes it increasingly clear that not only were many of Hus's characteristic and most influential ideas developed from those who had prepared the way for him in Bohemia, but also that he had read and studied the works of such men, and in particular the greatest of them, Matěj of Janov.[48] Hus's acquaintance with the theological works of Wyclif came first when he was some thirty-five years old, after he had spent some twenty years at Prague, which had already for half a century been the centre of a native reform movement. The university itself was a symbol of that nationalism which was to take so powerful a hold on Hus and to which he was to contribute so much. The spirit of Charles IV, its founder, the father of his country, and the first to attempt to restore religion in Bohemia, still pervaded the city he had so much enriched and beautified. It was Charles who had, in 1363, invited to Prague Konrad Waldhauser, whose work was to open the floodgates to that stream of reform which was to flow with ever-increasing majesty and power until Hus came to sail on its flood into the open sea of a Bohemia nationally and ecclesiastically free.

In the work of these early Bohemian reformers we can see the germ of all those ideas which are most characteristic of Hus,

[48] Cf. Bartoš, *Husitství a cizina*, p. 24.

and of the movement to which he gave his name, far more clearly than in the work of Wyclif. Waldhauser, though himself no Bohemian by birth, was a pioneer. He attacked the formalism of contemporary religion and preached the necessity of the religion of the heart; he decried the value of monastic promises of salvation in return for testamentary bequests; Waldhauser revived popular preaching in Prague, and at his denunciations the rich cast off their gay clothes, usurers relented and gallants were converted. His fiery zeal was directed against the avarice of the friars, the sale of favoured burial-places and the folly of making pilgrimages to the two rival heads of Saint Barnabas.[49] His writings were as effective as his preaching—he composed the *Postilla studentium pragensium*, a sermon handbook for the training of preachers, and his cycle of sermons on the Passion laid emphasis on the necessity of subjective qualification for the priesthood.[50]

The work so well begun by Konrad was taken up by his disciple, the former chancery clerk, Jan Milíč of Kroměříž, a product of the humanism of the court, cultured, and of an elegant latinity. He was converted in 1362 to a life of self-abnegation and devotion to the cause of reform. He gave to the movement an ascetic and apocalyptic character, and both preached and practised that clerical poverty which was to become one of the main items in Hus's remedial programme. Milíč too carried on the tradition of preaching and prepared the pulpit from which Hus was to preach so powerfully. As Hus was later to brave his enemies at Constance, so too Milíč went into the lion's den, first at Rome and later at Avignon, where he died. He preached the coming of Antichrist, he instructed young preachers in his *Abortivus* and in his sermons on the grace of God; he translated part of Gregory's *Moralia* and wrote prayers

[49] Compare with this exposure of the false claims of relics by Waldhauser, Hus's mission to Wilsnack to examine the genuineness of the miracles reported to have been performed by the Sacred Blood exposed there. ('Mag. Joannis Hus de sanguine Christi', edited by V. Flajšhans in *Mag. Jo. Hus Opera omnia*, i, fasc, 3, 33).

[50] For Waldhauser see F. Loskot, *Konrad Waldhauser*; Novotný, *Náboženské hnutí české*, pp. 157 ff.; F. Menčík, 'Konrad Waldhauser', *Abhandlungen der königlich-böhmischen Gesellschaft der Wissenschaften*, vi, Folge xi; F. Palacký, *Die Vorläufer des Hussitenthums in Böhmen* (1869), p. 16; 'Apologia Konradi in Waldhausen', ed. Höfler, in *Fontes rerum austriacarum*, 2, vi, 17-39. For complete bibliography see Zíbrt, *Bibliografie české historie*, ii, 1117.

both in Czech and German. He too gave to the movement a social character which it never lost, by the establishment of a very successful refuge for prostitutes. With Milíč begins the first timid criticism of an over-weening papacy; with him begins the movement which pointed to the bible as the first and ultimate authority for faith and morals; he continally directs men to the example of Jesus; and finally by instituting the practice of daily communion for his refugees in 'Jerusalem' he started a movement which was ultimately to become the distinguishing feature of later Hussitism. Milíč's writings were widely and freely copied and quoted, and it is inconceivable that he could have been without influence on Hus and Hus's friends.[51]

Milíč had done much to give its idiosyncratic form to the Czech reform movement, but it was to acquire one characteristic in particular which is not to be found in his writings, namely, its nationalism. It is here that the part played in forming the body of Hussite beliefs by Tomáš of Štítný is more important. Tomáš was born in the Tábor district, was married and widowed, and remained throughout his life a country gentleman. As a layman, and one who apparently never graduated at the university, he occupies a unique place in the movement. It is first and foremost as an interpreter of reformist ideas in the Czech tongue that he takes his place as a link between the generation of Milíč and that of Hus. He translated some of Augustine's works into Czech, and compounded for himself a mysticism based on a study of Hugo and Richard of Saint Victor, Bernard, Bonaventura, Robert Holkot of Oxford, and Henry Suso. These translations were not literal, but rather adaptations. Tomáš must have contributed to the general building up of the movement by conversation (often more effective than writing), for he was the friend of Matthias of Cracow, of Jan of Jenštejn and Vojtěch Raňkův. But his most evident influence is the educational treatises in the vernacular which he began to write for his orphaned children and then gradually adapted to a wider public; the *Knihy naučení křesť*-

[51] For Milíč see: Zíbrt, *Bibliografie české historie*, ii, 1117-18; *Fontes rerum bohemicarum*, i, 401-30; Matěj of Janov, *Regulae*, iii, 358-67 (Narracio de Milicio); Palacký, *Vorläufer*, pp. 39-46, and *Geschichte Böhmens*, iii, 1; L. Klicman, 'Studie o Milíčovi', *Listy filologické*, xvii; Novotný, *Náboženské hnutí české*, pp. 65 ff. Milíč's sermons are edited by Menčík in *Věstník královské české společnosti nauk* (Prague, 1890).

anského (Books of Christian Education) and the lay sermons of the *Řeči nedělní a svateční* (Sermons for Sundays and Saints' Days). Tomáš was the eloquent enemy of superstition, magic, relics, vain repetitions, fastings, masses for the dead, pilgrimages and indulgences. Before his death he had heard of Wyclif's eucharistic heresy of Remanence, and it is significant for our purpose that he rejected it and insisted on the merits and benefits of frequent communion. Also he foreshadowed Hus's rejection of Wyclif's doctrine of the inefficacy of the sacraments performed by evil priests.[52]

The growing reform movement which had its saint in Milíč and its philosopher in Tomáš of Štítný, had its theologian in Matěj of Janov,[53] whose monumental work the *Regulae veteris et novi testamenti* deserves to be placed very high amongst the achievements of the pre-Lutheran reformers. It is certain now that Hus was acquainted with his works,[54] and no one can have read the *Regulae* without being convinced that Hus's characteristic ideas were greatly influenced by Matěj. It is a work of profound scholarship, consolidated on a thorough knowledge of the scriptures, the fathers, and the schoolmen. It is replete with the spirit of Milíč; it has his biblical language, his mystical anticipation of the imminent advent of Antichrist; it anticipates Hus in its desire to return to the primitive simplicity of the apostolic church, its constant appeal to the crucified Jesus, to the bible as the sole source of faith, to the 'liberty of the Holy Spirit'. His learned and weighty exposition of the evils of hypocrisy, *adinventiones hominum*, papal provisions, reservations of absolution, the superfluity, idleness, avarice, pride and jealousy of the regulars, are all part of the armoury which Hus was to assume. But perhaps his most important legacy to the Hussite movement was, first, his doctrine of the church as the 'invisible communion of the elect', and secondly, his insistence on the daily, corporal participation of the laity in the sacrament of the altar as the supreme vehicle of the reformation.

[52] For Tomáš of Štítný see J. Durdík, *Tomáš ze Štítného*; J. Wenzig, *Studien über den Ritter Thomas von Štítný*; Novotný, *Náboženské hnutí české*, pp. 179-214.

[53] V. Kybal, *M. Matěj z Janova*; Matěj of Janov, *Regulae*; Novotný, *Náboženské hnutí české*, pp. 145-75.

[54] Bartoš, *Husitství a cizina*, p. 24; Sedlák, i (1914), 363.

In parenthesis it may here be noted how easy it is to ascribe to Wyclif what is the work of the Bohemian reformers from the fact that in a marginal note on the first page of Codex C of Matěj's *Regulae* there is a note: 'Tractate of John Wyclif. Therefore read cautiously lest you fall into a deadly snare.'

Of course we do not know that Hus ever met Matěj, who died in 1394. The final link in the chain is supplied pre-eminently by a lesser man, who had, however, much in common with both of them, Štěpán of Kolín. He was provost, dean of arts and rector of the university of Prague while Hus was a youthful graduate there. Hus may well have heard the sermons which Štěpán preached as cursor in theology, have heard him insist on the need for an educated priesthood, heard him inveigh against pluralities, indulgences, clerical immorality, and the wealth and luxury of prelates. In 1396 Štěpán was appointed preacher at the reformers' headquarters, the chapel of 'Bethlehem' in Prague, where Hus was to succeed him. Here too Hus may very well have heard him argue that a man may, in case of necessity, confess to another than a priest and that prayers to the saints are unavailing. At all points Štěpán's views look both backwards to Matěj and forwards to Hus: his conviction that a pure and simple priesthood is the first essential of reform; his violent attack on the simony that was rotting the Bohemian church; his alarm at the evils inherent in indulgences and papal jubilees; most of all by his acceptance of the freedom of the will, his emphasis on the necessity of renunciation and clerical poverty, and his combination of strict orthodoxy in the matter of transubstantiation with a passionate devotion to the saving and reforming virtues of the eucharist, he completes the chain which binds Hus undeniably to the work of his native predecessors.[55]

Waldhauser, Milíč, Štítný, Matěj, Štěpán—these are but the best known of a whole army of Bohemians who made some contribution to the mass of ideas, sentiments, theories, proposals, habits of thought, to the whole ethos of the Bohemian reform movement, into the thick of which Hus was plunged as soon as he came to Prague; it was the very air he breathed, the

[55] For Štěpán of Kolín see O. Odložilík, *Štěpán z Kolína* (Prague, 1924); Bartoš, 'Husovo kněžství', *ČČM*, xcviii (1924), 65-72.

constant conversation of refectory, dormitory, and corridor, the substance of lecture and sermon, of the literature, ephemeral and enduring, which was his constant reading. The mind and the views of Hus were already shaped and moulded before ever Wyclif's theological works came to Bohemia. When Hus first met those works he welcomed them gladly as confirming, developing, and enriching much that he had already long been thinking. The depth and breadth of Wyclif's philosophy, the vigour and courage of his criticism, his acute historical method, his remorseless logic, the perspicacity of his understanding, did not create in Hus a passion for reform; they merely were complementary to what he already knew and thought; they supplied fuel to an already fiercely burning fire; they gave an added impetus to an already swiftly moving current. But always it was his native inheritance which supplied the substance of Hussitism; Wyclif was never adopted as an ultimate and infallible authority; as his ideas and words were found to concur with those already accepted at Prague, they were eagerly adopted and incorporated. But always Hus and his companions maintained their independence, and it is only by an evaluation of the points on which they differed from Wycliff that the independence and autonomy of Hussitism can be appreciated. Those points of difference are neither few nor unimportant.

Wyclif looked always to the state and the secular arm to purify the church; Hus (and when the 'state' was embodied in so broken a reed as the hapless Václav, the fact is not surprising) saw the remedy for a corrupt sacerdotalism in a 'national church organised on the democratic principle of free election of parish priests and bishops, to realise in the church the basic sovereignty of the people'.[56]

Wyclif fully identified himself with the predestinarian position implicit in Augustine; but Hus, subconsciously realising how barren that forbidding faith must be, realising that Wyclif's predestinarianism had largely contributed to the unpopularity of his teaching, clung to his faith in the freedom of the will,[57]

[56] Bartoš, *Husitství a cizina*, 53. Cf. *M. Jana Husi O svatokupectví*, ed. Novotný (Prague, 1907), pp. 131-4.

[57] For Hus on predestination and free-will see: Hus, *Super IV Sententiarium* (vol. ii of *Opera omnia*), I, dist. 38 (p. 162); dist. 40 (pp. 165-6); dist. 17 (p. 110); dist. 41 (pp. 168-9). Cf. Kybal, *M. Jan Hus*, i, pp. 179-83.

and in so doing continued in the footsteps of Matěj[58] and Štěpán of Kolín.[59]

Wyclif taught that an evil priest was devoid of spiritual power and unable to effect the sacraments; Matěj, so strong had been his faith in the sacramental efficacy of the eucharist, had maintained that mortal sin in a priest did not invalidate his sacramental acts,[60] and here too Hus follows Matěj and not Wyclif.[61] It is fundamentally the ardent sacramentalism which underlies the whole Hussite movement which prevents Hus from conceding that the efficacy of the sacrament of orders can be destroyed by the sins of an ordained priest, or that his evil deeds render inoperative the words of consecration of the mass. And it is precisely in all that concerns the eucharist that the strength of the native influences on Hus can most clearly be seen.

Wyclif saw in the doctrine of transubstantiation a recent innovation for which there was no scriptural or patristic authority, an innovation which served to exalt the prestige and authority of the priest, the doctrinal basis of exaggerated sacerdotalism, which distinguished the priest as a perpetual worker of miracles, and therefore as different from the layman in kind as well as in degree. Against it he had brought the whole armoury of his realistic logic, pouring scorn on the neo-nominalists who had said 'credo quia impossible', condemning it as flouting the elementary axiom of logic that accidents cannot subsist even for a moment without a substance in which they could inhere. He had pursued his argument careless of consequences and had thereby forfeited all the support of those of his fellow-countrymen who had applauded his ecclesiastical but deplored his theological criticisms of the church. But it is an abiding witness to the essential practicality of the Bohemian reformers and to their basic sacramentalism, that though one or two of them toyed as realist logicians with Wyclif's doctrine of remanence, they ended by rejecting it and maintaining complete eucharistic orthodoxy.

[58] For Matěj's treatment of free-will and predestination see: *Regulae,* i, 22; ii, 10-11, 171, 307; iii, 150-1; v, 69-70, 247.

[59] See Odložilík, *Štěpán z Kolína*, pp. 41-2, and n. 165 on p. 68.

[60] Cf. *Regulae*, i, 58, 62, 129, 133, 287; v, 7, 162, 200.

[61] The whole question of Hus's view of spiritual lordship is discussed in Kybal, *M. Jan Hus*, ii, 380-401.

Long before Wyclif's doctrine of remanence reached Bohemia, the sacrament of the altar had become the palladium of the Bohemian reformers. Milíč, Vojtěch Raňkův,[62] Tomás of Štítný, and above all Matěj of Janov had all advocated frequent communion of the laity, as being in the first place an ever-ready, all-sufficient, ineffably delectable means of grace, a constant source of spiritual refreshment. The recent practice of denying to the laymen the right to communicate more than once a year was regarded as a cruel usurpation of a most glorious and saving privilege, typical of the contumely and disdain of the priesthood. To Matěj the eucharist is the very heart of his reform programme, it is his last and supreme rule drawn from the scriptures for the restoration of true religion. To it he returns again and again. It is manna in the wilderness, it is the principle of life, sweet and delectable, a river of pleasure, it is alpha and omega, the beginning and the end. Matěj confesses that he wrote his whole great work to promote the honour and glory of the sacrament of the body and blood of Christ, to prompt others to the love and desire of it.[63] He insists that it should be given to all, laymen as well as priests, sinners as well as saints, who came to receive it.[64] His most eloquent contempt is poured on the heads of those priests who in their pride and cruelty would deny to laymen participation in the mystical union of the soul to Christ.[65] And such participation by the laity must be frequent; indeed his ideal and goal is daily communion.[66] And though Matěj never consciously took the final step Jakoubek of Stříbro was to take, of demanding the chalice for the laity, the necessity therefor is implicit in all his reasoning, and on several occasions he seems vaguely to anticipate the whole fullness of Utraquism.[67] The whole of the fifth volume of the *Regulae* is devoted to extolling the virtues and expounding the lawfulness and necessity of that faith in the Eucharist which is perhaps

[62] Cf. quotation from him in *Regulae*, ii, 89, 90.

[63] Ibid., v, 35.

[64] Ibid., i, 105; v, 27-9, 36-7, 92-3.

[65] Ibid., i, 57, 59, 107; ii, 136; v, 38, 78, 83, 143-4, 148, 171.

[66] Ibid., ii, 137; v, 216-17, 218-19, 164-5.

[67] See R. R. Betts, 'The *Regulae Veteris et Novi Testamenti* of Matěj z Janova', *Journal of Theological Studies*, xxxii (1931).

the essence of the constructive side of the reform movement in Bohemia, both before and after Hus.

It is precisely here that the organic connexion between Hus and his compatriots, and his refusal to follow Wyclif blindly is most apparent. As Loserth himself admits,[68] Hus never erred in his orthodoxy in the matter of transubstantiation, never accepted Wyclif's doctrine of remanence.[69] More than that, the gradual publication of all Hus's works is making it ever more clear that Hus regarded the sacrament of the altar as Matěj had done, as the centre of the Christian life; he advocated communion of the laity, frequent communion, and the giving of the chalice to the laity.[70]

English Lollardy withered away largely because of Wyclif's difficult and unacceptable theology; it was made ineffective partly by his abstruse scholastic method, partly by the arid predestinarianism he inherited from Bradwardine, but chiefly by his premature attack on sacramentalism in general and transubstantiation in particular. The Bohemian reform movement of the fourteenth century survived and blossomed in the great national religious movement of the fifteenth, successful and permanent, precisely because Hus only adopted that in Wyclif which was congenial, which harmonised with the genius of Bohemia, and rejected all that was inapt and unsympathetic. Hus was a great and constructive religious genius, and the work which he effected, the national church which he created, was not the outcome of principles he slavishly adopted from Wyclif, but the result of the blossoming to genius in him of those ideals which had long been germinating in his own country.

[68] Loserth, *Huss und Wiclif* (1925), pp. 189 ff.

[69] See for a full discussion of this, Kybal, *M. Jan Hus*, iii, 244-7.

[70] See for a full discussion of this, Kybal, *M. Jan Hus*, iii, 241. Hus, *Super IV Sententiarium* (vol. ii of *Opera omnia*), pp. 580-2.

IX

Richard fitzRalph, Archbishop of Armagh, and the Doctrine of Dominion

THE doctrine that *dominium*, or lordship, is founded on grace was formulated by Richard fitzRalph in the middle of the fourteenth century, was elaborated by Wyclif in England, propagated by his admirers in Bohemia in the early fifteenth century, and became a disruptive instrument in the hands of Luther and Calvin in the sixteenth. Like all revolutionary and creative ideas it was both the offspring and parent of profound social change.

The doctrine was stated by Wyclif in this form:

> He who is in a state of grace can in his own person enjoy in perpetuity the inheritance of the kingdom and of every part of the world; but he who falls into sin, to which the use of every usable thing is repugnant, loses everything which he had before, even though he may seem to have much goods. And so grace is not irrelevant to, but is the basis of, lordship.[1]

The thesis maintained, that is, that the title to exercise office and authority and the enjoyment of property was to be a subjective one, namely, being in a state of grace; and the test of grace was to be freedom from mortal sin. Therefore no man, be he pope, bishop, priest or friar, king, judge, landlord or merchant, would have any right to exercise the functions implicit in his office or profession by virtue of any act of consecration, election, ordination, of coronation or appointment, of inheritance, purchase, conquest, gift, loan, licence, or charter. It was a doctrine which was able to unmake popes, to trample episcopacy underfoot, to mutilate monasticism; the fathers of

[1] Wyclif, *Tractatus de civili dominio*, ed. R. L. Poole, 4 vols. (London, 1885-1904), i, 24-5.

Constance, who condemned it in Jan Hus and Jerome of Prague, unconsciously used it to wrench the fisherman's ring from off the hand of John XXIII, 'simoniac, notorious dilapidator of the church, and a scandal to the church by reason of his evil life'.[2] Because the grace of God was not in him, the vicar of Christ became once more plain Baldassare Cossa. The same doctrine of lordship founded on grace was used by the Bohemians to reject the hereditary rights of King Sigismund in 1419 and to elect a worthy country gentleman, George of Poděbrady, as their king in 1458; it justified Henry VIII's dissolution of the monasteries, the Dutch revolt from Philip II, and is the basis of Locke's theory of a terminable contract between ruler and subjects. When Luther proclaimed the priesthood of every Christian man he was only saying, as fitzRalph had said, that the title to office is character, not rite. The Calvinists applied the principle to economics as well as politics, maintaining that only the elect, who alone are in a state of grace, have the right to rule men or control property.

Indeed, the development of the doctrine of dominion is merely an attempt to find a new basis for authority and wealth in a rapidly changing society. During the high Middle Ages authority in state and church had been solidly based on custom, law, investiture, and prescription. The fact of primogeniture or possession, the act of consecration or ordination, the physical taking of seizin, investiture with sceptre, by the gift of belt or willow-wand, all such outward acts had been deemed sufficient to give a just title. As long as right, possession, power, and ability were confined to the one small group of the territorial and ecclesiastical aristocracy, there had been little need to question the title of those who enjoyed authority and privilege. But by the fourteenth century new classes and groups were thrusting towards political and economic power. The merchants and bankers of Lombardy, the traders of the Rhineland, northern France and the Hanse, the wool growers of England, and the corn exporters of Poland, new families with-

[2] Decree of deposition, 29 May 1415, in Hardt, iv, 185-6. Jan Hus was quick to seize this point when during his trial at Constance his opponents maintained that the office of pope or priest was not dependent on merit: 'Why then', replied Hus, 'was Pope John XXIII, who is now Baldassare Cossa, deposed?' Palacký, *Documenta*, p. 300.

out roots in the past or hereditary fiefs, the Bardi, Ursini, Medici, the de la Poles and Philpots, able adventurers like the Visconti, the dukes of Burgundy (who expounded the doctrine of dominion by the practice and defence of tyrannicide), the new aristocracy of Bohemia and Hungary which emerged as the companions of such belated knights errant as King John of Bohemia and Kings Charles Robert and Louis of Hungary; the swarm of intelligent and ambitious parvenus who were the officials of the chanceries, exchequers, and councils of the new monarchs and the new oligarchic commercial republics of western and central Europe; able scholars of humble origin like Matthias of Cracow, bishop of Worms; or Pierre d'Ailly, cardinal of Cambrai, or Jerome of Prague, the first of the agitators among the reformers, all such as these were jealous of the established privilege and hereditary wealth of the great landlords and the richly endowed religious orders. They were asking by what right an atheistic lawyer like Boniface VIII could be pope; by what right the Cistercians held the best sheep pasture in England and the Premonstratensians the best farmland in Bohemia; by what title the perverted Joanna II ruled Naples and Sicily or the lunatic Charles VI was king of France? Everywhere men were searching for a new basis of right, which would justify the able and the virtuous (and in that commercial age virtue was already beginning to be identified with success) in taking over from the corrupt and effete.

Not that such a question was asked consciously in general terms; revolutions begin in assaults on particular abuses, not in the statement of general principles. The particular abuse which inspired fitzRalph and Wyclif to state the universal principle of dominion was the rapidity with which the mendicant orders, and particularly the Franciscans, had grown in influence, wealth, and pretensions. Hardly more than a century after the death of Francis, his followers, pledged to a degree of poverty which, as fitzRalph maintained, far exceeded that preached and practised by Jesus and his disciples, were one of the wealthiest and most influential corporations in Europe, and were using their power to oust the secular clergy from the influence and profits of the confessional, the churchyard, the pulpit, and the court. The Franciscans were challenging all the most powerful forces of fourteenth-century Europe: they flocked to the support of Lewis IV and threatened thereby to undermine the great edifice of the commercialised papacy that John XXII was building up at Avignon; they fought the Dominicans and the Dominican synthesis which Thomas Aquinas had created, by securing the condemnation of Thomism at Paris and Oxford; the friars were struggling to wrest the control of the universities of Prague and Oxford and Paris from the secular masters; they were emptying the parish churches by their skill in folk-preaching and the seductiveness of their indulgences and relics; they were enticing rich burghers to be buried, at a price, in their cemeteries, and seducing their daughters into the mendicant sisterhoods.

In the sermon which fitzRalph preached on 8 November 1357, at Avignon, in the presence of Innocent VI and the cardinals, the famous *Defensio curatorum*, he ably expounded the essence of the jealousy of the Franciscans that was felt by many of his contemporaries.[3]

In my diocese of Armagh every year two thousand of my subjects are excommunicated as voluntary homicides, public robbers, incendiaries, and such like, but hardly forty of them come to me to do penance; the rest are all absolved, or say they are absolved, by none other than the friars.[4]

Ever since these friars received the privilege of becoming confessors they have been building the most beautiful monasteries and regal palaces. But one never hears that the friars impose on those who confess to them the penance of giving alms for the repair of a parish church, of the public highway, or a bridge.[5]

Since the friars have had this privilege of hearing confessions almost all the young men in the universities, and those who live in homes where the friars are admitted as family confessors, make their confession to the friars. These youths are seduced by the frauds of the friars and their petty bribes (men of ripe age cannot so easily be bamboozled) to enter their order; nor are they afterwards allowed, as the friars claim, the liberty of leaving the order, but are detained

[3] 'Richardi Armachani, Defensio curatorum', in M. Goldast, *Monarchia sancti Romani imperii* (Hanover and Frankfurt, 1611-14), ii, 1392 ff., and in Orthuinus Gratius, *Fasciculus rerum expetendarum et fugiendiarum*, ed. E. Brown, 2 vols. (London, 1690), ii, 466-86.

[4] Goldast, ii, 1394. [5] Ibid., ii, 1395.

unwilling until they make their profession. Indeed, it is said that these boys are not allowed to speak with their fathers or mothers, except under the eye and fear of the friars. This very day as I was leaving my inn a worthy Englishman, who had come here to Avignon to get some redress from the Curia, told me that just after Easter last the friars at Oxford had in this way carried off his son, not yet thirteen years old, and when he went to Oxford he was not allowed to speak to the boy except in the friars' presence.[6]

This well-known passage is an example of the particular social facts which led fitzRalph to examine the question of the right of the Franciscans to wield the authority they claimed, and from that to study the whole question of the basis of authority. His conclusion that 'we are all born children of wrath . . . therefore until we have grace we are without lordship; so that no man receives lordship until he is conformed to his first parent in justifying grace. This lordship then does not flow immediately from man's specific nature, but mediately through justice, which without justifying grace is not to be had',[7] was the expression of a revolutionary social programme in theological terms. Its subversive character was realised by fitzRalph himself. 'Johannes', the interlocutor of 'Richardus' in the dialogue entitled 'Concerning the poverty of the saviour', puts the fundamental objection to the doctrine of dominion in these words:

From what you have said it seems to me to follow that heirs have no lordship in their fathers' goods if they succeed their fathers in mortal sin, nor have sinful grantees any lordship in what is given to them, or wage earners in the wages they receive, or sinful legatees in their legacies. So it seems to me, if your description of lordship is true, that it subverts all human laws which are made indifferently for the good and the bad that they may recover by legal process their legacies, gifts, inheritances, and the promised reward of their labour.[8]

The defenders of prerogative and prescription were quick to see the practical dangers of a doctrine which asked for a sub-

[6] Ibid., ii, 1397.

[7] Richard fitzRalph, 'De pauperie Salvatoris', books i-iv, in Wyclif, *Tractatus de dominio divino*, ed. R. L. Poole (London, 1890), p. 344.

[8] Ibid., p. 443.

jective qualification for office and property. If no man had any power from God, if he were in a state of mortal sin, what guarantee could there ever be that the sacraments were effectively performed? No man could be sure that he was not still in original sin for want of effective baptism, no woman could be sure that she was lawfully married; there would be no assurance of legitimacy, none that the sacrament of the altar was effectively performed; orders would be in doubt—absolution a conjecture, and supreme unction a gamble, if the celebrant's apostolic power depended on his state of grace. There was an even more serious ambiguity which would follow such a subjective criterion: if there was no sacramental power in a service, where then was the church? Not in the pope, the cardinals, and the hierarchy, for they might all be 'foreknown', or temporarily incapacitated, by a lapse into mortal sin; not in the whole body of the baptised, for either party to that sacrament might be disqualified for like reason. As Wyclif clearly saw and said in his *De ecclesia*, if the sacraments give no effective guarantee to membership of the church, then the church can be nothing other than the whole body of the predestined. The councils of Rome and Constance which condemned Wyclif's doctrines had no doubt that that doctrine of the church would be fatal not only to the wealth and power of the church, but also to its authority, for no corporation can survive if every member of it is uncertain not only of the right to membership of it of every one of his fellows, but of his own also.

If a bishop or priest is in mortal sin, he does not ordain, consecrate the elements, or baptise. If the pope is foreknown or evil, and therefore a limb of the devil, no power over the faithful is given to him unless perchance it be given by Caesar. No prelate ought to excommunicate anyone unless he first knows that he is excommunicate of God. No one is a civil lord, no one is a prelate, no one a bishop, while he is in mortal sin. The prayers of the foreknown avail nothing. Excommunication by pope or prelate is not to be feared, for it is the censure of antichrist. The church of Rome is the synagogue of Satan, and the pope is not the immediate vicar of Christ and his apostles. It is not necessary to salvation to believe that the Roman church is supreme above other churches.

So logically and remorselessly did the commissioners who were set up to examine Jerome at Constance enumerate the damnable conclusions of Wyclif which Jerome had been propounding over half Europe from Paris to Pskov. And they added one more, the most dangerous of all: 'Temporal lords may at their pleasure seize the goods of those habitually delinquent.'[9]

Wyclif, indeed, had advocated a disendowment of the church to relieve the burden of taxation on the gentry and merchants. But the Bohemian reformers saw more clearly than he that the doctrine of dominion works as much against the state as the church, and Hus and Jerome were not as successful as Wyclif had been in securing royal support to save them from their clerical enemies. The Emperor Sigismund was acute enough to realise that Jerome's violent attack on the unworthiness of the prelates, in the sermon he preached before Sigismund at Buda in 1410, was as dangerous to respect for the authority of a crowned king as it was for an ordained priest; that is why, probably, after the sermon he handed Jerome over to the archbishop of Esztergom to be detained in prison.

Sigismund also got to the heart of the difficulties inherent in the doctrine of dominion during the trial of Hus at Constance in June 1415. Hus was being charged with having written in his *Tractatus contra magistrum Stephanum Palecz*: 'If a pope, bishop, or prelate is in mortal sin, for the time being he is not pope, bishop, or prelate.'[10] Hus replied boldly, saying: 'Indeed a man who is in mortal sin is not worthily a king in the sight of God.' The fathers rejoicing that Hus had added sedition to heresy, hurriedly brought Sigismund from the embrasure where he had been talking with the Count Palatine and Frederick of Hohenzollern, to hear Hus repeat his words, whereon Sigismund said: 'Jan Hus, no man lives without sin.'[11]

[9] 'Articuli Johannis Wicliff quos Hieronymus Pragensis hodie revocavit', in Hardt, iv, 508-10.

[10] What Hus in fact had written was: 'A bad pope, bishop, prelate, or priest is an unworthy minister of the sacraments through which God baptises, consecrates, or otherwise operates to the profit of his church'—which is very different from Wyclif's and fitzRalph's denial of the efficacy of the sacraments of a priest in mortal sin. The correct version of Hus's statements is given by his biographer, Petr of Mladoňovice, in Palacký, *Documenta*, p. 299.

[11] Palacký, *Documenta*, pp. 299-300.

The Bohemian reformers themselves had realised the impracticability of strictly applying the doctrine of dominion, which in the fifteenth century would have left the church without pastors and the state without rulers or servants. Hus at Constance receded from the pure Wyclifitism of his *De ecclesia*, and stated his final opinion in the words: 'The power of a pope who is not conformed to Christ and Peter in morals and life is indeed frustrated in respect of any merit or reward which it might have earned, but does not earn, but he is not frustrated in respect of his office.'[12] Jerome on his final examination took up the same position: 'Though the pope be a usurer and a fornicator, nevertheless as a priest he effectively consecrates the elements, though he himself does not benefit thereby.'[13] This theory that an evil priest performs the sacraments to the salvation of the recipients, but to his own damnation, is a reversion by Hus and Jerome to the older Czech tradition which Matěj of Janov had expounded in the *Regulae veteris et novi testamenti* twenty years before Wyclif's *De dominio divino* and *De dominio civili* had reached Prague.

But Wyclif had known no such hesitation; his whole system of ethics and theology is penetrated with the conviction that right is based solely on righteousness. And it is obvious that he owed the idea to fitzRalph, for again and again he refers to and reproduces passages from fitzRalph's *De pauperie Salvatoris* and the *Summa in quaestionibus Armenorum*.[14] Though Wyclif disagreed with many of fitzRalph's opinions, especially with his somewhat lax views about predestination, he accepted the main body of fitzRalph's doctrine of dominion almost, but not quite, as a whole. It is obvious that it is to fitzRalph that the doctrine in its late mediaeval form is due, and it is worth while briefly to examine the career and character of the man who was the first to elaborate so potently revolutionary a doctrine.

Of course it was no novelty to insist that there should be some connexion between authority, virtue, and office. The apostles James and Paul had had much to say on the matter. But it was Augustine, 'our father and greatest doctor', as fitzRalph calls

[12] Ibid., pp. 291-2. [13] Hardt, iv, 752.

[14] *Summa domini Armachani in quaestionibus Armenorum*, ed. J. Sudoris (Paris, 1512).

him,[15] that the reformers found their favourite authority. The whole thesis is based on Augustine's statement: 'All the riches of the world belong to the faithful man, but the unfaithful has not a farthing',[16] and the parallel statement of Jerome: 'The avariciou man lacks as much what he has as what he has not; all the riches of the world belong to him who believes; the infidel has not a farthing. Let us then live as if we had nothing and yet possessed everything.'[17] But the doctrine was more readily applicable in the age of the fathers than in that of the high Middle Ages, when the church and churchmen, if they were to play the part in the government of the world which they believed to be their duty and their due, were bound to ensure themselves by the possession of landed property and regular incomes. Even Anselm discovered that the security of the Canterbury manors was a matter which he could not ignore; the programme of Innocent III could only be carried out if the church had a large and assured income from its estates, for in the thirteenth century power could only be based on land-holding. That is the reason why the appearance of the friars, claiming the right to live and work without property, and basing that claim in their thesis that Christ and his apostles lived in poverty, was bound to cause a great debate. There were elements outside the church which acclaimed this doctrine of apostolic poverty as highly desirable. The temporal power in the person of Lewis IV welcomed the Minorites and their doctrine as offering a hope of disendowing and thereby crippling the church. On the other side, John XXII was insistent to prove that the doctrine of the poverty of Christ was erroneous; for unless Christ had property the vicar of Christ would find it difficult to justify the immense wealth of the curia at Avignon and of the church in every part of Christendom. Here lies the fundamental importance of what superficially appears to be the barren and scholastic discussion about the poverty of Christ, and it is here that fitzRalph comes into the picture.

His life covers the first sixty years of the fourteenth century, and his career was characteristic of that of the able, successful,

[15] 'De pauperie Salvatoris', in Wyclif, *De dominio divino*, p. 364.
[16] 'Epistola xxxvii, ad Macedonium', quoted by Wyclif, *De civili dominio*, i, 5-6.
[17] 'Epistola i, ad Paulinum', quoted by Wyclif, *De civili dominio*, i, 20.

and conscientious ecclesiastic of his day. Born in Ireland,[18] educated at Oxford, spending his active life between his deanery of Lichfield, the court of Avignon, and those parts of his province of Armagh that the native Irish left accessible to him, he came into active contact with most of the contemporary problems of church and state. From 1337 to 1344 he was fighting at Avignon for the rights of the chapter of Lichfield to a prebend in Cannock Chase. In Ireland he was presented with a problem of grave disorder, not only in his own province, but also in the dioceses of Ossory and Dublin, where he was called upon by the pope to settle the violent and protracted quarrel between the Franciscan bishop Richard Ledred[19] and the much-excommunicated royalist and secular archbishop of Dublin, Alexander Bicknor.[20] The troubled state of the church in Ireland must have set fitzRalph thinking about the problem of unworthy priests and prelates; it is clear too that the presumptions of the friars exacerbated these obscure disputes. And also fitzRalph spent some fifteen years of his life in Avignon: 1334 to 1335 or 1336, 1337 to 1344, 1349 to 1351, and 1357 to 1360. There he saw the vices and virtues of the great administrative, financial, and judicial machine which the genius of the able series of lawyer popes was building up. He seems to have admired its efficiency; he explicitly bore witness to the fairness of its jurisdiction, and he himself owed his rapid and high promotion to the favour of papal provisions. His reputation as a former chancellor of the university of Oxford (1332 to 1334)[21] caused him to be increasingly employed by Popes John XXII,

[18] The doubts expressed by R. L. Poole in the *Dictionary of National Biography*, xix, 194 f., whether fitzRalph was born in Devonshire or Ireland are completely resolved by the Rev. Aubry Gwynn's discovery of fitzRalph's statement that Dundalk was his native city. Sermon preached at Avignon, 4 Oct. 1349. See A. Gwynn 'The Sermon-diary of Richard fitzRalph', in *Proceedings of the Royal Irish Academy*, xliv, sect. C, no. 1. Father Gwynn's reconstruction of the chronology of the sermon-diary is an invaluable contribution to fitzRalph's biography.

[19] Some account of Ledred's stormy career as bishop of Ossory, 1318 to 1360, is given by J. B. Leslie, *Ossory Clergy and Parishes* (Enniskillen, 1933).

[20] For the quarrel in the years 1347-9 and fitzRalph's connexion with it, see *Calendar of Papal Letters*, iii, 227, 231, 232, 253, and A. Gwynn in *Studies* (Dublin), March 1935, pp. 38-41.

[21] *Snappe's Formulary*, ed. H. E. Salter (Oxford Historical Society, lxxx, 1924), pp. 75-6. Also *Munimenta academica, or Documents illustrative of Academical Life and Studies at Oxford*, ed. H. Anstey, 2 vols. (London, 1868), i, 127.

Benedict XII, and Clement VI as consultant and rapporteur in the major controversial questions of the day, notably that of the beatific vision, the possibility of reconciliation of the Armenian church, the immaculate conception of the Virgin, and above all, the crucial question of Christ's poverty.

fitzRalph seems to have approached that last problem with an open mind. In 1349 he was still sufficiently friendly with the friars to be invited to preach in the Franciscan house at Avignon on the feast of St Francis, whom he highly praised. But in the next year, on 5 July 1350, he preached 'on behalf of the prelates and of all the curates of the whole church, before our lord the pope in full consistory', the first of his 'proposiciones' against the privileges of the friars, especially their claim to hear confessions and to give burial.[22] This 'proposicio' contains the principles of all the sermons against the friars, which he preached with increasing acerbity during the remaining ten years of his life. What is most significant in the first 'proposicio' for our present purpose is his argument that if a privilege has been got from the pope from motives of greed or ambition, that privilege is invalid and its use is sinful.[23] Such an argument anticipates the development of the doctrine of dominion founded on grace.

To that doctrine he was led by two investigations with which he was entrusted by Pope Clement VI, who in 1350 'entrusted to me and two other doctors of theology' the examination of the question debated between the two chief mendicant orders of the property, lordship, possession, and use of created things which was enjoyed by Christ and by the Friars Minor, and also the collation of the decretals of Nicholas III and John XXII on the same subject. 'But', fitzRalph adds, 'as the dispute went on

[22] MS Bodl. 144, f. 251b-255; New College MS (in Bodley), 90, f. 70 v ff.

[23] 'Ita enim inportune attendentes vexarunt quasi quoscunque summos pontifices sui temporis a tempore quo ad huiusmodi negocia habebant ingressum, ut amplieretur in eis talis facultas . . . Clarum est igitur quod ad peticionem et affirmacionem eorum non ad vocacionem ecclesie istud curatorum officium acceperunt. Petere vero sive desiderare istam facultatem fuit, ut videtur, contra divinum consilium atque apostolicum . . . Igitur non est dubium quin questus sit causa precipua execucionis facultatis istius, et cui dubium quin hoc maculat statum personarum sancti ordinis qui statum professionis et paupertatis altissime profitentur? . . . Item ista facultas in fratribus quia fuit acquisita mediante peccato non videtur posse exerceri ab eis sine peccato mediante quo fuerat acquisita.' (Bodl. MS 144, f. 253 r.)

ineffectively I resolved, encouraged by the good will of the cardinals, to examine the matter radically.' The result of this investigation, the *De pauperie Salvatoris*,[24] was completed not earlier than 1353, and not later than 18 December 1356.[25] The other commission entrusted to fitzRalph was to report on the differences between the Roman and the Armenian churches, revealed by the Armenian church council of 1342. The result of fitzRalph's investigation was the monumental exposition of Catholic dogma known as the *Summa in quaestionibus Armenorum*. He probably completed it somewhat before the *De pauperie*, and it contains a few interesting anticipations of his teaching about dominion and apostolic poverty.[26] There is also much of the doctrine of the *De pauperie* implicit in the series of sermons which fitzRalph preached against the friars in London and at Avignon during the years 1356 to 1357,[27] but these sermons and

[24] Liber Ricardi Archiepiscopi Armachani de pauperie Salvatoris, Bodleian MS, Auct. F, infra 1, 2. The text of books i to iv is printed in Wyclif, *De dominio divino*, ed. R. L. Poole (1890); books v to vii were transcribed by Miss Helen Hughes as part of her thesis for the Manchester doctorate. I have had the privilege of consulting this transcription.

[25] In his sermon of this date, fitzRalph says explicitly: 'Scripsi de ista materia septem libros quos nostro domino pape et quibusdem dominis meis cardinalibus approbandos seu discutiendos atque corrigendos si oporteret direxi.' The sermon is one of those printed at the end of the *Summa* (1512 ed.).

[26] See especially lib. xi, cap. 1 and lib. x, cap. 4. The latter has this passage on lordship and tyranny: 'Unde mihi videtur nullus existens in peccato mortali habet aliarum creaturarum verum dominium apud deum sed tyrannus aut fur sive raptor merite est vocandus, quamvis nomen regis aut principis aut domini propter possessionem seu propter successionem hereditarium aut propter approbacionem populi sibi subiecti aut propter aliam legem humanam retineat, nec verum habet dominium donec peniteat et penitencie gracia eum in statu deo acceptum instituat . . . quoniam sola approbacio populi ut super populum rex fiat aut princeps non sufficit nisi deus approbet eius statum.' *Summa* (1512 ed.), x, 4.

[27] These sermons are:

i. At St Paul's, 17 July 1356. Bodl. MS 144, f. 86 r ff.
ii. In the hall of the bishop of London, 18 Dec. 1356. Ibid., f. 92 v.
iii. At St Paul's cross, 22 Jan. 1357. Ibid., f. 98 v ff.
iv. At St Paul's cross, 26 Feb. 1357. Ibid., f. 106 r ff.
v. At St Paul's cross, 12 March 1357. Ibid., f. 112 v ff.
vi. At St Mary Newchurch, 25 March 1357. Ibid., f. 56 v ff.
vii. In consistory at Avignon (the famous 'Defensorium curatorum'), 8 Nov. 1357. Ibid., f. 255 r ff.

Nos ii, iii, iv, and v are printed as an appendix in Sudoris's 1512 edition of the *Summa*.

No. vii is printed in Goldast, ii, 1392 ff., and in Orthuinus Gratius, *Fasciculus rerum expetendarum et fugiendarum*, ii, 466 ff.

such others of the pastoral sermons contained in fitzRalph's sermon diary (Bodleian MS 144) as I have hitherto had time to read do not seem to me to add much to the exposition of his theory of dominion as set out in the *De pauperie*.

In that treatise there is much that today seems irrelevant and futile, though it is far more to the point than Wyclif's academic and ill-constructed *De dominio civili*. The *De pauperie* starts off with a long examination of God's original lordship, and of the lordship enjoyed by angels and by Adam and Eve before the fall. But even these questions of academic theology are not without interest to the student of political theory, for they represent fitzRalph's conception of the ideal state of man and society, and constitute his utopia. When he discusses what would be the state of society had there been no fall, he is in fact laying down principles which he conceives as being still valid if society is to be what it should and could be. For example, he says:

It seems difficult to know why communities or colleges, if the state of innocence had continued, should appropriate to themselves as private property those things which are the common goods of all sinless men in virtue of original lordship; I refer to the crops they grow on the land, the animals they have domesticated, the buildings they have built, the fish or the fowls of the air they have caught, and all that is necessary or useful for their livelihood and acquired by their labour.[28]

From the whole of his discussion of the nature of God's lordship fitzRalph is able to deduce the principle that all lordship is originally and eternally God's, and that God's lordship is not alienated or diminished when he gives lordship to men, any more than when a communal group admits another to share in its common ownership.[29] This theory, that true giving of property or authority creates a common lordship shared by giver and receiver, is an interesting and essential part of his argument, for it justifies the resumption by the giver if that which is given is abused, whether it be the estates of a religious order or the authority of a secular ruler.

From the principle that every gift of God, whether of lord-

[28] 'De pauperie Salvatoris', III, xvi, in Wyclif, *De dominio divino*, p. 398.
[29] Ibid., I, xvi.

ship, possession, property, or the right of use is in fact a loan given on condition,[30] fitzRalph is able to argue that a breach of the condition revokes the loan:

When anyone sins mortally, he loses in sinning natural lordship, at least over that creature with respect to whom he sins. Since, therefore, a whole and undivided original lordship over all lesser creatures was granted to that person in order to serve man, lordship having been lost by his sin against even one creature, lordship over all is taken away.[31]

Similarly the lower degrees of authority, possession and use, are conditional on the state of grace of the possessor or user,[32] though in one place fitzRalph seems to say that God may permit a sinner the use or abuse of things.[33]

fitzRalph sharply distinguishes between 'original' lordship which every man in a state of grace enjoys and the 'civil' lordship which is given by positive human law, which was made necessary by man's fallen state, but which does not revoke man's original and natural rights; royal authority was due to sin, and it conveys no right of possession or use over the property of the governed.[34] Such political philosophy is no novelty; it had been taught by Augustine and Ambrosiaster in the fifth century; but it is important that this philosophy with its denial of any absolute right in civil rulers should be thus reiterated in the revolutionary fourteenth century.

fitzRalph also revives the older doctrine that ideally all things should be owned in common, that a man might have the use of the fruits of his labour, but no property in them. Ownership, possession, use, he regards as right and laudable,

[30] Ibid., I, xxiv. fitzRalph is able to quote both the civil and the common law. He was well acquainted with both the Roman doctrine of 'dominium eminens' and the English law of 'dona conditionalia'.

[31] Ibid., II, 12, p. 354. [Translated from the Latin by Peter Brock.] 'Cum quis peccat mortaliter perdit peccando dominium naturale, saltem illius creature circa quam peccat. Cum igitur omnium propter hominem inferius creatorum fuerit illi simul simule et indivise collatum originale dominium, perdito per culpam unius creature dominio, omnium dominium est sublatum.'

[32] Ibid., III, iv; iii, vii, p. 392.

[33] fitzRalph, 'De pauperie Salvatoris', II, xiii, in Wyclif, *De dominio divino*, p. 355.

[34] Ibid., II, xxiv-xxvi.

but property as something inherently wrong.[35] Any right that is conferred merely by the civil law must give place to a right which proceeds from 'original dominion'. 'No one can doubt that a poor just man has a better claim to that which he needs than an impious man who has the legal right to it; a just judge ought, in such a case, to take the thing away from him who does not need it, and adjudge it to him who suffers penury.'[36]

The long and interesting discursion in the fourth book of the *De pauperie* on property, endowment, and use, brings fitzRalph closer to the practical question of wealth and poverty, particularly with reference to Christ and the friars who claimed to follow his example in this respect. He argues that in an age of innocence all would be wealthy, and equally wealthy, for wealth (*ditacio*) is inherently a good thing.[37] But since the fall wealth has existed only improperly, that is, unequally, and Christ himself was not rich in fact, though he was potentially so, for he did not wish to use his power.[38] Can it then be said that Christ was poor, as the friars maintained in order to justify their claim to live by begging? This question is dealt with in books VI and VII of the *De pauperie*, where fitzRalph argues that because poverty is an evil, Christ could not have been a pauper, and that the friars, if they do claim the right to practise 'altissima' or 'evangelica' poverty, can only do so on the express understanding that Christ did not practise it.[39] But fitzRalph was faced with the fact that Nicholas III had said that Christ and the apostles had no private or common property, while John XXII had declared such a doctrine to be heretical. fitzRalph is content to report the disagreement and to suggest that it was basically due to a confusion in the use of the terms 'dominium', 'proprietas' and 'usus'.

It was not till he came to preach the series of anti-mendicant

[35] 'Omnis autem propriacio iuris minuit aut privat aliqualiter ius utendi in aliis; igitur non potuit innocenter haberi.' Ibid., III, xiii, p. 402.

[36] Ibid., III, xxvii; III, xxxiv, p. 431.

[37] Ibid., V, xii-xvii.

[38] Ibid., V, xx-xxiii.

[39] fitzRalph again insisted that Christ was not a pauper in the 'Defensorium curatorum', and in the sermon preached at Paul's Cross on 22 Jan. 1357, where he said: 'Quod autem dominus noster Jhesus Christus non erat pauper nec propter se paupertatem dilexit taliter suadetur quoniam paupertas ad miserias pertinet . . . nullus autem prudenter diligit miseriam per se cum omnis miseria ex se sit omnino inutilis et ob hoc non est diligibilis propter se ipsam' (*Summa* (1512 ed.), sermo II).

sermons at St Paul's and the *Defensorium* at Avignon, that fitz-Ralph brought the two points of his doctrine together. Then by applying the theory of dominion founded on grace to the friars who made their evangelical poverty the excuse for idleness and the usurpation of the penitential and burial rights of the parish priests, he was able to set fire to a train of explosive material whose disruptive effect he could hardly have anticipated or desired.

X

Jan Hus[1]

FOR three hundred years two holy men have been rivals for the reverence of the Czech people. One of them, Saint Jan Nepomuk, was exalted by the Jesuits, who after the battle of the White Hill in 1620 sought to win back the Czechs to the Roman obedience. For this function Saint Jan was admirably fitted, for had he not been tortured and, bound hand

[1] BIBLIOGRAPHICAL NOTE. As has been mentioned in the text, the best short account of Hus in English is still [i.e. in 1939] that in M. Creighton's *History of the Papacy*, Book II, c. III-V (new edition, London, 1907). It may be supplemented by Count F. Lützow's *The Life and Times of Master John Hus* (London, 1921), and D. S. Schaff, *John Huss—His Life, Teachings and Death* (London, 1915). H. B. Workman, *The Dawn of the Reformation. The Age of Hus* (London, 1902), H. Rashdall, *John Huss* (Oxford 1879), and A. H. Wratislaw, *John Hus* (London, 1882), are more popular accounts, and somewhat out of date. Two other books in English are of great use: a translation of Hus's 'De ecclesia' entitled *The Church, by John Huss*, translated with notes and introduction by D. S. Schaff (New York, 1915), and *The Letters of John Hus*, translated by H. B. Workman and R. M. Pope (London, 1904).

Nothing like a complete edition of the works of Hus exists, and much of what he wrote still remains in manuscript. The following are the fullest editions: *Historia et monumenta* (1558); *Sebrané spisy české*, ed. K. J. Erben (1865-8); *Opera omnia*, ed. Flajšhans *et al.* (1903 ff.): Tom. i, *Expositio Decalogi*, etc., Tom. ii, *Super IV Sententiarum*, Tom. iii, *Sermones de sanctis*. Some of the other works fundamental to the study of Hus are: F. Palacký, *Documenta*; *Mistra Jani Husi korespondence a dokumenty*, ed. V. Novotný; C. Höfler, *Geschichtschreiber der hussitischen Bewegung*; H. Finke *et al.*, *Acta Concilii Constanciensis* (4 vols., Münster, 1896-1928); J. Loserth, *Huss und Wiclif* (2nd ed, 1925). (There is an English translation of the first edition by M. J. Evans, London, 1884.)

The most recent and authoritative work on Hus is Novotný and Kybal, *M. Jan Hus, život a učení*; unfortunately it has not been translated. The following books are useful for a study of the Bohemian reform movement in general and for the general background (I have omitted books written in Czech): Höfler, *Concilia Pragensia*; C. Ullmann, *Reformatoren vor der Reformation* (Hamburg, 1841-2); E. Denis, *Huss et la guerre des Hussites* (Paris, 1878); F. Palacký, *Geschichte von Böhmen*, 5 vols. (Prague, 1836-67). There is a mass of articles on Hus in learned periodicals in various languages; see, for instance, F. Žilka, 'The Czech Reformation in Its Relation to the World Reformation', *Slavonic Review*, viii (1929-30).

[Since the publication of Betts's article a number of studies on Hus's life and

and foot, thrown into the Vltava from the Charles bridge by the jealous Václav IV for his refusal to surrender monastic estates at the king's command? His rival for the position of national hero has been Jan Hus, who, during the reign and under the favour of that same king Václav, led the revolt of the Czechs against the ecclesiastical domination of Rome and the secular domination of Germany, and was martyred as a heretic and rebel at the council of Constance in 1415. From that date until the extinction of the independent Bohemian state by the forces of the empire and the Counter-Reformation in 1620, Hus was publicly honoured by his fellow-countrymen as the champion of national and religious liberty. From 1620 to 1918 his rival was exalted in his place; his followers were reconciled to Rome or driven into exile; Hus was remembered in sadness for the liberty which had been lost and in the hope of a national resurrection. From 1918 to 1938 the Czechoslovak republic restored Hus to his place of honour, and annually, with happy pride, celebrated during those brief years the man who symbolised the first and second birth of the Czech people. But now again in this present year[2] the compatriots of Hus have had to

teachings have appeared in English, French, and German, as well as in Czech. Particularly important are M. Spinka, *John Hus and the Czech Reform* (Chicago, 1941) and *John Hus' Concept of the Church* (Princeton, New Jersey, 1966). The same author has also translated and edited Petr of Mladoňovice's 'Account of the Trial and Condemnation of Master John Hus in Constance', along with other relevant documents, in *John Hus at the Council of Constance* (New York and London, 1965). A Belgian Benedictine, Dom P. de Vooght, published in 1960 in Louvain: *L'hérésie de Jean Huss* and *Hussiana*. Among numerous recent works in Czech which deal with Hus, the following, all published in Prague, deserve mention: F. M. Bartoš, *Čechy v době Husově, 1378-1415* (1947) and *Literární činnost M. Jana Husi* (1948); M. Machovec, *Husovo učení a význam v tradici českého národa* (1953); J. Macek, *Jan Hus* (1963); F. M. Bartoš and P. Špunar, *Soupis pramenů k literární činnosti M. Jana Husa a M. Jeronyma Pražského* (1965). For sources on Hus's activities at the university of Prague, see *Magistri Johannis Hus Quodlibet*, ed. B. Ryba (Prague, 1948), and *Johannes Hus: Positiones, recommendationes, sermones*, ed. A. Schmidtová (Prague, 1958). From *Magistri Johannis Hus Opera omnia*, now being continued in Prague by the Československá akademie věd a umění, two volumes have appeared recently, vii, *Collecta*, ed. A. Schmidtová (1959), and xxii, *Polemica*, ed. J. Eršil (1966). B. Ryba has brought out an edition of Hus's *Betlemské teksty* (Prague, 1951), and S. H. Thomson has edited his *Tractatus de ecclesia* (Boulder, Colorado, 1956), while M. Spinka has translated his Czech treatise 'On Simony' in *Advocates of Reform: From Wyclif to Erasmus* (Philadelphia, 1953). The early chapters of H. Kaminsky, *A History of the Hussite Revolution* (Berkeley and Los Angeles, 1967) and G. Leff, *Heresy in the Later Middle Ages* (Manchester, 1967), ii, c. IX, are important for Hus's thought.]

[2] [The study originally appeared in September 1939.]

shroud their act of national homage in the fearful secrecy of clandestine mourning; the festival of July the 6th has once more become an occasion for tears.

It is well that we should remember Hus and his people. The contribution of the Czechs to the civilisation of the late Middle Ages was not inconsiderable. The university of Prague was next only to Paris and Oxford in its reputation at the beginning of the fifteenth century; Germany and Poland owed much to the civilising influence of the teachers and scholars it sent out; it became a centre of humanistic studies while Petrarch was still alive. To the realism of the Bohemian king-emperor Charles IV Germany itself was deeply indebted for much of the achievement of its golden age, and the greatness of its cities was in no small measure due to civic officials who had been trained in the chancery of Prague. Frequently, too, history has brought the English and the Czech peoples close together: in Anne of Bohemia England had one of her most gracious queens, and the extent of her beneficent influence on her devoted husband we can only guess at. The names of Wyclif and Hus have always been closely associated, both by their enemies and their friends. No small part in the attempt to force back Bohemia into her allegiance to Rome and Sigismund was played by Henry Beaufort, cardinal bishop of Winchester, during the Hussite wars of the fifteenth century. And again, in the last hour of her independence England gave the Bohemians a queen in the person of Elizabeth Stuart, but deserted her and them in the interests of European appeasement. Finally, the debt which Hus owed to Wyclif was repaid with interest by the profound influence the Moravian church exercised on John Wesley.[3]

It is not merely coincidence which has brought England and Bohemia so often into contact, for, widely separated though they are in space, the situation of the two countries has much in common that has driven them frequently into parallel courses. Both countries lay on the periphery of the world of western Christendom. Neither had been permanently influenced by

[3] It is interesting that Hus rejected that predestinarianism of Wyclif which narrowed the acceptability of his teaching, and that it was Hus's spiritual descendants, the Moravians, who persuaded Wesley to reject Whitfield's and Toplady's predestinarianism, and thereby made Methodism widely acceptable.

imperial Rome. To both the Romance civilisation, organisation and language of mediaeval christendom were alien. As England but barely escaped being permanently incorporated in a Scandinavian empire, so too it was long uncertain whether Bohemia would be attracted into the Roman or the Byzantine orbit. In both there might be observed a constant tendency to kick against the authority of the papacy, as being too often identified in the one case with French, and in the other with German influence. Then, too, national consolidation and the awakening of national self-consciousness came earlier to England and Bohemia than to any other country in Europe, partly because both had geographical and economic advantages which provided a basis for the early development of a specifically nationalist economy. It is not therefore surprising that two of the earliest revolts against Roman authority should occur in countries as far apart as England and Bohemia, nor that Wyclif and Hus, Lollardy and the Bohemian sects, should be contemporaneous and have much in common.

It is not as yet possible to give anything like a definitive account of Hus and the Bohemian reformation. It is hardly more than a hundred years since Palacký, the father of the modern Czech renascence, began the scientific study of the subject. As long as Bohemia was but a part of the Habsburg empire, Czech studies were always carried on under the incubus of a Teutonic domination which inhibited to some extent the freedom of enquiry, and inevitably poisoned the atmosphere in which that enquiry was conducted with the bitter animosity of nationalism. However, even before 1914 much good work was done, for the dead weight of Austrian obscurantism was considerably lightened in the latter half of the reign of Francis Joseph. But, of course, when the liberation of the Czechs came in 1918, the floodgates were opened to a swift and sometimes turbulent spate of work. The years from 1348 to 1526 appeared as the golden age of the Czech nation and Hussitism as the characteristic manifestation of the earlier liberty and achievement of the Czech spirit. An immense amount of research, therefore, was devoted to these topics by Czech scholars during the twenty years of the republic; manuscripts were discovered, texts were edited, monographs composed, and syntheses undertaken. But the task was enormous, for not only had much new ground to be broken, but a great many rooted errors had to be laboriously eradicated, Little more than the preliminary work had been done when in March this year the night closed down again. The labourers in this field have many of them disappeared into the darkness; some are in prison, others in exile, and those that are left must surely be heavy in spirit, without enthusiasm and opportunity, even though their faith still lives. We do not and cannot know what will be the fate of Czech and Hussite studies in the next few years. Today, then, is perhaps a fitting occasion to attempt some estimate of Hus in the light of the work which has been begun and so rudely interrupted, acknowledging always that it can only be a reporting of progress, and by no means a final judgment.

Such an interim report must be based primarily on three recently published works, which enable us dimly to begin to see Hus as he was. The first is Flajšhans's edition of Hus's works, a modern and scholarly achievement, but unfortunately one that has been left far from complete. The second is the edition of Hus's correspondence by Novotný. The third is the five volumes of the *Life and Teaching of John Hus*, by Novotný and Kybal, which is the most authoritative biography and a most careful and complete synthesis of his teaching.

Also it is now easier to look at Hus as an historical phenomenon, freed to some extent from the haze of theological partisanship. An earlier generation of Englishmen was interested in Hus almost solely as a forerunner of the Reformation, as a Protestant champion to be put beside Wyclif and Luther and Calvin, extolled with more enthusiasm than discretion as one of the heroes of the intoxicating battle with the Scarlet Woman. But nowadays we flatter ourselves that we have put these Protestant heroes in their proper place: the iconoclasm of Professor Perroy has somewhat defaced the picture of Wyclif that Dr Workman painted; candidates for the higher certificate now either apologise for Luther or patronise him, while the dialectical materialists regard him as the scum which rose to the surface of the seething cauldron of social conflict. In this new spirit, though it is to be hoped without its excesses, we can now hope to look at Hus, and to see him divested both of the halo with which he has been endowed by his admirers and of the diabolic vestments in which his enemies have concealed the abhorred reality.

But it is not merely *odium theologicum* which has made it difficult to see Hus as he really was. He has been not only the subject of religious, but also of equally violent political controversy. To the Czechs he has become the personification of the greatness of their national achievement, the embodiment of their pride of race, the protagonist of their struggle for independence, the proto-martyr of their persecution, and the symbol of their hope and faith. Therefore they have tended on occasion to give to him qualities in higher degrec than the evidence seems to warrant; they have been suspicious and impatient of criticism, and have inclined to idealise him. On the other hand, to the Germans Hus has tended to appear as the false god in whose worship their Slavonic foes have intoxicated themselves and grown mad to hurl themselves against the superior civilisations of the Teutonic world. German historians have therefore been inclined to belittle Hus, to strip him of his claims to scholarship and originality, and to picture him as an idol of wood, the imperfect and lifeless copy of Wyclif, whose words he reproduced with all the soulless and mechanical unoriginality of a phonograph. It is, of course, very difficult even for an Englishman to be completely impartial in the controversy, but it is perhaps to some extent possible, after giving due weight to what Germans and Slavs have said on either side, and relying as far as possible on what Hus wrote, not only in Latin, but also in Czech, to arrive at an estimate of his character, abilities and influence, which shall be more or less uninfluenced by religious and political bias.

The historical significance of Hus is twofold: as a factor in the Reformation, and as a factor in the national history of Bohemia. In both these respects, like all those who have been powerful enough to influence the course of history, Hus was fortunate in the age in which he lived, just as the age was fortunate in having such a man to live in it. The spirit of reformation was spread all over Europe in the latter half of the fourteenth century, the period when Hus was growing up to maturity. The evils consequent on the materialisation of religion and the imprisonment of the faith in the cramping bonds of ecclesiastical organisation were apparent to those who had eyes to see and implicitly felt by thousands whose mute longing for salvation went unsatisfied. Pleas for reform went out from universities and royal chanceries, from monasteries and commercial towns, from ecclesiastics and from laymen alike. Not only in England had the chorus of criticism and the demand for reformation been swelling from Grosseteste to fitz-Ralph, but from France, from Sweden, from Germany, from Italy came a general demand for reform. Gerson and Nicholas of Clamanges, Saint Bridget, Gerard Groote, Saint Catherine of Siena, were but the clearest voices raised above the general cry. And in this movement, which was common to the whole of Europe, Bohemia played its part. It shared in the general disease whose symptoms were the worldliness of the clergy, the idleness of the monks, the ambition and avarice of the mendicants, and the preoccupation of the hierarchy and the curia with jurisdiction, administration and finance. In Bohemia, as everywhere, annates and jubilees, pilgrimages and indulgences were proving both a financial and a moral burden. The Babylonish captivity and the great schism were felt as disasters there as elsewhere.

But this mass of religious discontent remained vague and unco-ordinated except where there was a well-established civil authority to direct and unify it, and that meant only in England and Bohemia, for in the latter half of the fourteenth century those two countries alone in Europe were sufficiently centralised and free from internal and external weakness to undertake the task. France was distracted by English invasion and conquest, by the faction of Burgundy and Orleans, and by the lunacy of the king. Germany was notoriously cut up into small, sovereign principalities and divided by the rival ambitions of Luxemburgers, Wittelsbachs and Habsburgs, while the extensive and numerous sovereign ecclesiastical states of Germany created there a strong vested interest against radical reform. Italy too, without national consciousness or a national monarchy, straddled by the papal states and chronically disturbed by civil war in Naples, was in no position to attempt a national solution of the religious problem.

But with the Bohemian kingdom it was different. Charles IV was quick to realise the fact that Bohemia had the economic resources, the geographical unity and the centralised administration to make it an effective basis for his monarchy. He saw that ecclesiastical carelessness and religious disorder were among the evils militating against the efficiency of the state. That consideration, together with a genuine concern for religion, impelled him to give the lead to reform in Bohemia. He took the initial step by founding the university of Prague, which was to provide the educated leaders of the movement. To it he brought scholars from Germany and Poland; from it sent out scholars to Paris and Oxford, Cracow and Vienna. His second step was to invite to Prague Konrad Waldhauser, an Austrian preacher already distinguished by his eloquence and moral fervour. This was the beginning of a mighty religious revival in Bohemia. Konrad's sermons not only had immediate effect, but they were even more important in that they inspired a whole school of native preachers who carried the evangelical movement to all classes of the people. The outstanding names in this pre-Hussite reform movement are those of Jan Milíč, the ascetic, apocalyptic moralist, Matthias of Cracow, the critic and author of the *De squaloribus curiae romanae*, Matěj of Janov, a learned and evangelically-minded theologian, Tomáš of Štítný, a pious layman and publicist, and Vojtěch Raňkův (Adalbertus Ranconis), a great scholar and educationist. These men with many others of less distinction built up in Bohemia between 1365 and 1400 a very powerful movement, both critical and constructive. It accumulated a body of criticism against the corruption of the church, the gist of which was the accusation of having externalised religion and of having introduced '*adinventiones hominum*' to obscure its primitive simplicity. The reformers also evolved a constructive programme, preaching the need for a return to the purity and simplicity of the early church, and the importance of internal religion; they put at the centre of religious life five things: '*Jhesus crucifixus*', the scriptures, preaching, personal morality and the sacrament of the altar. In all this the state gave its active co-operation. Charles achieved the separation of the Bohemian church from the age-long control of the archbishop of Mainz by securing the establishment of an archbishopric at Prague; he secured benefices for the reformers; he was not even shaken in his support when Milíč accused him to his face of being Antichrist. His son and successor, Václav IV, continued his policy, and the reformers were favoured by the court, particularly by Queen Žofie. It is nowadays a commonplace to recognise the part played by the development of urban capitalism in the promotion of the Reformation, and we can see this influence working in Bohemia in the establishment and endowment of the chapel of 'Bethlehem', which was founded in 1391 by a group of middle-class property-owners and merchants to provide specifically for evangelical preaching. The preachers appointed to it were all reformers, and Hus himself became the incumbent in 1402.

Thus the atmosphere in which Hus grew up was one of intense religious activity. The whole air he breathed in his early years at the university of Prague was that of intense reformist agitation. When he emerged in 1402 as one of the leaders of the movement it was already thirty years old. He was not the creator of that movement, which would have been important had neither he nor Wyclif ever lived. It is our task to estimate what his contribution to it was.

He was of humble origin, born, probably in 1369, in the village of Husinec in Bohemia, near the Bavarian frontier.[4] Here the population even at that time was a mixture of Germans and Czechs, and thus Hus was from his earliest years brought up in the fatal atmosphere of racial antagonism. It seems that he began his education, not at the local school at Prachatice, but in Prague itself, whither he was sent in 1386. Therefore while still in his teens he was thrust into the centre of the reform movement. We get glimpses of him as a poor scholar, a normal youth, carefree except for his poverty. He was a little bit disgusted at the horseplay which accompanied the election of the boy bishop on Holy Innocents' day, and a little bit worried about the utility of oft-repeated formal prayers. He was interested in clothes and he liked to play chess (a

[4] He was known to his fellow-countrymen as Jan of Husinec. The name 'Hus' is not only a convenient abbreviation, but also a pun, apparently of his own devising, for 'hus' in Czech means 'goose', and Hus was fond of referring to himself as 'ansellus dei', 'God's little goose'.

weakness he enumerates among the sins he confesses in his last days at Constance). And so without any marked precocity of virtue or vice he passed through the normal curriculum of one preparing for an academic or clerical career. He became bachelor of arts in 1393 and master of arts in 1396. He was already reading avidly, the fathers, such as Augustine, Ambrose, Anselm, Gregory and Chrysostom, the canon law and the schoolmen, especially Gratian, Peter Lombard, Bernard and Hildgarde. Like all his contemporary reformers, he came to have an intimate and literal knowledge of the bible, and like many of his fellow-Praguers, he was influenced to some extent by the humanistic studies promoted by Archbishop Jan of Jenštejn; he knew some Greek and Hebrew words and quotes from Boethius; he learnt a smattering of ancient history, something of church history and of the earlier history of his own country. But outside theology his greatest achievement was in the development of the Czech language. One of the elements in the pre-Hussite movement had been the insistence on the importance of the vernacular. Charles IV had, with papal permission, established a monastery where the old Slavonic liturgy was used; the widespread appeal of Milíč was in a large measure due to the fact that he preached in the popular tongue; Tomáš of Štítný had written his great work on Christian education in the vernacular. Here, too, Hus is the perfector of what had gone before. He not only preached at 'Bethlehem' in Czech, but many of his most important writings are in that language.[5] Also he did a very great service to Bohemia by writing a dissertation on Bohemian orthography which did much to standardise spelling and the use of those diacritical signs which put the writing of a Slavonic language in Roman characters on a scientific basis.

It is important to remember that the university of Prague was not united in its philosophical and religious views. There were many eminent foreign scholars there, chiefly Germans, who not only had no interest in the national side of the movement, but also were almost all sympathetic with that nominalism

[5] e.g. 'O svatokupectví (On Simony)'; 'Výklad piesniček Šalomunových (Exposition of the Song of Solomon)'; 'Výklad Otčenaše (Exposition of the Lord's Prayer)'; 'O manželství (On Matrimony)'; 'O poznaní cesty pravé k spasení (On the Knowledge of the Right Way to Salvation)'.

whose centre was Paris. These foreign scholars had imbibed the materialistic, scientific and agnostic implications of the teaching of Occam, Duns Scotus and Pierre d'Ailly. With such a philosophy the Czech evangelicals had little sympathy, and there was already developing at Prague a reaction in the direction of realism. This native tendency received a remarkable fillip when the philosophical writings of the greatest contemporary realist, John Wyclif, began about 1390 to trickle through to Prague. The power and breadth of Wyclif's philosophical system made a profound impression on Hus, who copied and annotated the *De materia et forma*, the *De ideis* and the *De veris universalibus*. It is clear from Hus's notes that it was Wyclif's attack on the nominalists which particularly excited his lively interest and approval, not because such views were entirely new to him, but because they powerfully confirmed the opinions which the Prague realists had already been developing.

With the advent of the new century Hus emerges as one of the acknowledged leaders of the Czech party in the university. In 1401 he was elected dean of the faculty of arts for the first time, and in the same year was ordained priest, a step which must not be regarded as merely normal routine, but as the consequence of a vital personal resolve resulting from a conviction of the importance of the priestly office based on a study of the scriptures. It has been mistakenly suggested that Hus's ordination was due to the influence of his reading of Wyclif. This theory is part and parcel of a much wider thesis—namely, that Hus throughout his career shows no originality at all, but that he is always merely the mouthpiece of Wyclif, and that the whole Hussite movement is due solely to the adoption in Bohemia of English Lollardy. In any attempt to estimate the historical significance of Hus such a theory is crucial. It is a theory which has been adopted and preached by many German historians, and it finds its most complete expression in a great work by Johann Loserth [*Hus und Wiclif*], in which, by setting out parallel passages from the writings of the two reformers, he endeavours to prove that there is very little in Hus's work that is not a copy or paraphrase of Wyclif.

There is no opportunity here to go deeply into this great

controversy, which is merely a scholastic form of the secular conflict of Slav and Teuton. It must suffice to say that there is, of course, no question that Wyclif profoundly influenced Hus and his fellow-reformers in Bohemia. Many passages in Hus's writings are admittedly almost verbal reproductions of Wyclif's words. Hus himself freely acknowledged his debt and his admiration. In his *Replicatio contra Anglicanum J. Stokes* he said:

> I am moved by his fame . . . I am moved by his writings, in which he strives with all his power to bring back all men to the law of Christ, especially the clergy, that by putting off the pomp and lordship of this world they may live with the apostles the life of Christ . . . I am moved by the love which he had to the law of Christ, for when asserting its truth he said that not one jot or tittle should fail.

And on another occasion Hus boldly declared: 'I would that my soul were there where the soul of Master John Wyclif is.' Hus took the lead at Prague as the defender of Wyclif against the condemnation of his works to the flames by the chapter in 1403; he was burnt at Constance as a follower of Wyclif. Nevertheless to assert that such quotation and such admiration are a proof of the complete dependence of Hus is quite unsound. All mediaeval scholars, and not least Wyclif himself, quoted freely, and often without acknowledgment. They regarded the intellectual progress of man, not from the competitive, individualistic point of view of our own day, but as a co-operative act, the accumulation of a vast mountain of truth and wisdom, where each newcomer merely added a little to the accomplishments of his predecessors. Hus was no mechanical echo of Wyclif. He owed as much and more to his own native forerunners, to Milíč, Matěj of Janov, Adalbertus Ranconis and a hundred others. His ideas on most of the vital points of reform were already well developed before ever Wyclif's theological works were known in Bohemia. It was not until 1402 or 1403 that Mikuláš Faulfiš, Jiří of Kněhnice and Jerome of Prague brought back to Prague the first copies of the theological works of Wyclif (as distinct from his purely philosophical works, which had been known some ten years before). And Hus in his tractates and sermons had shown that he had formed his characteristic opinions before that date. Again, Wyclif's

Trialogus was welcomed in Prague, not because its views were something new, but because it showed that Wyclif had been concerned with problems long familiar to the Bohemians, and that he had proposed remedies analogous to those they themselves had long been considering. Wyclif was to the Bohemian reformers not so much an inspiration and a prime mover as an ally, coming late into the struggle, but nevertheless gladly welcomed.

Moreover, it must be recognised that Hus never hesitated to disagree with Wyclif. There were many analogies between the state of religion in England and that in Bohemia. But there were also many differences. Again and again Hus cut across Wyclifite doctrine and practice. For example, he would never accept Wyclif's strict predestinarianism. (This may be one reason why Hussitism proved more acceptable to large numbers of people than did Wyclifitism.) Again, Wyclif had maintained that the sacramental acts of a priest in a state of mortal sin were without efficacy; Hus would not accept so revolutionary a doctrine, for he saw that it could only lead to anarchy. Perhaps the most striking evidence of Hus's independence of Wyclif is that Hus refused to follow him into eucharistic heresy. Wyclif's historical and logical examination of the doctrine of transubstantiation profoundly interested the Czech reformers, who were already prejudiced against the nominalistic acceptance of the doctrine on the basis of *credo quia impossibile*. In the first flush of enthusiasm for Wyclif two Prague scholars, Stanislav of Znojmo and Jakoubek (Jacobellus) of Stříbro, declared their acceptance of Wyclif's heretical doctrine of remanence. But the dangers of this path were quickly recognised; Stanislav soon recanted his error, and Jakoubek refrained from publishing his acceptance of remanence. As for Hus, he never wavered from orthodoxy on this point. He wanted to discriminate in his acceptance of Wyclif. To Wyclif's plea for a return to the primitive simplicity and poverty of the church Hus gave his full and admiring consent; but he would have nothing to do with remanence. Hus was neither a schismatic nor a heretic by choice, and perhaps he realised that to go off into the barren fields of eucharistic heresy would be to forfeit royal and popular support, even as had proved to be the case with Wyclif. But, more certainly, Hus was too good a Bohemian, too much at one with his Czech predecessors, to be willing to undermine the sanctity of the sacrament of the altar. The peculiar feature of the Bohemian reformation and what distinguishes it from all other forms of Protestantism is its fundamentally sacramental character. Every one of the Bohemian predecessors of Hus, but above all Matěj of Janov, had urged that the pre-eminent means of grace, the certain way of reformation, was the sacrament of the eucharist. The demand for frequent communion by the laity had become part and parcel of the atmosphere in which Hus was brought up. The chalice was to become the symbol of his followers after his death, and communion in both kinds for the laity was to become the fundamental doctrine of the church which was to bear his name. Therefore when Hus refused to dishonour the sacrament by following Wyclif into heresy, he is proving both his own independence and that he was a Bohemian first and a Wyclifite afterwards. He rivalled Matěj in the honour he paid to the eucharist, he advocated frequent communion, and seems at the end of his life to have approved of giving the cup to the laity.

Another aspect of Protestantism which shows very clearly the relation between Hus and Wyclif is their attitude to the state. Both men were patriotic, the children of the new nationalism. It was the work of Charles IV which had made the Bohemian reformation possible, and that reformation was as much a protest against foreign domination as against purely religious evils. Hus therefore eagerly read the political views of Wyclif, his plea for ecclesiastical independence and for the disendowment of the church by state action. Hus saw that many of his arguments applied with great force to Bohemia. King Václav had been declared deposed by Boniface IX in 1403, and the civil war between Václav and his brother Sigismund which followed, the invasion and ravaging of the country by foreigners, the ignominious imprisonment of his king, profoundly disturbed Hus. He felt that the condemnation of the Wyclifite articles in Prague had only been made possible by the triumph of Sigismund with papal and German support. To Hus as to Wyclif the reformation of the church and national independence were closely bound up together. But Hus would not accept Wyclif's remedy of salvation through the state, partly because at the moment, under the not very effective Václav, the administration was very weak, and partly because the whole of Hus's political thinking was democratic, not aristocratic, as Wyclif's had been. Thus the remedy which Hus proposed is not to be found in the crown or the nobility, but in the people; the reformation both in church and state is to be popular; the church is to be re-created by a return to the primitive system of election of priests and prelates by the people. Here lies perhaps the supreme importance of Hus, for in the century which followed his death, it was not kings such as Václav and Ladislas who were to save Bohemia from papal and German attack, but the Czech people, Calixtines, Taborites and the Unitas Fratrum, and their popular leaders, Rokycana, Žížka, Prokop, Chelčický and George of Poděbrady. Had Hus been a tame follower of Wyclif, the Bohemian reform movement would have been driven underground as effectively and quickly as Lollardy in England; without his statesmanship and foresight the glories and greatness of the period between the council of Constance and the battle of Mohács could not have been. The democratic character of Hus's teaching and work is implicit in nearly everything he wrote, and it has borne rich fruit. Of all the sects which sprang up in Bohemia after his death none is more noteworthy than that of the Unitas Fratrum, the Bohemian Brethren. In ideals and organisation it is not unlike English Quakerism, and it was the vehicle for the preservation of much that was best in Hus, and through it was continued a tradition amongst the Bohemian people of democracy and sweet reasonableness which notably reappeared in the Czechoslovak republic of our own day.

Of the career of Hus from his appointment to be the preacher at 'Bethlehem' there is not space to speak here in detail; the story has been excellently told in English by Creighton; what he wrote of course needs much expansion and some correction, but it still remains substantially the best account in English, for Creighton shared with Stubbs the great gift of being able to divine by historical instinct the truth of much that later research has laboriously established.

The years from 1402 to 1409 saw the completion of Hus's

academic career and the production of the *Super quattuor sententiarum*, a commentary on Peter Lombard which establishes for ever the real eminence of Hus as a theologian and philosopher. He is not, admittedly, in these respects in the very first rank, but the commentary is a work of very fine scholarship, both acute and profound, Hus can use with great skill and learning the fruitful instrument of scholastic dialectic, but he also knows its limitations. Again and again he breaks into some academic discussion to plead for a more modern and practical approach to theology. His sermons at 'Bethlehem' and at provincial synods during these years were bringing him not only a well-deserved reputation as a preacher, but also the enmity of those who had a vested interest in the superstitions which he roundly attacked.[6]

In 1409 Hus reached the pinnacle of his political influence, when, with the collaboration of the king and queen, the decree of Kutná Hora gave to the Czechs a superiority of votes in the university, and the indignant foreigners (with the exception of the Poles), deprived of that control which their numbers had never warranted, departed to establish the university of Leipzig. This action has an unpleasant flavour, for when a university ceases to be international it loses its universality, and undoubtedly the decree of 1409 has done much to exacerbate the Germans against the Czechs and has provided them with an argument of persecution. But the action is understandable, for to Hus the Germans were identified with nominalism and the burning of Wyclif's books, and he regarded them with some justice as the biggest obstacle to religious and national regeneration.[7]

The years from 1409 to 1412 were a period of crisis in the career of Hus, and also in the history of Bohemia and of the Christian church. On the one hand, the opponents of Hus, led by the regulars, were now so fearful of the consequences of the

[6] For example, he was sent on a mission to investigate the miraculous cures which it was claimed had been effected by the holy blood of Wilsnack, and in consequence he wrote a pamphlet entitled 'De sanguine Christi' to demonstrate the falsity of those claims.

[7] The following remark of Hus is worth recording: 'Christus scit, quod plus diligo bonum Teutonicum quam malum Bohemum, etiam si frater meus germanus.' Palacký, *Documenta*, 168.

reform agitation that they did not rest until they had secured the full co-operation of the curia in the war against Hus. In 1410 he was excommunicated by Zbyňek, the archbishop of Prague. But his contumacious refusal to desist from preaching in 'Bethlehem' appeared the more dangerous in that it immediately became clear that he had both royal and popular support. The people of Prague refused to allow the publication of the excommunication in the churches of the city, and the king, the queen and the nobility stood by him and worked on the curia to get the excommunication removed. But then Hus committed the unforgivable sin, for when Wenceslas Tiem came to Bohemia preaching an indulgence to all those who would contribute to the expenses of Pope John XXIII in his war with Ladislas of Naples, Hus led what rapidly became a national protest against being bled to pay for the private ambitions of a foreign prelate. In 1412 there issued therefore a bull of excommunication with aggravation. Hus appealed from John XXIII to Jesus Christ. The pope ordered the closing of 'Bethlehem' and put Prague under an interdict. Hus, heartbroken at the misery which his presence was bringing on his beloved city, but yet feeling like the hireling who deserts his flock when the wolf comes, left Prague.

The next two years were invaluable in the development of Hussitism. Hitherto the main efforts of the reformers had been concentrated in the capital city. But now Hus extended his influence in the country districts and lesser towns of Bohemia. Here he continued his preaching, and won over not only ordinary people, but also many of the clergy and the nobility. The centre of his activity was in the southern part of the country, where a few years later was to rise up the armed camp of Tábor, the citadel of Hussitism in its long struggle to avenge the death of its proto-martyr and to defend the principles for which he had stood.

The religious struggle in Bohemia had now become a matter of general European interest, and even Gerson was writing: 'Against this error there ought to rise up every authority, both spiritual and temporal, to its extermination, and that rather by fire and sword than by nice argument.' Indeed, Hus was a symptom of a religious discontent so widespread and so justifiable that constituted authority could not afford to ignore it. Therefore when the council of Constance met in November 1414, one of its avowed objects was the extirpation of heresy. If Hus could be got to Constance and made to confess to Wyclifite errors, it was hoped that the danger would be scotched. Hus, confident in Sigismund's safe-conduct '*transire, stare, morari et redire libere*', was eager to go to proclaim the truth to the assembled parliament of Christendom, and to help, as he hoped, in the inauguration of a general reform. But he walked into a trap, for the only pulpit he was to find at Constance was the martyr's pyre. John XXIII saw in Hus a great opportunity: he would proceed at once to the trial and condemnation of the arch-heretic in order to divert the attention of the council from his own unsavoury past and in order to earn the applause of Christendom for destroying the enemy of the faith. But the pope could not have destroyed Hus without the help of Sigismund, and Sigismund was willing to keep faith with Hus until he came to realise that Hus was the enemy not only of the unity of the church, but also of the unity of the empire. At the second hearing, in the presence of the emperor, Hus was accused of stirring up strife in Bohemia, and declared: 'There are many lords in Bohemia who love me, in whose castles I might have hid, so that neither Sigismund nor Václav could have compelled me', and one of his supporters, Jan of Chlum, said, 'What he speaks is true . . . There are many great lords who love him and would keep him in their castles as long as they chose, even against both kings together.' Sigismund heard these words—not heresy, but treason, and henceforth abandoned Hus to the council.

On 6 July 1415 Hus was solemnly condemned as a contumacious heretic in the cathedral church of Constance. He endured the slow and terrible solemnity of being ritually divested of all the vestments which symbolised his academic and priestly status, the paper cap was placed on his head, and the ultimate words were spoken: '*Commendamus animam vestram diabolo.*' The same day he was burned to death at the stake in the suburb of Bruël outside the walls of the city.

Immediately the news reached Bohemia there were riots against the clergy, and within two months of his death the lords of the country had formed an armed league to defend the liberty of the preachers. The death of Hus convinced the people of Bohemia that if they wished to preserve their national independence and live their own religious life they must fight. The Protestant schism had begun, and the first great breach had been made in the ecclesiastical unity of western Christendom.

XI

Jerome of Prague[1]

THE Protestant writers of Bohemia, Germany and England of the sixteenth century honoured three men as the first champions of the assault on Rome: John Wyclif, Jan Hus and Jerome of Prague. The first two have been much studied and today are reasonably well known. But Jerome is still little more than a name to any except his Czechoslovak fellow countrymen, even though John Foxe recognised his importance by giving a full account of 'the tragical and lamentable history of the famous learned man and godly martyr of Christ, Master Jerome of Prague, burned at Constance for like cause and quarrel as Master John Hus was'.[2] Jerome's friends

[1] BIBLIOGRAPHICAL NOTE. The main sources for the life of Jerome are: The proceedings at Constance against Jerome, to be found in Hardt, or, less completely, in J. D. Mansi, *Sacrorum conciliorum nova et amplissima collectio*, xxvii (1784).

[See also] *Documenta Magistri Joannis Hus*, ed. F. Palacký (Prague, 1869), and V. Novotný, *M. Jana Husi korespondence a dokumenty* (Prague, 1920).

The few survivals of Jerome's speeches are to be found in Höfler, *Geschichtschreiber der hussitischen Bewegung*, II (Jerome's 'Recommendatio artium liberalium') and Sedlak, ii (the defence of Realism, and the 'Utrum a parte rei universalia', both of 1409).

The fifteenth-century accounts of Jerome were collected and published by J. Goll, *Vypsání o Mistru Jeronymovi z Prahy* (Prague, 1878).

The most important recent publications are: Novotný, 'M. Jeronym Pražský', *Naše doba*, xxiii (1916), 641-9, 742-8; his article on Jerome in *Ottův slovník naučný*, xiii, 259-63 and F. M. Bartoš, 'Paměti M. Jeronyma Pražského', *Lumír*, xliv (1916), 289-302. See also J. Vlček, *Dějiny literatury české* (2nd ed, Prague, 1945), I. There is much about Jerome scattered through the learned volumes of Novotný and Kybal: *M. Jan Hus, jeho život a učení* (Prague, 1919-31). [An important contribution to our knowledge of Jerome's biography is to be found in F. Šmahel, *Jeronym Pražský* (Prague, 1966). See also P. P. Bernard, 'Jerome of Prague, Austria and the Hussites', *Church History*, xxvii (1958), 3-22; Šmahel, 'Leben und Werk des Magisters Hieronymus von Prag: Forschung ohne Probleme und Perspektiven?', *Historica* (Prague), xiii (1966), 81-111; R. N. Watkins, 'The Death of Jerome of Prague: Divergent Views', *Speculum*, xlii (1967), 104-29.]

[2] J. Foxe, *The Acts and Monuments of the Church*, ed. M. H. Seymour (London, 1838), pp. 313-18.

and enemies admitted that he was a more learned man than Hus; his career and his end were far more exciting than those of Wyclif; the appeal of his courage and example to partisans of the fifteenth, sixteenth and seventeenth centuries was very great, as the most cursory examination of the woodcuts in polemical books will show. But modern historians, with their greater interest in ideas than actions, have neglected Jerome, for it is probable that Jerome wrote little. Certainly the materials that have survived for an estimate of his opinions, or even for an account of his life, are few and intractable. An attempt to reconstruct his biography must be largely based on the proceedings of his trials for heresy, first at Vienna in 1410[3] and later at Constance. Such ecclesiastical judicial records are necessarily *ex parte* statements, and the dating of the notaries is such as to obscure more often than to clarify the chronology of Jerome's life. Apart from these substantial sources there are one or two letters written by Jerome, a few references to him in Hus's correspondence, in the muniments of the university of Prague and in the so-called 'Old Czech' Chronicle; as first hand evidence of his distinction as a schoolman, theologian and polemist we have only the brief but invaluable account of his speeches in the great philosophical tournament held in the university of Prague in 1409. The accounts of Jerome's life written by his friends and opponents within fifty years of his death add little but confusion to the story deducible from the contemporary materials. Much work has been done on Jerome by modern Czech historical scholars and to that work this article is greatly indebted, though I am attempting here an independent account of Jerome's life and opinions.

We know nothing of Jerome's birth or social provenance, except that as he was always known as 'Hieronymus Pragensis' or 'de Praga', he was presumably a native of that city. The bishop of Lodi, in the sermon preached at Constance just before Jerome's condemnation, describes both Hus and Jerome as 'lowborn, base, of unknown origin',[4] and that enemy of all things Czech, Dietrich Niem, says they were

[3] The proceedings of the Vienna trial have been admirably edited by Klicman: *Processus judiciarius contra Jeronimum de Praga.*

[4] Hardt, iii, 59: 'Viles, plebeii, infimi, ortuque ignoti'.

born of the lowest common rabble and were squat yokels. However, then becoming unworthy and poverty-stricken young clerics at the university of Prague, they were fashioned or instructed with respect to piety by noble masters and graduates—chiefly in sacred theology and the arts—of the German nation.[5]

But such evidence is of as little value as Palacký's unsubstantiated statement that Jerome was born of a gentle family.[6]

As he was old enough to be Hus's fellow student at the King Wenceslas College of the university[7] and young enough to have been his pupil, he must have been a year or two younger than Hus, who was born probably in 1369. Jerome was promoted bachelor of arts in 1398, and at the same time Hus applied on his behalf for leave to postpone his lectures for two years. It seems probable that he wanted this postponement in order to study abroad,[8] and that he used it for a visit to Oxford, which possibly lasted almost two years. Perhaps he may have gone on the benefaction provided in the will of the Czech polymath Vojtěch Raňkův (Adalbertus Ranconis), who in 1388 had left money to provide for Czechs who wanted to study in Paris or Oxford.[9] This visit to Oxford, which may be dated to 1399 to 1400, is of great importance, for it was the direct means of making Wyclif's most important theological writings known in Bohemia.[10] The promoters of the cause against Jerome at Constance alleged that

Jerome, going to the land of the kingdom of England, zealously sought out the books of John Wyclif, either himself or by others, and having found them, he copied them with singular delight with his own hand, and having thus copied them he brought and published

[5] Ibid., ii, 454. [The citations preceding and in this note, as well as notes 27 and 46, have been translated by Peter Brock.] 'De vilissimis plebeiis geniti, et rustici quadrati, tamen in universitate studii Pragensis tunc indigni et pauperes clericuli, pietatis intuitu informati seu instructi fuerunt per nobiles magistros et graduatos, maxime in sacra theologia et artibus, nacionis Germanicae.'

[6] Palacký, *Dějiny národu českého* (1908), iii, 33.

[7] 'Nos quoque bohemi iuvenes in Praga studentes cum Johanne Huss et Jeronymo, item cum Jacobello [Jakoubek of Stříbro] et Marco [Marek of Hradec] et aliis constudentibus morabamur in collegio Regis Wenceslai.' Quoted from Jerome-John's tractate against the Four Articles of Prague by Bidlo, *ČČM*, lxix (1895), 246.

[8] Novotný, *M. Jan Hus*, i, 64.

[9] Novotný, *Náboženské hnutí české ve 14. a 15. stol.*, p. 144.

[10] Wyclif was known as a Realist philosopher in Prague at least as early as 1390. Novotný, *M. Jan Hus*, i, 58.

these works of Wyclif in divers lands, and especially in the kingdom of Bohemia, asserting in the hearing of different trustworthy witnesses that these books ought to be kept and loved by all those who aspired to true knowledge and understanding.[11]

Nor did Jerome deny the fact, for in his reply to the charge that he had taught Wyclifitism in Bohemia, he said:

It is false that I taught heresies and errors from Wyclif's books. But I admit, that when I was a young man and full of zeal for learning I went to England, and hearing the fame of Wyclif, that he was a man of subtle and excellent genius, when I could get hold of copies of his *Dialogus* and *Trialogus* I transcribed them and brought them back with me to Prague.[12]

Thus came to Bohemia highly explosive material; the *Dialogus* and *Trialogus* were the products of Wyclif's most revolutionary years, the former being a plea for the secularisation of church property, and the latter a summary of many of his views on endowments, the friars, the church and the dogmatic sufficiency of the scriptures.[13] These ideas found a soil well prepared by thirty years of intense agitation by native Czech reformers, such as Milíč, Matěj of Janov, Vojtěch Raňkův, and Tomáš of Štítný, who even if they had never heard of Wyclif. had nevertheless reached much the same conclusions as he about the need for moral reform and spiritual regeneration in the church. Other Czech students, such as Mikuláš Faulfiš and Jiří of Knĕhnice, followed Jerome to England, copied and brought back Wyclif's works, so that at a time when Oxford denied Wyclif and Henry IV was persecuting his followers, Prague was becoming his devoted apostle. So quickly did the new cult become popular that as early as 1403, at the instigation of the cathedral chapter during an archiepiscopal vacancy,

at Prague in the College of King Charles in the Faculty room there was a full and general convocation of all the masters of the university of Prague. And there forty-five articles extracted from the books of John Wyclif of damned memory were publicly read and con-

[11] Additional articles of accusation, 27 April 1416, Hardt, iv, 649.

[12] Articles against Jerome and his replies, 27 April 1416, ibid., iv, 635.

[13] A. W. Pollard dates the *Dialogus* to 1379. *Dialogus*, ed. A. W. Pollard (London, 1886), p. xx. The *Trialogus* was probably written even later in Wyclif's life. It was edited by G. Lechler, Oxford, 1869.

demned by the masters, and the rector of the university commanded that no member of the university should thenceforward hold, teach or defend them.[14]

The rector at this time was Walter Harrasser, a Bavarian, and he undoubtedly received the support of the numerous German masters of the university, while the champions of Wyclif in this debate were the Czechs Štěpán Páleč, Stanislav of Znojmo and Jan Hus.

Jerome was not present at this debate, for his *ardor discendi* had led him away once more. At his trial in 1416 he said: 'when the articles were condemned [in 1403] I was then in Jerusalem.'[15] That is all that we know of that pilgrimage.

He reappears next at the university of Paris, where he resided from 1404 until 1406, and where he became master of arts. As master he lectured in the university, and, as became a devoted admirer of Wyclif, he took up a strongly realist position: the articles of accusation of Constance allege that he maintained that there is in the trinity a common essence besides the three persons (this was construed as quaternitarianism), and that the three persons are not the same person, but that each of them is God and there are degrees of perfection between them; he also platonically divided the human soul into three parts: memory, understanding and will; he also was accused of having said that God of his absolute power could have not begotten a son, and that all things that will happen are conditioned by necessity; more dangerously, he maintained that God cannot annihilate anything, a doctrine which is the basis of Wyclif's formal attack on the doctrine of transubstantiation.[16] Such doctrines were most unpopular in Paris, which had followed Occam and Buridan into the extremes of nominalism, of which Jean Gerson, chancellor of the university, was then the greatest exponent. Peter Pergoschl, one of the witnesses at the Vienna trial, testified that he had heard Jerome at Paris 'respond' scholastically to the question whether forms in the divine mind were formally and really distinct, and 'everybody was satisfied, but he added certain corollaries on which he was ordered to remain silent; the masters said to him: "Master, stop that, or else you

[14] Hardt, iv, 652. [15] Ibid., 643. [16] Ibid., 645.

will be led into saying something even less becoming." And he answered: "willingly". '[17]

Jerome's realism ultimately became too much for the Paris nominalists: 'At last, when he had become well known to the Paris masters, zealots for the Faith, and was held by them suspect of heresy, they, and especially that honourable man Jean Gerson, chancellor of the university, would have compelled him to retract his errors. But Jerome, warned by someone unknown, secretly fled from the city and the university.'[18]

From Paris Jerome seems to have gone to the university of Heidelberg, and to have resumed there his exposition of realist philosophy, with similar results. It is at Heidelberg that we first hear of his daring attempt to illustrate the mystery of the trinity by a diagram, portraying a shield, at the three points of which were written the words 'ice', 'snow' and 'water'. A bachelor of arts of Heidelberg who gave evidence against Jerome in Vienna in 1410 deposed in these words: 'He was arraigned on four articles before the bishop of Worms, but certain difficulties prevented his recantation.' The witness added that he was present at a four-day disputation in the new schools at Heidelberg, in which Jerome 'strove to argue for a realist logic, and to prove that universal reals ought to be predicated in propositions, and therefore he maintained that masters Occam, Maulfeld, Buridan, Marsilius of Inghen and their followers[19] were not dialecticians, but diabolical heretics'.[20] It was said that Jerome had to escape from Heidelberg as clandestinely as he did from Paris.

Jerome's zeal for learning, or perhaps his delight in disputation, was not yet sated, for apparently in this same year 1406 he went on from Heidelberg to the university of Cologne; there, as at Heidelberg, he had himself inscribed as a master of arts. His stay in Cologne could not have been long, for he was back in Prague in time to be enrolled as a master there in January 1407. There seems to have been some opposition to his admission as a master, because he only reluctantly took the usual

[17] Klicman, p. 32. [18] Hardt, iv, 681.

[19] That is, the protagonists of late mediaeval Nominalism.

[20] Klicman, pp. 12, 13. For other references to Jerome's stay in Heidelberg see Hardt, iv, 218, 681.

oath not to 'sow discord between the nations'.[21] This is interesting, as it seems to indicate that Jerome was already disturbed about the constitutional position in the university of Prague. The four 'nations' which composed it were the Bavarians, the Saxons, the Poles and the Czechs, and because the Polish nation was largely represented by Silesians, the Czechs were outnumbered by the Germans by three to one in all university business. Inasmuch as Germany, Austria and Poland had by the beginning of the fifteenth century universities of their own, it is probable that the actual numbers of the foreigners were decreasing, while those of the Czechs were rising. The sense of injustice of the Czech masters was further aggravated by a growing national self-consciousness and also because this national disparity was emphasised by the fact that most of the Czechs were realists, Wyclifites and reformers, and most of the Germans were nominalists, anti-Wyclifite and conservative.

Political developments helped to bring the matter of the university votes to a head. Since the election of Ruprecht Count Palatine as anti-emperor in 1400 Václav IV had ceased to be anything more than national king of the lands of the Bohemian crown, and was inevitably driven towards a more purely Czech policy. Moreover Zbyňek, the archbishop of Prague, had been brought by the wealthy clergy of Prague and his chapter to oppose the reformist party led by Stanislav, Páleč, Hus and Jerome. In the course of the year 1408 the archbishop's party won a minor triumph by compelling one of the reformers, Matěj (Matthias) of Knín, to 'purge himself' of the suspicion of having maintained that Wyclif was an *evangelicus doctor* and that the bread and wine of the eucharist remain after their consecration.[22] The archbishop, concerned that the country was getting an ill-fame for heresy, also secured a repetition of the condemnation of the forty-five Wyclifite articles by the Czech masters in May 1408, though the reformers were able to modify the condemnation in the sense that the articles were not to be taught 'in their heretical, erroneous or scandalous sense', and

[21] According to the deposition at Vienna of Nicholas Czungl (Klicman, p. 23).

[22] See the testimonies of Johann Schwab of Butzbach and Conrad Kreuzer at the Vienna trial (Klicman, pp. 16, 17).

that mere bachelors were not to have or to read the *Trialogus*, the *Dialogus* or the *De corpore Christi*.[23]

The reformers, discontented at this partial defeat, struck back by electing Matěj of Knín, so recently arraigned as a Wyclifite, as *quodlibetarius* for the ensuing year 1409. The *quodlibet* was an annual dialectical tournament, and to open the debate was a high honour. 'And because Knín was willing to dispute', said one of the witnesses at Jerome's Vienna trial, 'many masters, namely Walter Harrasser, master Peter Storch, and master Johann Hofman and others did not wish to attend the *quodlibet*, publicly saying that they would rather leave Prague than attend the *actus* of one suspect of heresy, but the king ordered the three nations by letter to attend on master Matthias.'[24]

The great debate, which apparently lasted some days, began on 3 January 1409. The question at issue was officially the validity of the realist thesis that 'universals' or 'qualities' have reality apart from and antecedent to the sensible individuals in which they inhere, as against the more recent nominalist thesis that only sensible individuals are real, and that qualities or 'universals' are merely 'names', the mere product of abstraction by mental process. But in fact the debate resolved itself into a defence of and an attack on Wyclif, the modern champion of realism; it was Czech against German, reformer against conservative. Its interest for our purpose is that it was Jerome who concluded the debate and stole all the thunder. His speech was hailed by the Wyclifites as a most eloquent and learned statement of their case; it became the basis of the charges made against him both at Vienna and at Constance. It has been preserved in many manuscripts and affords us today the chief means of assessing Jerome's opinions and his intellectual stature and importance.[25]

Knín opened the debate on the question 'whether the unchangeable highest good is the creator of the individual entities

[23] The articles of condemnation of 1416 say that Jerome was present at this famous meeting of the Czech masters in their house of 'the Black Rose' (Hardt, iv, 652).

[24] Klicman, pp. 16-17.

[25] For the debate see Novotný, *M. Jan Hus*, i, 303 ff. For Jerome's part in it see Hardt, iv, 637; Klicman, pp. 15, 17, 19, 20, 22, 24, 28, 32, 33; Hardt, iv, 649-50. For the Oxford letter see Klicman, pp. 15, 22, 28, 31-2, 34; Hardt, iv, 644.

of the universe'. We have no record of the course of the debate until its last day, when Jerome went into the pulpit and expounded the theme 'whether it is necessary to posit universals apart from things for the comprehension of the harmony of the world'.

He again used his favourite illustration of 'the shield of the Catholic faith' to demonstrate the unity of the three persons in the Godhead. He concluded the first section of his thesis with the declaration: 'They are not logicians, but diabolical heretics, who say that universals are mere names.' At this an aged and much-beneficed master, Blažej Vlk (Lupus), attempted a reply, which in turn prompted Jerome to his famous *Recommendacio artium liberalium.*[26] He began by pouring his scorn on those masters who had insulted:

Their mother, the faculty of arts and her remarkable son, the worthy master *quodlibetarius*, by refusing to attend until they were forced to do so; 'they are', he said 'men whose fame is in outward show, which if it is stripped away reveals their foulness, lasciviousness, simony, error and faithlessness, as robbers of the poor and sacrilegious. These are the people who, themselves heretics in life and morals, attempt to hide their shame by innumerable insults against the noble and great of this honourable city, not stopping short of accusation of heresy against our most holy Czech nation, though there is an ancient saying that no true Czech can be a heretic, as, it is well known, has been true from old time. If then, as Solomon says, a good name is to be preferred above precious ointment, in the name of immortal God I call on each and all of you who love the honour of our most glorious prince, King Václav, and of this realm, and who bear love towards the good name of this most holy city of Prague, that each and all of you, as is your duty, seek to preserve that good and excellent name, which has hitherto been ours throughout all lands, and that you do not believe these deceitful and treacherous liars who would corrupt that good name and shame the members of our holy Czech nation . . .

'What a mark of ignorance in our midst is it that there are some insignificant priests who in their lying sermons are foolish enough to say that there are in this city many heretics, whom they call Wyclifites! As for me, I admit before you all that I have read and studied the books of master John Wyclif, just as I have those of other

[26] Text in Höfler, ii, 112-28 (ascribed there to Hus).

doctors, and I admit that I have learnt much that is good from them. But God forbid that I should be so stupid as to take for truth everything that I have read in his books or those of any other doctor. For to the Holy Scriptures alone do I apply the honourable rule: This says that so it is, therefore it is true . . . Let foolish smatterers realise that gold and silver and precious stones are often buried in foul earth, which the ignorant man thinks no more valuable than any other muck . . . Who then, you young men, is he who should forbid you to get to know the wealth of truth in Wyclif's books? And therefore for my part I admonish you above all that you study his books, especially his philosophical books, often and diligently; and if you find in them anything which, because of the insufficiency of your tender years, you cannot understand, as may happen, lay it aside until you are of riper years. And if there is in them anything which seems to be contrary to the faith, do not conceal it and do not hold thereto, but the more gladly be obedient to the faith.'

Jerome then launched into a laudation of Knín's steadfastness under persecution, and was so carried away by his own enthusiasm that he left his prepared text and 'went up to where master Knín was sitting and stroked him by the beard, and said in the vulgar tongue: "Ecce bone puer, Sie sind die nach deinem Leben nachgangen und wolten dich tött haben von des Wikleph wegen, und des pist unschüldig; modo ubi sunt nunc, qui confuderunt te?" '[27] [Behold, my good boy, they are after thy life and they want to have thee out of the way on account of that Wyclif, and thou art guiltless of that. Where are they now who have confounded thee?']

And now, when all thought the proceedings were over and were preparing to depart, Jerome, with a characteristic sense of the dramatic, cried out: 'See, my dearest children, I will tell you news of master John Wyclif, who some say was burned and condemned by the Church.' And he pulled out a letter from the university of Oxford, to prove that he had not been burned or condemned; he read the latter, and finally he said: 'Is it likely that so grave a doctor should have been so treated?' And in conclusion he said: 'Would that God would grant that my soul were where Wyclif's is.'[28]

[27] This is the evidence at Vienna of Kasper Weinstein (Klicman, p. 28). It is interesting that Jerome spoke these words in German, not in Czech.

[28] Evidence of Henry of Aura (Klicman, p. 33). The same wish was said to have

Jerome was now at the height of his name and fame, and for as long as he remained in Prague it is he rather than Hus who seems to have taken the lead. Jerome followed up his dialectical triumph by fateful deeds. He and his like-minded fellow Czech masters determined to reverse the constitutional position in the university, and to persuade the king to give the majority of votes to the Czechs. The story of that revolution has been often told; here we are concerned merely with Jerome's part in it. The report of his defence at Constance indicates that the initiative was his, for he is alleged to have said that

when he saw how things were in the university, Jerome, together with master Jan Hus, with other noble men of Bohemia, . . . wishing to make a stand, went to the king of Bohemia that now is, telling him how things stood, arguing that these things were a bad example, and were leading to the destruction of the Bohemian language. And he persuaded master Jan Hus that in his Bohemian sermons he ought to tell the Bohemian people that they should no longer allow themselves to be thus treated by the Germans.[29]

The moment was indeed favourable. The cardinals of the rival popes, Gregory XII and Benedict XIII, were about to meet in order to end the schism, and Václav had promised them his neutrality, in the hope that the new pope would annul the deposition that Boniface IX had pronounced. As Zbyněk and the German masters were still loyal to Gregory and opposed to the neutrality declared by Václav, the king was the more ready to listen to the Czechs in their plea for a reversal of voting power

been expressed by Hus. This notorious Oxford letter (text in Höfler, *Concilia Pragensia,* p. 53) dated 5 Oct. 1406, was brought from England by Mikuláš Faulfiš and Jiří of Kněhnice, with a piece of the stone of Wyclif's tomb, in 1408. G. V. Lechler, *Johann von Wiclif und die Vorgeschichte der Reformation* (Leipzig, 1873), ii, 69, 72, and Novotný, *M. Jan Hus,* i, 313, n. 1, argue that it was completely genuine. But the accusers of Jerome at Constance said explicitly 'quondam literam falsificatam legit' (Hardt, iv, 644), which seems to give some colour to the story that a number of Wyclifites in Oxford purloined the university seal in order to give an appearance of authenticity to their manifesto, and to make it appear as an act of the whole University. Jerome in his reply at Constance said that 'nescit an fuit falsa, vel non. Fuit enim sibi data, dum esset in cathedra, per quendam iuvenem, ut eam publicaret. Quod dixit se fecisse'; that is, he did not claim that this was the first time he had seen the letter.

[29] Hardt, iv, 758. At Vienna Johann Schwab, Conrad Kreuzer, Johann of Vohburg, Nicolas Czungl and Johann Tesser all gave evidence that the initiative was largely Jerome's (Klicman, pp. 16, 18, 20, 23-4, 25).

in the university. But characteristically he wavered, first promising the German rector of the university and his colleagues that he would maintain the order established by Charles IV, and when Jerome, Hus and the Czechs arrived at Kutná Hora and tried to persuade Václav the king was moved with anger and said to Hus: 'You are always disturbing me, you and your companion Jerome; and if those whose duty it is do not see to it, I myself will see that you suffer in the fire.'[30] When the Czech delegation returned to Prague Hus fell ill and could take no part in the development of events, but nevertheless the political current was set in the Czechs' favour. There was at this time at Kutná Hora an embassy from Charles VI of France seeking Václav's co-operation in the policy of neutrality in the schism. Soon after his abrupt dismissal of the Czech masters Václav became convinced that the Germans were set against the policy of neutrality, and therefore on 18 January 1409, the king published the fateful Kutná Hora decree,[31] whereby

> in future the Czech nation in the university of Prague is to be admitted to three votes in all the councils, courts, examinations, elections, and all other official acts, . . . since it is unfitting and very improper that the Czech nation, the rightful heir of the Czech kingdom, should have, as hitherto, only one voice, and that the German nation, which has no right of citizenship in the land, should have three.

Strong in the support of the university he had thus gained, Václav four days later renounced his allegiance to Gregory XII.

The witnesses at the Vienna trial who had been present in Prague at this time were unanimous in their affirmation that Jerome had played a leading part in this business. On him certainly must rest part of the praise or blame for a decision 'whence' said the witness Johann Schwab, 'arose schism and discord among the nations at Prague',[32] the result of which was the departure of the German masters to Leipzig and elsewhere. Henceforth the university of Prague lost much of its international character and reputation, and became an instrument of national policy and the Hussite schism.

[30] This is the account given by John Náz (Naso) at Hus's trial at Constance, according to Mladoňovice, 'Relatio' (text in Palacký, *Documenta*, p. 282).

[31] Text in Friedrich, *Dekret kutnohorský*.

[32] Klicman, p. 16.

Archbishop Zbyněk somewhat forlornly tried to renew the war against the triumphant reformers by renewing, probably in March 1409, his order that all who possessed Wyclif's books should surrender them. His order was completely ignored, and five students appealed against it to the pope. Zbyněk endeavoured to enforce his will by a general excommunication of those who had disobeyed. It was later charged against Jerome that he was excommunicated on this occasion and had failed to seek absolution therefor. Whether he was in fact excommunicated by name is doubtful; he himself denied that he knew of it if he was. But the witness Czungl at Vienna testified that

he saw the archbishop's mandate to all parish priests in the city of Prague that they should denounce as excommunicate all those who did not surrender to the archbishop books containing Wyclif's errors before the Sunday next following. Later, one Sunday, he was present at the sermon preached by friar Peter of the Order of Preachers at St Clement's, and friar Peter said: 'Beloved children, at the command of our lord archbishop I excommunicate each and every one who has not surrendered Wyclif's books and books containing his opinions, in the vulgar tongue, "die Keczrey" (heretics), and all those who maintain that there is a universal man and a universal ass, and I would like to name them to you specifically, but I have been forbidden to do so by the magistrates.' The witness believes, but he is not certain, that the friar did name four specifically, namely, Hus, Jerome, Jesenice and Stanislav. And he says that he is not clear in his own mind whether he did name them, but that he would rather take his oath that he did name them than that he didn't, because after dinner, when Jerome was told about the excommunication, it was the general belief in the market-places even amongst the lay folk, that master Jerome would have dragged the friar out of his house and convent if a crowd of laymen and craftsmen, especially the cutlers, had not been present.[33]

On the whole it seems more likely that Jerome did not care rather than that he did not know about the excommunication, for when he was charged at Constance with having taken into his service Peter of Valencia, one of the five who had appealed from Zbyněk to the pope, he 'confessed that he had done what good he could to the said Peter, not because Peter had been

[33] Ibid., p. 23.

excommunicated, though he did know of the excommunication'.[34]

About the same time, just after Easter, 1409, Jerome renewed his public disputation with master Vlk, his opponent at Knín's *quodlibet*; again the topic was nominally that of 'universals' but in fact that of Wyclif; but before this debate was finished it was broken up by a written order from the archbishop.[35]

During the rest of 1409 Hus comes again to the front of the stage,[36] and Jerome disappears from our sight. If he had been in Prague at the time when Zbyňek imposed an interdict on the city and formally charged Hus with heresy before the inquisition, we should certainly have heard of him. Where he was we do not know, but he next appears in a new field, as full of indiscreet zeal as ever—at the court of Sigismund, king of Hungary, in Buda. Perhaps it was a real missionary zeal to spread reformist ideals which was for ever urging him on his loquacious travels, as Andrew of Grillemberg suggested in his official condemnation of Jerome at Vienna.

How long he had been in Hungary we do not know, but on 20 March 1410 we find him addressing

> the most serene prince and Lord Sigismund, king of the Romans and of Hungary, in the royal chapel of the castle of Buda, and he a layman in layman's dress, with a long beard, in the presence of the lord king and of many reverend fathers, bishops and other prelates, and of other persons of diverse estates, publicly preached the errors of John Wyclif and many other scandalous and erroneous things, and also heresies about the sacrament of the altar, and other things against the clerical estate and offensive to pious ears, from which might ensue seditious and popular commotions against the clergy by means of the temporal lords.[37]

Jerome later replied to the charge that he, a layman, had preached a sermon by saying that this was not a sermon but an

[34] Hardt, iv, 642.

[35] The date and the circumstances are given in the evidence of Achacius Chenczl at Vienna (Klicman, 26). The text of Jerome's thesis is printed by Sedlák, ii, 229-58.

[36] Hus was elected rector of the reformed university in October 1409.

[37] Additional articles of accusation, 27 April 1416 (Hardt, iv, 673). The Vienna witnesses give no support to the charge that he preached eucharistic heresy at Buda.

'address' (*collacio*).[38] But whatever he called it, he took a text: 'A new commandment I give unto you', which he made the basis for the Wyclifite thesis that the present state of clerical morality demanded that the state should interfere to restore it to order and virtue. But Sigismund was as angry with Jerome as the prelates, and 'master Jerome was handed over as a prisoner to the archbishop of Esztergom on the authority of the king of Hungary by reason of certain letters which the archbishop of Prague sent to the king of Hungary, and so the king ordered Jerome to be sent to the archbishop of Prague. And therefore he was handed over to a certain knight who was to escort him to Prague.'[39] Jerome at Constance gave this version of his imprisonment:

Nor was I expelled from Hungary, but by reason of a letter of the archbishop of Prague of happy memory, which was written against me falsely, I was handed over to the archbishop of Esztergom, who entertained me kindly [*pie*] for a fortnight, and then the king directed me to a certain baron, and set me completely free, without security.[40]

We have no evidence that Jerome and his escort ever reached Prague; there is no sign of his having been there when Zbyněk solemnly burnt Wyclif's books in June 1410. The next place where Jerome appears is Vienna. To that town news of Jerome's 'collation' and imprisonment in Buda had come during the summer. Jerome heard that he was being defamed, and therefore boldly decided to go to Vienna to answer his accusers face to face.[41] He arrived in the city before the end of August,[42] and after a period of liberty which he spent in conversations with members of the university he was arrested and imprisoned by the official of the inquisition on the orders of the '*scriba causarum*' of the consistory court of the archbishop of Passau.[43]

On 29 August 1410, in his own house, Andrew of Grillem-

[38] Examination of 23 May 1416 (Hardt, iv, 753); Berchtold of Ruchwoser's evidence at Vienna (Klicman, p. 21).

[39] Evidence at Vienna of Johann Stuckler (Klicman, p. 30).

[40] Hardt, iv, 636.

[41] At the beginning of the Vienna proceedings Jerome said: 'I have come twenty-four miles to the venerable doctors and masters of this kindly university of Vienna because I heard that I was defamed amongst them' (Klicman, p. 4).

[42] Not December, as the articles of accusation said (Hardt, iv, 638).

[43] Hardt, iv, 638, 682. The diocese of Vienna was in the province of Passau.

berg, canon and official of the consistory of Passau, opened the trial of Jerome as one 'defamed in respect of certain articles contrary to the catholic faith and others which had been condemned in holy general councils and to which John called Wyclif had adhered'. As assessors Grillemberg had four professors, four doctors of canon law, and 'other masters, bachelors, and scholars of the university' of Vienna. Johann Gwerleich, bachelor of canon law, was appointed '*procurator fiscalis*' to prosecute the case. Jerome refused to have an advocate and swore on the gospels to tell the truth.[44] Then the forty-five Wyclifite articles, already condemned in Prague, were read out; some of them Jerome acknowledged as true, but most he denied having taught: for example, Jerome affirmed his orthodox faith in the matter of transubstantiation and affirmed his belief that the sacraments of a priest in mortal sin were valid; he denied that he had ever opposed auricular confession or said that God must obey the Devil, that an evil or 'foreknown' pope had no power, or that no pope should be recognised after Urban VI. Similarly he professed his orthodoxy about excommunication, church property, the right to preach, tithes, the vicariate and decretals of the popes, the supremacy of the Roman church, indulgences, reservations and the relations of state and church.[45]

In addition to the forty-five Wyclifite articles, twenty-two further articles were then charged against him. He was accused of having said that Wyclif was 'the evangelic doctor and destined for eternal life'; that 'in the mind of God there are several formal entities, which are both formally and really distinct'; he was charged with being an excommunicate and a perjuror,[46] with having, when in Hungary, denied the authority of the evangelists Luke and Mark, and having attacked the morals and immunity of the clergy; 'he asserted that every secular prince ought to rule the clergy'; that he had 'commended the life, morals, behaviour, teaching and learning of men vehemently suspect of heresy, such as masters Stanislav

[44] Klicman, p. 2. [45] Ibid., pp. 6, 7.

[46] The perjury consisted in having disturbed the harmony of the 'nations' in the university of Prague contrary to his oath on admission as a master to preserve it. [The Latin citations translated above run as follows:] 'doctor evangelicus et ad eternam vitam deputatus'; 'in mente divina plures essent formalitates formaliter et realiter distincte.'

[of Znojmo], Štěpán Páleč, Jan Hus, Marek of Hradec and many others in Prague'.[47]

To this second set of charges Jerome replied that it was not his business to say whether a man was damned or saved; if the church had condemned Wyclif, he agreed that he is condemned; he had called him 'evangelical' because he has written of the gospels, but had never said Wyclif was a saint. As to having taught that universals are present in the divine mind, he said that he had been dealing with the question scholastically and formally. He also replied that he knew nothing evil of Hus, and as to Stanislav, Páleč and the rest, let them answer for themselves, but he neither knew nor had heard any evil of them.[48] Further, Jerome denied that he had ever been excommunicated. The other additional articles he flatly denied.[49]

Gwerleich then asked for an adjournment until 2 September, when witnesses would be heard to prove the truth of the articles Jerome had denied.[50] On that day evidence was taken from fourteen witnesses, some of whom gave evidence of his having maintained realist positions at Paris, Heidelberg and Cologne; the majority of the witnesses testified as to Jerome's part in Knín's *quodlibet*, the excommunication of 1409, and the passing of the decree of Kutná Hora. The rest of the evidence was largely concerned with Jerome's recommendation of Wyclif and his preaching and imprisonment in Hungary.[51] The whole proceedings as recorded in the text published by Klicman are not only of great value for the chronology of Jerome's life and for his international reputation, but as an example of an examination for heresy in a court which was a curious mixture of an archbishop's consistory and a university court of discipline.

At this session of 2 September, on the petition of the procurator fiscal, Jerome gave an undertaking, not on oath, that he would not leave Vienna on pain of excommunication.[52]

On 5 September the hearing was resumed to take the evidence of one more witness, Berchtold Ruchwoser of Regensburg, professor of theology, of the order of the Augustinian Eremites. He deposed that Jerome had told him vaguely that

[47] Klicman, pp. 5, 9. [48] Ibid., p. 8. [49] Ibid., p. 10.
[50] Ibid. [51] Ibid., pp. 12-24. [52] Ibid., p. 11.

in his 'collation' at Buda he had 'spoken of the status of the clerical and secular power', and that he, Ruchwoser, had when on a visit to England heard that the archbishop of Canterbury had exhumed Wyclif's corpse[53] *propter hereticam pravitatem*.[54]

In the meantime news of Jerome's plight had reached Prague, and had impelled the university of Prague to write on 3 September to the magistrates of Vienna that

> this unforeseen misfortune which has befallen the honourable man, master Jerome of Prague, master of the universities of Paris, Cologne, Heidelberg and our own, has brought sadness to our hearts and affliction to our minds. Wherefore we humbly ask of your prudence that you deign to look graciously on the innocence of master Jerome and protect him from the insults of his enemies, believing us that he has conducted himself from his youth in those universities praiseworthily in his acts, learning and morals.[55]

It is noteworthy that the university of Prague thought it would be more efficacious to write to the city fathers of Vienna than to the university.

At the hearing of 5 September the court had adjourned for a fortnight, but Gwerleich had thought it prudent to ask that Jerome be kept in custody 'because Jerome said that these postponements gravely affected his position in Vienna and his affairs elsewhere were being neglected'. But Jerome strongly protested, and was therefore allowed to remain at liberty on renewing his undertaking not to leave Vienna until the case was ended.[56] But Jerome preferred not to wait; within a week of having given his promise, he fled from Vienna *clam, furtive et contumaciter*, to Bítov on the southern borders of Moravia. When he was later charged at Constance with having thereby made himself liable to excommunication and the penalties of perjury, he denied the jurisdiction of the official of Passau, and added: 'I did not flee contumaciously, but I was unwilling to remain to suffer violent treatment, nor was I bound to do so.'[57] He seems to have suffered no qualms of conscience, for on 12

[53] Ruchwoser was anticipating: the council of Constance ordered Wyclif's corpse to be exhumed and burned on 4 May 1415; this injunction was carried out by bishop Fleming in 1428.

[54] Klicman, p. 21.

[55] Text in Palacký, *Documenta*, p. 408.

[56] Klicman, pp. 11-12.

[57] Hardt, iv, 638.

September he wrote from Bítov an insulting letter 'to my venerable father, lord, and master the official of the church of Passau', saying that he was safe and happy among his friends in the castle of Bítov,

> at his service in all things . . . but, if you love me, don't ask me to stand alone among so many hundreds of enemies . . . Truly my soul like a sparrow has escaped from the snare of the fowler; the snare was broken, but we have been freed. Truly I thank you, and thank you again. Send the witnesses to Prague, and there I will conduct the case with them; or if you prefer it, we will take the case to the Curia, where they are as well known as I am in Prague. I am pleased to inform you that I have just been to your church in Laa,[58] and had a talk there with the schoolmaster and the notary of the town, so you see I don't forget your kindness, and I will be of service to your or yours whenever I can.[59]

This insult to his Viennese judges stood Jerome in very ill stead later, for some of them[60] were at Constance, and made sure that his imprisonment there should be a snare from which he could not escape.

But Grillemberg did not delay to pursue the cause; on 20 September a citation to Jerome to appear within eight days to answer a charge of contumacy, if he could, was posted on the doors of the cathedral of Vienna.[61] As he failed to appear the official proceeded to final judgment, and solemnly pronounced Jerome guilty of perjury, excommunicate, and vehemently suspect of heresy.[62] The sentence was published in Vienna, Prague and Cracow. Jerome admitted at Constance that he knew of its publication in Prague, but it does not seem to have worried him,[63] or prevented his participating in the services and sacraments of the church.

[58] Andrew of Grillemberg was incumbent of Laa in upper Austria.

[59] Text of letter in Hardt, iv, 683; Klicman, pp. 34-5; and Palacký, *Documenta*, p. 416.

[60] Nicholas of Dinkelsbühl, S.T.P., Peter of Pulka, S.T.P., and Caspar Maiselstein, Doctor of Canon Law.

[61] Hardt, iv, 638-9: Klicman, pp. 35-6, gives the text of the citation.

[62] It is difficult to date the excommunication definitely. The text printed in Klicman, pp. 36-9, directed 'to all to whom these presents may come', is dated 22 Oct. 1410: that printed in Palacký, *Documenta*, pp. 417-20 is directed to Zbyněk, archbishop of Prague, and is dated 30 Sept. 1410. The two texts differ in detail throughout and in the concluding paragraphs substantially.

[63] Hardt, iv, 639.

What Jerome did after his escape to Bítov does not appear. Throughout the rest of 1410 and the whole of 1411 there is very little trace of him, though there are indications that he was in Prague,[64] where stirring events were afoot. Hus's enemies had secured his excommunication by the pope's delegate, Cardinal Colonna, in February, and that excommunication had been published in all the churches of the city except those of the Teutonic knights and in Kříšt'an of Prachatice's church of St Michael. This attack on one who was rapidly becoming a national hero led to a violent outburst of anticlericalism; the mob interrupted church services and insulted the clergy, and on 28 April 1411 the king was induced to order the confiscation of all clerical incomes in the city. Zbyněk replied by excommunicating all who carried out the royal order and when the attacks on the clergy grew more violent the archbishop laid the city under an interdict and King Václav promptly forbad its observance. It is probable that Jerome had a hand in these events. At Constance he was accused of having taught and preached in the chapel of 'Bethlehem' at Prague that excommunication by pope or prelate is invalid except against one previously excommunicated by God, and that the pope has acted beyond his powers in forbidding preaching except in cathedral, collegiate, claustral and parochial churches, 'and in many places and towns in the diocese of Prague priests were forced by the temporal power to celebrate and hold services despite the interdict placed on Prague by apostolic authority'. And another article says: 'Jerome signed and posted up in many places a notorious libel against the lord Zbyněk, archbishop of Prague, and once, while Hus was preaching, Jerome stuck his head out of a window of the chapel of Bethlehem and abused Zbyněk of happy memory most gravely before a great crowd of people, and stirred up the people against him.'[65] Jerome admitted he had published a *querela* against the archbishop for his letter to Hungary which had led to Jerome's imprisonment there.[66]

The year 1412 was important in the history of Bohemia and

[64] If Novotný is right about the date of Jerome's conditional absolution by Kříšt'an of Prachatice.

[65] Hardt, iv, 670.

[66] Ibid., iv, 640-1.

of Jerome because it saw the crisis of the papal indulgence, which played almost as important a part in the Hussite Reformation as Leo X's indulgence did in the Lutheran. It was inevitable that an institution in which theory and practice were as patently divorced as they were in the case of indulgences should have in both cases provided one of the most effective bases for attack on ecclesiastical practice. The occasion of the indulgence of 1412 was Pope John XXIII's war with Ladislas of Naples; that war was a political struggle for the control of central Italy, one in which the Czech nation and king had no kind of interest. It is not surprising that Hus and Jerome found wide support in the attack they made, not only on the practices of the papal collector Wenceslas Tiem but also on the whole principle and theory of indulgences.

The sale of the indulgence began in Prague in May 1412; on the 29th of that month Hus formally condemned it in a sermon in 'Bethlehem'. On 17 June a disputation was held in the university in which Hus opened the discussion[67] and Jerome concluded it. The 'Old Chronicler' says:

Master Jerome entered on a very long speech and spoke eloquently. When he had finished he jumped from his place and said they should go to the magistrates and tell them that the indulgences were false; and the great majority of the students rose up and wanted to accompany him; with great difficulty the rector of the university was able to pacify them by a few well-chosen words. But master Jerome addressed master Marek (the rector) in the Czech language, saying: 'Listen, master Marek! you won't risk your neck for me, but I would be willing to risk mine for you.' And then he continued in Latin again . . . And when the disputation was ended many more of the students followed Jerome than Hus, for the speech of Jerome had pleased them more.[68]

Excited perhaps by this success Jerome flung himself into the

[67] The question he proposed was 'Whether according to the law of Christ it is lawful and expedient for the honour of God and the salvation of the people and for the well-being of the realm, for the faithful to approve the papal bulls about raising the Cross against King Ladislas.'

[68] The Czech text of the 'Old Chronicler' is quoted in Palacký, *Dějiny národu českého*, v, 292, n. 202. The text of Hus's speech has been preserved (Hus, *Opera omnia*, i, 174-89), but not that of Jerome. It is likely that Jerome had a faculty for exciting the passions of his hearers that was lacking in Hus's more sober treatment of indulgences.

agitation against the indulgence with great energy and hardihood. Layman as he was, he was now preaching continually[69]; perhaps in the excitement of the anticlerical campaign he committed himself in practice to the revolutionary doctrine of the priesthood of every Christian man.[70] He also used his talent for pasquinade and popular verse in the interest of what was rapidly becoming a popular faction. There is one series of charges made against him, which though they may be exaggerated and though Jerome denied them, yet undoubtedly have an element of truth in them. Their gist is that 'the said Jerome made or procured canticles and songs in the Bohemian tongue, containing in sense and effect the words of the canon prescribed for the consecrating of Christ's body, which mechanics learnt and sang . . . and he asserted that laymen and women of the Wyclifite sect who firmly held the teaching of Wyclif, could make [*conficere*] Christ's body, baptise, hear confessions, and perform all the other sacraments, provided they uttered the appropriate words'.[71] Jerome was well on the way to the establishment of an autonomous Protestant community.

Nor did his zeal stop at words. 'The same Jerome publicly boxed the ears of Beneš of Boleslav, a preacher of the order of the friars minor, in the street and in the presence of many. And drawing a knife, he would have struck him with it, and probably have killed him or wounded him fatally had he not been stopped by a certain master Zdislav of Zvířetice.' To this charge Jerome replied that 'when this friar spoke impudently to certain nobles, he, Jerome, reproved him, and Beneš then insulted him, so he struck him lightly on the mouth with the back of his hand'.[72] There was also probably some basis of truth in the charge made against Jerome at Constance that he had a hand in the notorious demonstration organised by Vok of

[69] 'Dixit et predicavit prefatus Hieronymus in sua nequicia persistens, errores Wicliff et Johannis Huss seminando et defendendo, quod nulla potestas dandi indulgencias residet apud papam, neque episcopos.' Hardt, iv, 670.

[70] 'Hieronymus . . . asseruit . . . quod licitum est cuicumque laico literato, vel alias intelligenti, ubique et in quolibet loco, sive in ecclesia sive extra, et sine pape, episcopi, curati, aut cuiuscumque alterius licencia, predicare verbum dei; prout idem Hieronymus pluries in diversis locis, diœcesibus et regnis fecit publice, tam in Bohemia, quam in Moravia, cum longa barba publice et notorie laicus existens.' Hardt, iv, 673.

[71] Hardt, iv, 669. [72] Ibid., 641-2.

Valdštejn, probably in August 1412, when a mob of 'Wyclifites, armed with staves and swords, conducted a cart on which stood a student dressed as a harlot with the papal bull hanging round his neck, importuning passers-by to buy indulgences by her smiles and lewd words. As the procession went from the Small Side of Prague by the archbishop's palace and through the streets of the Old Town past the king's palace, the escorting crowd shouted out that these were the bulls and indulgences of a heretic and a ruffian. Finally, the bulls were burnt in the middle of the market place of the New Town.'[73]

In such an atmosphere tragedy could not lag far behind comedy. On 10 July 1412 there occurred what appears to have been an organised heckling of the preachers of the indulgence; there is some reason to believe that Jerome may have organised it. Three youths, Martin, Jan and Stašek, who had been the interrupters at the church of the Hradčany, the Týn church and at St James's were arrested and thrown into the prison of the Old Town. Hus and a deputation from the university went to the magistrates, taking the responsibility for the campaign against indulgences on themselves, and got a promise that the young men would not be ill used. But the next morning they were hastily sentenced and beheaded.[74] When the news became known a body of men from the university came and reverently bore the bodies amidst a weeping concourse to the chapel of 'Bethlehem', intoning the antiphon '*Isti sunt sancti*'. There they were placed, and the next day they were honoured with the rites due to martyrs. At Constance Jerome was accused of having been the prime mover in these events, with what justice it is impossible to say, though the procession and the ceremony are in accord with his humour.[75]

Jerome carried the campaign of physical violence against the preachers of indulgences into the provinces:

In August 1412 in Jindrichův Hradec where Jan of Vysoké Myto and Beneš the altar priest of St Michael's in Opatovice had come to

[73] Ibid., 672.

[74] See Novotný, *M. Jan Hus*, ii, 116 ff. The execution could not be carried out in the usual place, under the pillory, because of the hostility of the common people to the magistrates.

[75] Hardt, iv, 676.

the parish church to publish the indulgences granted by Pope John XXIII, the aforesaid Jerome of Prague, as soon as he heard of it, inspired by the devil, entered the parsonage accompanied by many armed accomplices and with wrathful countenance and angry heart he burst out with these or some such words: 'Get out, you liars, with your lies. For your master the pope is a liar, a heretic, and a usurer, and has no power to grant indulgences.' Then they rushed at Jan and Beneš with arms in their hands, and with threats forced them to flee from the house to the parish church, . . . and from the church they drove them to the outer parts of the town.[76]

A month later we find Jerome extending his campaign to an attack on relics. On 29 September 1412 Jerome was present, perhaps by design, in the Carmelite church of St Mary of the Snows, when a dispute arose between a friar who was soliciting payment for displaying the relics of the friary and a citizen, who roundly declared the relics to be a fraud and then trampled the shrine and relics underfoot. Jerome joined in the affray that followed, snatching a sword from the hands of a rustic and wielding it with such effect that he captured three of the friars. Two of these he handed over to a magistrate, the third he kept prisoner in his own house for some days.[77]

Jerome's opinions were rapidly becoming more and more radical. Indulgences had led him to attack the power of the pope; relics had brought him into conflict with the mendicants; it was not far to a direct assault on monasticism. It is probably to this period that belongs an incident recorded in the Constance articles: 'The same Jerome induced a friar of the Order of Preachers of the monastery of St Clement of Prague to apostasy. With him and other armed men he came in to the prior and ordered the friar to put off his monastic habit, and there Jerome clad him in secular clothes. And he afterwards supported him in his apostasy, but later, as a result, he was drowned.' Jerome replied that he denied the article in respect of the armed men. 'But', he said, 'I admit that I was moved by pity, because the prior did not provide him with necessities;

[76] Ibid., 671.

[77] The incident has been reconstructed by Novotný (*M. Jan Hus*, ii, 160-1) from the charge made at Constance and Jerome's reply thereto (Hardt, iv, 641, 751, 752) and the dramatic narrative of Stephen of Dolan, 'Antihus' (in B. Pez, *Thesaurus anecdotorum novissimus* (6 vols., 1721-3), iv, 382).

and the boy placed his cowl at the prior's feet and left voluntarily. He was drowned accidentally while bathing.'[78]

We hear nothing more of Jerome for six months. Whether he shared Hus's voluntary exile from Prague in October 1412 we cannot say. He next appears in Cracow in March 1413. There was nothing of the fugitive about his presence there, for he came at the invitation of King Władisław Jagiełło of Poland and his famous cousin Witold, grand duke of Lithuania. What we know of the event is told in a remarkable letter of Albert bishop of Cracow written to Wenceslas Králík, patriarch of Antioch, on 2 April 1413.

Jerome of Prachatice [*sic*], who was invited here, as he himself said, by our lord the king and his brother Duke Witold (our pious and devout king was ignorant of what he was), came here in person, and the first day he appeared with a beard, but the second day, he appeared without a beard, in red tunic and hood lined with grey fur, and showed himself off before the king, the queen and a crowd of princes, barons and nobles. Though he stayed only a few days he caused a greater commotion among the clergy and people than has ever happened before in the diocese in human memory. And when he came to be examined before me as ordinary of the place, in the presence of the metropolitan of this province [the archbishop of Gniezno] and of the reverend father Bernardo bishop of Castello, nuncio of the apostolic see, and a great assembly of doctors of canon law, masters of theology and masters of arts, there were many and various disputations. And when I questioned him about those articles of the condemned Wyclif, he replied negatively to each of them execrating them and professing the catholic faith in all things. Finally he was sent back to his native place, there to work and till the earth in his own country for our land seems to be too arid to receive his seed and bear fruit, because the poor people [*plebicula*] cannot understand the teaching of so great a philosopher, much less the land of the Lithuanians and Russia.[79]

Jerome was not to be deterred from his mission. At this time Witold of Lithuania was seeking some means of reconciling his Orthodox subjects in White Russia and Ruthenia, and he found in Jerome a willing helper in this task. Therefore in April 1413 Jerome accompanied Witold and a great army on a journey to White Russia. When they arrived at Vitebsk two

[78] Hardt, iv, 642. [79] Palacký, *Documenta*, p. 506.

processions came to welcome the prince, one of Dominican friars, bearing flags and relics, the other of Orthodox clergy bearing their relics and icons; 'and Jerome, ignoring and spurning the procession of the Christian friars, went towards that of the Ruthenian schismatics, and there, in the presence of four or five thousand people, he knelt down and venerated the icons of those infidel and schismatical Ruthenians'. Also at Pleskov (Pskov) 'he not only personally entered the church or synagogue of these Ruthenian infidels during the time of their perverse sacrament, but in the presence of faithful Christians standing there, and in contempt of the keys and of the Christian religion, . . . he knelt down and there openly, publicly and notoriously adored their so-called sacrament'.[80] Witold and the bishop of Wilno asked Jerome his opinion about the necessity of rebaptising Orthodox Christians, and he replied that all that was necessary for their admission into the church was simply that they should be instructed in the Christian faith.[81] The fame of Jerome's activities in White Russia soon spread throughout Poland, Bohemia, Moravia and Austria.[82]

During the early months of 1414 Jerome was in Prague while Hus continued his work of preaching and writing in the provinces. Perhaps because Hus's moderating influence was removed Jerome took the lead in a number of demonstrations of which the object was now the crucifix. These are the specific charges as they were formulated at Constance:

On the Saturday before Palm Sunday [31 March 1414] in the monastery of the Friars Minor of St James at the desire and by the instructions of Jerome a certain smith, a Wyclifite, of Poriči in the New Town of Prague, went up to the crucifix during the sermon, and plastered it with human dung, saying that it was heresy to portray the image of the Crucified. The man was arrested, and admitted that he had been induced to do this by Jerome.

At the procuration of Jerome, a certain layman of the sect of the Wyclifites, on Good Friday [6 April 1414], in the monastery of the blessed Virgin Mary in the Desert, fouled the cross, which it was the custom to venerate, with dung.

[80] The only source for these events is the articles of accusation: Hardt, iv, 677-80. He was even charged with having been richly paid for his favour to the Orthodox Christians of White Russia. Ibid., iv, 643.

[81] Jerome's reply, ibid., 643. [82] Ibid., 680.

One day in May of the year 1414 he went to the monastery of the friars minor of St James, in the Greater City of Prague, and attacked the wooden image of the Crucified which stood in the corner opposite the house of one called Kreisse, to which much people were wont to come to remember the passion of Christ, and he fouled it all over with human dung and filth, saying that it is heretical to depict the image of the Crucified or of any other saint.[83]

That there was such an outbreak of iconoclasm is probable; it is impossible to control the statement made by the prosecution at Constance that Jerome played a leading part in it.

In November 1414 the council of Constance was begun, and from that time Jerome's history is bound up with that of the council, one of whose purposes was to eradicate heresy. It is probable that if Jerome had been content to stay at home he would have been preserved to play a leading part in the Hussite wars, for he was still little more than forty years old. But he had promised Hus before Hus left for Constance that he would come to aid and comfort him there.[84] When he heard that Hus was imprisoned at Constance he came in fulfilment of his promise, prepared to defend his faith and to pay the penalty if he should be found to have taught anything heretical or erroneous.[85] He arrived on 4 April 1415, but was at once advised by his friends there to leave if he did not want to follow Hus into prison. He therefore retired a few miles from the city to Überlingen, where on 7 April he composed a letter addressed to the council, affirming his readiness to defend his teaching before them, and demanding a safe conduct.[86] This document he had posted on the doors of the churches and the cardinals' lodgings in Constance.[87] On April 9 a group of Bohemian lay delegates to the council published an open letter testifying to the fact that Jerome had asked for a hearing and a safe conduct and had been refused it[88]; with this letter to justify him, Jerome, with greater prudence than courage, set off home. Two days later, 11 April 1415, a congregation of the deputies of the four nations of the council granted a safe conduct to Jerome, which, however merely[89] guaranteed him safety 'as far as in us lies and

[83] The only source is the articles of accusation (ibid., 674-5).

[84] Ibid., 759-60. [85] Ibid., 684-5. [86] Ibid., 103.

[87] Ibid. [88] Ibid., 685-6.

[89] 'A violencia, iusticia semper salva, omnem tibi salvum conductum nostrum,

orthodox faith demands'. Six days later, on 17 April, the sixth general session of the council cited Jerome to appear within fifteen days to answer as one suspect of teaching many errors; if he did not appear justice would be done in default.[90] The next day Michael de Causis published the citation at the Minorite Friary and at St Stephen's and St Mary's churches in Constance.

Meanwhile Jerome was on his way through Bavaria, making for Bohemia; but on either 24 or 25 April he was arrested by the castellan of Hirschau, and handed over to John, duke of Bavaria and count palatine, who took him to Sulzbach and wrote to the council to report his capture.[91] But before the letter arrived the citation had run out and proceedings against Jerome for contumacy were begun at the seventh general session of 2 May, and the president of the council, the cardinal of Ostia, gave orders for a new citation and further process.[92]

When it later received the palatine's letter the council wrote back instructing him to bring his prisoner to Constance. On 23 May 1415 'Duke John sent master Jerome bound to Constance. His brother, Lewis duke of Bavaria, led him through the whole city to the refectory of the Friars Minor in Constance where the princes and priests were waiting for his arrival. Master Jerome was wearing iron manacles to which was attached a long chain, and as he walked the chain rattled; and for his greater humiliation the gentlemen of Duke Henry led Jerome at a distance at the end of the chain. And so they brought him bound into the refectory.'[93] There the Palatine John's letter and the citation were read, and Jerome explained why he had sought safety in flight.[94] At once several of his former colleagues and opponents began to accuse him of having taught the realist doctrine of universals at Paris, Cologne and Heidelberg; his sharpest critic was Jean Gerson, the chancellor of the university of Paris and the most learned and eminent champion of the conciliar programme.

Another rose up and said: 'when you were in Heidelberg you main-

quantum in nobis est, et fides exigit orthodoxa, tenore presencium offerimus.' (Ibid. 687.)

[90] The citation is in ibid., 686-7. Cf. ibid., 119.

[91] Ibid., 760. [92] Ibid., 142. [93] Ibid., 215-18. [94] Ibid., 217-18.

tained many things about the Trinity which were heretical. And there you painted a shield, comparing the Persons of the Trinity to water, snow and ice:' and Master Jerome said: 'What I wrote and painted there I am willing to say, write and paint here. If I am taught that it is erroneous I am willing humbly to recant.' Meanwhile some were shouting: 'Let him be burned, let him be burned,' to whom he replied: 'If my death is what you want, in God's name let it be.' And the archbishop of Salzburg said: 'No, Jerome, for it is written: "I require not the death of a sinner, but rather that he may live and be converted." ' . . . When the tumult had subsided they handed over master Jerome bound to the officers of the city of Constance.

His (and Hus's) gaoler was Walenrode bishop of Riga, who shut him up in the tower of St Paul's cemetery 'and ordered him to be closely chained. He was bound by fetters to a post, too high for him to sit on, in such a way that his hands, which were shackled to the fetters, were dragged above his head.' In this agonising position he was kept for two days, fed only on bread and water, until Petr of Mladoňovice (the pupil and biographer of Hus), discovered his plight and managed to persuade his guard to alleviate it.[95]

Jerome remained in his prison for almost a year; at first we hear of him only from Hus's letters written from his prison during the month of June. As early as 6 June 1415 Hus expressed his fear that Jerome would be put to death,[96] and later in the month Hus dreamed of Jerome in prison and recalled that Jerome had once said: 'If I go to the Council, I think I shall not return.'[97] When the hearing of the case of Hus was completed on 8 June, the Emperor Sigismund said to the fathers of the council: 'And you will also make an end of his secret disciples and supporters, for in a short time I am going away, and especially you will deal with that man, that man

[95] Ibid., 218. Poggio said of this imprisonment: 'Here is a wonderful example of a good memory: for 340 days Jerome was in the bottom of a foul dark tower, where not only could he read nothing, but he could see nothing. Add to this the mental anxiety which must daily have agitated him and might have been expected to blot out his memory. But [at his trial] he quoted so many learned and wise men in support of his opinions that would have more than sufficed if for the whole of this time he had been at leisure and in a position to devote all his time to study.' (Letter to Leonardo of Arezzo, Palacký, *Documenta*, p. 628.)

[96] Palacký, *Documenta*, p. 106. [97] Ibid., p. 110.

[repeating the words 'that man'] who is here in prison. And they said: "Jerome?" And he replied: "Yes, Jerome. We will make an end of him in one day; for his case will be easier, for Hus is the master, and this Jerome is his disciple." '[98] Jerome was always in Hus's mind during his last days. On the 10 June Hus wrote 'to all the people of Bohemia' a letter in Czech in which he said: 'About master Jerome, my dear comrade ['towařiš'], I hear nothing except that he is in close confinement, expecting death, as I am, and that for his faith which he bravely showed to the Czechs—and it is Czechs who are our most cruel enemies and have given us into the hands of other enemies to be put in prison. I beseech you that you pray the lord God for me.'[99] Hus's last reference to Jerome, in a Czech letter of 27 June, is prophetic: 'I say to you, that God knows why they delay to kill me and my dear brother master Jerome, who, I trust, will meet his death holily without guilt and conduct himself and suffer more bravely than I, wretched sinner that I am.'[100]

On 6 July 1415 Hus was sentenced and burned outside the walls of Constance. On the 11th, John the 'Iron' bishop of Litomyšl, a protagonist of the anti-Wyclifite party, wrote to King Václav in Czech telling him that the case against Jerome was being prepared.[101] A commission of the council of which cardinal Pierre d'Ailly was the chief member was engaged in drawing up articles of accusation against him. But, as with Hus earlier, the council was much more anxious to secure the recantation than the death of Jerome; a penitent sinner would be a far more valuable asset to the council than a martyr, especially as the death of Hus had already let loose a storm of national protest in Bohemia. Therefore d'Ailly, Zabarella and others of the conciliar leaders laboured hard to secure Jerome's submission, and Jerome, genuinely frightened by what had happened to Hus and probably overwhelmed for the moment by the weight of authority against him, consented. He drew up in his own hand a form of recantation which on the 11 September 1415 he read in a congregation of the four nations. The recantation is pathetic; he submitted himself completely to the wisdom of the church and of the council 'which now represents

[98] Ibid., p. 315 ('Relatio' of Petr of Mladoňovice).
[99] Ibid., p. 116. [100] Ibid., p. 140. [101] Ibid., p. 563.

the Church'; he denounced the forty-five articles of Wyclif[102] and agreed that Wyclif had been justly condemned. As to the thirty articles of Hus, he said that at first he had refused to believe that they were his, but when he was shown the books containing them written in a hand which he knew to be that of Hus, he was convinced, and agreed that they had been rightly condemned; but he did so 'without prejudice to Hus's person, or what I believe to be his good character and the very many truths which I heard from him in the schools and in his popular sermons'. Finally he declared that this recantation was his own composition.[103] The council instructed Jerome to report his recantation by letter to the king, the lords and his friends in Bohemia, for it hoped that the news that their leader had surrendered would help to allay the storm of indignation that the news of Hus's death had caused. Later the council accused Jerome of having broken his promise,[104] but certainly not with complete accuracy for there survives one letter which he wrote in Czech on 12 September 1415, the day after the recantation, to the Lord Lacek of Kravář, an influential friend of the reformers, wherein he said:

I beg to inform your grace that I am alive and well in Constance. I hear that a great storm has arisen both in Bohemia and Moravia on account of the death of master Hus, on the grounds that he was wrongly condemned and straightway burned . . . I am writing this that you may know no wrong was done . . . At first I thought Hus had been wronged, but when I was given the articles of which he was accused to examine, having looked at them carefully and discussed them backwards and forwards with more than one master, I came to see that some of the articles were heretical, some erroneous, and others liable to cause offences and harmful. But I still doubted whether the articles had been accurately quoted from his writings, and therefore the Council gave me his books written in his own hand, and I was forced to recognise that Hus had in fact uttered these heresies and errors. And I who had been his friend and who had with my own voice defended his error on all sides, seeing this,

[102] Enumerated in Hardt, iv, 508-10.

[103] The recantation of 11 Sept. 1415 is quoted by Theodoric de Vrie in his 'Historia concilii Constanciensis', Dist. XII (Hardt, i, 171 ff.). See also the 'Anonymi relatio' in Palacký, *Documenta*, pp. 596-7, and the *ex parte* account given by the prosecutor in Hardt, iv, 688-9.

[104] Ibid., 688.

and being unwilling to defend those errors, I voluntarily disowned them at length before the whole Council.[105]

Jerome's recantation was so great a victory for the conciliar leaders, who were anxious to demonstrate that a council would be no less jealous of the orthodoxy of the church than any pope, that they deemed it prudent to give it even greater publicity by having it solemnly repeated amidst all the pomp of a general session. Therefore on 23 September 1415 in the Cathedral of Constance at the nineteenth general session of the council Jerome was made to read his revocation again. Indeed he amplified it, prefacing it with a rhetorical and subservient introduction and adding to it a formal renunciation of his now famous illustration of the 'shield of faith', and a recantation of the heresy that the saints in heaven have faith, whereas the church teaches that they have 'the beatific vision which excludes all enigmatic knowledge and which far exceeds faith'. Finally he swore by the trinity and on the gospels to remain always in the truth of the Catholic church.[106]

If Jerome hoped by his abject recantation to secure freedom he was sadly deceived, for he was sent back to his prison, and though he received somewhat more lenient treatment and better food, it soon was made clear to him that he must expect to spend the rest of his days there. Undoubtedly his conscience began to trouble him and his visitors were made aware that he was beginning to regret the betrayal of his dead friend. There were other things too that began to make the council wonder whether it had finished with Jerome. The indignant recalcitrance of the Bohemians showed no signs of abatement as a result of Jerome's defection. During the winter a number of Carmelite friars arrived from Bohemia bringing stories of Jerome's encouragement of sacrilege and iconoclasm during 1412 and 1414. And also on 19 October 1415 Gerson, the acknowledged intellectual leader of the council, gave a public lecture on the whole subject of recantation in which he came to the conclusion that no recantation can wipe out the guilt of having once been a heretic, and that therefore repentant

[105] Palacký, *Documenta*, pp. 598-9. Jerome at his last hearing again said that scripsit in Bohemiam suam abiuracionem' (Hardt, iv, 761).

[106] Hardt, iv, 499-514.

heretics ought to be kept in perpetual imprisonment.[107] There was no reference to Jerome by name, but his hearers when they heard it and Jerome when he heard of it must have made the particular application of Gerson's generalisations. On 19 December the German nation at the council urged that Jerome's case be reopened,[108] and when on the 30th a letter of protest against the burning of Hus signed by 452 nobles and gentlemen of Bohemia and Moravia was read to the council, the desire to deal with Jerome finally must have been increased.[109] This time the council was determined that there should be no more leniency; in place of the former commissioners, among them the reasonable and moderate d'Ailly and Zabarella, the task of collecting the evidence against Jerome was now entrusted to John, the Latin patriarch of Constantinople and Nicholas of Dinckelspühel, who had been one of the assessors whom Jerome had flouted at Vienna five years before.

The commissioners evidently did their work with a despatch that was rare in ecclesiastical proceedings, for by 27 April 1416 they were ready for the hearing to begin. On that day in a congregation of the four nations, in the absence of Jerome, the patriarch and Dinckelspühel repeated the articles of accusation. The Fransciscan John Rocha then read thirty-one articles which dealt with Jerome's activities as a propagandist of Wyclifite opinions, with his activities in Hungary and Austria, the *quodlibet* of Knín and Jerome's campaign against Archbishop Zbyněk; they recited all the scandals connected with the indulgences of 1412, Jerome's favouring of the Orthodox in Lithuania and Russia, and ended with accusations that he had taught the quaternity of the trinity, predestination and remanence.[110] To this first group of articles witnesses had already testified. Now the congregation ordered them to be shown to Jerome so that he might admit or deny them one by one. The prosecution then produced, apparently at the same session, a further batch of 104 articles, which were also to be shown to Jerome, and witnesses were to be heard in respect of any of

[107] Text of Gerson's dissertation in Hardt, iii, 39 ff.

[108] Hardt, iv, 556.

[109] On 20 Feb. 1416 the whole 452 were cited by the Council as suspect of heresy (ibid., 607 ff., 839-52).

[110] Ibid., 629-31, 633-56.

them which he denied. These 'additional articles' also ranged over the whole of his career from his journey to England, through thirteen years of his activities in Prague, Paris, Heidelberg, Cracow, Vienna and in Russia, and finally his relations with the council of Constance. They conclude by accusing Jerome of having broken his promise to repeat his recantation to King Václav, Queen Žofie, the university and others, with having refused to confirm his recantation, having demanded to be released, and having reaffirmed his admiration for Hus. The prosecutor then demanded that Jerome be made to fast, and that as a layman he be merely allowed to answer *Credo* or *Non credo*, that he be put to the torture,[111] and that, if he persisted in denying what was proved against him, 'then without delay he shall be handed over to the secular arm to be dealt with in accordance with the canons as a pertinacious and incorrigible heretic'.[112]

Apparently Jerome replied in writing to the first group of articles, denying most of them, admitting some to be true in whole or in part,[113] but not to the second group, for he was insistent that he should be given a public hearing. This was not in accord with the strict procedure of the inquisition, but the cardinals knew the value of publicity, and Jerome's request was granted. On 23 May 1416 at a general congregation held in the cathedral under the presidency of John of Vivari, the cardinal bishop of Ostia, Jerome was brought to face his accusers, one from each nation: the patriarch of Constantinople for the French, Caspar abbot of Perugia for the Italians, John Welles prior of St Mary's, York, for the English and Lambert of Geldres for the Germans. Jerome was asked to take an oath, but refused to do so on the grounds that he was not to be allowed to speak freely, but merely to reply to the articles affirmatively or negatively.[114]

[111] He was not in fact tortured; see Hardt, iii, 60.

[112] These 'additional articles' are in Hardt, iv, 646-91. All the 142 articles have provided much of the material for this essay, and therefore I refrain from reproducing them in detail here. They are well summarised in C. J. von Hefele and H. Leclercq, *Histoire des conciles*, iii (2), 377-87; see also ibid., 394-408.

[113] His replies are appended to the articles as recorded under the proceedings of 27 April. See Hardt, iv, 633-46.

[114] Ibid., 751: 'Poggii Florentini ad Leonardum Aretinum epistola', in Hefele-Leclercq, vii (2), 405-8: Palacký, *Documenta*, p. 624 ff.; Hardt, iii, pt v, 64-71.

It seems that at this hearing of 27 May 1416 the council was concerned with the 104 additional articles to which Jerome had not yet replied. There was present one of the ablest journalists of the time, the eminent humanist, Poggio of Florence; in his well known letter[115] to Leonardo of Arezzo he says:

I have never seen anyone, particularly in a capital case, who got nearer to the eloquence of the ancients whom we so much admire. It was wonderful to behold with what words, what eloquence, what arguments, with what a countenance, voice and confidence he replied to his adversaries; . . . it is sad that so noble a mind and so excellent should have strayed into the field of heresy—assuming that those things he is charged with are true . . . After some discussion it was decided that he should first publicly reply to the errors with which he was charged and then be given the opportunity to say what he liked. Therefore the heads of the accusation were read from the pulpit, and then he was asked whether he wanted to object to any of them; after that they were proved by evidence. It is unbelievable with what skill he replied and how he argued in his defence. He said nothing unbecoming to a good man; if he really believed what he professed, then no just cause of death could have been found in him . . . When he was asked what he believed about the Sacrament, he said: 'before the consecration it is bread, afterwards it is the body'. Then one said: 'But some say that you said that after consecration the bread remains.' He answered 'the bread remains at the baker's' . . . To another who swore by his conscience he said: 'That is the easiest road to deception' . . . Since the number of the charges and the weightiness of the affair made it impossible to finish that day, the case was adjourned for three days.[116]

The hearing was resumed on 26 May; the remaining articles were read, and Jerome replied to them one by one. The patriarch of Constantinople then invited Jerome to address the assembly, which he did in a speech whose eloquence, learning and courage moved Poggio to declare:

His voice was pleasant, well used and resonant, and he had the dignified gestures of an orator . . . He stood there fearless, undismayed, not merely despising death but welcoming it, so you would have said that here was another Cato. O man, worthy to be always

[115] See preceding note.

[116] 'Poggii epistola' in Palacký, *Documenta*, pp. 624-6.

had in memory! I do not applaud him if he believed anything contrary to the Church; but I admire his learning, his knowledge of many things, his eloquence and his skill in reply: but I fear that the very gifts nature had given him were his worst enemies.[117]

Jerome began his speech by calling on those present to pray for him. He then launched into an exposition which revealed that he was a humanist as well as a schoolman, telling how Socrates, Plato, Anaxagoras, Zeno, Virgil and Seneca, Rutilius and Boethius had suffered as martyrs for the truth, as also had Moses, Elijah, Daniel and Susannah, John the Baptist, Stephen and the apostles. He then described the origin and development of the quarrel of Teuton and Czech in Bohemia, out of which he said had sprung his present persecution. After an account of his coming to Constance, his escape, arrest and imprisonment Jerome continued:

I do not believe Jan Hus was justly condemned; when I formerly admitted that he was I acted against my conscience, for his teaching was just and holy, as was his life, and I shall keep to him and hold to him firmly, to confirm which I here and now revoke the letter which I wrote to Prague in which I denounced the opinions and teaching of Jan Hus. As to the books and teaching of Wyclif, I have never known anyone who wrote so well and profoundly as he. When I denounced the teaching of Jan Hus I did not do so because I was willing to desist from that teaching, but I recanted from fear, because I was afraid of the fire. But what Wyclif and Hus[118] said about the sacrament of the altar contrary to the opinions of the doctors of the church, so far I do not follow them.[119]

Poggio comments:

Great was the sorrow of those who stood by, for they were anxious that so exceptional a man should be saved, had he been of a good mind. But he persisted in his own condemnation and seemed to welcome death; for he praised Hus, saying that he had not attacked the church, but only clerical abuses, the pride, luxury and pomp of the prelates. For the patrimony of churches was originally in-

[117] Ibid., pp. 628-9.

[118] There is no more evidence that Hus ever accepted Wyclif's heretical views about the eucharist than that Jerome did.

[119] Hardt, iv, 752-62, contains the official version of this speech, certainly not accurately, for at one point Jerome is made to say that he and Hus 'una die cooperati fuerint tantum, quod multi Teutonici a Bohemis fuerunt interfecti'.

tended for the poor and strangers and for the fabric, and it seemed wrong to that good man that it should be spent on harlots, feasts, horses, dogs, vestments and other things unbecoming to Christ's religion.[120]

'He was given two days in which to repent, during which time the most erudite men visited him to try to move him from his conviction, among them the cardinal of Florence [Zabarella].'[121]

The last scene was enacted on Saturday 30 May 1416, when in the cathedral early in the morning the council met for its twenty-first general session again under the presidency of the cardinal bishop of Ostia; there were thirteen other cardinals present 'and also the ambassadors of the illustrious princes the kings of France, Aragon, Naples, Cyprus, Poland, Norway, Dacia and Sweden, and of many other princes, dukes, margraves, counts, prelates, universities, and nuncios and proctors in great number'.[122] A mass of the Holy Spirit was celebrated and then James, bishop of Lodi, went into the pulpit and preached a sermon on the text 'He rebuked them for their unbelief and the hardness of their hearts'.[123] That sermon is an enlightening illustration of the attitude of the fifteenth-century church towards heresy and the heretic[124]; it is a scholarly, eloquent, logical, bitter and merciless exposition of the thesis that 'the more pestilent the disease, the more violent must be the remedy'. Professing his own charitable love of lenity and that he did not wish 'to poke the fire with a sword', the bishop addressed himself directly to Jerome and hurled the harsher sayings of Augustine, Isidore and Gregory at his head: 'Open crimes ought not to be punished in secret'; 'It is better that the guilty should be punished to save many, than that through the license of one man many should be put in danger.' It was not Jerome's lack of faith or his honest errors, but his hardness of heart and presumptuous pride which were being punished.

Ye catholic lords, behold the bold temerity of these men, Jan Hus and Jerome, lowborn, base, of unknown origin, who have dared to

[120] 'Poggii epistola' in Palacký, *Documenta*, p. 628. Cf. Dietrich Niem in Hardt, ii, 449 ff.
[121] Palacký, *Documenta*, p. 629.
[122] Hardt, iv, 764-5.
[123] Mark, xvi, 14.
[124] Text in Hardt, iii, 55 ff.

assault the whole realm of Bohemia, to incite the barons and nobles to strife and dissension, to provoke the knights, to subvert its ancient and useful constitution, . . . to promote dissension among the citizens; they became mob leaders of armed bands of satellites, committing or procuring murders, spoiling churches and profaning altars. O happy Bohemian realm, had this man never been born . . . Not even Arius, or Sabellius, Faustus or Nestorius were of greater ill-fame than you, Jerome. The evil report of your heresy has spread through England, all Bohemia, France, Hungary, Poland, Lithuania, Russia and Italy. You were taken prisoner, as such, as you ought to be, brought back to the Council, and shut up only because it was necessary; while you were thus imprisoned my most reverend lords the Cardinals of Orsini, Aquileia, Cambrai [Pierre d'Ailly] and Florence [Zabarella] personally sought to have you put in some more comfortable place. And had they not been afraid you would run away, each one of them was willing to have you not only in his house, but in his chamber and at his table . . . Nor were you tortured. Would that you had been, for then you would have spewed out all your errors. Such punishment would have opened those eyes which guilt had closed.

The sermon ended, Jerome was permitted to address his judges. Dietrich Vrie, who was present, describes how 'he stood up in the midst of them, his voice clear, with pale face and long black beard'.[125] He began by strongly denying the bishop of Lodi's charge that he had ever done harm to Bohemia; he thanked the first commissioners, especially Zabarella, for their patience and good instruction. He then made a confession of faith and obedience to the Catholic church, but denounced again the pomp and luxury of the clergy. He repeated his confession of loyalty to Hus, and again revoked the letter he had written to Lacek, saying that he had done so against his conscience 'for fear of the fire, whose heat is most cruel'.[126]

When Jerome had finished the proctor of the synod, Henry of Piro, asked that definitive sentence be passed on him. The patriarch of Constantinople then read the sentence from a paper he had in his hand. The sentence recited Jerome's recantation of his belief in the articles of Wyclif and Hus, 'heretical, erroneous, blasphemous, scandalous, offensive to pious ears,

[125] Theodoric de Vrie in Hardt, i (1), 203 ff.

[126] Jerome's speech is in Hardt, iv, 766-8.

temerarious and seditious', and his subsequent relapse. Having explicitly recorded Jerome's profession of orthodoxy in the matter of the eucharist, the sentence concluded: 'From the aforesaid it is clear that the said Jerome adheres to the said Wyclif and Hus already condemned and to their errors, and that he was and is a favourer thereof. Wherefor this holy Synod has decreed and doth decree that the said Jerome shall be cast out as a rotten branch that is dry and dead, and it pronounces and declares him to be a heretic and relapsed into heresy, excommunicate and anathema, and it condemns him.'[127] The deputies of each of the four nations were then asked to vote, and one by one the Italian Antonio, bishop of Concordia, the German Nicholas, bishop of Merseburg, the Frenchman Vital, bishop of Toulouse, for the English nation Patrick, bishop of Cork, and for the cardinals John, bishop of Ostia, answered *Placet*. 'And when this was done the council or synod of Constance asked and called on the secular arm to carry out the sentence against master Jerome.'[128] There was brought to him a great tall paper hat painted round with red devils. When he saw it he pulled off his hood and threw it on the ground among the prelates, and put the hat on his head, saying: 'Our lord Jesus Christ when he was about to die for me wore a crown of thorns on his head. And I in place of such a crown will gladly wear this hat for the love of him.'[129]

An eyewitness and a compatriot describes the last scenes in these words:

After these things he was led out of the cathedral to suffer execution of death and as he passed through the door of the church he began to sing, joyfully and in a loud voice and with his eyes raised up to heaven, '*Credo in unum deum*' as it is wont to be sung in church. Then as he went along he sang the whole Litany. When that was ended, at the city gate which leads to Gottleben, he sang '*Felix namque es, sacra Virgo*.' And when that canticle was ended, after he reached the place of execution where master Jan Hus had earlier suffered death, he knelt down before the stake which had been prepared for master Jerome in the likeness of that of master Jan Hus,

[127] Text of sentence ibid., 766 [*sc.* 768]-71.
[128] Ibid., 766 [*sc.* 768].
[129] Theodoric de Vrie in ibid., 764-5.

and said a prayer leisurely [*morose = cum mora*?]. But the executioners raised him from the ground while he was yet praying and stripped him of all his clothes until he was naked, and then girt a linen cloth round his loins, and bound him to the stake, which was in the form of a thick post and fixed in the earth, and he was fastened to it with ropes and iron chains, with his feet on the ground. And when they began to pile the wood around him he sang: '*Salva festa dies.*' When that hymn was finished again he chanted in a loud voice '*Credo in unum deum*' to the end. Then he spoke to the people in German to this effect: 'Beloved children, as I have just sung, so and not otherwise do I believe. This creed is my faith. I die now because I would not agree with the Council and assert with it that master Jan Hus was rightly and justly condemned by the Council. For well I know that he was a true preacher of the gospel of Jesus Christ.' And when the wood was heaped up as high as the top of his head they put his clothes on top of the pile[130] and set fire to the wood with a torch, and as it began to burn he sang in a loud voice: '*In manus tuas Domine commendo spiritum meum.*' When that was ended and the fire burning fiercely he said, in the Bohemian tongue: 'Lord God, Father almighty, have mercy on me, and pardon my sins. For thou knowest how sincerely I have loved thy truth.' And then his voice was stifled by the fierce fire and from that time could not be heard, but his mouth and lips continued to move quickly, as if he were speaking rapidly to himself or were praying. But when almost his whole body, together with his beard, was burning, then, owing to the excessive heat a great blister as big as an egg appeared on his body. While he was yet burning he lived in the fire in great martyrdom for as long as one might walk slowly from St Clement's [in Prague] across the bridge to St Mary the Virgin's, so great was his natural strength. But when he had expired in the fierce fire, they brought his bed, blanket, breeches, hood and other belongings from his prison and burnt them all to dust in the same fire. And when the fire had burned out they took the dust and ashes in a cart to the river Rhine which flows nearby and threw them in.[131]

'And so', relates the German papal official Dietrich Niem, 'he remained obstinate in his errors as long as he could open

[130] Poggio here adds the detail: 'Here is the greatest proof of his brave spirit, that when the executioner was going to light the fire behind Jerome's back so that he should not see it, Jerome said: "Come round here, and light the fire where I can see it; if I were afraid of it I would never have come to this place"' (Palacký, *Documenta*, p. 629).

[131] Hardt, iv, 770-1.

his mouth to speak, persisting in his diabolical and damnable presumption as in life so in death.'[132] The Florentine humanist Poggio wrote:

With joyful mien, with happy face and eager countenance he went to his death; he feared not the fire, nor the manner of his torment, nor death. None of the Stoics ever endured death with so constant and strong a spirit . . . Thus died this man, excellent in all but the faith. I saw his end; I observed his every action: whatever may have been his dogmatic errors, whatever his obstinacy, you would assuredly have said that here died a man from the school of philosophy. I have told a long tale, for having nothing to do I wanted to do something, to tell you of things a little like the stories of the ancients. For Mutius of old did not give his one limb to be burned with as confident a mind as this man did his whole body; nor did Socrates drink the poison as readily as this man embraced the fire. But enough of this: forgive me if I have been too long; but the thing itself demanded a full account; but I did not mean to be so loquacious. Farewell.

From Constance on the day in which Jerome paid the penalty.[133]

[132] Ibid, ii, 454. [133] Palacký, *Documenta*, p. 629.

XII

Peter Payne in England

SOME sixty-five years ago an English Protestant clergyman named James Baker happened to read the German version of Palacký's *History of the Bohemian Nation*. There he found, to his surprise, many references to an Englishman named Peter Payne, who for forty years had played a leading part in Hussite Bohemia. Baker at once began eagerly to enquire of the most eminent English historians of his day what they knew of Peter Payne; but they one and all, even the greatest of them, Freeman and Maitland, confessed their ignorance even of Payne's existence. Baker therefore set to work to try to do justice to this *Forgotten Great Englishman* by learning what he could about Payne's life and work. He came to Bohemia and visited Prague and other places which he knew from Palacký had been the centres of Payne's activity. He also discovered from other English historians such as Thomas Gascoigne, John Foxe and Anthony Wood some meagre details about Payne's life in England before he left his country; but he was able to add nothing to the history of Payne's share in the Hussite revolution.

But Baker's pioneer work appeared in 1894 just in time for the Dictionary of National Biography to give Payne his proper place in the volume of 1895, where C. L. Kingsford wrote his first scholarly account of him. Kingsford used the information about Payne which was to be gleaned from the chronicles of Petr of Žatec, Charlier, Długosz, Ebendorfer and Jean of Tours and he also used the documents in Wilkins' *Consilia*, in Martère and Durand, Höfler and Loserth.

No further work was done by English scholars on Payne during the next thirty years, until Alfred Emden wrote his history of *An Oxford Hall in Mediaeval Times*. Emden was for many years the principal of St Edmund Hall in Oxford, a college where students have resided and worked under the supervision of the principal of the hall from the beginning of the fourteenth century to the present day. Peter Payne was principal of St Edmund Hall for the last four years of his life in England and therefore Emden set out to incorporate in his history of the hall all that he could discover about the early life and activities of his distinguished but heretical predecessor. He was able to find in the archives of the university and city of Oxford some few details which help to some small extent to fill in the picture of Payne's career in Oxford. Since Emden's book was published in 1927 nothing has been added to our knowledge of Payne's life before 1414, and I have to acknowledge my indebtedness for what I write today to Alfred Emden, not only because I depend on his researches, but also because he was my first teacher in these studies.

To all students of the history of Anglo-Czech relations, the great interest of Peter Payne must be the fact that he provides another link in the chain which has bound our distant countries intermittently together from the days when Václav IV made a diplomatic and marital alliance with King Richard II, through the era of Wyclif and Hus, of Elizabeth Stuart, queen of Bohemia, of Jan Amos Komenský, to the time when England was able to repay the Czechs for the refuge which they gave to Payne when he was forced to flee from the persecution of the English prelates and king, by providing a refuge for Masaryk and Beneš from the tyranny of the Habsburgs and terrorism of the Nazis.

To those who look merely at the surface of history, it may seem strange that two countries more than a thousand miles apart, widely separated by racial origin, by speech and historical development should have so often come into fateful contact. But a comparison of the political, social and economic development of England and Bohemia at the end of the fourteenth century will, I think, explain why it was that an Oxford theologian who was in peril of his life because of his opinions, should find a secure refuge and place where he could continue to work for what he believed to be the truth, not in the Netherlands or France or Germany, but in distant Prague.

In both countries there was a struggle for supremacy between a would-be autocratic monarchy and a nobility which sought to use its social privileges and economic power to seize and exploit the government of the country: in England there was the revolt of the lords appellant against the king; in Bohemia there were the coups d'état carried out by the magnates against Václav IV. The end of the fourteenth century also saw in both countries a maturing social and economic crisis: the struggle of the English peasants and townsmen to throw off the burden of heavy rents and services which culminated in the peasants' revolt; in Bohemia, particularly in the south and south-west, the increasing demands of the landlords for payments and services of all kinds. Finally in both lands there was the deep stirrings of a religious revival and the beginning of a revolt against the spiritual and moral weaknesses of the prelates, the monks and friars and the financial demands of the church, a revolt which had culminated in England with John Wyclif and the Lollards, and which in Bohemia had been built up by Waldhauser, Vojtěch Raňkův, Jan Milíč, Matěj of Janov and Tomáš of Štítný into a potentially explosive force.

It is in the light of these considerations that we can understand the circumstances which brought Payne from Oxford to Prague.

Peter Payne, or Peter Clerk as he usually called himself, was born probably between 1380-90 in the village of Hough near Stamford in Lincolnshire, so that, like Wyclif, he was a north-country man. He probably came to Oxford as a student a year or two before the end of the century, more than ten years after Wyclif's death, but in time for it to have been possible for him to have met Jerome of Prague and, later, Mikuláš Faulfiš and Jiří of Kněhnice when they came to England. That he met Jerome in Oxford, as Professor Margaret Deanesly says, is possible but unproven. At Oxford Payne studied the usual course of the liberal arts and secured the degree first of bachelor and before 1406 that of master of arts. He never took any degree in theology, though as a resident master he almost certainly lectured in logic and dialectic, perhaps also he began to lecture as *cursor* on the bible.

At this time the teaching of Wyclif in Oxford, as well as elsewhere in England and Scotland, was still influential, despite the persecution which the church, led by the archbishop of Canterbury, had been conducting spasmodically for twenty-five years. Though king and parliament enacted the statute *De hereticis comburendis* in 1404 and the burning of the Lollards had begun, there remained in Oxford a group faithful to the ideals and programme of the great reformer. We have evidence that Payne was one of this party and from Petr of Žatec's *Diarium* we know that he was introduced to Wyclifitism by the man, Peter Partridge, who was to be Payne's bitterest antagonist at the council of Basel. It is possible that one of Payne's first open appearances as a follower of Wyclif was as a protagonist in the dispute which was then at its height in the Oxford schools about the propriety of publishing the bible in the English language, for we know that Purvey, one of the Lollard translators of the bible into the vernacular, secured the services of a 'certain doctor' to defend the English bible, and though Payne was not a doctor, it may well have been he. The unique manuscript of Purvey's tractate *De versione bibliorum* today exists in Vienna, and it may be that it was brought to central Europe by Payne himself. We have, alas, nothing that Payne certainly wrote while he was in England, and our knowledge of his activities is very meagre. However, the report of the trial for heresy of the Lollard, Ralph Mungyn, in St Paul's Cathedral in 1428 records

that the said Ralph knew a certain Master Peter Clerc [i.e. Payne] while Master Peter was still in England. The same Master Peter was then a man of evil fame in respect of certain errors and heresies which had originated with John Wyclif, and in the university of Oxford and in London and in divers other places he had publicly been known [as a follower of Wyclif]. Further it was charged against Ralph Mungyn that he had adhered to Master Peter and his teaching and was his disciple and had frequent communication with him in the university of Oxford and in the city of London and in other places in the kingdom of England. Furthermore, that the said Ralph, after he came to London, had with him various books of John Wyclif and other books, written in English, which contained erroneous opinions of Master John Wyclif and Master Peter Payne.

Mungyn confessed that twelve years earlier he had sold a copy of Wyclif's *Trialogus* to a certain chaplain of the county of Surrey named John Botte.

The arch-enemy of the Oxford Wyclifists, Thomas Netter or Walden, also throws a little light on Payne's Oxford activities. He records in his *Doctrinale* that he and his fellow friar, William Beaufeu, were invited by a certain *nobilis vir* to dispute with Peter Payne concerning pilgrimages, the eucharist, monasticism and mendicancy, but, says Walden, even before the debate began, Payne retired *vecordia suffocatus*. There is also good evidence that Payne, like his master, was critical of the greed of the mendicant friars, for Petr of Žatec records that at Basel Payne was accused of speaking of the friars with hatred. Payne admitted that when one day some friars came begging to his hall in Oxford he refused to give them anything and said some things to them which they did not enjoy hearing.

Less certain, but still quite probable, is Payne's part in one of the most famous incidents of these turbulent years at Oxford. In the year 1406 the Wyclifite party in Oxford compiled a testimonial in favour of Wyclif, declaring him to have been a man of great probity, who had been without a peer in the university—in all his writing on logic, philosophy and moral and speculative theology; the testimonial further declared that Wyclif had never been convicted of heresy nor had his books been burned after his death by the English prelates. This letter was clearly intended to give the lie to stories of Wyclif's heresy and punishment which his enemies were spreading throughout England and Europe. It is difficult to know how the university seal came to be affixed to this testimonial, for the majority of the regent masters at Oxford in 1406 were not Wyclifites. Indeed, an almost contemporary writer, Thomas Gascoigne, in his famous *Dictionary* says: 'and this Peter [Payne] the heretic was master of arts of Oxford, a very cunning man, who stole the common seal of the university, under which he wrote to the heretics of Prague that Oxford and all England were of the same faith as the Praguers, excepting only the mendicant friars.' It probably was not necessary to steal the seal; what probably happened was that an ill-attended congregation of masters was rushed into allowing its testimonial to be sealed quite lawfully. Gascoigne, on the other hand, was probably quite right in thinking that it was precisely intended for the Wyclifites of Prague, for this was the famous Oxford letter which Faulfiš took to Prague and which was so dramatically produced and read by Jerome at the end of Knín's *Quodlibet* in January 1409.

It was about this time that Peter Payne became the principal of one of the Oxford halls of residence. The Oxford students usually lived in a hall, that is a house rented from a landlord, where six to twelve students shared a dormitory and a refectory; the university authorities, for the sake of discipline, insisted that every such hall should be run by a resident principal, who would collect residence fees from the students, provide them with food, pay the rent and be responsible to the university for their good behaviour. In the year 1408 an Oxford burgess, named Nicholas Bishop, who fortunately for us kept careful accounts, granted a lease of his house, called White Hall, in the High Street, to Master Peter Clerc, for 28/4 a year. Next door to White Hall was St Edmund Hall, and the two houses seem to have been run together, for in 1410 Payne was the principal of both.

St Edmund Hall already had become a strong Wyclifite centre. Payne's last predecessor but one was William Taylor, who almost certainly was one of the leaders of the reformers. Taylor had been principal of St Edmund Hall from 1405 to 1408. During those years he preached a sermon at Paul's Cross in London which led to his citation for heresy by Thomas Arundel, archbishop of Canterbury; Taylor was charged with having advocated the seizure of property of the church *quasi per violentam seditionem populi*. He failed to answer the archbishop's summons and was therefore excommunicated. He seems to have had to leave Oxford and to have gone underground. But in 1417 Taylor was arrested, and after a series of trials, recantations and re-arrests Taylor was found guilty at a trial at Blackfriars in London of errors about the secular lordship of the clergy, mendicancy and adoration of the Cross and the saints. Archbishop Chichele condemned him and on the 2 March 1422 William Taylor suffered death by burning at the stake at Smithfield 'with a marvellous constancy and boldness'.

Such was the man whose work and ideals Peter Payne inherited when he became principal of St Edmund Hall in 1410.

It was a dangerous inheritance. Archbishop Arundel, a scion of one of the richest and most powerful aristocratic families in the land, was ambitious of power and determined to purge the realm of heretics. The king, Henry IV, was too old and ill to be able to stop the hand of the fierce prelate; the prince of Wales, the future Henry V, was filled with a pious zeal and willingly gave his support to the campaign which Archbishop Arundel launched against the Wyclifites.

And so, at the same time that Archbishop Zbyněk was raging against Hus and his fellow-Wyclifites in Prague, Archbishop Arundel started his campaign. He went down to Oxford where he held a convocation of the province of Canterbury which forbade the use in the schools of the university of any work by Wyclif which had not been approved by both archbishop and the university; all heads of colleges and principals of halls were instructed to enquire every month into the orthodoxy of their students. In 1409 another convocation at St Paul's in London drew up the famous list of Wyclif's heresies and errors, and in 1410 the archbishop induced the king to write to Oxford ordering that all who held these errors should be imprisoned. But it seems that the Wyclifites were still strong enough to prevent the carrying out of this decree. Therefore the archbishop came down to the university to hold an official visitation; the university protested against this as a breach of its academic privilege, but at last, before the end of 1411, the university submitted and promulgated a decree which was to put an end to open Wyclifitism in the university. The decree declared that no doctor, master, bachelor or scholar should dare to teach or defend any of the 267 articles which had been condemned by convocation, under penalty of imprisonment, degradation and excommunication. The university further decreed that copies of the condemned articles should be placed in the university library and that all principals of halls were to have copies of them; further all future graduates were to swear on the gospels never to teach these heretical doctrines or to give in to those who did so; finally once every year all wardens, provosts and rectors of colleges and all principals of halls were to take an oath that they knew of no master, bachelor, scholar or servant in their college or hall who was suspect of heresy or Lollardy.

This decree of the university was bound to make Payne's position extremely dangerous. He was now the leading Wyclifite in the university; his commentaries on Wyclif's writings were, as the evidence of the Lollard Mungyn shows, already current. However Payne for two years more stuck to his post as principal of St Edmund Hall. The account books of Osney Abbey, which was the landlord of the hall, show that he paid 30s. rent for it in 1412. But the landlord of White Hall, Nicholas Bishop, seems already to have been nervous of having so rebellious a man as Payne as his tenant, for Bishop served notice on Payne that he wished himself to occupy White Hall before October 1412.

In the following year the archbishop of Canterbury decided that the university must be finally purged of heresy by action against Peter Payne. We have the evidence of Payne's antagonist, Peter Partridge, that Payne was suspected of having persuaded John Oldcastle, Lord Cobham, the leading Lollard layman, to attempt an armed insurrection. This charge helps us to date events which led to Payne's departure from England. Oldcastle was arrested on a charge of heresy in the summer of 1413, and on 25 September was found guilty of heresy by a provincial synod held by the archbishop. Oldcastle however escaped from the Tower of London, where he was in prison, and on 10 January 1414 the Lollard rising began. But the attack on London was a pathetic failure. Oldcastle fled and became an outlaw, hunted by the officers of the king and the church for three years, until at last he was captured in a fight near Welshpool, and on 14 December 1417 he was hanged and his body burnt on the scaffold at Smithfield.

Partridge's suggestion that Payne and Oldcastle had worked together was probably based on fact, and is all the more interesting in view of Oldcastle's active interest in the Bohemian Wyclifites. It seems then that soon after the condemnation of Oldcastle in September 1413 Archbishop Arundel cited Payne to appear before him to answer charges of heresy and treason. Did Payne answer the summons? Partridge declared at Basel, twenty years later, that he had seen Payne face to face when he was cited. Payne made the somewhat ambiguous reply: 'As for my refusal to abjure the condemned Wyclifite articles, anyone who likes can believe me to be suspect. But as to the charge that when I was summoned I refused to appear, I reply that if I was cited after I had left England what could I do about it? And as to the charge that I was a traitor, who sought the life of the king, I say, that from my boyhood I was never willing to consent to taking anyone's life; how then could I seek the king's life?' This account of the dispute at Basel between Partridge and Payne was recorded by Petr of Žatec; another of the chroniclers of the council, Jean of Tours, also says that Payne denied that he was ever before a judge in England on a charge of heresy or anything else. John of Ragusa in his narrative gives a curious and interesting account of the matter. He says: 'The doctors of the university of Oxford asked Payne to swear an oath that he did not hold, and would not teach the articles of Wyclif, but he had refused to do so.' He had therefore gone to the king of England to complain of unjust pressure and had taken to the king his reply on the subject of the condemned articles. 'Payne asserted', says John of Ragusa, 'that when the King had heard what he had to say, he not only agreed that Payne should not take the oath but actually forbade it.' It seems to me inherently improbable that so fanatically orthodox a king as Henry V should have gone out of his way to protect a heretic like Payne; and also it leaves unanswered the question of why, if he had the king's protection, Payne thought it prudent to leave the country.

But though there must remain some uncertainty about what actually happened, this much seems probable. Payne was first asked by the university of Oxford to take the oath not to teach Wyclif's opinions. He may have had some sort of interview with King Henry V; but when the archbishop used the opportunity provided by Payne's involvement in the Oldcastle conspiracy to cite him for heresy, Payne decided that if he was to be any further use to the cause of church reform he must seek another field of activity where there was still freedom to proclaim the truth.

We have the evidence of Friedrich Reiser that Payne spent some months on a leisurely journey through the Rhineland. Payne tells us that he never saw Jan Hus in person, and therefore it seems likely that he did not reach Prague before Hus's departure for Constance on 11 October 1414. But Payne was almost certainly in Prague early in 1415, if, as Professor Bartoš thinks, Payne wrote the tractate *Quia nostri temporis homines* in support of Jakoubek of Stříbro and communion in both kinds. We can, then, follow Emden in thinking that Payne left England late in 1413 and that he arrived in Prague a year later, at the end of 1414.

It was a critical moment in the history of Bohemia. The nation's champion, Jan Hus, had already been thrown into the damp darkness of the dungeon under Lake Constance by the pope's orders and in defiance of the emperor's promised word. Hus's friends in Bohemia, the masters of the university, his pupils in the pulpits of the Prague churches, his devoted hearers in the Bethlehem Chapel, the queen, the lords and gentry of Bohemia and Moravia, the workmen of Prague and their wives who had heard him preach the saving word of God, the farmers and peasants of south Bohemia among whom he had lived and taught during his exile from Prague, all were awaiting with anxiety and growing anger the news from Constance. Already Jakoubek had taken on the mantle of the departed master, and he and some other priests were beginning to assault the fortress of priestly privilege by administering the chalice to the laity. The reform movement was young, inexperienced, not yet provided with a sound basis of doctrine and a clear programme. The arrival of Payne was therefore of the greatest value. He came as the leading English exponent of the older reform movement, bringing with him more books written by the English master and probably some of his own expositions of the fundamentals of Wyclifitism, perhaps too the draft of his famous and much used index to Wyclif's writings. He may even have brought with him one or two of his Oxford students like that John Penning, the English scholar who later was living in the College of All Saints in Prague and who was thrown into prison by Sigismund in 1437.

Peter Payne also brought with him from England a clear-cut and well thought-out plan for the revival of evangelical religion and the reform of the church. He had learnt from Wyclif first a hatred of the selfishness, greed and worldliness of the mendicant friars, secondly a radical view of the all-important question of the eucharist. He seems to have accepted Wyclif's doctrines of the remanence of the substance of the bread and wine in the consecrated elements, and to have been prepared at once to embrace Jakoubek's doctrine of communion for the laity in both kinds. But most important was the zeal with which he had accepted Wyclif's programme for the disendowment of the church. Payne's belief that the wealth of the church was the cost of its ineffectiveness and corruption was to be his most important contribution to the Hussite programme, and at Basel it was the article condemning the temporal power and wealth of the church which Payne was chosen to defend.

This then was the English refugee who came to Prague just after Jan Hus left it for ever. Peter Payne came to forge a link between England and Bohemia that has sometimes been strained almost to the breaking point, but never broken. Payne came to Bohemia as the only place where he could find tolerance and a sphere of activity where he could work for the cause of truth and righteousness.

XIII

Society in Central and in Western Europe: Its Development towards the End of the Middle Ages

THIS year—1948—Hungary celebrates a glorious anniversary, the centenary of the rebirth of the Hungarian people.[1] For all the peoples of central Europe 1848 was marked by a vitally important demonstration of national consciousness. It was the year when noble aims were formulated in noble language, when every good patriot, every citizen conscious of his rôle in society, demanded political rights and social justice. In Budapest, in Vienna and in Milan, in Venice and in Prague, there took place a powerful upsurge of peoples aspiring to liberty. This was the year of the great heroes of the sword and of the pen, of the Magyars Kossuth and Petöfi, of the Czech Palacký, of the Pole Libelt and of the Italian Garibaldi. In many respects the ends pursued were actually attained—we see the birth of the Hungarian constitution and the publication of the manifesto addressed by the Slav congress in Prague to the European nations. On the other hand, failure was undeniable too. The war for Hungarian independence meets with total defeat from the sinister alliance of Habsburg and Romanov. Radetzky overcomes the Italian insurgents at Novara and Custozza, and Windischgraetz triumphs in Prague and Vienna. Yet, notwithstanding so many hopes cruelly deceived, the year 1848 brings one victory, the results of which were to be of inestimable value: the final emancipation of the peasants from

[1] [This study was originally published under the title 'La société dans l'Europe centrale et dans l'Europe occidentale: Son développement vers la fin du Moyen Âge'. No English version was found among Professor Betts's papers: the article has been translated from the French by Peter Brock.]

serfdom throughout all the lands of the Habsburg monarchy—in Austria, in Hungary, in Bohemia and in Galicia. In central Europe only Russian Poland must wait nearly another two decades for this salutary reform.

The question that I want to raise today, and which in some measure I shall try to answer, runs as follows: why is it that the Danubian region has to wait until 1848 for liberation from serfdom when in western Europe serfdom had finally disappeared in the previous century? To answer this question is not a simple and easy task; indeed, generally speaking, answers to the basic historical questions are rarely simple. In this case it is not enough to say that the more rapid and longer political evolution of the west by itself led to the disappearance of serfdom there: all assertions of this sort would collide with the factual evidence. In Hungary kings like St Stephen, Coloman and St Ladislas created a united monarchy that was peaceful and well governed from the twelfth century, that is, at a period when France was still a conglomeration of feudal provinces: the dukes and counts of Normandy and Aquitaine, Brittany, Burgundy, Champagne and Blois, Toulouse and Provence were as powerful as the king of France in his little territory around Paris. The political evolution of Spain was much slower than that of the kingdoms of Bohemia or Poland. Until 1870 all Italy's efforts to lay the basis for national unity failed; it had no dynasty comparable to the Árpáds, Přemyslids or Piasts, no dynasty that could preserve it from division into small states and rival cities. Nevertheless, in Italy, in Spain, in France and in England, serfdom gives way to peasant proprietorship from before the end of the Middle Ages. On the other hand, Bohemia which, even though it was a united, powerful and politically mature state from the thirteenth century, and Poland, which became great and powerful under Mieszko I and Bolesław I in the high Middle Ages, have to wait until the nineteenth century before achieving serf emancipation. In short, the answer to our question cannot be supplied by comparing the political development of the states in central and in western Europe.

The only method which will allow us to solve this problem is to place ourselves round about the year 1400. First we must survey the state of the peasantry in Europe at this period, and then we must examine in what measure during the course of the fifteenth and sixteenth centuries the history of serfdom in central Europe diverges from that of serfdom in western Europe. By proceeding in this way we may perhaps arrive at a partial explanation of events.

The fourteenth century, it has been said, was the golden age of the peasant of central Europe. Of course, this does not at all invalidate the fact that at this period, whether in Hungary, Bohemia or Poland, almost all peasants belonged to a lord, who might be a nobleman, a royal official, a bishop, an abbot or the king himself. The peasant fulfilled his obligations towards the lord either in money or in kind; he could be required besides, within a framework of set services, to till the soil, to sow and to reap for a given time on the lord's domain. Other obligations were laid upon him too: the duty of transport, and especially of cartage, according to the lord's needs, not to speak of the employment of peasants on the construction of houses and in domestic service. In addition, seasonal work could be doubled, at least in certain cases, by regular weekly labour, and the peasant was often placed under the lord's jurisdiction, that is, his misdemeanours had to be tried by an official of the lord, who pronounced sentence in the name of the seigniorial court.

However, in the fourteenth century the peasant in central Europe was still a free man enjoying the same freedom as an English farmer or a small French proprietor in the nineteenth century. In so far as liberty is compatible with a seignioral régime, the fourteenth-century peasant was free in Hungary, Bohemia and Poland, since his tenure had the character of free proprietorship. First of all, he had the right to leave his land if he was not satisfied there. In many cases he could sell his holding or exchange it with another; he also had the right to leave it to his children at his death. In a word, the peasant was not *adscriptus glebae*, i.e. bound to the soil, since, in the absence of any law saying that runaway serfs should be returned to the lord's demesne, he could try his fortune either in the towns, continually growing in size, or in the service of lay or ecclesiastical authorities. In the second place, the peasant of central

Europe in the fourteenth century could be considered a free man because his obligations were limited and carefully demarcated. He knew exactly what work he had to perform and what he had to pay—the courts protected him against every arbitrary demand in excess of his obligatory services. Bracton, that great English lawyer of the twelfth century, had defined the serf as a man who, at sunset, does not know what he will be required to do on the morrow. In this sense the peasants of central Europe in the fourteenth century were certainly not serfs; according to the law and the opinion of the royal courts, they were free men. Although lords of the manor had acquired certain rights of jurisdiction over their farmers, they did not possess the right to maim or to kill them, or to sell or to exchange them like cattle.

The relative liberty of the peasants in central Europe was due to several factors. In Bohemia and in Hungary the fact that the sovereign had for some time been powerful enough to entrust local government to his own officers, whom he placed in charge of the strong castles, retarded the development of feudal power. Monarchs of the Árpád dynasty and later of the house of Anjou preferred to leave the peasant free in order to prevent the formation of a feudalism comparable to that which had characterised England in the reign of Stephen (1135-54) and France during the eleventh and twelfth centuries before the accession of Philip Augustus in 1180. On the other hand, it should be remembered that in the west the basic cause of the development of serfdom lay in the incessant civil wars and in foreign conquest. In England the chief reasons for the relatively early appearance of serfdom were the bloody conflicts between the petty kingdoms of Anglo-Saxon England and, above all, the occupation of the country first of all by the Danes in the tenth and eleventh centuries and then by the Normans in 1066. In times of civil war and foreign domination the peasant was forced to sell his land and liberty to the nearest lord in order to gain the latter's protection. We should recall, too, that Christianity and the church had reached western Europe three hundred, indeed seven hundred years earlier than north-eastern Europe. Assuming that the peasants often submitted to becoming serfs of the church in order to obtain from it benefits in this world as in the next, there thus followed a much more rapid development of serfdom in the west than in the east.

There is another reason explaining the relatively greater freedom enjoyed by the peasants in central Europe compared with that enjoyed by the peasants in the western countries—and that brings us on to speak of the numerous German colonies which were founded in central Europe from the twelfth to the fourteenth centuries. We know today how this influx of German colonists was organised. Society, as then in full swing in Bohemia, Hungary and Poland, observed with regret that, owing to insufficient manpower, large fertile areas remained unexplored. At the same time the king, the church and local lords strove in common to increase their income by enlarging the area of arable land. On the other hand, the rise of population in Germany and the Low Countries, the imposition of ever more burdensome feudal obligations, and the lack of internal order and good government in Germany after the death of Frederick Barbarossa, had coincided to force the Germans to seek prosperity and more freedom elsewhere. Thus there ensues a whole series of population transfers, one of the greatest colonising movements in the world's history. The organisers, known as *locatores*, carried out the transfer of whole villages in order to establish German colonists in the uncultivated regions of Bohemia, Hungary and Poland. An essential feature of the process was that these Germans were settled in their new country by virtue of written contracts. Generally speaking, the settlers were exempt for a certain period from all levies. After having broken in the land for ten or fifteen years and made it fit for cultivation, they were required to pay fixed dues, either in kind or in proportion to the yield. In most cases they received a written document, which set out their legal rights and which protected them against extortion and unjust treatment. As we know, the rights of these German peasants were soon extended to indigenous peasant communities, which often succeeded in obtaining as clear a limitation of their obligations as was made in regard to the newcomers. No other factor contributed more to safeguard the liberty of the peasants in central Europe than this extension of the legal status of the German colonists to the whole of the agrarian population.

Up to the fifteenth century, then, the peasants of central Europe had never experienced serfdom similar to that of the English villein of the twelfth century or the French and west German peasant of the thirteenth century. The latter were already tied to the soil and delivered over to the mercy of the lords of the manor and their officials. As for services and dues, here custom alone fixed limits. In the west the legal status of the serfs was such that the royal courts refused to take any responsibility in this respect.

Another phenomenon should be mentioned at this point that presents two contradictory aspects. While in the west, from 1250 to 1550, the status of the peasants was evolving progressively from serfdom towards freedom, in central Europe the peasantry over the same period, after their previous freedom, were being reduced to a servitude that was much more humiliating and tyrannical than anything western countries had ever known.

In England the first signs of the decline of serfdom go back to the thirteenth century; certain services attached to servile holdings begin to be payable in cash. In some instances lords find it advantageous to accept from their peasants sums of money in exchange for weekly labour services and the *corvée*. This method of converting labour into cash payment depended exclusively on the lords; nevertheless there resulted in England, as in Bohemia, from the first half of the fourteenth century a system within the framework of which the economic autarky of the village and production for local consumption yielded slowly to production for the market and cash profit. The lord needed money to fulfil his military obligations to the king, to pay what he owed to the church and to satisfy the increasingly large demand for luxury goods which the expansion of European commerce had made essential in regard both to clothing and finery and to military equipment and armour. So the lord tended to transform the obligations of his serfs into rents payable in money. Very often even the serfs obtained written documents, such as a copy of the receipt confirming payment of a sum registered by the manorial court. Thus began to crystallise a legal form that became characteristic of the rights of the English peasants: tenure by *copy-hold*, i.e. tenure distinguished by a copy of the receipt for rent paid. This kind of tenure became the typical form of peasant proprietorship in England from the fourteenth century until the disappearance of the yeoman-farmers and smallholders at the beginning of the nineteenth century. Curiously enough, payment in money was preferred not only by the French and English territorial lords of the fourteenth century, but also by many Czech, Polish and Hungarian lords of the same period. Poland and Hungary were inclined to welcome *hospites* on the basis of a system of money payments and to extend this 'German law' to indigenous serfs as well. In England the emancipation of the serfs, that is, their liberation from the *corvée*, made considerable progress during the fourteenth century. But setbacks occurred.

After the black death in 1348 and 1349 had killed off a third of the population, and manpower in the countryside had declined catastrophically, the lords of the manor naturally tried to impose compulsory labour again on their tenants who had survived the epidemic. And this was all the more comprehensible since, despite all the efforts of parliament, the pay of agricultural labourers continued to rise. This attempt at re-establishing the predial labour of the serfs was one of the causes of the peasants' revolt of 1381. But the failure of the revolt did not interrupt for long the progress of emancipation. The lords leased uncultivated land to anyone, provided the farmer agreed to pay in money the rent demanded by the owner. Towards the end of the fourteenth century villeinage scarcely existed any longer in England: the legal status of a villein disappeared altogether towards the end of the sixteenth century. The serf was now transformed either into a copyholder paying a hereditary rent or into a lease-holder paying rent on the basis of a lease. In many cases the status of the copyholder was particularly advantageous; the rent to be paid, having been fixed in the fourteenth century at the trifling sum of fourpence per acre, became quite insignificant in view of the great depreciation of money in the sixteenth century.

In France the history of the emancipation of the serfs, and the transformation of their predial services into money payments, unfolded simultaneously with the analogous process in England. However, one should add that this emancipation was less complete in France, for, until the reign of Louis XIV, the political power of the French landed nobility was much greater than that of the English landowners. The political and juridical decline of the latter dates back to the Tudor period. That is why, right up until 1789, the French peasant is subject to a whole series of obligations and levies (obligations in regard to marriage, inheritance, milling: levies on rabbits, pigeons or game, etc.). Nevertheless, he could be considered a free man because he had the right to leave the lord's demesne and to sell his own land. In addition, he was protected by the royal courts against any injustice committed to his hurt by the civil authorities as well as in regard to any criminal action.

In Spain, where internal development was of a quite different character, the peasants, once liberated from the Moorish yoke, soon entered into a relationship with the new Christian lords that had nothing in common with serdom. Without doubt the Spanish peasant of the fifteenth century was very poor, but at least he was treated as a free man.

It was the same in Italy. In the Middle Ages one does not find serfdom there in any form: the fairly early triumph of the Italian towns over the landed nobility had prevented the establishment of various predial services. True, the Italian nobility and burghers treated the *contadini* in a very harsh manner, but they imposed on them a régime of financial exploitation rather than of servile *corvées*.

In the sixteenth century, then, serfdom was almost nonexistent either in England, France, Spain, Italy, the Low Countries or in western Germany. In central Europe the situation was quite different.

One can say, generally speaking, that in the fifteenth century the liberty of the peasant had taken on the same form in all countries of Europe. This may be attributed to the fact that in western Europe serfdom was tending to disappear, while in central and eastern Europe it had not yet reached its full development. Let us observe first the process by which the relatively free peasant of Bohemia, Hungary, and Poland became the wretched serf of the sixteenth century, who has to wait until the nineteenth century for emancipation. (We are not dealing here with the history of serfdom in Russia, but it is well known that it unfolds there in a manner almost analogous to its development in central Europe.)

As we have seen, the introduction of serfdom into western Europe relatively early, during the Dark Ages, was in large measure the result of foreign invasion and internal disturbances. The same factors contributed in large measure to aggravate the lot of the peasants in central Europe towards the end of the Middle Ages. The first invasion was that of the Mongols around the middle of the thirteenth century. In Bohemia its results were minimal: the Mongols who crossed Moravia from north to south took only a fortnight to do so. Poland had to suffer more. After the defeat and death of the Polish prince Henry at Lignica, the presence of the Golden Horde near the country's south-eastern frontiers constitutes a fresh ordeal. Tatar raids devastate Poland and Volhynia for two hundred years. During this whole period the Galician or Volhynian peasant, menaced incessantly with pillaging, arson and murder, can expect no protection from the king of Poland, the Polish monarchy undergoing a process of disintegration until the beginning of the fourteenth century. In these conditions the peasant's only possible protector was the local lord, always ready to demand from his subjects the price of the protection he offered. In 1323 the extinction of the princely house of Galicia deprived the peasants of this province of their last hope of finding at length a strong bulwark against the Tatar and Lithuanian raiders.

But, of all the states of central Europe, it was undoubtedly Hungary which suffered most from the Mongol invasion. It was in fact a question not only of the material damage caused by the hordes of Batu Khan, but even more of the harmful influence of the Cumans who, having found refuge from the Tatars in the very heart of Hungary, brought about the decline of the Árpád dynasty and a lamentable revival of barbarian customs. It was as if their aim had been to revive ancestral paganism throughout the entire land. The year 1301 was marked by the extinction of the house of Árpád; Hungary and its peasantry fell into the hands of several ambitious and unscrupulous adventurers like Matthias Csák, Ladislas of Transylvania, and the Aba family. It is impossible not to be struck by the fact that within a decade we see the disappearance of three ancient dynasties of central Europe: the Árpáds in 1301, the Přemyslids in 1306, and the Piasts reigning in Great Poland in 1296. In all these countries the period that followed was marked by civil wars and the accession of foreign rulers.

The kingdom of Bohemia was the object of keen competition between Rudolf of Habsburg and Henry of Carinthia, only to fall in 1310 to John of Luxemburg, who was then still a minor. But even after the accession of King John, Bohemia knew neither order nor the benefits of a solidly established government, since its king regarded it simply as a source of revenue. He was nearly always away from the country, squandering his time in extremely costly chivalric enterprises in Prussia, Italy and France. Until the regency of his son Charles in 1333, Bohemia remained at the mercy of certain unscrupulous nobles; the latter's oppression of the peasants continued to increase throughout this sombre period.

In Poland and Hungary we may note analogous developments. In Poland it was not the power of a dynasty, but the primitive character of economic life that delayed the establishment of feudalism and serfdom. Poland had been divided into some half dozen autonomous statelets and Silesia into some twenty duchies. This state of affairs lasts a century. After the extinction of the senior branch of the royal house at the end of the thirteenth century, the Czech Václav had been elected king of Poland in 1300. In 1306 his son, also Václav, who had succeeded his father in the previous year, was murdered in mysterious fashion during his journey to his new country. For around two decades and a half, that is, until the coronation of Kazimierz III in Cracow in 1333, Poland was the scene of a long conflict with the Teutonic knights. It is unnecessary to say that during this period the territorial lords seek to establish their power. The oppressed classes reply with disturbances among the German colonists settled in Little Poland (1311). At the same time, in Hungary, the extinction of the house of Árpád with the death of Andrew III in 1301 was followed by a fierce struggle between Václav II of Bohemia and Charles Robert of Naples for possession of the crown. As elsewhere, only the local tyrants profited by these disorders.

At a certain period the triumph of the territorial lords over the peasants was moderated by the formation of powerful modern monarchies. In Poland Władysław I and Kazimierz III, in Bohemia Charles IV both as regent and later as king, in Hungary Charles Robert, in Hungary and Poland Louis the Great, were all rulers too farsighted to permit territorial lords with their immense domains to become kinglets. But the struggle was hard. Although Charles IV succeeded in securing the peasants settled in the lands subject to the Czech crown in their right to take their complaints against their lords to the provincial courts, his efforts at checking the expansion of the lords' customary rights by inserting these rights into the *Majestas Carolina* were set at nought by the tenacious resistance of the nobility, who were sensible enough to know that *definitio est limitatio*.

It is true that in Hungary Charles Robert breaks the power of the oligarchs, who had sprung up during the period of the Cumans. But neither he nor his son, Louis, were able to prevent the formation of a new aristocracy composed of great landowners, who were either former tenants of the oligarchs or royal retainers loaded with important donations. Of course there also existed a free nobility. All these elements, brought together in *una eademque nobilitas*, had only one care: to subject the *jobbágy*, i.e. the serfs, to their economic and judicial authority.

In the middle of the fourteenth century the lot of the Polish peasant was still more harsh, for the kings of Poland did not equal the Luxemburgs or the Anjous either in power or ability. Silesia fell to the Czechs and Pomerania to the Teutonic knights; in both provinces the peasants were subjected to the direct control of foreign lords. Even on the territory of Poland proper the nobility succeeded in imposing on the peasantry an increasingly harsh régime. Still, the serfs were not yet bound to the soil, and they had the right to appeal from the judgment of the seigniorial court to a royal tribunal. But the charter of Košice (1374), which recognised the privileges of the *szlachta* class, had disastrous consequences for the future of the peasants.

The enfeebling of the monarchy could only hasten the success of the territorial lords of the three countries. When Charles IV of Bohemia died in 1378, his son Václav IV was still a child;

and later he showed himself incapable of checking the ambition of the lords. Rebels threw him into prison on two occasions, in 1394 and 1401, and although he regained power in 1404, his barons could not be reduced to obedience. But for the peasants of Bohemia, Moravia, Silesia and Lusatia, the Hussite wars and the anarchic epoch following them were the most critical period. Václav IV died in 1419. A coalition formed by burghers and territorial lords under the Calixtine standard prevented Sigismund, brother of Václav, for twenty years from succeeding him on the throne. During this period the territorial lords and the burghers direct the affairs of the country. At the outset the Bohemian peasants had hoped that the champions of Hussitism would bring Christ's kingdom upon earth; but soon they were forced to recognise that the Utraquists in no way differed from the Catholic lords when it was a question of extorting from the poor peasants their last penny and the last minute of time set aside for the *corvées*. Petr Chelčický raised a solitary protest; his successors, the Czech Brethren, were persecuted by the Hussites, who remained masters of the situation. Even the end of the Hussite wars did not in the least diminish the power of the Czech lords. Sigismund died in 1437, that is, a year after he had come to the throne for the second time; and his successor, Albert of Austria, died in 1439. The latter's son, Ladislas, being a posthumous child, the Bohemian lords were able to keep power for a further period of twenty years. Nobles and burghers now gave the tone to the diet: the country was divided into twelve provinces and the nobles who governed them assumed the title of *hejtman*. For the peasants there was very little difference between the Catholic lords of Rožmberk and Hussites like Hyněk Ptáček or George of Poděbrady; the peasants had to bear increasingly heavy impositions. This process was all the more grievous for them since it involved a progressive dimunition of their rights. Until the death of Ladislas, a king lacking in energy, or more accurately, until the election of George of Poděbrady in 1458, no attempt was made to arrest the growth of feudal power and the enserfment of the peasantry. Although George's reign was comparatively short—about thirteen years—it permitted the rehabilitation of the country after the destruction caused by the Hussite wars and the arbitrary governmental régime of the aristrocrats; for a moment even, the peasants could breathe more freely.

Hungary after the death of Louis the Great in 1382 suffered a similar fate to that of Bohemia after the death of Charles IV. The murderous civil war, which then took place between Maria and Charles of Durazzo, lasted five years; it was followed by another war between Sigismund of Luxemburg and Ladislas of Naples for possession of Hungary and then by a third war, this time with Venice. The approach of the Turks, the disaster of Nicopolis (1396) and the bad administration of Sigismund, the Hussite wars, and the imperial ambitions of the sovereign deprived Hungary for a half century of good government and its peasantry of all protection. During this period the new nobility continued to increase its power; it entrenched itself firmly in the provinces, exercising an increasingly heavy economic and judicial pressure on the peasants. Even if it is true that the peasants were not yet serfs in the legal meaning of the term, nonetheless the various ecclesiastical pretexts for oppression, the royal tax known as *nona*, predial services and dues in kind constituted such a mass of obligations that the Hungarian peasant slipped fairly swiftly into the same kind of serfdom as that from which the English and French peasants were already freeing themselves. Even Sigismund's death does not alleviate in any way the lot of the Hungarian peasant. Albert of Austria reigned only two years; Ladislas Jagiellon lost his life on the battlefield at Varna (1444), and Ladislas the Posthumous was simply a puppet in the hands of the Hungarian lords. The rehabilitation of Hungary had to wait until 1458, as long—that is—as was the case with Bohemia: in that year Matthias Corvinus was elected king of Hungary. But he soon raises by 18 dinars the taxes imposed on the peasantry, and he too, like George of Poděbrady, fails to found a dynasty.

In Poland the course of events following Louis the Great's death was more or less the same. The coronation of Jadwiga took place only after a troubled interregnum lasting two years: until the queen's marriage to the Lithuanian prince Jagiełło there was no one strong enough to check the greedy and ambitious *szlachta*. Even during the long reign of a king as severe as Jagiełło, the *szlachta* showed itself capable of following the example of the Hungarian nobility and of strengthening its position within the provincial dietines (*sejmiki*). These, having become detached from the central government, became thereby the more efficacious instruments for oppressing the peasantry. Jagiełło's successor, Władysław (Ladislas) III, reigned for ten years, but during this period he lived more in Hungary where he had to fight the Turks. His death at Varna was followed by an interregnum: the Poles, once they were certain that Władysław was actually dead, elected Kazimierz IV as king of Poland. He reigned from 1447 to 1492; during this time he attempted to create an autocratic government based on the royal bureaucracy. This régime was more or less similar to the régimes introduced at the same period by Matthias Corvinus in Hungary and by Louis XI in France. But in Poland serfdom was already in full swing, and Kazimierz, while he succeeded in slowing down its progress, was unable to reverse the course of history.

Around the end of the fifteenth and the beginning of the sixteenth centuries the three countries met with a serious disaster. The trends and practice of the preceding hundred and fifty years were now given a legal form: the rights of the lords in respect to the peasants were formulated without equivocation and the latter transformed into serfs according to the letter of the law. In all three countries the control exercised by the monarch was weakened to a dangerous degree. In Bohemia George of Poděbrady, who died in 1471, was succeeded by the feeble and indecisive Vladislav II from Poland, a new puppet of the nobles, nicknamed 'King *Dobře*', since he had the habit of answering with this particular affirmative all requests made to him. When in 1490 Matthias's strong hand ceased to control political life in Hungary, this same Ladislas succeeded him in Hungary, Moravia, Silesia and Lusatia; but in fact it was now the nobles who governed these lands. And after Kazimierz IV of Poland had left the scene in 1492, Vladislav's brothers, Jan Olbracht, Alexander and Sigismund I, proved as weak as Ladislas himself. This did not prevent them from occupying the Polish throne successively from 1492 to 1548.

In Bohemia the year 1497 brought the first blow against the interests of the peasantry. The diet passed a law which made the peasants *adscripticii*, that is, serfs tied to the estate on which they had been born. At the same time they were deprived of the right to sell or even to leave their holdings. They constituted henceforward a part of the demesne and, if they tried to flee in order to escape from a particularly brutal lord, they ran up against the opposition of the public authorities, who had only one aim—to return the fugitives to the estate from which they had originated. But even this law did not satisfy the nobles. Three years later, i.e. in 1500, the diet accepted the famous land ordinance, which raised considerably the *robota* (*corvée*) due the lord.

In Hungary, where the peasants were subjected to extortion by the church, king and nobility, and where they were already under the jurisdiction of the territorial lords, complete enserfment was achieved only at the price of bitter struggles, as the *jacqueries* of 1437 and 1445 prove. Later, in 1514, when the Hungarian peasants were mustered for a crusade against the Turks, malcontents turned their arms against the representatives of oppression. This peasant revolt set in motion the population of very large areas; but, despite the rebels' heroism, it ended in a bloody failure and an atrocious massacre. The nobles' triumph was complete and lasting; the diet also passed a law tying the peasant to the soil.

In Poland the final scene in this drama was still more instructive. Not only does the all-powerful *szlachta* dare to banish the king and exclude the burghers from all the privileges of, and all participation in, power; in addition, the Polish territorial lords discovered that their fertile fields could produce much more than was necessary for themselves and their household. They saw that it was easy to sell Polish cereals in the west, especially in England and the Low Countries, as well as the products of Lithuania (e.g. wood for building, furs). In England, where sheep-raising was practised on a grand scale, domestic agriculture could no longer satisfy the needs of a growing population: it was necessary, therefore, to import cereals. In these conditions the Polish gentry had one aim: to produce as abundant crops as possible in order to send their produce to Danzig and sell it there to English, Dutch or Swedish merchants.

There existed, however, still another factor which, to a

certain degree, determined development in Poland as well as in Bohemia and Hungary. In the course of the fifteenth century feudal armies were replaced by armies of professional mercenaries. The territorial lords, who found both their amusement and their principal occupation in warfare, were demobilised—this allowed them to devote themselves to the exploitation of their estates. This changed orientation proved fatal to the peasants: everywhere in the countries of east central Europe, and above all in Poland, they became the most easily exploited instruments for capitalist agriculture. This degradation is reflected clearly in the legislation of the Polish *sejm*. In 1493 Polish peasants were transformed into *adscripticii*, with the exception of one member in families having several sons, and in 1496 the diet at Piotrków makes serfdom general: all peasants were subjected to the jurisdiction of the territorial lords.

Should one not see in these facts, then, the chief cause of the very different evolution of the peasantry in eastern Europe from that in western Europe? In England, the Low Countries, France, Spain, Italy and the Rhineland, the most ancient form of capitalism possessed a commercial and industrial character. England preferred sheep-raising, cloth-making and overseas commerce to agriculture. Manufacturing and commerce also transformed the style of life both in Flanders and the Low Countries and in seaports like Florence, Venice and Genoa. Spain likewise neglected agriculture and concentrated its attention on the riches of lands overseas. France became the principal source of luxury items. This kind of capitalism gives birth to a proletariat of an urban and not an agrarian character. But in central and eastern Europe the oldest form of capitalism appears in the domain of agriculture, that is, in the production of cereals, timber and furs for export. That is why the western nations demand money rents from their peasants, while the landowners of central Europe require manual labour from their serfs. In central Europe rents were replaced by compulsory labour in the fields and in the forests. Thus, at the very time when the peasants in western countries had already begun to free themselves from their obligations in this respect, in eastern lands like Hungary, Bohemia, Silesia, Poland, Prussia, and Russia too, their counterparts were being reduced to a serfdom that their ancestors had never known, a serfdom from which they were to gain liberation only three and a half centuries later.

XIV

Social and Constitutional Development in Bohemia in the Hussite Period

Aberrations from the normal course of national development are often interesting. They are not uncommon: England during the years 1642 to 1660, France between 1552 and 1594, Hungary between 1241 and 1306 and Bohemia between 1419 and 1471, with which this paper is concerned, are examples. Such periods of aberrancy are not only intrinsically interesting in respect of the causes and results of the deviation from the usual path of political and social evolution, but also because the character of the deviation may well illuminate the history of neighbouring and contemporaneous societies both by contrast and similarity.

The aberrant period of Bohemian history may well be taken to have begun with the apoplectic death in 1419 of Václav IV, king of Bohemia, margrave of Moravia, lord of Silesia and Lusatia and titular king of the Romans, and to have ended with the election to the Bohemian crown in 1471 of a foreign, Catholic prince, Vladislav Jagiellon, eldest son of Kazimierz IV, king of Poland. During the half century between these two events Bohemia stood outside the normal current of European history in two ways, ecclesiastically and politically. This paper is an attempt to examine the way in which this double idiosyncrasy affected the constitutional and social development of the Bohemian nation.

The ecclesiastical separation of Bohemia from the body of the western church was occasioned by its refusal to accept the authority of either general council or pope after the burning of Jan Hus at Constance on 6 July 1415. Its defiance of the council of Constance was manifested by the practice of giving the eucharistic cup to the laity despite the fact that the council had explicitly condemned that practice as heretical in the same year. Even when in 1436 a tripartite agreement between the Bohemians, the Emperor Sigismund and the council of Basel was made at Jihlava on the basis of the 'Compactata', that did not entail a permanent return of the nation to the obedience of the council, for the compactata were only a partial and interim compromise on the crucial question of communion in both kinds, and when, in the following year, the fathers of Basel refused to admit that the giving of the cup to laymen was a binding ordinance of Christ or that the cup should be given to infants immediately after baptism, the Hussites again suspended their allegiance to the council. Indeed when, in 1439, Pope Eugenius IV declared the council of Basel to be illegal and dissolved and when in its turn the council declared the pope to be deposed, some of the Hussites continued to give a nominal obedience to the pope which it denied to the council and the anti-pope whom it set up. For a time the whole nation, Catholic as well as Hussite, was united in its refusal to recognise any ecclesiastical authority outside the realm. The Catholics were devoted adherents of the council of Constance and continued to acknowledge the authority and legitimacy of the council of Basel for a time even after its deposition of Eugenius IV. In 1442 we have the anomalous situation that while the Bohemian Catholics rejected both rival popes, the more extreme Hussites, the Taborites, theoretically recognised Eugenius as the only lawful head of the church. The degree of the ecclesiastical independence of the whole Bohemian nation can be observed in its unanimous rejection of the archbishop of Prague provided by the council of Basel in 1440, Mikuláš Jindřichův, who was not only rejected by all the Hussite factions, but also by the Catholic chapter of the archiepiscopal cathedral church of Prague.

Throughout almost the whole of this period there was no archbishop of Prague. Konrád of Vechta, who was archbishop when Václav IV died in 1419, after some havering made common cause with the Hussites, and after his death in 1431 the see remained vacant for a century and a quarter. There was only one bishopric in Bohemia other than Prague, that of Litomyšl. But Litomyšl lay in the middle of the most convincedly Hussite part of the country; its lands were among the first to be seized and secularised, and its bishop, John the Iron, had been one of Hus's bitterest enemies. Neither he nor the titular bishops and administrators of the diocese whom councils and popes nominated to succeed him was ever thereafter able to occupy and govern his see. During the first twenty years, therefore, after the beginning of the ecclesiastical revolt the Catholic minority in Bohemia was without head or leader. Even when, after the restoration of Sigismund to the Bohemian throne in 1436, the Catholics were to some extent able to recover and stabilise their position, they did so merely under the authority of the Catholic chapter of the cathedral of Prague and of the administrators whom it appointed; the Catholic clergy, like their Hussite rivals, had to seek ordination in Moravia from the bishop of Olomouc or from foreign bishops.

The schismatic Hussite majority of the nation also gradually acquired an ecclesiastical organisation and government of its own. During the years of foreign and civil war from 1420 to 1434 there were very many religious assemblies which issued doctrinal and ecclesiastical ordinances, but they were only occasional, partial and haphazard congregations; it was a matter of chance what clergy, masters of the university, officers of state, lords and gentry attended them. Usually if they embraced all the factions they decided nothing; if they were homogeneous, their decisions were obeyed merely by the adherents of the party present at the meeting. In such circumstances it was easy for supreme ecclesiastical authority to pass into the hands of the one body which, in the absence of a king, had any sort of authority in the nation as a whole, the diet or assembly of estates of the realm. By negotiating the compactata with the council of Basel, it came to occupy the position of a parliament whose authority, at least in theory, was supreme in matters spiritual as well as temporal. As early as 1435 the parliament nominated Jan Rokycana to the archbishopric of Prague and Martin Lupáč and Václav of Chocen as his suffragans. The fact that none of the three was ever consecrated or ever exercised any episcopal functions illustrates the ineffectiveness of parliament, but does not derogate from the completeness of its claims to be the supreme governor of the national church.

It was King Sigismund's failure to fulfil his undertaking to procure recognition from the church of Rokycana's title to the archbishopric and the understandable refusal of council and pope to recognise the canonicity of episcopal elections made by a lay parliament which kept Rokycana and his colleagues from their episcopal chairs. Nevertheless such ecclesiastical organisation as the Hussite church attained was entirely of parliamentary authority: the Hussite consistory which was the ecclesiastical governing body of the national church, and the two clerical Administrators who were its executive organ were nominated by the parliament and continued to be so until the reign of Ferdinand I of Habsburg.

Thus there was a national, schismatic church in Bohemia, the first in western Europe, which survived outside communion with the church of Rome until it fell in common ruin with the national state before Tilly's victorious assault on the White Mountain in 1620. It is true that from the accession of Vladislav Jagiellon in 1471 the Bohemian kings were Catholics, but they were the Catholic rulers of a nation which for the most part manifested its ecclesiastical independence by maintaining the condemned and schismatical practice of communion in both kinds and by acknowledging no religious authority superior to its own consistory and the national parliament.

The second aspect of the aberration of the Bohemian nation in the fifteenth century is political. In an age when the principles and practice of absolute monarchy were making rapid advances towards that position of supremacy which it was to achieve almost universally in the following age, Bohemia was for most of the time without a king at all. In the age of great supranational dynastic agglomerations like those of Philip the Good of Burgundy, Kazimierz IV of Poland, Sigismund of Luxemburg, Albert II of Habsburg, Henry V of England, Eric of Scandinavia and Mohammed the Conqueror, Bohemia remained an isolated national state, rejecting the rule of native and foreign princes alike. For thirty-two years of the fifty-two with which we are concerned there was no king in Bohemia; the other twenty years were occupied with the brief reigns of the restored Sigismund and of his son-in-law Albert of Habsburg, which together only occupied three years, and the seventeen years of the reign of George of Poděbrady, from 1453 to 1457 as administrator for the juvenile Ladislas Posthumous, from 1458 to 1471 as king. Neither Sigismund nor Albert was able to do much to re-establish the authority of the crown. During the twenty-two months of Albert's reign as king of Bohemia, from his election in December 1437 to his premature death in October 1439, he did nothing to arrest the development of oligarchy which had been going on ever since the death of Václav IV in 1419. Albert was recognised as king only by the Catholic and Austrian party; he spent most of his brief reign not in Bohemia, but in Silesia, Lusatia and Hungary, while Bohemia itself was torn by civil war and despoiled by invading Polish armies. The reign of the native king, George of Poděbrady, might at first sight seem to have restored Bohemia to the normal course of contemporary development, for King George shared many of the aims and adopted many of the methods which characterised the new monarchy; he has much in common with his contemporaries Matthias Corvinus of Hungary, Kazimierz IV, Louis XI and Edward IV. Yet the aberration of Bohemia can hardly be deemed to have been rectified before his death. George of Poděbrady was not a member of any of the great dynastic families of his day; he had not a drop of Luxemburg, Habsburg, Jagiellon or even Přemyslid blood in his veins; he was a native Czech, merely the most successful of the newly enriched landed nobility, who by his eminent ability, application and good fortune, outlived or outdid his fellow oligarchs in taking aristocratic polity to its culmination, making the whole realm his estate. George's accession in 1458 was not the triumph of the monarchical principle, but of the essentially oligarchic principle of elective monarchy; it was the last defeat of dynasticism, and it is remarkable that though George, once elected, inevitably behaved like a king, he was no dynast; he made no attempt to secure the succession for his son. Not until King George's death and the election to the Bohemian crown of a foreign prince, a Catholic and the eldest son of one of the great European dynastic houses, was Bohemia brought back into the main stream of European history. But it was then too late for the country to resume the normal course which had been interrupted in 1419 by the accident of the childlessness of Václav IV. In the ensuing half-century of civil war and foreign invasion, of interregnum, anarchy and oligarchy, of ecclesiastical rebellion and isolation, the history of the nation had been distorted in a way which the Jagiellonian kings were too feeble and the Habsburg kings too late to correct. The failure of the Bohemian nation to preserve its political and ecclesiastical independence under Ferdinand I and Ferdinand II was determined by the twist which was given to its development during the Hussite aberration.

The development of the Bohemian kingdom during its golden age of the thirteenth and fourteenth centuries had seemed to presage for it a development parallel not to that of Poland and Hungary, but to that of the Netherlands, France, Spain and England. Its geographical position brought it into closer contact with the west than Poland and Hungary were. Its great natural wealth, especially in silver, provided the material basis for the empire building of Přemsyl Otakar II, Václav II, John of Luxemburg and Charles IV, and provided the foundation for an urban development which again made Bohemia more like a western state than its eastern neighbours, where urban life was suffocated in its infancy. The four able Bohemian kings of the thirteenth century had laid a firm foundation for monarchical government and those central institutions of finance, administration and royal judicature which were firmly planted by the last Přemyslid monarchs and carefully elaborated by Charles IV. Even Charles's son, Václav IV, though, like his brother-in-law Richard II of England, he had had to suffer from the ambitions of his closest male relatives and the attempt of the magnates to subject the crown to conciliar control, had, like Richard, survived the storm and done something to reassert monarchical authority. Had Václav been survived by an adult son, had the religious revolt not kept his brother and heir, Sigismund, off the throne for seventeen critical years, the history of the country might have continued on the course already set.

There were in Bohemia, as in all late mediaeval states, strong currents making for the growth of the political and economic domination of the landlords, though the country had been fortunate, as compared say with France, Germany, Poland or Hungary, in that the political power of the landlords had developed comparatively late. It was not till the fourteenth century that the ownership of land had come to be synonymous, *eo facto*, with the exercise of political power. But the disastrous extinction of the Přemyslid dynasty in 1306, the ensuing absence of a resident monarch during most of the reign of John of Luxemburg, and the early weakness of Václav IV had given the magnates and gentry some opportunity to exercise political power both in their own estates and in the arrogation to themselves of the influential and lucrative offices of the central government. It was this tendency towards the oligarchy of the landowners which was hastened and confirmed by the absence of a monarch after 1419.

The primary opportunity which the interregnum afforded to the magnates was that of arrogating to themselves the great offices of state. There was no king to give office to his own servants and favourites, men of no estate dependent on the crown for their appointment and continuance. Here was an opportunity for which the great landlords had been struggling throughout the forty years of the reign of Václav IV with limited success. Now there was no one to deny them the enjoyment of power and profit. In as far as great offices of state were filled at all during the years 1419 to 1458 we find it is the members or clients of the richest families—Vartemberk, Rožmberk, Lobkovic, Šternberk, Hradec, Pirkštejn, Kunštát, some of them Catholic, some Utraquist, some mere politiques, who occupy the offices of chamberlain, high burgrave, marshal, hejtman, or chief justice, treating them too often as the instruments of power exercised in the interest of individual or class, and valuing them chiefly for their emoluments.

The magnates confirmed their political power by increasing their wealth. They secured for themselves royal estates and castles which they held in almost perpetual pawn from the crown to such an extent that the royal demesne almost completely disappeared. The impoverishment of the crown during this period was such that it proved almost impossible to get anyone to accept it. After the death of King Albert in 1439 parliament and the political parties hawked the once rich crown of St Wenceslas over half Europe with an ignominious failure to find any takers that has only been matched by the desperate effort of the Greeks to find a king in the middle nineteenth century. The Bohemian crown was offered to Albert duke of Bavaria, Albert of Hohenzollern and Frederick III of Habsburg and refused by them all, primarily because the crown lands of Bohemia were almost all in pawn and none of the invited princes could hope to redeem them. Only Władysław III and Kazimierz IV of Poland showed any willingness to enter into the impoverished inheritance, and when in 1471 Kazimierz's son did become king of Bohemia he found that he was so poor that there was no economic source of strength he could use to stand against the power of the nobles who had grown fat on crown lands.

The increased wealth of the magnates was derived not merely from crown lands. They were also the luckiest beneficiaries of the secularisation of church property, which was perhaps the most influential result of the premature religious revolt of Bohemia. More than a century before Henry VIII seized the land of the English monasteries the first iconoclastic fury of the Hussites had sacked and razed to the ground half the monasteries in Bohemia and Moravia. Nearly all the monks were expelled; many of them were murdered. Within five years of the death of Václav IV practically all monastic land had been confiscated. The land of those religious houses which were destroyed by the Hussite zealots of the towns of Prague, Tábor, Hradec Kralové, Slaný, Písek and others was seized and kept by the municipalities. The lands of other monasteries, nunneries and friaries were coolly taken by neighbouring landlords, by Catholic lords like the Rožmberks as much as by Hussites like the Šternberks, Žampachs and the family of Kunštát. By the seizure of the lands of four of the richest of the south Bohemian houses, Milevsko, Zlatá Koruna, Zvíkov and Sedlcany, Oldřich of Rožmberk, the most powerful of the Catholic lords, was able to complete his vast principality which made him the independent ruler of most of southern Bohemia; it was monastic lands which were largely the basis of the great Hussite lordships in the north and east of the country, such as those of Kolda of Žampach, Ptáček of Pirkštejn, and of George of

Poděbrady himself. It is interesting to observe the future Hussite king receiving the grant of twelve monastic manors from the arch-enemy of the Hussites, King Sigismund. The lands of the Franciscans of Hradec Kralové (Koniggrätz) went to the enrichment of the leading politique, Menhart of Hradec. The Catholic town of Plzeň and the Hussite citadel of Tábor alike profited from the spoils of the monasteries. Even when the Catholic minority was in power after the restoration of Sigismund and some of the abbots and monks were reinstated in monasteries on Catholic lands, very little of their property was restored to them even by their co-religionists. It is important too to remember that during the vacancies which occurred after the death of Archbishop Konrád of Prague most of the vast estates of the archbishopric were seized by the lords and the towns. The estates of the bishopric of Litomyšl were almost the first victims of the religious revolt, for the Hussites had no mercy for Bishop John the Iron, the agent of the council of Constance for the repression of the revolt. Most of the estates of the bishopric of Litomyšl fell into the hands of the Kostkové lords of Postupice. As in England a century later the property of the parish churches was, it seems, left to them; for one thing, it was not extensive, and for another the advowsons of the parish churches were usually held by the corporations of the towns or by the local landowners. The Hussites often assumed control of the churches and put in clergy of their own persuasion, but neither they nor their Catholic rivals were interested to deprive the incumbents they nominated of all sources of revenue. It is probable however that the more extreme Hussites, the Taborites, Horebites and Orphans, may have taken over parish revenues and paid a salary to their clergy.

The enrichment of the powerful few by the acquisition of crown and church lands was in many cases further increased at the expense of the lesser landholders. In the anarchy of the period it was inevitable that the war of every man against his neighbour should have its victims as well as its victors. Some of the gentry and knights were skilful and unscrupulous enough to win for themselves a share of the plunder; some of them grew rich on the spoils of civil war and of the great raids which the 'warriors of God' made into Germany, Austria and Hungary.

The whole period down to the accession of King George is filled with incessant and often petty civil war between great and lesser landlords, often but thinly disguised as religious conflicts, from which the greater normally profited at the expense of the lesser. It is probably in this confused struggle that the poorest class of freeman, the lordless *svobodnici*, virtually disappeared from the social scene, so that in the next century there were only a few hundreds of them left. A few freemen flourished during the Hussite period and became gentry; but most of them were brought under lordship and sank into villeinage.

The acquisition of monastic lands by the towns is an interesting phenomenon. It was hardly to their ultimate advantage, for as landowners they were forced into competition with the lords both as primary producers and in the diminishing labour market. It was a competition in which the advantages were almost all with the lords, and in the struggle between the lords and the towns which was waged in the sixteenth century the landlords, with their control of the legislature and their greater capital resources, were victorious.

The increase in the economic resources and political power of the lords at a time when the crown was virtually in abeyance transformed the character of the Bohemian monarchy. The lords were able to clinch their victory over the crown by virtue of a series of personal accidents: only one of the kings of the Hussite period was survived by a son, and that was King George, but even he was so strongly convinced of the impossibility of the survival of a small nation in dynastic isolation that he made no attempt to secure the succession for his son Viktorín and was content to leave it to the nation to decide to which of the neighbouring dynasties the kingdom should pass. As for the others, Václav IV was ultimately succeeded by his brother Sigismund and he by his son-in-law Albert. Albert's wife was pregnant when he died, but the posthumous Ladislas was not even acknowledged as Albert's successor in Bohemia until four years after his father's death, and then he was kept out of the country by his guardian, Frederick III, from 1443 to 1453. Even after Ladislas came to Prague and was crowned he was still but an ineffective youth, a puppet in the hands of the lords and the governor, George of Poděbrady. Ladislas died childless in 1457.

This series of accidents robbed the Bohemian nation of the chance that its monarchy might have become as unquestionedly hereditary as that of France in an age when hereditary monarchy and succession by primogeniture was the best guarantee against oligarchy. The hereditary character of the crown of St Wenceslas which had seemed to be assured by the terms of Frederick II's Golden Sicilian Bull of 1212 and Charles IV's Golden Bull of 1356 was ruined by the fact that there were five elections to the crown in the fifteenth century. This was a series of opportunities which the estates were quick to seize; four of the elected kings were made to purchase the throne by capitulations: Sigismund in 1436, Albert in 1437, Ladislas Posthumous in 1453 and Vladislav Jagiellon in 1471. Each capitulation meant the acceptance of limitations on the freedom of the crown in its choice of ministers, control of the executive and public finance and in its ecclesiastical supremacy; each capitulation meant a *de facto* confirmation of the rule of the oligarchy of landlords. The Bohemian monarchy which had in the middle of the fourteenth century seemed as well set on the road to absolutism as that of France had by the end of the fifteenth become less powerful than the monarchies of Poland and Hungary. Even the Habsburg kings of Bohemia were not able to break the power of the Czech lords until they had ruled the country for almost a century, and even so, by 1620, it was too late for absolutism to save the country from bastard feudalism and belated serfdom.

It would not have been so bad for the country had the functions and powers of the monarchy passed into the hands of an efficient and patriotic parliament, truly representative of the nation. To a limited extent the Bohemian *sněm* or parliament was the beneficiary of the demise of monarchy. In the periods of interregnum, as far as there was any exercise of national government it was the parliament which was legally sovereign. But its meetings were at irregular intervals; it was not summoned unless it was in the occasional interest of the political and religious factions that it should be; it rarely represented all those factions at the same time, but was often little more than a party caucus arrogating to itself sovereign functions. The meetings of parliament were usually very brief; it made little pretence at legislation in the interest of the community as a whole. The membership of parliament was undefined and inconstant. Writs of summons were sent out by those magnate officials of state who at the moment wanted a parliament to meet for their own immediate and usually selfish purposes, and were sent only to those whose presence was for those purposes thought to be desirable. Most parliaments were predominately composed of magnates and the richer landlords. There was no clerical estate, and the two lower estates, the knights and the burgesses, found the expense of attendance intolerable and the proceedings frustrating and often opposed to their particular and class interests. Such parliaments could not justify their existence or become a centralising force of permanent good governance; they did not achieve effective sovereignty because they did not earn it. The parliament which Hussite Bohemia bequeathed to the sixteenth century was therefore little more than an organ of class domination, an interested assembly of nobles and knights wherein the burgesses played an ever diminishing part, a body which was to prove quite incompetent successfully to maintain national autonomy against Habsburg absolutism.

The tasks which the crown could not and the parliament did not perform could not be entirely neglected if society was to survive at all. Even during the worst times of civil and religious strife the need for some ordering of relationships and for the perservation of life and property was felt by the mass of the people. It is only the powerful few who can afford the luxury of anarchy. At first it was the need for defence against foreign invaders which compelled the creation of local organisations for defence and war. The invading armies of crusaders organised by the councils and the emperor and led by Sigismund, Albert of Austria, Frederick of Brandenburg, Cardinal Beaufort and Cardinal Cesarini fostered the development of military political communities based on the Hussite towns such as Tábor, Prague, Písek, and Hradec Kralové. These local and sectarian organisations of Taborites, Horebites, Praguers, 'Orphans' and the rest were the instruments of coercive government within the territories their field armies controlled. And when foreign invasion was interrupted and succeeded by intestinal religious and social strife the Catholic districts and the Catholic landlords set up in their turn their own local defence organisations such as the Plzeň *landfrid* and the league of Strakonice. These organisations, both Hussite and Catholic, soon found it necessary to supplement military provisions by assuming many functions of government which were left unperformed by the central authorities or which the Catholics of the Plzeň *landfrid* in south-western Bohemia would not allow the Hussite rulers of the country to exercise in the area which it controlled. Even when the victory of the moderate Utraquists at the battle of Lipany in 1434 and their agreement with Sigismund at Jihlava in 1436 brought the civil war and the danger of invasion to an end, the tendency for local units to crystallise out of the national confusion continued. The incipient local government of the *kraje* or *Kreise* provided almost the only refuge for the *menu gens* against the greedy aggression of the magnates, especially when after 1439 the central court of common pleas, the *zemský soud*, was suspended from operation until the realm should have a king again. The division of the country into political and religious factions also facilitated the development of more or less autonomous local units, especially where a district was predominantly of one political or religious persuasion. For example, after the death of King Sigismund in 1437 we find that the strongly Hussite districts of Chrudím and Kutná Hora negotiated as if they were sovereign bodies with Władysław III of Poland to promote the candidature of his brother Kazimierz for the Bohemian throne in opposition to the candidate of the Catholic and moderate lords, Albert of Habsburg.

The decisive year for the development of provincial autonomy was 1440, after the death of King Albert. His heir was yet unborn and no foreign prince was willing to assume the impoverished and schismatic Bohemian crown. Even if Ladislas Posthumous was to become king the country was faced with the prospect of a long minority. The mass of the people who had no interest in anarchy, that is, the yeomen, knights and gentry, the artisans, miners and traders, therefore gave their support to the only public authorities who could give any assurance of peace, order and justice, the local governments of the *kraje*. This solution was accepted by the parliament of 1440 which virtually confessed its own inability to provide good government for the whole realm and abdicated its sovereign position by completing and regularising the pattern of local government. The kingdom was apportioned into districts, significantly called 'peace districts' (*landfridy*), the number of which varied at different times from 12 to 14. Each landfrid had its local parliament, the 'estates of the *kraj*'; the constitution of these local parliaments seems never to have been strictly determined, but they were attended by a fluctuating number of local landholders and municipal councillors and officials. The parliament of the landfrid elected a council, whose members were usually lords and knights and sometimes burgesses, and also the *hejtman* of the landfrid. In those landfrids which were predominantly Hussite or predominantly Catholic there was a single hejtman; if the landfrid was confessionally mixed there were two hejtmans, one of either confession. The hejtmans and the councils composed the executive of the landfrid: it provided arms for the semi-professional military force which each landfrid maintained; it built castles and garrisoned them, collected the land tax in the countryside and the house tax in the towns; justice for the most part continued to be administered in the village, manorial and municipal courts, though the council of the landfrid apparently exercised some of the judicial functions which had in better days been performed by the royal courts. Sometimes the local parliaments elected the delegates to the national parliament. This last function indicates well how nearly the Bohemian landfrids were coming to approximate to the Hungarian county courts and the Polish local assemblies (*sejmiki*). Indeed the emergence and the importance of the landfrids is the clearest indication of the way in which Hussite Bohemia was assuming the pattern of development of the retarded states of eastern Europe and how fatally far it was diverging from the road which the more advanced states of the west were travelling. The system of local government survived, with many modifications, as long as the kingdom of Bohemia lasted. Nevertheless it never had that importance as an enduring embodiment of political power which the county organisation in Hungary maintained. This was in large part due to the fact that the Bohemian landfrids became themselves the instrument for the restoration of central authority. The power of the Catholic pro-Austrian faction led by Oldřich of Rožmberk in the years immediately after the death of King Albert drove the predominantly Utraquist landfrids of eastern Bohemia to seek security by common action. Four of them, Chrudím, Časlav, Kouřím and Hradec Kralové, elected a common over-hejtman, Hyněk Ptáček. He was almost unique among his fellow magnates in that he put the interests of the nation above those of sect or faction, and he made of this eastern union the instrument of a truly national policy. He used it to repress the intransigence of the Taborites even more vigorously than against the Catholics. When Ptáček died in 1444 the hejtman of the neighbouring landfrid of Boleslav, George of Poděbrady, succeeded him as over-hejtman of all five landfrids, and it was on the basis of this solid block of Hussite provinces that George was able to proceed successively to the occupation of Prague, the assumption of the governorship of the realm and finally to the crown. But though George as king dispensed to some extent with the governmental functions of the landfrids, his feebler successors allowed them to recover a measure of the power which they had enjoyed during the interregnum, a power which was thenceforth exercised in the interests of the landlords, who, with the decline of the wealth and influence of the towns in the sixteenth century, dominated the local councils and courts of law.

All these constitutional and political developments in Hussite Bohemia profoundly affected and were themselves conditioned by the fortunes of the mass of the people. Probably the most influential factor was the falling off in the supply of labour. This was in large part due to the destruction wrought by civil war, foreign invasion and expeditions into foreign lands. Native and foreign armies lived in and on the land, unproductive and destructive, consuming food and destroying crops. Starvation, premature death and pestilence decimated the towns. Thousands of men who should have been tilling the soil or practising their crafts learnt no other trade than that of the soldier. Many of them became professional mercenaries in foreign armies or departed for good to serve in the bands which for two generations battened on northern Hungary. Evidence of the resultant shortage of labour is afforded by the efforts made by the landlords to keep their peasants on their estates. Already in the fourteenth century there had been legislation designed to prevent tenants from leaving the land or selling their holdings. The lords' anxieties were increased by the readiness of the towns, themselves afflicted by the shortage of labour, to seduce the peasants and their sons. Therefore it was that the Hussite period is marked by further restrictions on the mobility of labour. In 1437 the land court ruled that 'subject people who leave their holdings and go to the towns or elsewhere should be returned to their lords or else should provide for the occupation of the land they have deserted by suitable persons. If they do not do so, the lord may bring them back by force.' In 1453 the Bohemian parliament enacted that 'no one shall harbour any rent paying tenants or servants of a lord unless they have been given his due permission to depart', and that 'labouring men or servants who are without employment must within two weeks provide themselves with a lord, for whom they shall work and whose servants they shall be'. Thus was the way prepared for the complete ascription of the serfs which the landlords secured by the statute of 1497 and the land ordinance of 1500.

Before the Hussite wars the Bohemian peasant had been in the eyes of the law a free man and a citizen, with the right of appeal from the village or manorial court to the king's court or the king himself. The absence of any royal government and the political domination of the oligarchy of landlords during the Hussite period gravely worsened the juridical and economic position of the peasant. The state to which he was reduced by the end of the fifteenth century was described by Viktorín Kornel, an eminent and humane jurist, in his *Nine Books of the Law* as follows:

The lords buy their tenants and servants with their own money and have full power of life and death over their people as if they were their servants, as the laws prove; but the lords themselves are only the voluntary servants of the king, for he has not bought them with his money, and they are voluntarily subject to him. And each king swears an oath to the Land; but the lords promise nothing to their people, servants and labourers, though they exact oaths and promises from them. In fine, all their rent paying tenants, labourers and servants are not free, but bound and unfree.

It is an interesting, difficult and disputed question how far the material condition of the peasants was worsened, if at all, during the Hussite period. On the one hand must be placed the indisputable deterioration of their legal status: they now swear an oath of homage to their lords, they are almost completely at the mercy of the lord's court; they cannot leave their lands without his written permission, for which they have to pay a fee. But on the other hand there are reasons for thinking that the material condition of the peasants at the end of the fifteenth century was not much worse than it had been at the beginning. For one thing the peasant was the chief beneficiary from the decline in the purchasing power of money which was a feature of the period in Bohemia as elsewhere. The peasant's heaviest monetary expenses were his rent and taxes. Rents were mostly customary, and there is reason to think that, though they were arbitrarily increased by some lords, the peasant, who normally sold more than he bought, would generally be spending a diminishing proportion of his income on rent. It is an interesting phenomenon of this period, too, that far less was levied by the state in the way of taxes during the Hussite period than had been done in the fourteenth century or was to be in the sixteenth, for the simple reason that there was often no central authority to demand and collect a tax. The general land tax (*berně*), the whole burden of which fell on the peasants, and which had been before 1419 an annual tax equal nominally to half what the peasant paid in rent, was levied only five or six times in the whole period from 1419 to 1458. But this does not mean that the peasants' financial immunity was complete; they suffered from the requisitions of both friendly and hostile armies, and we know that the landfrids organised in 1440 had the power to raise local taxes, and presumably they exercised it.

Marxist historians regard Hussitism as fundamentally a self-conscious revolt of the serfs and the urban poor against their exploitation by the landlords and the merchant patricians.[1]

[1] The Marxist view of this period of Czech history which holds the field in Czechoslovakia today [i.e. in 1955] has been recently and succinctly stated by Josef Macek in chapter 7 of *Přehled československých dějin* (pp. 28-36), published by

They point to the primitive communism practised by the small farmers and peasants in 1420 and 1421 in southern Bohemia in their enthusiastic expectation of the immediate second coming of Christ which, they believed, would be accompanied by the abolition of all rents and services. They also lay great stress on the almost equally short-lived proletarian revolution in Prague, under the able leadership of the ex-monk Jan of Želiv, who incited the people to the destruction of monasteries and brothels and to the defenestration of the patrician consuls of the New Town of Prague in 1419. But both these movements were of short duration, perhaps partly because the oppression of the poor had not been heavy or prolonged enough to become the

the Czechoslovak Academy of Sciences as a supplement to volume ii of the *Československý časopis historický* for 1954. I translate some of what Macek there writes:

'The evaluation of Hussitism in the work of K. Marx and F. Engels is the basis for the scientific exposition of the history of the Hussite revolution.

'The world importance of the founding of Tábor consists in this that there for the first time in the history of humanity extensive progress was made towards the building up of a society of equals based on the socialisation of consumer goods. Chiliasm became the dominant and practical expression of the ideology of revolutionary Tábor . . .

'In Prague there was put into the foreground a social programme (the Four Articles of Prague), accepted by the poor as the beginning of the revolutionary reconstruction of society . . .

'Jan of Želiv was one of the most devoted fighters for the rights of the revolutionary people. Exemplary too was his attitude to the nationality question. As long as Želiv was the leading person in Prague there was no fear of the Praguers being able to betray the revolution. Želiv became therefore one of the most important personalities, though he has been vilified or ignored by the bourgeoisie . . .

'The Hussite revolutionary movement was a peasants' war (Marx) and a prelude of the bourgeois revolutions, because for the first time in history it threw off the power of the greatest feudatory, the Church, and because it was fought out by the country people and the urban poor under the leadership of the town leagues.'

To illustrate that current view [i.e. in 1955] about the effect of the Hussite movement on the condition of the peasantry I quote F. Graus, *ČsČH*, I, 2 (1953), p. 211: 'The greater part of the Czech people were serfs whose position as a result of the Hussite revolutionary movement was recognisably improved; the most important acquisitions of the serfs were that they were freed from heavy Church imposts, chiefly tithes.' Macek in his *Husitské revoluční hnutí* (*Hussite Revolutionary Movement*), p. 173, says: 'Bourgeois historiography—especially the work of Josef Pekař—endeavoured to maintain that the Hussite Revolutionary Movement worsened the situation of the serfs . . . In fact however at the end of the Hussite Revolutionary Movement after the battle of Lipany, the country people and the poor were on the whole, after their defeat by the counter-revolution, brought back roughly to the position of the pre-Hussite period.' [In the original version this note was inserted in the text.]

incentive to permanent revolution. Within a year or two the chiliastic enthusiasts who had left their lands and their lords to found the city of refuge they christened Tábor were soberly and successfully engaging in profitable crafts and even more profitable crusades, their early communist enthusiasm so far forgotten that the Utraquist chronicler who describes their bloody extermination, under the leadership of Jan Žižka, of the Adamite sect could end his narrative of the massacre with the words: 'Thanks be to God.' After the overthrow in Prague of Jan of Želiv in 1422 the Hussite movement was directed by and for the gentry and the solid majority of the townsmen. How far peasants' rents were raised and their predial services increased it is hard to say because of the absence of fifteenth-century manorial rolls and cadasters. The evidence provided by contemporary publicists seems to indicate what we should expect from the analogy of the behaviour of politically powerful landlords elsewhere. Kamil Krofta summed up his conclusions from his careful examination of the problem in these words:

The majority of rents and services had been permanently fixed by agreements and were not liable to alteration. As most of these agreements dated from the pre-Hussite period the peasants' obligations in the fifteenth and sixteenth centuries ought not to have been greater than they were before the Hussite wars. Nevertheless it is certain that payments and services did increase markedly during this time. Sometimes the increase was made illegally: the lords imposed on their subjects greater payments and services than were due, having no other justification for so doing (apart from their right to extraordinary aid 'in great need') than their power over them. Both the great Hussite moralists, Rokycana and Chelčický, complain of this. In his protest against the oppression of the serfs by the lords Chelčický accuses them of acting against their poor people unjustly by imposing on them field services, hunting services, newly devised night patrols and other burdens. Rokycana speaks even more explicitly in his sermons. 'The gentry', he says, 'flay the labouring folk, imposing illegal taxes on them designedly, burdening them as if they were pack horses . . . they devise new carriage and building services . . . This too they have devised, that every peasant who has a cow must pay to his lord one groat for each horn . . . You have to pay to the king the equivalent of half your rent in tax, but to the lord the equivalent of the whole of it . . . Who has to supply the means to support the pride of the lords? Why, the peasants! Who pays for their tournaments, their dances, and their lovemaking, their feasts and banquets? The peasant, alas, must bear it all! He, alas, must eat dry bread and drink water, and give to the lord that he may feast.'

There is little statistical evidence to confirm these allegations. As far as the documents go it is only in the sixteenth century that we can demonstrate any increase in predial service (*robota*) above the few days' boon work of the pre-Hussite period. The evidence of sixteenth century legislation, land stewards' instruction books and fragmentary tax rolls shows that by that time servile incidents had grown considerably in number and weight; by the end of the sixteenth-century the peasant was far advanced on the road to complete serfdom, closely bound to the soil, unable to sell or mortgage his holding, to send his son to school or to learn a trade, or to marry his daughter without purchasing his lord's permission; he was forbidden to sell beer and often to brew it, and he was liable to be expelled without compensation for bad husbandry. While it is true that the position of the Bohemian peasants in the sixteenth century was not nearly as abject and wretched as it was to become in the seventeenth and eighteenth centuries, yet it was already so much worse than it had been before the Hussite wars that there is a presumption that it had degenerated during the Hussite period. While it is possible that the research at present projected by Czech historians may yet prove the truth of their thesis that the Hussite period was one of social progress, the evidence that is available at the moment seems to indicate that the sixteenth century made explicit and gave legislative sanction to a worsening of the position of the peasants which had come about during the earlier period for which evidence is lacking.

It is well known that the belated subjection of the peasantry of central and eastern Europe was in large measure due to scarcity of labour at a time when the landlords were turning from subsistence agriculture to production for local and foreign markets. Labour was short during the Hussite period; but how far the lords were already in the fifteenth century capitalising their estates and producing cereals, wool, beer, flour and fish for the market is a problem on which research still remains to be done.

There is indeed much that still awaits investigation in the history of Hussite Bohemia, but we already know enough to begin to understand that that period was critical in the history of the country. Anarchy, oligarchy and isolation from the body of western Christendom diverted the development of the country from the lines on which it seemed to have been set. Thenceforward it was forced into the pattern provided by the retarded societies of Hungary and Poland, with whom its history thereafter ran closely parallel and whose political and social fate it has since largely shared.

XV

Masaryk's Philosophy of History[1]

WHEN Thomas Garrigue Masaryk, already president of the republic he had created, published his war memoirs in 1925 under the title *World Revolution*, he said this:

> I stayed more than eighteen months in London—from the end of September 1915, to the end of April 1917 . . . The university offered me a Slavonic professorship which Seton-Watson pressed on me again and again on behalf of Dr Burrows, the principal of King's College; and even though I was reluctant to take it, because I am not a Slavonic specialist [that from a man who two years before had published the two volumes of *Russia and Europe*] and because I feared that I should have no leisure for scientific work, I ended by accepting it, and did well to follow the advice of my friends . . . The subject of my inaugural lecture on 19 October 1915, was *The Problem of Small Nations in the European Crisis*. It was our first big political success. Above all, the fact that the Prime Minister, Mr Asquith, had agreed to take the chair, accredited me to the wide public in London; and as Mr Asquith fell ill, Lord Robert Cecil represented him, and thereby provided a political background which gave our cause great prestige.[2]

In that record are linked not only the philosophy and creative statesmanship which make Masaryk one of the small number of those who have combined *δυναμίς πολιτικῄ καὶ φιλοσοφία*, but also the two men whom it is my privilege to succeed in this Chair, Masaryk and Seton-Watson, the father and the midwife of the Czechoslovak republic.

[1] Inaugural Lecture delivered as the Masaryk Professor of Central European History in the university of London, 4 Jan. 1947. [R. R. Betts's predecessor in this chair, R. W. Seton-Watson, held a professorship of Czechoslovak Studies at the university of Oxford from 1945 to 1949. He died in 1951.]

[2] T. G. Masaryk, *Světová revoluce* (Prague, 1925), pp. 105-6. Translated by C. Paul, *The Making of a Nation* (London, 1927).

Those of us who are young enough to think of the Austro-Hungarian empire merely as an historical phenomenon as irreparable as the empire of Attila, sometimes forget that when Seton-Watson first set off on his crusade as 'Scotus Viator' forty years ago the Austro-Hungarian state was one of the potent realities of world politics, and that the Czechoslovaks, the Croats, the Slovenes and the Ruthenes were even to the scholars and statesmen of western Europe but half-remembered names of oppressed and neglected subjects of the Habsburgs. That they are today constituent parts of independent and powerful states, strong in their restored pride in their past and their plans for the future, is in large measure due not only to Masaryk, but also to Seton-Watson. Both men are apostles of the Platonic gospel that philosophy which does not ripen into action is but barren scholasticism. Seton-Watson, during the twenty years before 1914, laboured not only to know the peoples of central Europe, but also to make them known, and during the period of the first war he seconded the efforts of Masaryk and Beneš, Trumbić and Pašić, with such effect that Balfour's recognition of the Czechoslovak provisional government and the pact of Rome which saw the birth of Jugoslavia were in no small measure his work. Since 1918 Seton-Watson has watched over the growth and growing pains of his god-children with anxious care; as occupant of this chair he expounded the history of the Czechoslovaks, the Rumanians, the Magyars and the southern Slavs by voice and pen, and also in three notable volumes he told the story of that British foreign policy which during the last hundred and fifty years has so often been fateful for the central European nations of whom, but for him, not only our prime ministers would have known nothing.

And now he has gone if not to a higher, at least to another sphere, to endeavour to stir the university of Oxford out of its omphaloscepsis to have an intelligent and scholarly concern for those Czechs in whom it has shown but little interest since the day in the reign of Henry IV when a group of dissident Oxford scholars purloined the university seal to forge a letter to the Bohemian reformers averring that Wyclif was no heretic. We may hope that Seton-Watson, who wrestled so triumphantly with the obscurantism of Vienna and Budapest, will succeed even in Oxford.

Seton-Watson's achievement as scholar and politician is, I believe, due not only to his own genius and devotion but also to the fact that he is a disciple of Masaryk and has practised the gospel of political philosophy which was Masaryk's most valuable contribution to his own country and to the world. It is the purpose of this lecture to describe the powerful influence which Masaryk exercised on the development of the philosophy of history. That influence was beginning to make itself felt just at the time when Seton-Watson was beginning to shape his life's work.

Masaryk himself speaks of 'the so-called lucky accident which springs from the inner logic of life and history',[3] and the world must deem it a lucky accident that Masaryk appeared just when he did. His considered judgment of the nature of the historical process was completed in its main features and formulated in an authoritative book during the last decade of the nineteenth century, that is, just at the period which he himself rightly designated one of political, scientific and philosophical crisis.[4]

The liberal world of the nineteenth century was already showing signs of dissolution; the golden age of Britain's free trade hegemony was nearing its end; commercial rivalry between Britain, the United States, and Germany was filling the air with threatening storms; the sun of Japan had risen over the horizon in blood-red dawn; the threatened autocracies of Austria, Russia, and Turkey were hurrying themselves and their subjects towards war and revolution. Hypertrophied and unregulated capitalist development was driving by its innate momentum towards imperialism and imperialistic conflict.

In conformity with this catastrophic progress the philosophy of history was finding justification and explanation for the journey towards Armageddon in a philosophy which rejected reason and ethics in favour of scientific fatalism and the amoralism of organic evolution.

Two systems, rivals in fact, but sprung from common parents

[3] *The Making of a Nation*, p. 289.

[4] Masaryk, *Otázka sociální*, ed. V. K. Škrach, 2 vols. (Prague, 1946), ii, 360.

and nurtured in the same environment, were clamouring for men's allegiance. The parent of both was Hegel, who had rationalised reason out of all rationality and set it on the throne of the Hohenzollerns, and who had formulated a dialectical method of thesis, antithesis and synthesis. This method Marx and Engels had used to construct a philosophy of history which was determinist, materialist, objectivist, catastrophic, and revolutionary, one which taught that ethics, religion, ideals, liberty, law, and love were mere ideological superstructures, mere fetishes and illusions. The other school of historical philosophers of the nineties learnt from Hegel to think of the state as omnipotent and omniscient, and had married the fashionable German *Korporationslehre* to immature Darwinism and senile Platonism. Gobineau, Lagarde, Seeley, Treitschke, Bosanquet and Houston Stewart Chamberlain were trying to persuade their generation that every corporation and especially the nation and the state was a living organism, more than and greater than the sum of the individuals that composed it, an organisation with a will, a reason, a soul of its own; an organism in which the function of the individual was no more than that of an unconscious specialised biological cell.

Such were the two doctrines, the dialectic of economic materialism and the pseudo-biology of organic totalitarianism, which Masaryk in his early middle age found were being offered as philosophies of history and political panaceas to his students in the university of Prague, and he set himself to examine the validity of their claim to be able to rescue his own nation from the danger of suffocation in the Habsburg hot-house and the world from the danger of war and dissolution.

The nature of the case, his own modesty, and his philosophical training made it inevitable that Masaryk's approach to the problem of the nature and direction of the historical process should be critical rather than expository. Therefore in all the many and voluminous writings of Masaryk there is nowhere a full and systematic account of his own philosophy of history. It has to be culled from a study of his books, articles and lectures, and put together piecemeal from his critical, historical and political works. That he had a positive philosophy of history is apparent to anyone who reads his great treatise on the development of Russia during the hundred years before 1913, published in Czech under the title *Rusko a Evropa* and in English as *The Spirit of Russia*, or his account of the birth of the Czechoslovak state which he wrote under the title of *Světová revoluce*, translated into English as *The Making of a Nation*. Nearly everything which he wrote that I have read throws some light on his historical philosophy, especially *The Czech Question* (1894), *Palacký's Idea of the Czech Nation* (1897), *The Problem of the Small Nation* (1905), and his inaugural lecture in this university, *The Problem of Small Nations in the European Crisis* (1915). But his greatest book and the one from which above all his detailed philosophy of history must be quarried is *The Social Question*, first published in 1898.

The Social Question was the first systematic critique of Marxism, and still remains a book that every disciple and every opponent of Marxism ought to study most carefully. It was based on an exhaustive knowledge not only of all Marx's writings, but also of those of Engels and the first generation of their followers: Lasalle, Kautsky, Cunow, Konrad Schmidt, Bebel, Liebknecht, Vollmar, Plechanov, Belfort Bax, William Morris, Lafargue, Enrico Ferri, but not of course, those of Lenin, whose importance as a philosopher Masaryk did not begin to appreciate until after 1917.

With the rightness or wrongness of Masaryk's criticism of Marxism I am not now concerned. I use *The Social Question* merely to elucidate what Masaryk's positive opinions about the historical process were, supplementing it from the incidental light thrown by his other writings, particularly *Russia and Europe* and *World Revolution*.

Fundamental to an understanding of Masaryk's philosophy of history is the fact that he did not regard history as *vitae magister*, laying down laws for all the other arts and sciences. He has nothing but contempt for the 'pure' historian of the universities of his day 'who masters palaeography and the so-called historical sciences, and then trots out a series of individual facts in accordance with some extraneous system of chronology, but who never learns anything about the substance of society, the state, the church, or anything else'.[5] The theory that the

[5] *Otázka sociální*, i, 178.

answer to all political or social problems is to be sought in history, that all sciences are ultimately history, Masaryk brands as 'historism', 'which looks for and finds in history reasons for what, in its own opinion, ought to be'.[6] 'The historian', he says, 'must be a specialist. He will be a specialist if, in addition to his auxiliary historical sciences, he is trained in philosophy and sociology; he must also be an historical specialist, for example in political history, which again presupposes a special study of political science.'[7] The Marxists, Masaryk felt, chiefly erred in making history supreme over the present and the future. 'Rather', he said, 'should the historian learn to observe the present in order that he may explain that which is more remote by means of that which is near, the less known from the known.'[8]

It must be remembered that Masaryk had had no professional historical training; he never professed to be a 'pure' historian, in my opinion truly enough, for it seems to me that his historical judgments are not always well founded; he is too ready to take his historical opinions at second hand from the latest doctoral theses, and very rarely had the time or the patience to go to the original texts. I feel that he misjudged and undervalued the Middle Ages and that he was too ready to assume that the Renascence and the Reformation were the cataclysmic beginning of all that has been influential in the making of the world of today. It is true that as a young man he had taken steps to set up a society for the publication of the texts of the Czech reform movement, and that by his high-minded and unpopular labours in exposing Hanka's forgery of the Zelenohora and Královė Dvůr manuscripts he performed an heroic and enduring service to historical truth, but that does not alter the fact that Masaryk's approach to the philosophy of history was not primarily that of an historian.

It was the insistence of Marx and Engels that the past reveals the working of a process of historical dialectic which drove Masaryk to counter their historism with what he calls 'realism', by which he meant the study of things as they are, not as they were, or how they came to be what they are. He said:

Over against excessive historism I place realism: first things, after-

[6] Ibid., i, 181. [7] Ibid., i, 179. [8] Ibid., i, 180.

wards development. And if I have to decide which is the more important I shall say, things . . . The static, not the dynamic, aspect of the world seems to me to be the chief and especial object of our thinking. Realism, then, stands opposed to Marxism, but not in absolute opposition, for there is no thing which has not developed, and that which develops is things.[9]

Masaryk refused to resolve the world and life into the droplets of Heraclitus's river; the world is more than mere movement and mere becoming. 'From history I cannot discover what I ought to do, and what I ought to do is what really matters.'[10]

This scepticism about history is part of Masaryk's indecision about causation and determinism in the historical process; indeed, it is part of his fundamental metaphysical agnosticism. He is constantly charging Marx and Engels with trying to construct a *Weltanschauung* without first establishing its metaphysical and epistemological basis. But Masaryk is not himself guiltless in this respect; he was sufficiently a child of his time to dislike formal philosophical and theological systems, and indeed once said: 'The philosophy of the schools estranged me, for it was a survival and continuation of mediaeval scholasticism. Metaphysics I did not like, for I found no satisfaction therein. In my eyes philosophy was above all ethics, sociology and politics.'[11]

Therefore we search Masaryk's works in vain for any formal statement of his views about appearance and reality, or about the nature of existence and of truth. This deficiency makes it the more difficult to state precisely his philosophy of history. But there are enough hints and negative statements to compensate for the absence of a formal exposition.

Masaryk takes the reality of mind and matter and of the time process for granted. But when he asks himself what is the relationship between events in time he finds himself in a dilemma. He does not want to accept the Marxist ascription of all social phenomena to economic causes, but at the same time he is so much a child of nineteenth-century science that he accepts the universality of causal connexion, what he calls 'the scarlet thread of cause and effect'.[12] 'The question whether the

[9] Ibid., i, 103. [10] Ibid., ii, 311.
[11] *The Making of a Nation*, p. 291. [12] Ibid., p. 288.

will is determined or not', he says, 'is a matter for empirical psychology, and empiricism proves that it is always determined. Therefore theism, criminal law, and education must recognise this fact.'[13] But while Masaryk maintains that everything has a cause he refuses to see cause only in 'conditions of production'. The essence of his philosophy of historical cause is the doctrine that causes are manifold, complicated, and never simple. He says:

The attempt to give a causal explanation of history is quite justified. But in practice a causal exposition of history demands great caution and methodological care. As a rule an historical event has not one cause, but many, often very many. The individual is constantly being acted on by heaven and earth, by the whole environment, and by the past; causes are closely and mutually connected with each other; results too are not simple but complex; a complex of effects will have a complex of causes and it is not easy so to isolate individual elements that the connexions of real causes and their working can be discovered with certainty.[14]

That needed saying in 1898; it needs repeating today. But besides the problem of the nature of cause there is the problem of how causality works. Of that Masaryk says:

Beside the multiplicity and complexity of causes we must observe how they work: we must carefully distinguish causes which operate always and without interruption from those which operate only intermittently; those which operate at certain periods from those which operate only once. Also we must measure, or at least estimate, their strength, the intensity of the effect, and we must distinguish those causes which are substantial and therefore deserving of attention from those which are negligible.[15]

In the same passage Masaryk warns historians against the temptation to see a causal relationship between every pair of successive and contemporary events. Like causes do not always produce like results[16]; what was or is does not necessarily determine what is or will be.[17] For example, vice and misery are not always and solely caused by poverty,[18] nor is poverty the only cause of pessimism, which more often afflicts the rich than the poor.[19]

[13] *Otázka sociální*, i, 308. [14] Ibid., i, 195. [15] Ibid., i, 196.
[16] Ibid., i, 161. [17] Ibid., i, 182. [18] Ibid., i, 162. [19] Ibid., i, 163.

Masaryk's opinions about historical causation may be illustrated by quoting what he has to say about the causes and effects of the Protestant Reformation:

There can be no doubt that the great reform movement in Bohemia, Germany and everywhere else sprang from religious and moral needs. This is proved by an historical and psychological analysis of the process of the reform. We see how the Reformation changed ways of life and ecclesiastical order. Dogmas changed, the substance of the Church changed, the relations of church and state changed; the whole life of the individual and of society was transformed. It is not true that in the Reformation it was only a matter of conflict between the bourgeoisie and the feudal aristocracy, and that the Reformation was only a 'costume', a 'change of dress': the religious revolution is the fundamental and chief part of all those changes which were wrought by and with the Reformation. The religious movement was prepared by attempts at reformation made at a time when there was not even a suspicion of the bourgeoisie of Marx and Engels; also the Reformation was established long before the bourgeoisie had developed so far that the new religion could be described merely as its 'costume', 'reflex', or anything of that sort.[20]

That passage illustrates not only Masaryk's method of historical analysis, but also his imperfect historical equipment. He does not realise how early in the Middle Ages the bourgeoisie begins to be influential, and like Palacký and most of the Czechoslovak historians, he underestimates the influence of economic factors. It also illustrates the idealism of Masaryk's philosophy of history of which I shall have more to say later.

The problem of human freedom and of the place of creative will in the history of man psychologically determined is one with which Masaryk never seriously grappled. He is content to say:

Here we stand before the question of questions. While a brain like that of Kant helped itself out with a wonderful dualism of empirical unfreedom and of the freedom postulated by pure reason, and Marx and Engels saw the answer to the problem of the world and of life in materialistic fatalism, . . . I for myself expound the world and history theistically: theistical determinism is for me a synergism not only social, but also truly metaphysical.[21]

[20] Ibid., ii, 196-7. [21] Ibid., i, 309.

How this co-operation of man's free will with the determining providence of God works Masaryk does not explain, except to say that he is a determinist but not a fatalist,[22] but again without elucidating the distinction. Determinism he regards as a Protestant attitude, indeterminism, with its provision for miracles, as a Catholic attitude.[23] That providence plays a part in man's destiny he has no doubt. To it he ascribes those 'lucky accidents' which preserved him and Beneš during the first world war, and he also quotes:

> There's a divinity that shapes our ends,
> Rough-hew them how we will

and adds: 'Yet a belief that Providence watches over us and the world is no reason for fatalistic inactivity, but rather for optimistic concentration of effort, for a strict injunction to work determinedly, to work for an idea. Only thus are we entitled to expect the so-called "lucky accident" that springs from the inner logic of life and history, and to trust in God's help.'[24] That, presumably, is 'synergism'.

As on the one hand Masaryk revolted against the strict historical materialism of the Marxists, so on the other he protested against making a fetish of modern science in the fashion of those who saw in history the evolution of cellular organisms. 'The cult of science', he said, 'by reason of its one-sided positivism has become more than a cult; it is sheer idolatry.'[25] And again:

> It cannot be disputed that natural science is helpful, indeed necessary, for the philosophical sociologist. But on the other hand, it cannot be too often emphasised that there is a danger of confusing sociology with zoology and natural history. Social and historical laws, the laws of social organisation and development must be established by a strict study of human society and human history themselves; zoology, botany, biology, even cosmology and so forth may give to sociology much instruction and many hints, but that is all. Natural science, at the most, provides sociology with analogies; but it proves absolutely nothing.[26]

[22] Ibid., ii, 306. [23] Ibid., ii, 199.
[24] *The Making of a Nation*, p. 289.
[25] *Otázka sociální*, i, 113. [26] Ibid., i, 108.

'Society is not an organism, but a *collectivum sui generis*.'[27] 'There is no such thing as a collective consciousness; there are only individual consciences.'[28] In another place Masaryk says:

This conception of society as an organism is anthropomorphic in a high degree. It is a mythical habit of thought which Marx and Engels get from Hegel. The organic assumption usually leads sociologists to make the mistake of using analogies with individual organisms for an unwarranted simplification of sociological and political problems. This is the error of all organicists, beginning with Plato, down to Spencer and Marx.[29]

Marx had constructed a scientific philosophy of history on the analogy of the physical, mechanical, geological science of Marx's youth; since then the biological sciences had been brought to the forefront by the work of Darwin, Schwann and Wallace. Masaryk is scornful of Engels's attempt to spatchcock evolutionary concepts into the Marxist system. He says: 'Modern evolutionism, even Darwinism, are irreconcilable with Hegel's teaching; Darwinism cannot be reconciled with Marx's teaching: Marx and Engels did not perceive that evolution is in opposition to their dialectic and historical materialism.'[30] Masaryk says that he believes in evolution, but not in Darwinism; that means presumably that he regards the human race as having evolved from a lower to a higher state, but he rejects the doctrine that the evolution has been accomplished solely by the principle of the survival of the fittest. Masaryk has as little use for the philosophy of the war of every man against every man as he has for the philosophy of the class war.

Confessing himself a determinist and evolutionist, Masaryk could not but believe that in some measure the past gives us a guide to the future, nor could he help believing in progress. Again I quote from the *Otázka sociální*:

The demand that socialists should give a picture of the future is quite justified; it applies also to non-socialists, and in general to all who study society historically. Grillparzer in one of his epigrams smiles at our latest historians who write the history of the future; but

[27] Ibid., i, 285, n. 1. [28] Ibid., i, 249.
[29] Ibid., i, 251. [30] Ibid., i, 70-1.

in fact the ability to write future history is the peculiar criterion of true historical knowledge. In this sense it may still be said that history is *vitae magistra.*[31]

He continues:

Faith in progress and the exposition of history as development and completion leads necessarily to the determination of the future, to a foresight of that which will develop from the known past. This foresight comes from the determinism of development; it is the conclusion from the premises of the past; it is strictly scientific prophecy. But we must not wander off into the thirtieth century; we will be content to lift a corner of the curtain that veils the next few years.[32]

But a little later he adds a characteristic warning: 'History, if it is exact, enables us in some, but always in a limited measure, to foresee, but it does not enable me to determine what in a given case I ought to do or not to do. Foresight is not action. Action springs from the will; not only from knowledge.'[33] Again Masaryk's intellectual determinism is in conflict with his ethical voluntarism.

Even as late as 1925 Masaryk was still talking about the moral and philosophical crisis of his generation, as he had done thirty years before. But he never lost his fundamental faith in progress. He will have nothing to do with circular or cyclic theories of history, whether they be Platonic or Marxist. He visits Engels's doctrine of a primitive communistic society from which civilisation has aberred and towards which it will catastrophically return with trenchant and detailed obloquy. Despite occasional and local periods of decadence, mankind has gradually risen from the savage, 'whose only communism was the communism of those who have nothing', to his present position of civilisation, which, despite war, oppression and vice, he believed in 1925 at least, to be bright with hope for the future.

But if Masaryk rejects the Marxist philosophy of history, and refuses to accept what he calls the 'hocus pocus' of dialectical materialism, what does he offer in its place? If he rejects economic forces, 'conditions of production', as the *primum mobile* of the historic process, what does he suggest as the alternative?

The problem of *Triebkraft*, *ženoucí síla*, *vis motrix* is fundamen-

[31] Ibid., i, 290-1. [32] Ibid., i, 291. [33] Ibid., i, 298-9.

tal to any philosopher of history who believes in something more than an unrelated succession of events. Masaryk begins his answer to it by saying:

The principles of exposition adopted by historians may be unificatory, but they are not simple. This is true of those who, for example, see the unique explanations of history in 'religion'; it is true of Ranke's 'ideas', and of Buckle's 'reason', of the 'egoism' of others; it is also true of 'economic conditions'. All these theories have this in common, that they see one chief, or indeed, a single social motive force whereby historical development can be explained. But in fact none of these motive forces is simple. For example, if it is said that reason is the unique cause of historical movement, it is nevertheless necessary to compare and evaluate accurately the intellectual activities of varied origin that are to be found in science, in art, in technique, and so forth. Similarly, religion, the state, and also economic conditions, are complex historical and social activators; and, too, Marx's 'conditions of production' are a synthesis of different and varied forces. The explanation of social phenomena cannot be as simple as that of mechanical operations; the sociologist in particular must not be afraid of very complex formulas; the number and complication of causes and effects in the sphere of social life is great.[34]

Masaryk in one place enumerates the more important of the motive forces of the historical process: cosmic and tellurial forces; biological forces, especially those that regulate the growth of population; division of labour; natural sympathy, personal properties; belief in fate or belief in God.[35] And scattered throughout Masaryk's writings are passages which indicate that he ascribed a primary effective part to human kindness, to kinship, to political momenta, to reason, emotion and will.[36] Masaryk considers art to be no less an efficient historical cause than economic production. 'Byron alone', he says, 'did more for the political emancipation of the nations than hundreds of secret societies.'[37] And again: 'Not only literature, but music and the representative arts have a powerful educative and cultural influence. Plato knew that, as can be seen from his exposition of the place of art in his *Republic*. Not

[34] Ibid., i, 197-8. [35] Ibid., i, 199-200.

[36] Ibid., i, 237; ii, 33, 101, 133. Cf. Masaryk. *The Spirit of Russia*, 2 vols, (London, 1919), i, 210.

[37] *Otázka sociální*, ii, 242.

merely among the Greeks, but also today poets and artists are the creators of gods and the dogmatic oracles of the nations.'[38] Marx and Engels erred, says Masaryk, in ascribing all human action to greed and love of power; joy in service can be equally powerful. 'Perhaps everybody would like to be a small Napoleon, but normal men like equally to obey, and they obey gladly.'[39] Masaryk refuses to arrange these manifold and complicated moving forces in any hierarchy of logical or causal precedence; nor does he agree that any one of them is supreme; he rejects utterly Engels's thesis of a *Triebkraft der Triebkrafte*, a *motor motorum*, or supreme historic cause. Even more emphatically does he reject instinct, the revolutionary instinct or the ambitious instinct or what not, as an historical motive force. He says:

The revolutionary instinct? I have very little respect for such instincts, very little use for instincts at all, for they probably don't exist . . . If revolutionary instinct is the moral justification of the claim to equality, then the ambitious instinct would be a justification not only of Napoleon I but also of Napoleon III, and, by the same argument, of capitalism. Instinct would justify Nietzsche and all aristocrats without distinction. Instinct—that is moral chaos.[40]

Masaryk refuses to simplify the historical process into either a Marxist class war or a Darwinian jungle conflict of every man against his neighbour. All war is not class war, nor is all economic conflict war. 'The French Revolution', he says,

had its parents not only in the Physiocrats, but also in Pascal and the Jansenists, in philosophers and politicians. Misery was indeed a very powerful cause of the French Revolution, but not its only or even its strongest cause. Modern revolutionism exists not only in the proletariat, but also in all classes, and it has its origin in discontent with the religious, ecclesiastical, philosophical, political, and social, as well as with the economic régime.[41]

Masaryk maintains that the class structure is not nearly as simple as Engels would have it, and that factors other than economic are determinative of class; nor is all vice to be found

[38] Ibid., ii, 249.
[39] *The Making of a Nation*, p. 296.
[40] *Otázka sociální*, ii, 142.
[41] Ibid., i, 236.

in the capitalists and all virtue in the proletariat. Anyhow, he asks, why is a class system as such morally wrong?[42]

But this is all negative criticism. What was Masaryk's own positive theory of the nature of the historical process? It is difficult to say concisely, just because he so stoutly rejected the temptation to over-simplification. But out of the critical arguments of the *Otázka sociální* and *Rusko a Evropa* a positive and concrete, even if not systematic, philosophy of history emerges. Using his own words as far as possible I would summarise it thus:

There is no objective dialectical process in history, and no dialectical opposition in things themselves.[43] In history, as in nature, there is a process of gradual development, a process which is not catastrophic[44]; violent revolutions more often have retarded than advanced the development of society. This development is driven by a great variety of motive forces. That which develops is not things but conscious man[45]; even economic development proceeds from subjective motives, from human needs. Once you abstract consciousness from science and philosophy, you destroy science and philosophy altogether, and with them economic science and also economic materialism.[46] There are indeed catastrophes in history, but catastrophes have not the epochal and universal importance which Marx ascribes to them, nor are they all merely economic. We today more rightly appreciate the fullness of social development, and posit an infinite number of infinitesimal modifications by means of which development, and in the long run, progress, are realised.[47] There must be some metaphysical basis of this development, and because it is the development of human beings, that basis cannot be materialism; and because it is a progressive development the metaphysical basis cannot be atheism. Despite all his professed dislike of antiquated teleological theories, Masaryk confesses that he cannot subscribe to a doctrine of absolute accidents.[48]

If history is the story of the development and progress of man, it must therefore be the story of the development and the pro-

[42] Ibid., i, 228-30, 381; ii, 142.
[43] Ibid., i, 69. [44] Ibid., i, 388. [45] Ibid., i, 203.
[46] Ibid. [47] Ibid., i, 277. [48] Ibid., i, 288-9.

gress of minds, of ideas. Masaryk is first and last an idealist, both in the political and philosophical sense of the word. His whole approach in his historical writings is that of a man who believes that ultimately thought is the only real and the only creator. That can be seen from the way he approached Russian history in his monumental *Rusko a Evropa*. How the concatenation of thought from generation to generation works he tells us in *Otázka sociální*: Every thinker and worker is psychologically linked with his predecessors and hands on his ideas and the results of his work to other thinkers. That is the rational thread of history. But the work of one generation is not merely a continuation of that which has already developed, for progress is not mere summation. Every man who thinks critically collates what his predecessors have bequeathed to him with what he can add thereto; he criticises, selects, makes a synthesis and transforms what he has selected, welding it into a whole in the furnace of his own spirit. Progress is not achieved merely by the adding up of given units; progress is not to be found in eclecticism and syncretism, but in organically creative synthesis—that is the only way that new ideas and deeds can grow out of the old. History is not only our logical laboratory; it is also the scene of action of our feelings and strivings. In history our desire and longing for achievement are realised.[49]

Since history is the history of thought it is the history of individual men and women, for masses and classes, states and nations cannot think; only the individual has a mind. And because of the inevitable inequality of men, history is largely made by individuals who are eminent in virtue, courage, genius or assiduity, not solely by mobs and masses.[50] To emphasise the individual's part in history is not to ascribe all human action to egoism, for individualism and egoism are not synonymous; there is not only antagonism between the individual and society, they also have common interests in well-being.[51]

Masaryk further assumes that because history is the history of thinking individuals it must have an ethical basis. One feels on reading his critique of Marxism that the most damning fault of Marxism in Masaryk's eyes is its positivist amoralism,

[49] Ibid., i, 303. [50] Ibid., i, 257-8. [51] Ibid., ii, 226.

its attempt to eliminate right and wrong and the moral purpose from history.[52] Masaryk's ethics is based on the observed fact that we make moral judgments (as indeed do Marx and Engels themselves); everyone engaged in politics, and in political economy, makes moral judgments, for his aims are determined ethically. Ethics is as necessary to action as logic is to thinking. Socialist planning, any planning, makes ethical assumptions.[53] The problem of revolution is not one of social dynamics but the ethical problem of the morality of force and violence.[54] The state has an ethical basis; its purposes are ethical and cultural, as well as economic[55]; if the nation has any absolute rights, they are based on ethics[56]; religion too is concerned with the relations of man to man as well as with the relations of man to God.[57] Even socialism and communism are and must be based on ethics. 'Why', says Masaryk,

are Marx and Engels against capitalist exploitation? Merely because the capitalist system is economically unsound? Or because it is wrong, because it offends the feelings of humanity? If capitalism was merely unsound economically Marx would probably never have written *Das Kapital.* If capitalism, as Marx admits, was economically better than the earlier system—*why* must we change it for a communist system? *Why* must we strive for equality? *Why* and by what right must we accept communism? Merely because the Communist Manifesto threatens the 'rebels'? Why are they rebels? Unless we have some internal argument for equality, springing from our own souls, then Marx will only be able to oppose capitalistic violence with communistic violence—whence then is to come that kingdom of liberty which Engels so exaltedly offers us? From violence and still more violence?[58]

The fact of conscience, the sense of a moral imperative cannot be explained away by Engels's doctrine of a morality relative to the economic conditions which create it.[59]

Masaryk sees in the historical process not only a great moral drama, but also the necessary counterpart of morality, religion —religion, not theology. Masaryk disliked theology and

[52] Ibid., i, 156. [53] Ibid., i, 300-1.
[54] *The Making of a Nation*, p. 200.
[55] *Otázka sociální*, ii, 124.
[56] Ibid., ii, 160. [57] Ibid., ii, 189-90.
[58] Ibid., ii, 222. [59] Ibid., ii, 219-22.

ecclesiasticism with all the fervour of the rationalist radicalism of the nineties. But yet he clung to what he called 'religion' with almost desperate zeal; and nothing is so amorphous and evasive as religion without theology or a church. Of religion's part in human history Masaryk has no doubt; he knows its strength in primitive societies[60]; he sees the basis of many of the differences between the nations not in mystical national characteristics, but in the different ethos of Catholic, Protestant, and Orthodox; he exaggerates the influence of the Protestant Reformation; he believes that today religion still plays a great part, and that it will continue to do so. He says:

> Goethe and Kant saw better and further than Marx. Leaving aside the impossibility of materialism in general, it is *a priori* most unlikely that religion, which has hitherto played so great a rôle, should just cease to be and be replaced by positivist science; every analogy makes it more probable, even from the evolutionist point of view, which Marx and Engels profess, that out of the present religious crisis will come a further and higher development of religion.[61]

I find it one of the weaknesses of Masaryk's teaching that, though he always insists on the importance of religion, he never tells us what his religion is. An admiration of Jesus and a somewhat vague belief in providence seem to be the substance of his theology. To him religion is primarily ethical and practical. In as far as it affects his view of history it appears in his faith that the two superior moving forces in history have been and will be work and love. I quote two memorable passages to conclude this lecture:

> Work, real work, is small jobs, everyday work. Just as every science is built upon everyday phenomena, so the real worker is he who knows how to do detailed, everyday essential work, and who does it willingly . . . The so-called great deeds, heroic actions, heroic revolutions are greater in idea than in fact. Utopia comes by patient labour . . . The heroes of the future will declare themselves by care for that which interests no one, by doing what is tedious and humdrum. Hitherto there have been few such; people would rather sacrifice their lives than work. Great epochs are not made in a moment; history, no more than nature, proceeds by leaps. Revolutionary changes, though they appear to happen suddenly, have been

[60] Ibid., ii, 57. [61] Ibid., ii, 192.

long prepared in obscurity . . . On the one side is lack of method and order, the occasional appearance of what is called genius, Bohemian disorderliness, excitement, nervous agitation; on the other, certainty of aim, clear thinking, beauty and purity of life and deed, and actual activity; not fantasy, but poetry; not muscularity but strength.[62]

But to praise work for work's sake, says Masaryk, is to make a fetish of labour, as Marx did. Work must be for an object ethically determined, and the ultimate ethical determinant, of politics as well as history, is love.

Love, which is effective, active; not sentimentality or philandering; muscular Christianity—as the Yankees say. True love is persevering, constant, considerate. It does not suffice that I should feel pity merely when some wretch comes into sight momentarily to trouble my complacency. True love will never know peace and contentment while physical and moral misery exist. Love means to work continuously and with open eyes against misery, even when we don't directly see it, since it is mere sentimental egoism to be stirred up to moral indignation only once in a Hungarian month. Occasional benevolence is not love . . . Love does not ask for martyrs . . . for love is mutual and demands no sacrifices . . . Long ago Havlíček said: 'In the past men have died for their country, for the well-being of their nation—but we today for the same cause will live and work.'[63]

Such in summary form is what I believe to be Masaryk's philosophy of history. With much of it I cannot agree. I believe he failed to appreciate the fundamental strength of the Marxist argument and the potency of Marxist politics. But what I believe is not to the point. Whether Masaryk was right or wrong in this argument or that cannot take away from his eminence nor derogate the greatness of his influence. His teaching and work became the basis of social democracy and modern liberalism in his own country and profoundly affected political thought and practice in the whole of Europe. None will deny, be he Marxist or agnostic, Czechoslovak or Englishman, that that influence, the influence of Masaryk's work and love for humanity, has been for good.

[62] Ibid., ii, 304-5. [63] Ibid., ii, 231-2.

SELECT LIST OF WORKS CITED BY R. R. BETTS ON LATE MEDIAEVAL CZECH HISTORY

The books and articles listed below have been selected from the footnotes of Professor Betts's studies. Only items directly relating to late mediaeval Czech history have been chosen, and works mentioned in the long bibliographical notes (see Ch. II, n. 1; X, n. 1; XI, n. 1) have been omitted unless cited elsewhere. Bibliographical information on works quoted by Betts but not included here and on those added by the editors is to be found in the notes above.

Bartoš, F. M., *Husitství a cizina*. Prague, 1931.

—, 'Husovo kněžství', *ČČM*, xcviii (1924).

—, *Literární činnost M. J. Husi*. Prague, 1948.

Bidlo, J., 'Čeští emigranti v Polsku v době husitské a mnich Jeronym Pražský', *ČČM*, lxix (1895).

Chaloupecký, V., *The Caroline University of Prague*. Prague, 1948.

Daňhelka, J. (ed.), *Husitské písně*. Prague, 1948.

Durdík, J., *Tomáš ze Štítného*. Prague, 1879.

Friedrich, G., *Dekret kutnohorský*. Prague, 1909.

Goll, J., *Quellen und Untersuchungen zur Geschichte der böhmischen Brüder*. 2 vols., Prague, 1878-82.

Graus, F., *Český obchod se suknem ve XIV. a počátkem XV. století*. Prague, 1950.

—, *Chudina městská v době předhusitské*. Prague, 1949.

—, *Dějiny venkovského lidu v době předhusitské*. 2 vols., Prague, 1953-7.

Hardt, H. von der (ed.), *Magnum oecumenicum Constanciense concilium*. 7 vols., Frankfurt, Leipzig, Berlin, 1696-1742.

Höfler, C., *Anna von Luxemburg*. Vienna, 1871.

—, (ed.), *Concilia Pragensia, 1353-1413*. Prague, 1892.

—, (ed.), *Geschichtschreiber der hussitischen Bewegung in Böhmen*. 3 vols., Vienna, 1856-66.

Hrejsa, F., *Dějiny křesťanství v Československu*. 6 vols., Prague, 1947-50.

Hus, J., *Historia et monumenta Joannis Hus atque Hieronymi Pragensis*. 2 vols., Nürnberg, 1558; new ed. 1715.

—, *Magistri Iohannis Hus Quodlibet* (ed. B. Ryba). Prague, 1948.

—, *M. Jana Husi sebrané spisy české* (ed. K. J. Erben). 3 vols., Prague, 1865-8.

—, *Opera omnia* (ed. V. Flajšhans *et al.*). Prague, 1903 ff.
Janov, Matěj of, *Matthiae de Janov dicti magister Parisiensis Regulae veteris et novi testamenti* (ed. V. Kybal and O. Odložilík). 5 vols., Innsbruck and Prague, 1908-26.
Klicman, L., 'Studie o Milíčovi', *Listy filologické* (Prague), xvii.
—, (ed.), *Processus judiciarius contra Jeronimum de Praga habitus Viennae a. 1410-12*. Prague, 1898.
Krofta, K., 'Jan Hus', *Cambridge Medieval History*, viii. Cambridge, 1936.
Kybal, V., *M. Jan Hus, život a učení*: II. *Učení*. 3 vols., Prague, 1923-31.
—, *M. Matěj z Janova. Jeho život, spisy a učení*. Prague, 1905.
Lechler, G. V., *Johannes Huss*. Halle, 1890.
Loserth, J., *Huss und Wiclif*. 2nd ed., Munich and Berlin, 1925.
Loskot, F., *Konrad Waldhauser*. Prague, 1909.
Macek, J., *Husité na Baltu a ve Velkopolsku*. Prague, 1952.
—, *Husitské revoluční hnutí*. Prague, 1952.
—, *Tábor v husitském revolučním hnutí*. 2 vols., Prague, 1952-5.
—, 'Zdeněk Nejedlý a husitství', *ČsČH*, I, i (1953).
Mansi, J. D. (ed.), *Sacrorum conciliorum nova et amplissima collectio*. Florence and Venice, 1759 ff.
Menčík, F., 'Konrad Waldhauser', *Abhandlungen der königlich-böhmischen Gesellschaft der Wissenschaften*, VI, Folge xi, Prague, 1881.
Nejedlý, Z., *Dějiny husitského zpěvu za válek husitských*. Prague, 1913.
—, *Počátky husitského zpěvu*. Prague, 1907.
Novotný, V. (ed.), *M. Jana Husi korespondence a dokumenty*. Prague, 1920.
—, *M. Jan Hus, život a učení*: I. *Život a dílo*. 2 vols., Prague, 1919-21.
—, *Náboženské hnutí české ve 14. a 15. stol.* Prague, 1915.
Odložilík, O., *Štěpán z Kolína*. Prague, 1924.
Palacký, F., *Dějiny národu českého*. 5 vols., Prague, 1848-76; new ed. 1908.
—, (ed.), *Documenta Mag. Joannis Hus vitam, doctrinam, causam ... illustrantia*. Prague, 1869.
—, *Die Vorläufer des Hussitenthums in Böhmen*. New ed., Prague, 1869.
Paulová, M., 'Styky českých husitů s cařihradskou církví', *ČČM* (1918-19).
Pekař, J., *Smysl českých dějin*. Prague, 1936.
—, *Žižka a jeho doba*. 4 vols., Prague, 1927-33.
Sedlák, J., *M. Jan Hus*. Prague, 1915.
—, (ed.), *Studie a texty k náboženským dějinám českým*. Olomouc, 1913 ff.
Šembera, A. V., *M. Jana Husi Ortografie česká*. Prague, 1857.

Spinka, M., *John Hus and the Czech Reform*. Chicago, 1941.
Štítný, Tomáš of, *O obecných věcech křesťanských* (ed. K. J. Erben). Prague, 1852.
Urbánek, R., *České dějiny*, part iii. Prague, 1915-62.
Wenzig, J., *Studien über den Ritter Thomas von Štítný*. Leipzig, 1856.
Young, R. F., 'Bohemian Scholars and Students at the English Universities from 1347 to 1750', *English Historical Review*, xxxviii (1923).
Želivský, J., *Dochováná kázání z roku 1419* (ed. A. Molnár). Prague, 1954.

A SELECT BIBLIOGRAPHY OF THE PUBLISHED WRITINGS OF R. R. BETTS

1931

'The *Regulae Veteris et Novi Testamenti* of Matěj z Janova', *The Journal of Theological Studies* (Oxford), xxxii, pp. 344-51.

1939

'English and Čech Influences on the Husite Movement', *Transactions of the Royal Historical Society* (London), 4th series, xxi, pp. 71-102.

'Jan Hus', *History* (London), New Series, xxiv, 94, pp. 97-112.

1947

'Jerome of Prague', *University of Birmingham Historical Journal* (Birmingham), i, 1, pp. 51-91. [A Czech translation appeared under the title 'Jeroným Pražský' in *Doklady a rozpravy* (Ústav Dr Edvarda Beněse, London), i, 7 and 8 (1952), pp. 26-72. Another Czech translation by J. Polišenský appeared under the title 'Jeroným Pražský' in *Československý časopis historický* (Prague), v (1957), pp. 199-226.]

'Masaryk's Philosophy of History', *The Slavonic and East European Review* (London), xxvi, 66, pp. 30-43.

'The Place of the Czech Reform Movement in the History of Europe', *SEER*, xxv, 65, pp. 373-90.

1948

'La Société dans l'Europe centrale et dans l'Europe occidentale: Son developpement vers la fin du Moyen Age', *Revue d'histoire comparée* (Paris), New Series, vii, 2, pp. 167-83.

'The University of Prague: 1348', *SEER*, xxvii, 68, pp. 57-66.

1949

'Richard fitzRalph, Archbishop of Armagh, and the Doctrine of Dominion' in *Essays in British and Irish History in Honour of James Eadie Todd*, ed. M. A. Cronne ,T. W. Moody and D. B. Quinn (London), pp. 46-60.

'The University of Prague: The First Sixty Years' in *Prague Essays*, ed. R. W. Seton-Watson (Oxford), pp. 53-68.

'The Great Debate about Universals in the Universities of the Fourteenth Century' in *Prague Essays*, ed. R. W. Seton-Watson (Oxford), pp. 69-80.

1950

(Ed.) *Central and South East Europe 1945-1948* (London), with Chapters 6: 'Czechoslovakia', pp. 163-95, and 7: 'The Revolution in Central and South-Eastern Europe', pp. 196-214.

1951

'The Influence of Realist Philosophy on Jan Hus and His Predecessors in Bohemia', *SEER*, xxix, 73, pp. 402-19. [A Czech translation appeared under the title 'Vliv realistické filosofie na Jana Husa a jeho předchůdce v Čechách' in *Doklady a rozpravy* (Ústav Dr Edvarda Beněse, London), i, 7 and 8 (1952), pp. 3-25.]

1952

'The Social Revolution in Bohemia and Moravia in the Later Middle Ages', *Past and Present* (London), 2, pp. 24-31.

'Some Political Ideas of the Early Czech Reformers', *SEER*, xxxi, 76, pp. 20-35.

1955

'Central and South-Eastern Europe' in *The Fall of Constantinople, A Symposium held at the School of Oriental and African Studies 29 May 1953* (London), pp. 18-24.

'Correnti religiose nazionali ed ereticali dalla fine del secolo XIV alta metà del XV' in *Relazioni del X Congresso Internazionale di Scienze Storiche* (Florence), iii, pp. 485-513 [in English].

'Social and Constitutional Development in Bohemia in the Hussite Period', *Past and Present*, 7, pp. 37-54.

1957

'Peter Payne in England', *Universitas Carolina, Historica* (Prague), iii, 1, pp. 5-14. [A Czech translation appeared in the same issue, pp. 15-23, under the title 'Petr Payne v Anglii'.]

1958

'The Reformation in Difficulties: Poland, Hungary and Bohemia', chapter VI (2), pp. 186-209, and 'Constitutional Development and Political Thought in Eastern Europe', Chapter XV, pp.

464-77, in *The New Cambridge Modern History*, ii, ed. G. R. Elton (Cambridge).

1961

'The Habsburg Lands', Chapter xx, pp. 474-99, in *NCMH*, v, ed. F. L. Carsten (Cambridge).

1966

'Europe at the Beginning of the Fourteenth Century', Chapter II, pp. 13-25, and 'The Central Monarchies', Chapter IX, pp. 212-40, in Denys Hay, *Europe in the Fourteenth and Fifteenth Centuries* (London).

INDEX

Note. This index is solely of names; persons referred to only cursorily and authors of works mentioned in footnotes have been omitted.